Horizons Blossom, Borders Vanish

פרץ מארקיש

שוועלן

Peretz Markish, *Shveln* (1919), Kiev: Idisher folks farlag.
Cover by Joseph Chaikov.

Horizons Blossom, Borders Vanish

ANARCHISM AND YIDDISH

LITERATURE

◆━◁◦◎◦▷━◆

Anna Elena Torres

For Margaret ~
with abundant
comradeship!
AE Torres

Yale UNIVERSITY PRESS

New Haven & London

Published with assistance from the foundation established in memory
of Henry Weldon Barnes of the Class of 1882, Yale College.

Uncaptioned art is from Yosef Chaikov from *Shveln (Thresholds)*, a collection
of poetry by Peretz Markish (Kiev: Yidisher folks farlag, 1919). Images
were scanned from the copy held by the New York Public Library.

Yale University Press books may be purchased in quantity for educational,
business, or promotional use. For information, please e-mail
sales.press@yale.edu (U.S. office) or sales@yaleup.co.uk (U.K. office).

Set in Adobe Garamond type by Integrated Publishing Soutions.
Printed in the United States of America.

Library of Congress Control Number: 2023937895
ISBN 978-0-300-24356-7 (hardcover : alk. paper)

A catalogue record for this book is available from the British Library.

This paper meets the requirements of ANSI/NISO Z39.48-1992
(Permanence of Paper).

10 9 8 7 6 5 4 3 2 1

For Jewlia Eisenberg z"l

Contents

Acknowledgments

I give my first thanks to Chana Kronfeld, my doctoral advisor at the University of California, Berkeley. Many readers shared their insights throughout the evolution of this manuscript. David Shneer (z"l) read the first draft, and his suggestions informed its direction. During the manuscript symposium and after, Amelia Glaser, Kathy Ferguson, Jesse Cohn, Na'ama Rokem, Faith Hillis, Jessica Kirzane, and Andy Drucker read the entire manuscript. Juno Richards offered key feedback on chapters regarding translation, law, and deportation. Ania Aizman, Raya Shapiro, Kenyon Zimmer, Nathaniel Deutsch, Juana María Rodríguez, Zohar Weiman Kelman, Harriet Murav, Devin Hoff, Ruth Kinna, Denise Grollmus, Yael Chaver, Naomi Seidman, and Nina Gurianova read chapters and sections over the course of this project's emergence from my dissertation. My editor Heather Gold and staff at Yale University Press, especially Elizabeth Sylvia, Margaret Otzel, and Elizabeth Casey, were abundantly gracious throughout the process of revision.

I am grateful to my colleagues at the University of Chicago, members of the Junior Faculty Working Group hosted by Kaneesha Parsard, and to Ingrid Sagor, administrator in Comparative Literature. I thank the Frankel Fellowship cohort on Jewish Translation at the University of Michigan, especially Maya Barzilai, Adriana X. Jacobs, Jeffrey Veidlinger, Roni Mazal, and Sasha Senderovich. Julie Herrada, a stellar archivist, supported this project during a summer Heidrich Fellowship at the Joseph A. Labadie Collection Special Collections Research

Center, University of Michigan Library. I deeply appreciate research assistants Raya Shapiro and Nick Wilkins and my creative collaborators and visiting artists Dan Kahn, Tadhg O'Sullivan, Ella Ponizovsky Bergelson, Nikita Kadan, Margaret Killjoy, Zhenya Fiks, and Mónica Gomery, for their inspiring conversation. For helping to further this research I thank Hayyim Rothman, Moshe Goncharok, Barry Pateman, Itzik Gottesman, and Kenyon Zimmer, and Ayelet Brinn.

My students at the University of Chicago, especially each "Poetry and the Human" cohort, brought playfulness and joyful commitment to the classroom. Students in the seminar Stateless Imaginations visited Waldheim Cemetery on May Day each year, and I appreciate their openness to exploring the fields and corners of anarchist studies together.

I am grateful to the librarians and archivists at the International Institute for Social History (Amsterdam) and Amanda Miriam-Khaye Seigel of the Dorot Division of the New York Public Library. Robert Adler Peckerar, leader of the Helix program, was a learned guide through Yiddish sites of Belarus, Latvia, and Lithuania; I am glad to have shared this memorable summer with fellow travelers in Yiddishland, including Erin Faigin, Joseph Heller, Jessica Rosenberg, Mindl Cohen, Isaac Bleaman, and Helix's historians and artists in residence.

John Zorn and AnMarie Rodgers permitted me to quote Jewlia Eisenberg's lyrics and warmly shared materials from her archives. David Markish and his son Peretz Markish kindly granted permission to translate *The Man of Forty* and Markish's other works. Eva Belavsky generously spoke with me about her father Lev Syrkin's artwork, offering precious insight. Yael Chaver, Marcia Falk, Martín Espada, Shirley Kumove, and Larry Rosenwald graciously allowed citations of their translations and poetry.

As Jacques Rancière writes: "Human beings are tied together by a certain sensory fabric, a certain distribution of the sensible, which defines their way of being together; and politics is about the transformation of the sensory fabric of 'being together.'"[1] I am grateful to these communities for being together and engaging with this work: JEWDAS (London), JFREJ (New York City), the cultural festivals Yiddish New York and KlezKanada, AVODAH (Chicago), and Di Rozeve Pave (Glasgow), and house parties hosted by Ezra Berkley Nepon and April Rosenblum in Philly.

The friendship, comradeship, and scholarship of many has sustained me: Beezer de Martelly, Sally O'Brien, Shayn Smulyan, Emilie Hardman, Aryeh Bernstein, Molly Crabapple, Jeremiah Lockwood, Dean Spade, Ayelet Adelman, eliui damm, Kai Zhang, Harrison Magee, Jorell A. Meléndez-Badillo, Theresa

Warburton, Anastasiya Lyubas, Selina Makana, Mimi Portilla, Simone Stirner, Eman Abdelhadi, Uri Gordon, Raphaël Koenig, Annie Cohen, Ianna Owen, Benay Herzel, N. O. Bonzo, Zoé Samudzi, Hadar Ahuvia, Christoph Hanssmann, Maia Deutsch, Karen Underhill, Sam Brody, Alexis Pauline Gumbs, Rachel Hui-Chi Hsu, rosza daniel lang/levitsky, Alejo Arroyo, Faith Jones, J of Tamago, and others. I thank Irena Klepfisz, Suzanne Toren, Noam Chomsky, Yuri Kochiyama, and Audrey Goodfriend (z"l) for sharing their memories. Ben Meyers and Jenny Romaine are dear chumrades in midnight dumplings and East Broadway stargazing. Tanuchka Floaker sparked much inspiration. Shira Mitchell, Itamar Haritan, Shadi Rohana, Anna Tomi, and Dove Kent welcomed me to write at their porches, rooftops, and kitchen tables. David Massey and Debbie Rose opened their homes and archives. Shirley Kumove warmly introduced me to Toronto's Yiddish world; I arrived in search of a copyright permission and left as a *shifshvester*. My neighbors in the Amalgamated Housing Cooperative of the Bronx taught early Yiddish history lessons. I am grateful to the high school classmate in stage crew who casually remarked through a cloud of sawdust that I might enjoy reading Kropotkin. I lovingly thank my family William Torres, Beth Adelman Torres, Sam Torres, Sophia Subbayya Vastek, Karin Drucker, Ron Drucker, Erica Buhrmann, and Andy Drucker.

Anarchist Constellations

In 1907 in the Netherlands, two conferences occurred simultaneously with rival visions of the political future: the Eighth Zionist Congress at The Hague and the International Anarchist Congress in Amsterdam. Serving among the Zionist delegation was the journalist and literary critic Reuben Brainin.[1] In a Yiddish article, Brainin recalls strolling through Amsterdam's "dozing streets blessed by Baruch Spinoza" toward the Jewish Quarter. There, at a coffeehouse, he encountered a prominent delegate from the rival International Anarchist Congress:

> Sitting with my steaming cup of tea and gazing into empty space, I noticed not far from my seat a lady by a table, engrossed in a heap of manuscripts and brochures laying willy-nilly around her. The woman was ruminating over the newspapers and various journals with feverish movement, taking notes in a small notebook. The lady's face was hidden in her notes. I did not know her, but the scene itself had caught my interest: at midnight, in a coffeehouse in Holland, sits a woman alone except for her parcel of printed brochures and newspaper clippings. In her hand was a long pencil, with which she made notes unusually quickly.... Her Jewish eyes expressed her energetic being and distinct chutzpah. Spiritual—intellectual daring was engraved on her full face.[2]

This woman sitting alone with her piles of pamphlets was none other than Emma Goldman, the firebrand intellectual dubbed "Queen of the Anarchists" by the North American press.[3] The anarchist and Zionist began to argue immediately:

> Suddenly, the woman raised her head and observed me with her nearsighted eyes. In a calm tone she asked me her question:
> "Are you, sir, a Zionist?"
> She had probably noticed my lapel symbol from the Zionist delegation.
> "Yes!"
> I briefly answered, anticipating a new question. I sensed in my blood that a second question would soon come, and I was right.
> "My gentleman was perhaps a delegate of the Zionist Congress in The Hague?"
> . . . The lady would not abandon me with her questions, as though she were a cross-examining judge:
> "Zionism is already dead, so what did you do in The Hague? You assembled there to bring Zionism to the gravedigger?" . . .
> The lady picked herself up from her place and sat down near my table. Her calm gaze suddenly ignited, as though she found me to be a hostile enemy. With an energetic voice and sharp emphasis on each word, she asked me:
> "You truly plan, Zionists, to establish a Jewish country in the Land of Israel . . . ?"
> "All of us certainly think so."
> "Yet the nation, the state, is the main source from which come all people's trouble and misery!"
> The woman accompanied her last remark with an energetic bang on the table, awakening the waiter from his doze. His eyes popped open. The lady continued:
> "We people have enough trouble from the state without establishing another one and becoming like the old bandits. You want to come up with a new, Jewish state. No, I think that the task of the Jews and their assignment in the world is to demolish and make a furnace of the states."

The stakes of their debate were no less than defining the political essence of Jewish history. Brainin passionately defends Zionism in terms of life and death: "When the lady reckoned the Zionist movement dead, she denied a vital movement amongst the Jews. No, as long as the Jewish people have not returned to the land of their forefathers, and as long as the world has not recognized our right to independence in the promised land, the Zionist movement cannot die." Goldman, meanwhile, excoriates all forms of nation-states, whether their government is left- or right-wing, forged by revolution or ethnic independence movement; in this, anarchism differs from other factions of the Left, which maintain that state power can be transformed or reformed. To this critique, Brainin suggests that Jewish anarchists might create a temporary Jewish state in Asia for the sole purpose of abolishing it, birthing world revolution from within an established state.[4] Goldman responds:

> "You cannot call a people to struggle to establish their own country, only for them to destroy it all with their own hands. We anarchists have long recognized that every government—whether an aristocracy or a democracy—robs people of freedom, subjugates their wills, and protects the powerful. The state is an obsolete, rusted institution that stands while collapsing. We see with our own eyes that the so-called promised land will bring us closer to our end, while you, Zionist, fantasize about a Jewish state in Asia. . . . No, we will not permit that!"

The midnight debate between Brainin and Goldman in an Amsterdam cafe in 1907 dramatizes a historical moment when European Jews imagined multiple avenues to liberation, with dozens of variants of Zionism, socialism, anarchism, and other political formations. Their dispute centers on Goldman's claim for a Jewish genealogy of anarchism:

> "Dear sir, your Excellency, Jesus of Nazareth was the first anarchist: not just the first, but the greatest and the most extreme. And the first Zionist, Moshe Hess, was first an anarchist. The construction of states and their perfection is an art far away from and alien to the Jewish spirit. . . . Also in Hasidism, if I remember correctly, there are anarchist elements."

Goldman casts statehood as "alien to the Jewish spirit" and interprets statelessness as an ethical and revolutionary position. Her opposition to Jewish statehood is bound up with her critiques of antisemitism. In her speech at that same International Anarchist Congress in Amsterdam, she denounces the "brutal treatment of the Jews in Russia" along with anti-Black racism and the persecution of Japanese Americans in both the North and South in the United States.[5] This articulation of anti-statism not as a universalist dissolution of difference but as a perspective emerging from a specific minoritized genealogy intervenes in both "classical" European anarchism and in rival discourses of Jewish politics centered on state sovereignty.

Anarchism is a prefigurative ethics of anti-authoritarianism. As Goldman declares, it envisions the undoing of power and restructuring of social relations toward comradely attachments. Its constellation of aspirations includes the dissolution of national borders, cessation of war and militarism, and abolition of prisons and police forces. Rather than prescribing a single platform or policy blueprint, anarchism critiques hierarchy as a structure; its praxis consists of artistic freedom, mutual aid, and direct action. As Ruth Kinna writes, "The anarchists' colossal ambition is to combat domination." Anarchism furthermore critiques the framework of human rights as dependent on state protection, instead seeking the fulfillment of human needs regardless of citizenship. As Giorgio Agamben notes, "the status of the refugee is always considered a temporary condition that should lead either to naturalization or to repatriation. A permanent status of man in himself is inconceivable for the law of the nation-state." Thus anarchism challenges the model of state-granted human rights and critically centers the refugee rather than citizen.[6]

When Goldman announces that "we people have enough trouble from the state without establishing another one and becoming like the old bandits," she articulates a particularly Jewish critique of iterative statehood while drawing on European anti-statist arguments predating the French Revolution. Jean Varlet (1764–1837), for example, denounced "revolutionary government" as an oxymoron: "What a social monstrosity, what a masterpiece of Machiavellianism is this revolutionary government! To any rational being, *government* and *revolution* are incompatible."[7] One hundred years later, after the Congress of the First International in 1864, the Russian anarchist Pyotr Kropotkin argued that it was not enough "to overthrow the government, to put ourselves in its place and decree the revolution," thus "setting ourselves up as an army of conspirators, with all the characteristics of the old secret societies with their leaders and deputy leaders."[8] Rather than putting faith in a totalizing revolutionary event, Kropotkin argues, "the role of the anarchist must for a long time be one of permeation," when activists "apply their principles in the organization of social life here and now."[9] In Brainin's account of their debate, Goldman expressed a method of "permeating" liberation through Jewish political vocabulary of diaspora.

To describe Yiddish-speaking radicals' translation and reinvention of "classical" anarchism, I offer the term "anarchist diasporism." Goldman and other Jewish deportees, immigrants, and refugees critiqued citizenship as the primary guarantor of human rights. Instead—through mass mobilization and revolutionary strategy, popular cultural and artistic production, over long years of imprisonment and exile—they cultivated stateless imaginations, elaborated through literature. Against the antisemitism of other European anarchists, Jewish radicals articulated this specific anti-statist critique. The term "anarchist diasporism" describes how they resignified classical anarchism. It foregrounds the specific anti-nationalist critique born of migration, deportation, and exile rather than the transnationalism of happenstance. Studies of Yiddish literature often approach historical transnationalism as politically undetermined. Migration deeply informed the emergence of Jewish modernism, as Allison Schachter writes in *Diasporic Modernism:* "A diasporic approach to literary history captures the mobility of twentieth-century literary culture through specific and locally grounded networks of literary production and reception. Diaspora offers new avenues for theorizing the vexed relationship between modernism and literary history, illuminating how modernist literary networks operated outside national borders in minor and non-national languages, by which I mean languages that do not fit within the borders of a nation-state."[10] This approach aptly describes Schachter's subjects, though modernism is not the sole expression of Yiddish transnationalism; circuits of migration occurred long before and continued after the 1920s. The Yiddish anarchists sought kinship with the ancient world and constructed genealogies long predating the rise of European nationalism, identifying their own statelessness and dispossession with biblical, medieval, and futuristic imaginaries of justice. The persistent focus on "transnationalism" as a defining feature of diasporic Jewish modernity elides the impact of deportation and censorship on literary culture, highlighting instead a valorized—and often masculinized—idea of mobility. This book employs the lens of "migratory aesthetics," centering multiple experiences of stillness, containment, detention, and deportation rather than a singular romanticized figure of the agentic, cosmopolitan immigrant.

Horizons Blossom, Borders Vanish examines the forms and aesthetics of Yiddish anarchist diasporism, focused on four aspects: Elegy, Genealogy, Modernism, and Language Politics. My approach counters the erasure of Jewish anarchism from both literary studies and anarchist historiography, which largely centered atheist universalism. This book spans 130 years of anarchist history and several literary movements. It begins with the fiery Proletarian (Sweatshop or *Svetshop*) poets, who immigrated to England and the United States from Russia in the 1880s and composed Romantic visions of a world without factories. It moves to the Chicago and New York modernists of the 1910s, elegizing their "martyrs of labor," and from there to the expressionist and avant-garde poetry of Warsaw and Moscow in the 1920s and 1930s, bent on exploding form. It then travels to Tel Aviv of the 1970s and 1980s, when the last Yiddish anarchist editors reckoned with the meaning of their Israeli citizenship. Finally, it documents the persistence and presence of Jewish anarchism in the work of contemporary composer and ethnomusicologist Jewlia Eisenberg. Throughout this research, I encountered writers from a multitude of anarchist positions and fields: rabbis and militant atheists, pacifists and assassins, ethnographers and doctors, and women who advocated dismantling the state while simultaneously fighting for universal suffrage.

This book takes up the questions: How did Jewish experiences of stateless-ness inform anti-statist literature? How did anarchist writers use Yiddish—a diasporic language bearing the imprint and mutual exchange of its dozen con-tact languages—to forge antifascist aesthetics and poetics? What was the role of translation in the Yiddish radical press, and how did translators negotiate with "classical" anarchist texts to express new forms of diasporic anarchism in Yiddish? What happens when a monolingual state attempts to regulate multi-lingual speech, and how did immigrant dissidents make use of the minor lan-guage to evade censorship and surveillance? The project understands anarchism not as an individual's identity but as a *strategy* of action and form of social relat-ing that holds comradeship as its highest ideal. Nearly all the authors considered here explicitly allied themselves with anarchism; others were strongly informed by anarchism and cited its thinkers in their manifestos.

Despite a bounty of primers on anarchist thought, the term continues to be used colloquially as a synonym for chaos. Yiddish anarchists defined and refined their credo through iterations of speeches and pamphlets, notably Alexander Berkman's *Now and After: The ABC of Communist Anarchism* (New York, 1928) and Dr. Y. A. Merison's *Principles of Anarchism* (New York, 1935). In 1919, an article by H. Burgin in the popular Yiddish newspaper the *Forverts* (Forward) titled "What Is Anarchism?" began with the term's etymology: "In common speech, one uses the word 'anarchy' to suggest disorder, chaos [*toye-voye*], dis-cord. But there is another meaning...." The article explains that "the anarchism of Kropotkin is not the same as that of the American Benjamin Tucker," dis-tinguishing between individualist and collectivist strains of anarchist thought. Burgin offers a positive definition: "Anarchism is a teaching or movement to-ward social order, where a person will not dominate another, that is to say, an order where people will do without government.... Anarchism calls for such coexistence where each will have the right to all, so long as it will not harm another."[11]

Despite popular misunderstanding and scholarly neglect, we can still at-tune our ears to the anarchist frequency that ran through twentieth-century Jewish art movements in other languages and media, surfacing in the work of such artists as Franz Kafka, Alfred Stieglitz, Allen Ginsberg, Camille Pissarro, and Grace Paley.[12] Historicizing Yiddish anarchism reveals its presence and persistence through English, Russian, Hebrew, and other Jewish literatures. No one book can represent the fullness, multilingualism, and heterogeneity of anarchism's voyages; this examination of anarchist diasporism offers a single port.

THE TRANSNATIONAL YIDDISH ANARCHIST PRESS AND ITS LITERATURE

By the time of Goldman's appearance at the International Anarchist Congress in 1907, self-identified anarchist labor movements had been growing for thirty years, in large part organized by immigrant workers. Their presence in the United States was so formidable—and their association with border-crossing so entrenched—that three years earlier the U.S. Supreme Court had ruled Congress possessed unlimited power to deport philosophical anarchists.[13] As Kenyon Zimmer notes, "Anarchism was the principal ideology of global radicalism between the collapse of the International Working Men's Association (the First International) in the 1870s and the consolidation of the Communist International, or Comintern (the Third International) in the 1920s." Zimmer estimates that anarchists outnumbered Marxists in the United States in the 1880s, peaking in 1910 at over 100,000 primarily Jewish and Italian immigrants, which "inextricably link[ed] anarchism and immigration in the American experience and popular imagination."[14] Anarchists remained significant in the labor movement through World War II.

The Yiddish anarchist press shaped the language of its readers. Few East European Jews had heard the word "anarchism" before arriving in England or the United States in the 1870s, when political expatriates and refugees from Russia and across Europe sought shelter there. London functioned as a site of radicalization through which Russians passed en route to the Americas, and, despite surveillance from Scotland Yard, anarchist editors organized mutual aid societies for refugees and opposed conscription. As Goldman described that period, "England was the haven for refugees from all lands, who carried on their work without hindrance. By comparison with the United States the political freedom in Great Britain seemed like the millennium come."[15] The prominent editor and theorist Rudolf Rocker emphatically centers London as the "motherland" for anarchist diasporic circuits: "London in this time was a clearing house for the Jewish revolutionary labour movement. . . . The threads went out from London to all countries where there were large numbers of Jewish immigrants, and later even to their original homes in Russia and Poland, when the first anarchist underground groups began to form in Bialystok, Grodno, Vilna, Warsaw, Lodz, and other places."[16] Among those militant groups was the Black Banner (Chernoe Znamiia) of Białystok, Poland, composed largely of young Jewish men committed to revolutionary violence against pogromists and the ultranationalist Black Hundreds.[17]

In 1886, the Haymarket Affair in Chicago galvanized broad support for labor. Likely framed for the anti-police bombing that followed a May Day demonstration, four anarchists died by execution and one by suicide.[18] Goldman hailed the so-called Haymarket martyrs as "pioneers" whose memory, she said (using a Jewish idiomatic formula, *dor l'dor*), "perpetuates itself from generation to generation." Haymarket radicalized many thousands, including the prolific Russian-born Yiddish poet and editor Dovid Edelshtat, who had attended lectures by one of its martyrs and had become radicalized by his death, which he elegized in a suite of poems. Edelshtat's poems appeared in radical papers nearly every week from 1889 to 1892, helping originate the genre of the Yiddish "newspaper poem."[19] His sister Sadie Edelshtat organized Goldman's lectures in Butte, Montana, and took joy in singing his poems around the house and to family for the rest of her life.[20]

These Haymarket-era papers, though labeled anarchist, were often heterogeneously leftist and unpreoccupied with ideological orthodoxy. From the 1880s onward, the Yiddish radical press foregrounded Yiddish verse, juxtaposing all genres of literature and theories of political action on the same page. Yiddish anarchist poetry of the 1880s–1890s maintained a highly social purpose and was composed in forms suited to public performance, such as the ballad and elegy. The poets Morris Rosenfeld (Moyshe Yakov Alter, 1862–1923), Dovid Edelshtat (1866–1892), Yosef Bovshover (1873–1915), and Morris Vinchevsky (1856–1932) primarily comprised the Proletarian poets, who held varying positions within anti-capitalist groups. Rosenfeld was first drawn to anarchism upon visiting London, where his parents had immigrated.[21] After moving to New York City in 1886, Rosenfeld published socialist writing, and his later work included Zionist poems. Vinchevsky founded both the first Yiddish socialist newspaper and the first Yiddish anarchist newspaper.[22] The anarchist archivist Moshe Goncharok notes that "not all knew that Edelshtat was an anarchist, although his poems were known and sung by the workers of many parties."[23] While these writers may have had partial and multiple dogmatic allegiances, they inhabited a shared social world formed from opposition to capitalism. In their political heterogeneity, the Sweatshop poets reflected the world of the Yiddish radical press: the first Yiddish anarchist newspaper in the world, Vinchevsky's *Arbeter* fraynd

(Worker's Friend, London, 1885) had a mixture of anarchist and socialist writers until 1892. *Vorheyt* (*Truth*, also spelled *Vahrhayt*, 1889), the first Yiddish anarchist newspaper in the United States, published both Edelshtat and Rosenfeld.[24]

The anarchist and socialist press in New York City only truly differentiated after an attempt to publish a joint newspaper at the first conference of Jewish radicals in the United States on December 25, 1889. Almost fifty delegates representing thirty-one organizations met in the hall of the Essex Street Market on the Lower East Side, "decorated for the occasion with red flags, portraits of the Haymarket martyrs, and a banner inscribed 'Neither God Nor Master!'"[25] Paul Avrich describes their collaboration as doomed from the beginning: "The anarchists, favoring a joint newspaper, argued that the workers should acquaint themselves with all streams of radical thought, if only to choose intelligently among them. The socialists, however, branded a nonparty paper as '*pareveh lokshn*' [that is, neither dairy nor meat], a term imported from London, where it had been used to deride the *Arbeter Fraynd*."[26] The socialists maintained that such heterogeneity would not unite workers but only confuse them, and the anarchists were defeated by a single vote. This incident illustrates how the two camps clashed only when they tried to establish a joint written project; practical organizing occurred collaboratively across leftist identifications. After the conference of 1889, socialists founded the weekly *Arbeter-Tsaytung* (Worker's Paper). Likewise, the *Pyonirn der frayheyt* (Pioneers of Liberty) began plans for an anarchist newspaper and invited Morris Vinchevsky of London to edit. Vinchevsky, who was "as much a socialist as an anarchist,"[27] declined their offer, and the Russian Roman Lewis became the first editor of the first Yiddish anarchist newspaper in the United States.

The Yiddish anarchist press grew from 1889 onward, counting more than fifty periodicals across North America to Argentina, Palestine, Poland, France, and Russia's Pale of Settlement.[28] The earliest Yiddish anarchist papers appeared in London, giving an audience to David Edelshtat and other Proletarian poets, who expressed the humiliations of daily factory work and their dreams of a world without exploitation. Between 1904 and 1914, *Arbeter* fraynd reached a circulation of 5,000 copies. London anarchists "achieved such popularity that they became almost respectable" within the Jewish community and labor movement.[29] The grandest Yiddish paper was *Fraye arbeter shtime* (Free Voice of Labor), which was founded in 1890 in New York City and remained in print for nearly ninety years—the longest-running anarchist paper in any language.[30] In Mandatory Palestine and the early years of Israeli statehood, the Yiddish press was highly regulated and taxed by a young government eager to establish Hebrew-language hegemony, which rendered experimental writing in Yiddish a subversive act.[31]

Jewish writers contributed to transnational anarchist papers in non-Jewish languages as well.[32] In Germany, the philosopher Gustav Landauer's *Der Sozialist* (1893–99) was hailed by radicals in fin-de-siècle Berlin. Ernst Friedrich's weekly *Die schwarze Fahne* (The Black Flag) pilloried militarism—and individual ministers, leading to Friedrich's libel trial in 1928. With support from a Jewish greengrocer, Friedrich built the Anti-Kriegs-Museum in 1925. Its title was intended to be glossed as both *Anti-War* Museum and the *Anti* War-Museum, questioning the valorization of militarism. In 1933, the Nazis shut down Friedrich's museum and converted its space into torture chambers.[33] In Russia, anarchist movements arose during the revolutions of 1905 and 1917. Just after the 1917 Russian Revolution, about two dozen anarchist newspapers circulated, among them the avant-garde *Anarkhiia* published by the brothers Abba and Volf Gordin—until Bolsheviks firebombed their office one year later. The Gordins' manifesto attacked the collusion of racism, colonialism, and gender, calling for "the complete liberation of people from property, children from schools, society from the state, nations from empire, and women from men."[34] Members of the Russian Jewish diaspora founded the Union of Russian Workers, the largest anarchist federation in the United States; many of them were deported on the USAT *Buford* during the Red Scare. The Russian Jewish radical diaspora extended to Argentina as well, surging through Buenos Aires until the 1970s, when it was finally repressed by the juntas. *De'ot* (Opinions), the first Hebrew anarchist paper, appeared in Tel Aviv in 1952, followed seven years later by the bilingual Hebrew-Yiddish *Problemen/Problemot,* which continued publication until the 1990s.[35]

Radical newspapers produced new forms of materiality, as well as sociality. Kathy Ferguson emphasizes the materiality of the press and the arduous physical labor of printing:

> I propose to encounter the print shops' physical objects, pungent smells, and laboring bodies as actants that are mutually constitutive of each other and that enable anarchism's politics. The printers' swift hands and sharp eyes, and the presses' mechanical operations and physical components, knit together chains of events in which each element acts upon and is acted upon by others. Printers and presses acted as nodal points, horizontal linkages among the objects, persons, desires, and ideas constitut-

ing anarchist assemblages. The printers' bodies and the printing apparatus were ubiquitous aspects of anarchist organizing, their materiality
central to the merger of intellectual and physical labor prized by anarchists in their schools and communities. The printer-press relation, re-
framed with the conceptual tools of the new materialism, provides a
crucial supplement to older materialist analyses in accounting for the
remarkable persistence of anarchism in the face of sustained onslaughts
by authorities. While the stock image of the bearded, black-clad, bomb-
toting anarchist prevails in the public eye, a more representative figure
for the classical anarchist movement would be the printer, composing
stick in hand, standing in front of the type case, making and being made
by the material process for producing and circulating words.[36]

Ferguson comments that anarchists "cherished the interactive process of making
and being made by the creative process of printing. The assemblages of printer-
press-publication constitute a diffuse technology of the community, spreading
across surfaces, confusing causes and effects, facilitating the emergence of something new."[37]

Phenomenologies of the print shop are found in many accounts of the radical press. The anarchist organizer Isidore Wisotzky plays upon the English-
Yiddish newspaper divide in his narrative of a violent fight on the Lower East
Side of Manhattan, in which a committeeman with a rolled-up newspaper hit
the boss:

> Mother asked whether a person who is hit with a newspaper falls down.
> "It was an English paper and when one is hit by an English paper, one
> can even get his head split open." So Mother asked again and the lands-
> man answered, "That is when in the paper is wrapped an iron pipe." "Oh,
> so you could have said that in the first place," Mother chided him.[38]

In Wisotzky's account, the symbolic object of the "English paper" becomes a
literal weapon. The exchange with his immigrant mother demonstrates the slippage between categories of language and object, here producing a kind of slap-
stick violence.

In the United States, more than one dozen Yiddish anarchist newspapers
circulated between 1890 and World War I, constituting a significant economic
sector.[39] The press functioned further as an engine of translation, bringing "classical" anarchist texts, philosophy (particularly Spinoza—in serial!), and works
of world literature. In the first half of the twentieth century, Jews also edited

more than a dozen English-language anarchist newspapers. Women had more editorial power in the English press than the Yiddish, and Emma Goldman's *Mother Earth* was particularly influential for a generation of modernist writers, artists, and activists—as were her unceasing lecture tours, which reached from 50,000 to 75,000 people per year. *Mother Earth* and other papers championed realist novels, and back-page ads attest to the great popularity of Tolstoy, Multatuli, Ibsen, and others in translation. The most influential modernist journal in North America, Margaret Anderson's *Little Review,* was "largely an anarchist publication" for its first three years.[40] Wryly admitting Goldman's influence, Anderson quipped, "I heard Emma Goldman lecture and had just enough time to turn anarchist before the presses closed."[41] As a U.S. citizen, Anderson could not be deported; however, her magazines were repeatedly confiscated by the postal service in 1917 and 1921 for publishing an anti-militarist short story by Wyndham Lewis. Anderson also serialized James Joyce's *Ulysses* in twenty-three installments, from 1918 to 1920, until the Society for the Suppression of Vice charged the magazine with obscenity; the U.S. Post Office burned it during four separate incidents. Anderson and co-editor Jane Heap lost the obscenity trial and were forced to discontinue the novel amid Joyce's notorious Episode Fourteen ("Oxen of the Sun"), costing them much of their funding. During this time, Anderson and the paper were supported by Yiddish anarchists such as Leon Malmed, one of Goldman's lovers. In this sense, modernist writing—even in English—functioned as a transgressive dialect, censured as though it were an anarchistic foreign language. A study of "language politics" in censorship and free speech law, then, ought to consider both linguistic difference (non-English languages) as well as transgressive forms of literary experimentation.

Although studies of Yiddish modernism largely exclude the presence of anarchist thought and imagery, the significance of anarchism for modernism in other languages is better documented. Patricia Leighton, Theresa Papanikolas, Mark Antliff, and other art historians have revealed the intimacy between anarchism and modernism. Félix Fénéon, the French anarchist curator of Henri Matisse and Pierre Bonnard, similarly hailed the future dissolution of the division of artist and worker: "Day'll come, Goddam, when art will fit into the life of ordinary Joes, just like steak and vino. Then plates, spoons, chairs, beds—the whole works, what d'ya think! Everything, great guns, will have nifty shapes and fabulous colors. When that happens, the artisse [*sic*] won't look down his nose at the worker: they will be united. But before we get to that point, the old Union will have to get up some steam and we gotta be slap-dab in the middle of anarcho civilization."[42] For Fénéon, the harmonious color of Neo-Impressionist painters such as Paul Signac "had a related scientific basis in its systematic use of color and brushstroke, wherein individual touches of paint combine in the viewer's eye to create secondary colors, with luminous results. . . . And he believed that these aesthetic effects were psychologically powerful enough to guide the viewer toward an equivalent social harmony, echoing Kropotkin's blueprint for a future society."[43] The French poet and artist André Breton (1896–1966) also remarked on the close relation between anarchism and art: "It was in the black mirror of Anarchism that surrealism first recognized itself, well before defining itself, when it was still only a free association among individuals rejecting the social and moral constraints of the day, spontaneously and in their entirety."[44] While much remains to be recovered about specifically Jewish anarchist modernism, Yiddish mischief runs through the linguistic play of the surrealists, and the anarchism of Tristan Tzara, a Jew from Romania, has been well studied.[45] Born Samy or Samuel Rosenstock, his chosen name resembles the Yiddish word *trishtshen* (to crack or burst), the French *triste* (sad), and the Hebrew *tsara* (calamity)—a striking multilingual pun for an anarchist absurdist.[46]

In contrast to more doctrinaire papers, anarchist editors cultivated experimentalism. The poet Menke Katz, for example, was repeatedly disciplined and expelled from the communist group Proletpen for work they deemed too "decadent" and erotic. As Dovid Katz notes, "This was the New York *secular* equivalent of the religious Jewish *kheyrem* (*herem*) or Ban of Excommunication. It meant that *no* publication in the leftist movement would publish his work any more. It seemed he was finished at twenty-six."[47] The communist *Frayheyt* (Freedom) succinctly dismissed Katz's poema *Dray shvester* (Three Sisters, 1932): "An example of rottenness and degeneracy."[48] The anarchist paper *Fraye arbeter shtime* championed it, however, in a review by the paralyzed poet Chaim Krul, who wrote with pen in mouth. While the Proletpen group banned Katz from publishing such "degeneracy," Krul observed its shock value calmly and compared Katz favorably to the national Hebrew poet: "True, [Katz] is a bit shocking when you see phrases like *táyre* [ritual cleansing of the corpse] in the book, and blood and death and dozens of similar expressions. But this is secondary. The main point is that the poem is good. . . . The poet has had his say. These poems by Menke Katz are as strong as Bialik's 'sorrow and anger' poems. But there is this difference between Bialik and Menke Katz. Bialik stirs the national beat, Menke Katz stirs the human beat."[49] Though Katz was not formally aligned with anarchist literary or political movements, these reviews show how anarchist reading practices allowed space for expressionism and the grotesque beyond the constraints of communist literary programs.

From its earliest decades through avant-garde eras, then, Yiddish anarchist papers emboldened literary experimentalism. Anarchist editors fought for artists' and writers' free expression against censors and charges of sedition, and the short lifespans of many of these papers resulted from state seizures and their editors' incarcerations.[50] The experience of producing radical newspapers—written and printed by what might today be called affinity groups—restructured sociality across lines of comradeship.

ANARCHIST DIASPORISM

I introduce the term *anarchist diasporism* to name a specific stance emerging from and interpreting diasporic experience. Anarchist diasporism converges with and diverges from "classical" European anarchism, which informed Jews' worldview even as it often cast them outside humanism. The term offers a name for a particular mode of Jewish anarchism of the Ashkenazi diaspora, distinct from the anarcho-Zionism of Bernard Lazare, Martin Buber, and Gustav Landauer, which might be historicized in relation to German and French philosophy.[51] This lens acknowledges the consequences of deportation, detention, migration, and statelessness for Yiddish literature, rather than positing a neutral or circumstantial "diasporic" network of writers or valorizing their mobility. The recently coined term "deportspora" describes an "abject diaspora," capturing the lack of agency and circularity in forced mobility.[52] "Mobility" itself, as Harsha Walia notes, is an etymologically charged term: "the word 'mob,' a criminalizing vocabulary used to link large groups of poor, racialized people to social disorder, including in inner cities and at the border, derives from the word 'mobility.'"[53]

Studies of diaspora have long contrasted individuals' transit with the stability of borders, yet empire is inherently "transnational": it exists in transit, moving and displacing its subjects. Anarchist diasporism does not theorize a stationary nation antagonizing transnational ethnic subjects; rather, it traces how borders themselves move and capture their subjects, as those living in borderlands testify. Further, I intend the term "anarchist diasporism" to reject a binary of "Indigeneity versus diasporism" and to emphasize instead how the violent intra-state displacement of Indigenous peoples is no less "diasporic" than the "cosmopolitan" transnational immigrants often centered in studies of diasporism. As political identities that describe a relation to the state, *Diasporic* and *Indige-*

nous are not mutually exclusive and may also overlap by appealing to a temporality before, beyond, and after the state.[54] Yiddish anarchists sought to establish the origins and lineage of ethical anti-domination from within ancestral memory, not positing Jewish anarchism as a symptom or rupture of modernity. Likewise, the Yiddish anarchists' genealogical rhetoric appeals to a deep memory of the transience of empire, while it imagines the state's undoing. Anarchist citations of Jewish antiquity—from Gideon's refusal of kingship to Judith's vigilantism to Essene (all-male) horizontalism—undermined the sense of empire as exceptional, novel, or modern. Nonlinear temporality is not merely a jagged avant-garde aesthetic but a political technique for representing memory, ritual, and ancestry in resistance to colonial and nationalist temporalities.

Anarchist diasporism posits language politics as not only cultural or ethnic habitus but *strategy,* a means of negotiating surveillance, censorship, and assimilative pressures via diasporic language's creative possibilities. It extends beyond imprinting modernism and modernity as the epitome of mobility by taking in nineteenth-century political movements. Studies of Jewish literary transnationalism often portray modernism as epitomizing or exceptionalizing the condition of diaspora. These migratory formations were not unique to modernist experience, however, and I trace anarchist diasporism through Proletarian, realist, romantic, futurist, expressionist, and other movements. Migration, deportation, and other mobilities across nation-states are not the hallmark of modernity alone, though the anarchists were singularly intent on undermining structures of nationalism.

A key distinction between Yiddish anarchist diasporism and European "classical" anarchism emerges through their relation to structural antisemitism. Anarchist diasporism critiqued antisemitism, prevalent among European anarchists who articulated their atheism through anti-Jewish language.[55] The French "father of anarchism," Pierre-Joseph Proudhon (1809–1865), published the first positive defense of anarchism in *What Is Property?* (1840). Recent scholarship has shown that Proudhon's "seemingly occasional hostile remarks agglomerate into a fully-fledged antisemitic worldview, undergirding everything from his critique of authority to his eventual embrace of patriotism."[56] The Russian social anarchist Mikhail Bakunin (1814–1876) likewise invoked the full range of virulent antisemitic canards from parasitism to vampirism and even advocated for Jews' expulsion from France—or, failing that, extermination.[57] His paranoid hatred of Jews is made clear in *God and the State:* "This whole Jewish world, comprising a single exploiting sect, a kind of blood sucking people, a kind of organic destructive collective parasite, going beyond not only the frontiers of states, but of political opinion, this world is now, at least for the most part, at the disposal of Marx on the one hand and Rothschild on the other."[58] Bakunin links Jews and capital ineffably: "where there is centralisation of the state, there must necessarily be a central bank, and where such a bank exists, the parasitic Jewish nation, speculating with the Labour of the people, will be found." Bakunin does not celebrate the revolutionary potential of transnationalism but excoriates Jews for "going beyond the frontiers of states." Contradictory stereotypes accumulate here, without negating each other. Inflammatory antisemitic imagery appears throughout *God and the State,* and Bakunin sets the foundation of European anarchism upon rejection of Jewishness. Nonetheless, Bakunin did achieve some popularity among Jewish revolutionaries, particularly in Kiev and Mogilev.[59]

How did his radical Yiddish readers and translators negotiate the dissonance of Bakunin's antisemitism? Against such vitriol, Jewish anarchists articulated another ethical interpretation of statelessness. Bakunin portrays Jews as essentially abject because of their political condition. He characterizes Jews as possessing "that exclusive national spirit which distinguishes them even today" and becoming "the most international people of the world": "urged on by that mercantile passion which constitutes one of the principal traits of their character, they had spread through all countries, carrying everywhere the worship of their Jehovah, to whom they remained all the more faithful the more he abandoned them."[60] Bakunin reads Jewish diasporism as motivated by near-atavistic capitalist impulses ("driven by their passion for commerce"). The Yiddish translation resignifies these passages into an example of Jewish self-critique. Saul (Shoel) Yanovsky's addition of "Jewish theologians" to Bakunin's polemic suggests an attempt to read himself into European texts—even critical ones—from which Jews had been excluded.[61] In Part II of this book, I examine genealogical narratives constructed from Jewish text and tradition in partial response to Bakunin's and Proudhon's antisemitism.

Yiddish anarchists expressed another anarchism in their own vernacular, drawn from lived experiences of literature, diaspora life, and folkways. Anarchist diasporism became a major current in nineteenth- and twentieth-century Jewish artistic and political production. Ashkenazi diasporic relations to the state have long been modeled as either Zionist aspirations to statehood or Bundist entry into Russian, Lithuanian, and Polish governments. Though the Bund was transnational—announced in its name, Der Algemeyner Yidisher Arbeter Bund in Lite, Poyln, un Rusland (The General Union of Jewish Workers in Lithuania, Poland, and Russia)—its organizers contended with the particularities of each state, achieving some electoral success.[62] Through labor agitation and political party campaigns, the Bund fought for Jewish workers, not for the abolition of militarism and the state.

"Anarchist diasporism" describes anarchism as a structure of relating to time and territory. By and large, theirs was not a farming settlement or land freedom movement. This theorization of anarchist diasporism is rooted in the specificity of Yiddish culture. While European Jewish anarchists were radicalized by immigration and deportation, Jews in the Ottoman Empire related differently to state power. As Sarah Abrevaya Stein writes, "The story of Jewish protégés and their descendants pushes us to consider citizenship as a spectrum: a range of conditions or positions that Jews could access rather than a singular possession they could or could not claim," when European citizenship "bespeaks cacophony rather than harmony."[63] Rather than the "rule by deportation" that Goldman describes, Abrevaya Stein explains the experience of Sephardim: "No rigid doctrine, protection emerged from negotiation and experimentation, and ultimately proved to be a measure of the diffuse and unruly nature of state power." In her nuanced study, Abrevaya Stein portrays the protégé as "neither pawn nor victor" in relation to state power.[64] The mercurial, precarious citizenship status of Ottoman Jews differed from those in the Russian Empire or United States.

Another aspect of Jewish anarchist history requiring further research is the role of Sephardim in Spain during the Spanish Civil War. Of the solidarity volunteers in the Abraham Lincoln Brigade who came from the United States, more than one-third were Jewish; yet from a list of thousands of volunteers published by a veterans' group, only a single American individual is noted for her Sephardi identity.[65] Among the British battalion, one Sephardic man is listed.[66] The veterans' list notes that fighters from Yugoslavia, Czechoslovakia, and Bulgaria were "mostly Sephardim"; however, this list "was fraught with difficulties as during the McCarthy era many records were hidden and lost."[67]

Among the exceptions to predominantly Ashkenazi Jewish anarchism is Sephardic painter Camille Pissarro, whose curator called him "the only impressionist with a big police file."[68] Raised on the Caribbean island of St. Thomas in multiracial schools, Pissarro had anarchist impulses and sympathies since his youth. He was inspired more formally by anarchist writing in the 1880s, which he read voraciously; even when his financial situation was precarious, he continued subscribing to anarchist newspapers such as *La Révolte*.[69] Pissarro maintained that art should be bartered and shared, rather than sold, and his paintings uplifted archetypal laborers of field and market. As a radical Sephardic Caribbean painter working in antisemitic France, Pissarro embodied complexities of ethnicity, culture, and political exchange.

The term "Yiddish anarchism" includes both Jews and non-Jews and fore-grounds the language of literary production, rather than received identities. I use this rather than a pan-religious term such as "Jewish anarchist movement," since Sephardim, Arab Jews, and others negotiated citizenship through their own languages and strategies.[70] Nineteenth- and early twentieth-century anar-chists of white European ancestry were at times racialized as non-white on ac-count of their politics. During the Paris Commune, white Communards were referred to as "negroes."[71] During the Red Scare in the United States, newspapers ran antisemitic caricatures with exaggerated facial and bodily features, casting Jewish men as unassimilable and animalistic. Clare Hemmings documents the racialization of Emma Goldman by the press, which occurred hand-in-hand with her sexualization.[72] The racialization of European anarchists as non-white—and the ascription of essential criminality and anarchism to people of color—emerged from eugenics discourses elaborated by Cesare Lombroso and others.

Even though they are grounded in Yiddish particularity, these anarchists' critiques resonate with other movements, and my readings are inevitably in-formed by contemporary pedagogies. Recent scholarship by Saidiya Hartman, William Anderson, and Zoé Samudzi critiques Black nationalism and instead studies the password of statelessness in Black radical thought. Anderson casts statelessness as "more than a lack of citizenship: it renders you nonexistent, a shadow. So why not embrace the darkness we're in, the darkness we are, and or-ganize through it and with it?"[73] This embrace of statelessness resonates with the concept of *hefker*, a Yiddish term for multiple forms of abandonment. Ruth Wilson Gilmore's term "organized abandonment" recognizes the condition of *hefker* as foundational to abolition.[74]

Anarchist diasporism is both historically bound to classical anarchism and critical of its limitations. In some ways, the refusal of anarchist diasporists to appeal to the state as guarantor of human rights resonates with contemporary Black radical and Indigenous critiques, rather than classical European anarchist formations. In other ways, the anarchist diasporists theorized primarily from ex-periences of migration, rather than colonial subjection. Anarchist diasporism, invested in recovering a particular historical record and literature, is subject to critiques of Eurocentric anarchist history. William C. Anderson notes:

> I'm not doing this work to rescue classical anarchism from its whiteness. As I've said before, the existence of Black anarchism represents a failure of European anarchist movements because they couldn't overcome their own lack of appeal to Black communities. To this day, classical anarchists

have a race and racism problem they struggle with like any other faction of the white left. The anarchism of Blackness is about pointing out the historical struggles of Black people that were anarchic without simply plastering anarchism onto them. Instead we can draw parallels and as Russell Maroon Shoatz said when describing something similar, "the affinity between anarchism and the following is not rejected; on the contrary, it's welcomed as a sister set of ideas, beliefs and concepts."[75]

The history of Jewish anarchism is not innocent of sexism, racism, or settler formations. Some anarchist arguments for birth control engaged in eugenic logics that sting the ears: one of Goldman's lectures asked "Should the Poor Have Children?" and Margaret Sanger's affiliations with eugenicists have been well documented. Anarchist abolitionists, too, found promise in eugenics' claim that criminality is genetic—for if lawlessness is an inheritable trait, what good is prison reform? Thus Cesare Lombroso's prescription of a Mediterranean island—rather than incarceration—for unreformable, congenital anarchists had a certain appeal.

Yet anarchist diasporism theorized ethics as prefiguration. Walter Benjamin describes the psychological disjoint produced by practicing such prefigurative ethics, inherently at odds with the world:

> The more antagonistic a person is toward the traditional order, the more inexorably he will subject his private life to the norms that he wishes to elevate as legislators of a future society. It is as if these laws, nowhere yet realized, placed him under obligation to enact them in advance, at least in the confines of his own existence. In contrast, the man who knows himself to be in accord with the most ancient heritage of his class or nation will sometimes bring his private life into ostentatious contrast to the maxims that he unrelentingly asserts in public, secretly approving his own behavior, without the slightest qualms, as the most conclusive proof of the unshakable authority of the principles he puts on display. Thus are distinguished the types of the anarcho-socialist and the conservative politician.[76]

The schism is produced by living a prefigurative ethics "nowhere yet realized," which demands one elevate his or her actions above the status quo.

Mutual aid and direct action may be understood as *prefigurative* social forms. Although the term "prefiguration" rarely appeared in nineteenth-century anarchist writing, it has emerged as a keyword in the past three decades.[77] Cindy

Barukh Milstein defines prefiguration as "the idea that there should be an ethically consistent relationship between the means and the ends. . . . Anarchists participate in the present in the ways that they would like to participate, much more fully and with much more self-determination, in the future—and encourage others to do so as well."[78] Prefiguration has roots in Christian theology as "a recursive temporal framing . . . in which a future radiates backwards on its past," as Uri Gordon's genealogy shows.[79] In the anarchist tradition, prefiguration strategizes an interruption of the present and refuses deferring action until "after the revolution." Prefiguration is thus an important concept for anarchist temporalities in literature. As Jayna Brown notes, literary strategies of anti-linear time use "temporal disruptions as a key way to intervene in dominant regimes of power."[80]

Broadly stated, anarchist and communist temporalities differ in their orientation toward genealogy versus futurity. Amelia Glaser writes that Yiddish communist poets "to varying degrees put their faith in a future, liberating, world revolution at a time of rising nationalist movements."[81] While anarchists shared such revolutionary thinking, what distinguishes their *poetics* is rigorous study of the past to prove the immanence of mutual aid within this world, rather than deferral to a post-revolutionary temporality.

Benjamin's interior psychological description of prefigurative schism speaks to the temporality of dispossessed subjects. For some Jewish anarchists, prefiguration demanded mobilization against assimilation and antisemitism. Contemporary Indigenous activists and scholars describe decolonization not as the possibility of another world, but the sovereignty to practice one's own traditions. As Theresa Warburton notes, the book titles of Nick Estes's *Our History Is the Future* and Leanne Betasamosake Simpson's *As We Have Always Done* signify "this orientation toward the existence of worlds that live with the land and its people here."[82] Brandon Benallie similarly emphasizes that rejecting tradition cannot support processes of Indigenous liberation.[83] Their critique of European, Christian, and settler anarchist definitions of *prefiguration* resonates with Jewish anarchist resistance to hegemonic time—including revolutionary time.

LITERATURES OF MUTUAL AID AND COMRADESHIP

Anarchism is not the product of a single thinker or sacred text: there is no Marx for anarchism (though there is much of Marx in anarchism).[84] Beyond the principles of mutual aid and direct action, anarchist thought ranges from individualism to communism, militant atheism to ascetic mysticism, pacificism to retributive terrorism. Jewish anarchists drew inspiration for the principles of mutual aid and comradeship from two non-Jewish writers, the Russian geographer Pyotr Kropotkin (1842–1921) and the North American poet Walt Whitman (1819–1892). Whitman and Kropotkin shared lyrical forms: breathlessly long sentences, litanies that embed humanity within ecology, a vocabulary of natural sciences, and themes of comradeship and kinship with all the world. They write like Bellini's St. Francis, turning from his open manuscript to regard the animals in a beam of light.[85]

In 1902, Kropotkin published *Mutual Aid*. The word "anarchism" never appears in the book, as Kropotkin aimed to disrupt the perception that exploitation is natural through scientific observation rather than political argument. David Graeber notes that when *Mutual Aid* first appeared, "there were few scientists courageous enough to challenge the idea that capitalism and nationalism were rooted in human nature, or that the authority of states was ultimately inviolable."[86] Kropotkin was informed by a series of anthropological expeditions funded by the Russian Empire's geographical society. Although his sponsors had intended for him to gather information on borderlands and Indigenous societies to advance imperial ventures, he returned instead with research that provided the basis of an anarchist theory derived from the lifeways of non-state societies. Throughout *Mutual Aid*, Kropotkin musters anthropological, historical, and zoological data to argue against Social Darwinism. He asserts that cooperation was a determining factor of evolution and seeks to reclaim Darwin's insights from capitalist competition. Kropotkin's model of mutual aid embeds humans within the natural world and in relation to animality. The lists of mutual aid formations accumulate to show the reality of non-competitive social arrangements. He emphasizes mutual aid as a law of nature, not an emotion or "mere" affective bond, even while his authorial voice keens with longing for comradeship:

> It is not love to my neighbour—whom I often do not know at all—which induces me to seize a pail of water and to rush towards his house when I see it on fire; it is a far wider, even though more vague feeling or instinct of human solidarity and sociability which moves me. So it is also with animals. It is not love, and not even sympathy (understood in its proper sense) which induces a herd of ruminants or of horses to form a ring in order to resist an attack of wolves; not love which induces wolves to form a pack for hunting; not love which induces kittens or lambs to play, or a dozen of species of young birds to spend their days together in the autumn; and it is neither love nor personal sympathy which induces

many thousand fallow-deer scattered over a territory as large as France to form into a score of separate herds, all marching towards a given spot, in order to cross there a river. It is a feeling infinitely wider than love or personal sympathy—an instinct that has been slowly developed among animals and men in the course of an extremely long evolution, and which has taught animals and men alike the force they can borrow from the practice of mutual aid and support, and the joys they can find in social life.

In short, Kropotkin sought to prove that *mutual aid is not love, but science;* not utopianism, but the very substratum of life, human and other animal. Kropotkin envisioned an anarchist society rooted in organic harmony "obtained, not by submission to law, or by obedience to any authority, but by free agreements," as he elaborated in his 1905 entry in the *Encyclopaedia Britannica.*[87] Kropotkin's prose on mutual aid profoundly informed anarchist literature, seeking genealogy and immanence rather than utopian deferment. In brief, the strategy of anarchist genealogy is to reveal that another world is possible because another world is already here in this one.

Unlike Bakunin and Proudhon, Kropotkin was not antisemitic, and he cultivated relationships with Jewish anarchists. He was one of the few non-Jews to receive the honor of a *zaml-bukh,* a kind of posthumous festschrift.[88] More than two dozen of Kropotkin's works were translated into Yiddish, and he enjoyed close comradeship with Jewish anarchists, from whom he learned to understand Yiddish.[89] *Arbeter fraynd* (Worker's Friend), edited by the anti-militarist rabbi Yankev Meyer Zalkind in London, ran serialized Yiddish translations of *Mutual Aid* in the early 1920s, and the poet Sholem Shvartsbard likened him to "the *Rebbe,* the Baal Shem-Tov," calling him "that noble Russian heart" and "the Buddha of our time."[90] The poet Anna Margolin (Rosa Lebensbaum) brought Jewish political debates to Kropotkin's attention during his time in London exile. In 1901, Emma Goldman arranged his tour of the United States. He made a tremendous impression, and in private gatherings he met with Yiddish anarchists and writers, including the playwright Jacob Gordin, the editor Saul Yanovsky, and the physician Hillel Solotaroff, who discussed with him "the Dreyfus case and other important questions of the day."[91] In a letter to his Yiddish editors in March 1904, Kropotkin salutes Jewish revolutionary participation and hopes for "one great confraternity" of workers:

> The Jewish workers took a prominent part in the great movement which began in Russia during these last years. . . . And not only have the young

heroes stepped forth bravely, unafraid of death and annihilation in lonely prison cells, in the snows of frozen Siberia, but also a great number of Jewish working-men in the large and small towns have not feared to rise bravely and vigorously against the hundred years' oppression, declaring frankly and freely before the entire world their demands and hopes for the final liberation of the hundred-year-old slavery. I heartily wish that my "Memoirs" may help the Jewish youth to read the divers problems of the present movement against the all-destroying power of existent capitalism and authority. I will consider myself fortunate if one of the downtrodden of Capitalism and Authority, wafted to one of the distant nooks of Russia, will find upon reading those lines that he does not stand quite alone on the battlefield. May he know that, on going into battle for liberation of those who create all wealth and receive as reward nothing but poverty, he becomes, by this alone, a participant of the great cause—of the great struggle which is conducted everywhere for the freedom and happiness of all mankind, that he enters into the family of the workers of the entire world who are united in one great confraternity demanding freedom and equality for all.[92]

First published serially in English between 1890 and 1896 in the journal *The Nineteenth Century*, Kropotkin's opus entered Yiddish through a three-volume edition, which also circulated in *Arbeter fraynd* (London). Y. A. Merison translated *Mutual Aid* as *Gegenzaytige hilf: bay khi's un menshen, als a faktor fun entviklung*, published in New York City in 1913 by the Kropotkin Literature Society, a social group founded by Merison and a prolific engine of translation. The Germanic (*daytshmerish*) term *gegenzaytige hilf* has a technical ring, appealing to a high register to underscore the biological basis of Kropotkin's work. Merison chose the most Germanic or "international" terminology, avoiding terms more commonly used in Jewish discourse for mutual aid: *gemakh*, for example, are traditional mutual aid societies, which Kropotkin references obliquely ("the Whitechapel alliance of mothers"); he similarly passes up *mithelf* (collaboration) and *mesaye*, a Hebraic term for help or aid. Merison writes in the translator's introduction that he turned to the 1907 Russian translations, which were "improved" by the author after publication of the English version, and he includes supplements on newly emerging science.[93] As he notes, he aims to reproduce the "precision/perfection" of Kropotkin's English style.

While the original English editions of *Mutual Aid* avoid the word "anarchism" (and only briefly mention "unionism"), Kropotkin's introductions to the

Yiddish editions are forthright about the work's political aims.[94] Kropotkin's
seven-page introduction to the 1913 Yiddish edition comments on his recent
work, including the pamphlets "The Origin of the State." Kropotkin writes in
that introduction:

> I will say that it is the greatest pleasure to me to see my work appear in
> Yiddish. In the present moment, the idea of centralisation and centralis-
> ing states is so much in fashion, admittedly even amongst socialists, that
> we hear all too frequently people saying that the little nationalities have
> no reason to exist; rather, that they will become gobbled up by the larger
> nations, and so rapidly forget their mother-tongue—which would be all
> the better.
>
> My whole life's experience has taught me exactly the opposite. All
> that I have learned in my life, on the contrary, convinced me that the
> most certain path to bring about harmony from the striving of various
> nations, is—for each part of humanity to develop and enrich the language
> spoken by the masses of that part of humanity. . . . [Multilingualism] is
> the surest way to enrich our general heritage [*yerushe*] from all national-
> ities and tribes, which have special value for philosophy, theory, poetry
> and art.

Kropotkin's reference to "the little nationalities" may be a calque of the Russian
phrase *malochislennye narody* denoting ethnic minorities, particularly of Indigenous peoples.[95] He concludes the Introduction: "I am filled with a special pleasure to see *Mutual Aid* appear in a language spoken by a considerable part of humanity which already has their own original literature, and which contributes
their national characteristics to humanity's broad treasure."[96] Just as Goldman's
remarks differed when expressed in Yiddish rather than English, Kropotkin
writes differently through Yiddish than in English, where he addressed "universal" scientific audiences; here, he discusses the value and preservation of what are
now called "minor" languages. Kropotkin's Yiddish introduction may have been
informed by his conversations with the poet Anna Margolin (Rosa Lebensbaum), particularly his enthusiastic affirmation of Yiddish as a "mother tongue"
worthy of radicals' attentive preservation.

Kropotkin's framing of mutual aid, harmonious social attachment, and noncoercive association was widely taken up by Jewish anarchists, including Gustav
Landauer. A translator of Kropotkin, Landauer wrote: "The state is a social relationship; a certain way of people relating to one another. It can be destroyed by

creating new social relationships; i.e., by people relating to one another differently."[97] Erich Mühsam described his friend and comrade: "Landauer never saw anarchism as a politically or organizationally limited doctrine, but as an expression of ordered freedom in thought and action. . . . His revolutionary activity was never limited to the fight against state laws and social systems. It concerned all dimensions of life."[98] Part II of this book examines mutual aid as the basis of feminist thought for Katherina Yevzerov Merison, who likely worked with her husband, Y. A. Merison, to translate Kropotkin's opus. Judith Butler's recent lectures echoed Landauer's and Mollie Steimer's definitions, terming anarchism "an ethos of sociability."[99] For Yiddish anarchists, sociality was cultivated in the form of balls, picnics, fundraisers held on steamboats sailing up and down the Hudson River, spaghetti events, free medical programs, Ferrer Modern Schools, and mutual aid societies. Although mutual aid practices can and do exist without anarchism's specialized vocabulary, mutual aid is central to anarchism.

Stylistically, *Mutual Aid* became a model for anarchist writing: inclusive of many disciplines, lyrical, ecological, and genealogical. Its *form* thematized mutual aid, seeking ancestry, a submerged present, and recognition of labor already performed to serve survival. In the passage about ruminants, kittens, deer, and hosts of other creatures, Kropotkin's long sentences stretch out this litany; there is no jaggedness, rupture, or declamation in his prosody. Rebecca Solnit describes mutual aid after natural disasters in prose that echoes Kropotkin's cadence:

> On the warm night of August 15, 2003, the Milky Way could be seen in New York City, a heavenly realm long lost to view until the blackout that hit the Northeast late that afternoon. You can think of the current social order as something akin to this artificial light: another kind of power that fails in disaster. In its place appears a reversion to improvised, collaborative, cooperative, and local society. However beautiful the stars of a suddenly visible night sky, few nowadays could find their way by them. But the constellations of solidarity, altruism, and improvisation are within most of us and reappear at these times. People know what to do in a disaster. The loss of power, the disaster in the modern sense, is an affliction, but the reappearance of these old heavens is its opposite. This is the paradise entered through hell.[100]

At his centennial, Kropotkin's works were freshly taken up by ecologists, Black radical theorists, and scholars of animal studies, among other disciplines.[101]

Saidiya Hartman writes of Black women's social worlds in the early twentieth century: "Collaboration, reciprocity, and shared creation defined the practice of mutual aid. . . . Mutual aid did not traffic in the belief that the self existed distinct and apart from others or revere the ideas of individuality and sovereignty, as much as it did singularity and freedom."[102] Mutual aid flows from an understanding of the self as shared.

The vocabulary and methods of mutual aid have spread widely through contemporary leftist discourse and practice, even as Kropotkin's entanglement with colonial anthropology bears new critique.[103] In his popular handbook *Mutual Aid: Building Solidarity During This Crisis (And the Next!)*, Dean Spade defines mutual aid as "work that directly addresses the conditions the movement seeks to address, such as by providing housing, food, healthcare, or transportation in a way that draws attention to the politics creating need and vulnerability."[104] Rather than citing Kropotkin, Spade constructs a contemporary genealogy including the Black Panther Party's free breakfast program, the Young Lords' "hijacking of New York City's tuberculosis testing mobile unit," and "feminist organizing to provide underground abortions in the 1970's." Beyond anarchism's specific vocabularies of mutual aid, Marxists such as the abolitionist Ruth Wilson Gilmore also insist upon its immanence: "Abolition is not absence, it is presence. What the world will become already exists in fragments and pieces, experiments and possibilities. So those who feel in their gut deep anxiety that abolition means knock it all down, scorch the earth and start something new, let that go. Abolition is building the future from the present, in all of the ways we can."[105] Named or not, Kropotkin's observation of mutual aid as the world's substratum persists in leftist scholarship.

If anarchism is a prefigurative ethics—an "ethos of sociality," as Kropotkin and Judith Butler affirm—what ought that sociality look like? What literary practices did anarchists develop to cultivate comradeship? As Colin Ward argues, "Anarchists are people who make a social and political philosophy out of the natural and spontaneous tendency of humans to associate together for their mutual benefit."[106] They endow the principle of comradeship with spiritual intensity; for some, "comradely affection" might even become the root of a new currency.[107] Anarchist commitment to friendship rejected the utilitarian view of comradeship as the mere basis of militarism or movement-building. Instead, they strove to make all forms of social relation egalitarian, from farming to education to family and romantic partnerships—with attendant ecstasy and heartbreak amply expressed in their correspondence.

Walt Whitman lit their imaginings of a new sociality and provided its poetic vocabulary. Yiddish anarchists devotedly studied him, recognizing their own ethos within his rumbling language. In 1899, the revolutionary anarchist Yosef Bovshover dubbed him "a Moses of free thought."[108] The journalist Leonard Abbott claimed that the "central motive" of Whitman's poetry was "revolutionary."[109] Gay anarchists such as Oscar Wilde thrilled to Whitman's erotic cadence of comradeship, as Abbott noted: "Homosexuals all over the world have looked toward Whitman as toward a leader."[110] Anarchist journals rallied to reprint Wilde's most galvanizing verses; for this they sometimes faced censorship, as when *The Firebrand* attempted to publish "A Woman Waits for Me" in 1897.[111] Whitman was translated into Yiddish in 1934, but his work was read widely before then in English; indeed, the poet Malka Heifetz Tussman received a volume of Whitman upon immigrating to the United States.[112] Though Whitman's poetry effused nationalism and Western expansionism, settler anarchists adjusted their lens to include it.[113] Like Ibsen and Strindberg, Whitman was ushered into the anarchist canon by the reading practices of his audience, if not by self-avowal.

Emma Goldman hailed his verse as prefiguring horizontal democracy and planned to name her paper *The Open Road* after a Whitman line. Had she not been in jail at the time, Goldman would have presented at the annual Whitman gathering. Her unfinished manuscript criticized how "Classicists" interpreted Whitman and how biographers elided his homosexuality. She dubs *Leaves of Grass* "Whitman's song of sex" and names the queerness of his idealized comradeship: "It was his sex differentiation which enriched his nature, hence enriched his knowledge of and his understanding for human complexities. Walt Whitman's idea of universal comradeship was conditioned in his magnetic response to his own sex. So was his extraordinary sensitiveness to the nature of woman conditioned in the fact that he had considerable femininity in him." Goldman notes that he twice calls himself "the poet of comrades" in *Leaves of Grass* and parts by reaching out to readers' bodies: "Comrade, this is no book, / Who touches this touches a man."[114] Reading Whitman as comrade, Goldman melds his language with anarchist visual tropes:

> We need Walt Whitman now more than ever. We need his indomitable courage, his beautiful comradeship, his stirring song, that we may not falter in our efforts to build the new life out of the ruins of the old, for the new city stands "Where no monuments exist to heroes but in the common words and deeds."[115]

Goldman cites Whitman's romantic anti-monumentality of "The Great City" within the anarchist phrase "living among ruins." Her citational practice represents another form of anarchist close reading, gesturing against Emerson to claim genealogy otherwise. Her absence from the Whitman gathering and inability to finish or publish the Whitman essay further represent the material exclusion of her voice from literary discourse, even as she continued to lecture in Yiddish and attended others' speeches on Whitman.

Goldman does not critique Whitman's imperial westward gaze or his exoticized images of Black and Indigenous male bodies. Whitman upheld comradeship as a structure of brotherhood inseparable from territory, as he apostrophizes feminine "democracy":

I will plant companionship thick as trees along all the rivers of America,
    and along the shores of the great lakes, and all over the prairies;
        I will make inseparable cities, with their arms about each other's necks
        By the love of comrades,
            By the manly love of comrades.
        For you these from me, O Democracy, to serve you ma femme![116]

This aspect of Goldman's essay expresses what Theresa Warburton terms "settler anarchism": the replication of colonial structures of race and land relation even within a critique of state domination.[117] Goldman instead identifies with Whitman as a victim of homophobia and censorship. Goldman extends Whitman's vision of democracy without troubling it: "Democracy as conceived and sung by Walt Whitman, is still far from come. Whatever some of her admirers have once thought of democracy, they have recanted, sacrificed to the rule of dictatorship. Mr. George Bernard Shaw and many others have now become the pall-bearers of democracy, slain by the Tcheka and Fascism. What Walt Whitman wrote to a European Revolutionair, holds good for the revolutionair of the whole world today." Goldman references "To a Foil'd European Revolutionaire" in *Leaves of Grass,* eliding the failure of Whitman's addressee and the avowal of "Nationality" that precedes the quoted passage. More remarkable is the appearance of "the Tcheka," the Soviet secret police, in an essay universalizing Whitman: she places him within a genealogy of antifascism.

Among Whitman's anarchist devotees was the philosopher Gustav Landauer, who translated the poet into German in 1916, having earlier translated Kropotkin. Landauer praises Whitman's "sometimes visionary capacity for imagination" and claims he "shared a common intellectual bond" with Proudhon. Landauer extols Whitman's "cosmic love and exuberance of feeling," arguing that this "love between people, for the development of this spirit and for his artistic vision, isn't some general, blurry love of humanity." Landauer affirms the truth of affect and the value of sentimentality: "It is in the context of this love that feelings of solidarity, as reflected in Whitman's most beautiful and searching poems, converge with his dreams of new life and social forms. It is a fruitless endeavor, smacking of fashionable pseudo-scientific psychology, to regard these feelings of brotherhood as something perverse, pathological, or even degenerate. We must learn again that personalities and momentous times are also sentimental; and that it is in times of weakness and among dissolute generations that people shrink from the giving of unreserved and fervent feelings for one's loved ones, intimate friends, or the sea, the landscape, the cosmos."[118] Landauer's philosophical model of comradeship echoes his reading of Whitman:

> One can throw away a chair and destroy a pane of glass; but those are idle talkers and credulous idolators or words who regard the state as such a thing or as a fetish that one can smash in order to destroy it. The State is a condition, a certain relationship between human beings, a mode of behavior; we destroy it by contracting other relationships, by behaving differently toward one another—One day it will be realized that socialism is not the invention of anything new but the discovery of something actually present, of something that has grown. . . . We are the state, and we shall continue to be the state until we have created the institutions that form a real community and society of men.[119]

Landauer's elaboration of anarchist ethics follows from this recognition of the contingency of power. In Whitman's visions of comradeship, Landauer saw the lyrical flowering of this idea. Defining anarchism/socialism as "not the invention of anything new but the discovery of something actually present" harmonizes with Kropotkin's location of mutual aid as immanent.

From Goldman to Landauer, anarchist readings of Whitman offered a poetic methodology of comradeship. Mark Doty remarks that Whitman's ideal of an anti-classist gay erotic life among equals was, for his era, "entirely new."[120] Among Whitman's radical acolytes was the gay activist Edward Carpenter, whose adoring account *Days with Walt Whitman, with Some Notes on His Life and Work* appeared in London in 1906. Carpenter describes the effect of Whitman's presence: "I was aware of a certain radiant power in him, a large benign effluence and inclusiveness, as of the sun, which filled out the place where he was—

yet with something of reserve and sadness in it too, and a sense of remoteness and inaccessibility." Doty notes that Carpenter "wants the like-minded to find in Whitman their experience reflected, their voices—their soundless voices—carried."[121] Whitman's vision of comradeship formed the basis of Carpenter's politics and placed gay men and women at "the vanguard of the utopia to come."[122] Contemporary abolitionists such as Mariame Kaba cite Whitman as inspiration, and the performance artist Taylor Mac's recent "Whitman in the Woods" dramatizes *Leaves of Grass* as a new queer eco-poetics.[123]

Carpenter and Doty emphasize the force of Whitman's physical presence. In rhetoric and fervor, these accounts resonate with the anarchist genre of recounting luminous social encounters, often across differences in age and language. Goldman, for example, narrates meeting the French Communard leader Louise Michel: "The afternoon with Louise was an experience unlike anything that had happened till then in my life. Her hand in mine, its tender pressure on my head, her words of endearment and close comradeship, made my soul expand, reach out towards the spheres of beauty where she dwelt."[124] Michel herself was a French poet who learned the Kanak language during her exile in New Caledonia, whose work heralded a futurity of comradeship.[125] A muse to poets, Michel was "nearly Joan of Arc" to Paul Verlaine, and Victor Hugo sang of "Your long look of hatred to all those who are inhuman, / And the feet of children which you warm between your hands," she who possessed "the divine chaos of starlike things."[126] Margaret Anderson, the lesbian editor of the experimental modernist *Little Review,* similarly described Emma Goldman with an erotic thrill: "Life takes on an intenser quality when she is there, something cosmic in the air, a feeling of worlds in the making which Hardy once put into a single line: 'while universe after universe drifts by.'"[127] These openly homoerotic accounts describe an anarchist *presence* that obviates speech and makes new forms of relating possible, promising an even more luminous comradeship-to-come.

Yiddish anarchist ideals of comradeship at times obstructed romantic love. Edelshtat, for example, publicly espoused "free love" as a philosophical human right while scorning personal romance. Saul Yanovsky, later the literary editor of *Fraye arbeter shtime,* wondered: "Were Edelshtat and Bovshover ever in love? I don't know. In all probability yes. But I am sure they suppressed it with all their strength as something sinful, as a sort of betrayal against their only love, freedom. Therefore, you would be wasting your time looking for a love poem by Edelshtat."[128] Regardless of their actual domestic lives, anarchists' *openness* toward passionate comradeship fascinated writers across the political spectrum and invited literary representations often more lurid than lucid.

LOVER, AVENGER, TERRORIST: REPRESENTATIONS
OF ANARCHISTS IN YIDDISH LITERATURE

Anarchists appear in Yiddish literature as sometimes charming, sometimes oversexed, sometimes terrifying, but always fascinating creatures. Some portrayals merely recirculate caricatures of bomb-throwing, beard-growing terrorists, while others elaborate the authors' philosophical and social dilemmas through dialogue with anarchist characters. The Bundist writer Zusman Segalovitsh, known for his middlebrow-to-lowbrow (*shund*) prose, published a trilogy titled *Dos anarkhistishe meydl* (The Anarchist Girl, Warsaw 1925–1929). Translations of anarchist texts edited by socialists also tended to highlight the most scandalous aspects of their source material: the *Forverts* (Forward) newspaper canceled its serialized Yiddish translation of Goldman's memoir after the crowd-pleasing chapter about her living arrangements with two lovers.

Anarchists appear in Isaac Bashevis Singer's short stories amid a menagerie of dreamers and unsavory oddballs, as in "Job" (1970) and *Der tate vert an anarkhist* (Papa Becomes an Anarchist).[129] The latter is an autobiographical piece first published in *Forverts*. When the narrator's pious father encounters a group of anarchists on the way home from synagogue, the story makes merry with the convergences and tensions between religious and militant futurities, as both rabbi and anarchist fervently envision the world to come. The rabbi declares his newfound reasoning to his family: "Of course Jews long for the Messiah, but while we're in Exile it would be quite a good thing. We wouldn't have to pay rent. There would be no thieves. . . . We wouldn't need policemen or thieves to lock the gates, and there wouldn't be any soldiers or wars. Because why do kings wage war? For money." His wife grills him with skeptical questions, but the son is enthralled. Bashevis Singer's father analogizes "ancient times" with an anarchist society in which all would work a trade without shame, resolving both workers' poor education and rabbis' poverty: "[Workers nowadays] have no time to study, but with a four-hour day everyone would be a scholar. In the Talmud we learn about the sages Rabbi Yochanan the shoemaker and Rabbi Joshua the blacksmith. . . . Our forefather Jacob was a shepherd, and so were Moses and King David." The father's enthusiasm for anarchism cools, however, once "someone in the Radziminer *shtibl* had told him that this entire philosophy was incompatible with Judaism. He no longer wanted to discuss it. When I asked him, he responded, 'Be a Jew and the Messiah will come.'" The story ends with the young narrator realizing the "awful truths" of poverty and abjection. Singer's narrative arc descends from the heights of rabbinic and anarchist hope to the boy's inner turmoil caused by ceaseless social misery. Yet the reasoning behind his father's dissuasion from anarchism is never explicated, and any actual conflict presented by the idea of Jews biding their time in an anarchist society until the Messiah arrives remains unspoken. If there is truly no bottom to human depravity, he seems to ask, why ought there be a limit to human idealism?

In her comic novel *Diary of a Lonely Girl, or the Battle Against Free Love* (Tage-bukh fun a elende meydel), Miriam Karpilove lances anarchist rhetoric of "free love" as a self-serving scheme devised by men. The novel was serialized from 1916 to 1918 in the New York paper *Di vorheyt* (The Truth). Its heroine endures her boorish caller's "radical" monologues, transparently cloaking ulterior motives:

> "I will never tire of explaining to you what we are and what we were created for," said C., "until you understand and come around to my point of view. You'll say: 'Here I am. I live for today. I won't hold anything back for tomorrow. Let anarchy, full anarchy reign here, where until now only dark thoughts ruled. My young body will no longer serve my old spirit. Let me separate from myself, or let my spirit follow my body, as science decrees it must.'"
>
> "That's ridiculous. I'll never say that," I replied skeptically.
>
> "Yes you will," he said with a certainty that didn't permit me to respond, "you will have to say it."
>
> "Why will I have to?"
>
> "Science says so."
>
> "Science can say what she likes. I don't know her, and she can't hurt me."[130]

The self-righteous suitor parodies Kropotkin's investment in "scientific" laws of behavior or, more broadly, anarchist reifications of a natural order. Karpilove's witty prose emphasizes the dissonance between C.'s purported aim to "let full anarchy reign" and his coercive behavior. Her novel resonates with the irate letters of wives whose husbands have wandered libidinously into the anarchist movement; their fury and abandonment still blister in the archive.

Although Yiddish writers in North America such as Karpilove and Bashevis Singer cast anarchists as naïve or calculating romantics, those in Europe tended to represent Jewish anarchists as more sinister figures during the period of assassinations at the turn of the century, which were often met with violent antisemitic backlash.[131] Their work reiterated the tropes of the French "Age of Attentats" of 1892 and 1894, when four young anarchists were guillotined. One of them, François Koenigstein, was assumed by antisemites to be Jewish based upon his last name. Koenigstein had become an atheist after reading Eugene Sue's novel *The Wandering Jew* (1844). In this era, some Jewish assassins were crowned heroes by the broader community, who saw them as avengers for trauma. In 1926, the poet Sholem Shvartsbard murdered the Ukrainian Cossack Symon Petliura to avenge the pogroms of the Russian Civil War (1917–1920). Shvartsbard searched for Petliura in the streets of Paris for months, pistol in his pocket, and finally shot him point-blank in the street. He was acquitted in a 1927 trial, defended by the flamboyant lawyer Henri Torrès. Torrès also defended the teenage assassin Herschel Grynszpan a decade later, to great acclaim; Albert Einstein hailed his "masterly speech, vibrant with a sense of humanity and justice, [which] has built a monument to the cause of Law that time will not erode."[132] Between Shvartsbard's self-mythologizing courtroom speeches and Torrès's oratory, they succeeded in turning the jury and audience's focus to Ukrainian antisemitic brutalities. Shvartsbard then toured the world, reportedly disappointing audiences with his strange lack of charisma and weak handshake. In his poetry, correspondence, and memoirs, however, Shvartsbard portrays himself as a philosophical soul plotting Jewish utopia.

Contra Shvartsbard's poetic self-portraits and his comrades' identification with the "Jewish avenger," he enters as an ambivalent figure in Yiddish modernist literature. Shvartsbard's archetype appears in the Soviet writer Dovid Bergelson's short story *"Tsvishn emigrantn"* (Between Refugees) and Alter Kacyzne's 1935 play *Shvartsbard: a sintetisher reportazh* (Shvartsbard: A Synthetic Reportage), which was produced in Los Angeles in 1940. Both works portray a psychologically twisted character. Kelly Johnson characterizes the Shvartsbard of Kacyzne's play as "a Jewish Hamlet."[133] Bergelson's expressionist short story *"Tsvishn emigrantn"* (Between Refugees) portrays the "Jewish terrorist" with trepidation and anxiety—and not a little fascination with this character, so out of joint with time. Bergelson first composed the story in the early 1920s and then rewrote it after Petliura's murder. Although he was likely first inspired by the Armenian assassin Soghomon Tehlirian, Bergelson revised *"Tsvishn emigrantn"* after Shvartsbard's case gripped the public and a few years after the height of support for the Russian revolutionary Grigory Gershuni. Bergelson's story explores the traumatized psyches of the narrator, a writer living in a boarding house, and the "Jewish terrorist" who moves into a room on the same corridor. The narrator describes his first encounter with this fellow boarder in tones of expressionist horror:

> He had broad cheekbones, but they were not the same, and therefore the two sides of his face looked different. The right cheek was smooth

and even, like everyone else's—a cheek that wanted to take pleasure from the world, it let you know,

"I want to live with people."

And his left cheek was crooked; as if it were his and not his. It looked like a cheek that fought with the world—life had thrust displeasure at it, and it would sling displeasure at the world. Thanks to his left cheek, the young man was ugly, but as it seemed to me, the young man took the left cheek's side, he was like a mother whose one child was bright, but whose other child was a monster—and out of a sense of justice he took the side of the ugly left cheek, carrying its meanness in himself [*getrogn in zikh ir beyzkayt*]. Because of this ugly cheek he had a mustache—to hide its ugliness a bit. I noticed his mustache and it seemed to me that his right cheek was not satisfied with it, because of its unusual dirty copper color, which seemed to say, "Leave me alone. I am a mean one. Better you go your way and I mine."[134]

The description of the refugee's face echoes visual tropes of German expressionism, which Harriet Murav likens to Otto Dix's lithograph "Skin Graft" (1924).[135] Bergelson's description of the scar also evokes the face of Ukrainian anarchist commander Nestor Makhno, whose prominent facial scar was likely inflicted not by trench warfare but by his wife, Galina. In Bergelson's story, the would-be assassin's acquaintance attempts to get him a psychiatrist, pathologizing rather than sympathizing with Jewish violence.

"Among Refugees" embodies crooked temporality. The stranger's face resembles a clock, evoking Shvartsbard's occupation of watchmaker, or perhaps making literal Mikhail Bakhtin's "time made fleshy." Bergelson's wandering would-be assassin appears as an unsettling embodiment of modernity's trauma, not the glamorous avenging angel that Shvartsbard professed to be in his memoir and courtroom testimony. Though Shvartsbard's poems and letters cite Judith and Deborah to justify collective vengeance, Bergelson replaced his self-fashioned persona with expressionist symbols of misguided revolutionary impulses.

While Shvartsbard acted alone, G. A. Gershuni founded the Russian Socialist-Revolutionary Party and led its Combat Organization, which assassinated high officials in the tsarist government. In Gershuni's Russian-language memoir *Iz nedavniago proshlogo* (From the Recent Past), which was translated into Yiddish, he also constructs himself as a Jewish hero. After Gershuni's trial in 1904 and subsequent escape from Siberian prison in 1906, he became a touring celebrity on a much grander scale than Shvartsbard. In earlier decades, Jewish anarchists

hotly debated assassination and "propaganda of the deed" after the 1901 assassination of President McKinley by Leon Czolgosz. Saul (Shoel) Yanovsky, the editor of *Fraye arbeter shtime,* denounced Czolgosz's act, weighing it against the
repression that followed. Yet as Zimmer notes, this perspective was considered
high-handed: "on the night of September 16, three days after Yanovsky's words
saw print and a day after McKinley succumbed to his wounds, a mob of 'Jewish
school boys' ransacked the offices of the *Fraye Arbeter Shtime* at 185 Henry
Street and chased down and beat Yanovsky. In his 1902 pamphlet *Der olef beys
fun anarkhizmus* (The ABCs of Anarchism), Yanovsky reiterated, 'Anarchism is
not a doctrine of assassination and the anarchists are not murderers.' Rather, the
foundational principle of anarchism was 'peace between men.'"[136]

The father, the lover, the neighbor, and the terrorist: Jewish anarchists appear in many guises in Yiddish literature. Despite anarchist ambivalence toward
assassination as strategy, the image of anarchist as terrorist persisted as a trope
in Yiddish literature. Shvartsbard, Gershuni, and other militants appear as troubling muses. For Karpilove, Bashevis Singer, and Bergelson, the Jewish anarchist
is a proxy figure for grappling with Jewish identity, failures of masculinity, and
immigrant precarity. These characters—picaresque, charismatic, philosophical,
or blunt forces of destruction—are mere refractions of the complexity of Yiddish anarchist thought and literature itself.

YIDDISH ANARCHIST AESTHETICS:
EDELSHTAT TO PALEY

Yiddish anarchist aesthetics are constituted by the proliferation, rather than
codification, of heterogeneous forms. A unifying aspect of Yiddish anarchist
approaches across literary trends and historical eras, however, was the ethos of
radical immanence and pleasure-taking in the everyday world. In a manifesto
from 1907, Gustav Landauer declares that artists, poets, and scientists belonged
to a category of work that does not serve life, but is life itself.[137] This approach
suffused anarchist aesthetics beyond the Yiddish radicals: in a letter written in
1920 from the Leavenworth Penitentiary, the Mexican revolutionary Ricardo
Flores Magón scorned the idea of art removed from the realm of the everyday:
"Life, with its myriad manifestations, is against that absurd school."[138]

Few of these Yiddish poets enjoyed enough material privilege to achieve philosophical detachment, in any event. Dovid Edelshtat thematized the struggle to
produce authentic art within proletarian conditions, extracting verse from his
own suffering. "Two Painters" expresses his highest values: in a competition be-

tween artists, "a canvas full with manufactured paint can't match one drop of
blood drawn from the heart."[139] Another poem titled "To the Muse" discloses
how conditions of rough living shape his poetry. In Aaron Kramer's translation, Edelshtat opines, "I never learned how to polish my rhymes, / how prettily
thoughts can be dressed":

> Stop knocking, Muse, at the door of my heart!
> No lamps of hope are alive;
> it's crowded with tears, and terribly dark.
> —Go to the poets who thrive!
>
> To them who know about golden noons,
> Who've reached the rapturous isle;
> and me, with my fetters and my wounds,
> leave me alone for a while![140]

The poet is hounded and tortured by creativity, captive to its "fetters and
wounds"; the speaker bids his Muse visit other poets "who know about golden
noons," whose afternoons unfold at leisure. Despite this call to be left at peace
by inspiration, the poem performs a defiant assertion of a worker's subjectivity:
nonetheless, the worker is a poet, and the muse knocks.

This study of Yiddish anarchist stylistics ranges from Edelshtat's Sweatshop
romanticism to the Russian avant-garde, without attempting to overdetermine
a single aesthetic. The art historian Nina Gurianova identifies a "golden age" of
anarchist aesthetics between 1910 and 1918 in Russia, characterizing it as a key
liminal period for experimental, heterogeneous aesthetics, before the hegemony
of socialist realism and repression of the Kronstadt uprising. Gurianova documents the links between anarchism and the Russian avant-garde, which "created
an aesthetics attuned both to Mikhail Bakunin's anarchist theory of 'creative
destruction' and to the anti-utopian philosophy of Dostoyevsky's *Notes from
the Underground.*"[141] This heterogeneity encouraged Peretz Markish's "multiple and partial affiliations" with various trends of modernism, including both
futurism and expressionism.[142] In his essay collection of 1921, Markish's declaration of art as a simultaneously creative and destructive force references Bakunin.
His linguistic patterning, however, deepens rather than severs an aesthetic bond
to Jewish literary tradition: to do so would result in assimilation and surrender
to antisemitic erasure.

Across these heterogeneous movements, Yiddish anarchist literature remains
invested in genealogy and elegy as paradigmatic forms. Anarchism is frequently

framed as a utopian project, deferring realization of "the Idea" into the future; thus studies of anarchist literature focus on speculative and science fiction, genres which imagine the cosmic mechanisms and mundane details of fantastical future societies. Western and Romance-language literatures have a long tradition of such utopian fiction. In 1770, Louis-Sébastien Mercier's novel *L'An 2440, rêve s'il en fut jamais* (The Year 2440: A Dream If Ever There Was One), written several years before the French Revolution, depicted a revolution of the enslaved who overturn all colonial relations.[143] Kropotkin hailed William Morris's serialized novel *News from Nowhere* (1890) as "the most thoroughly and deeply anarchist conception of future society ever written."[144] More recently, the editors of the anthology *Octavia's Brood: Science Fiction Stories from Social Justice Movements* propose: "Whenever we try to envision a world without war, without violence, without prisons, without capitalism, we are engaging in speculative fiction. All organizing is science fiction."[145] The anarchist novelist Margaret Killjoy notes that "[Utopias] can simply be the exercise by which we free our imaginations, by which we escape, if even only for a moment, the confines of global capitalism, and see the possibility of something different—even if we don't know quite what that thing will be."[146] These approaches frame utopian fiction as a realm for imagining anarchist societies of the future, rather than recovering diasporic history or ethnic sovereignty.

In the context of the late nineteenth and early twentieth century, utopian Jewish writing is more strongly developed as a Zionist form, from Edmund Eisler's *Ein Zukunftsbild* (A Picture of the Future, 1885) to Theodore Herzl's *Altneuland* (The Old New Land, 1902). In 1901 the Zionist paper *Die Welt* serialized a utopian novel written by Sholem Aleichem.[147] Jewish anarchists were more committed to the construction of genealogy than speculation of futurity, apart from rare works such as Edelshtat's short story "One Hundred Years in the Future" and Russian anarcho-cosmism. The contrast between speculative and genealogical utopian literature reveals cultural differences in temporality. Jayna Brown's *Black Utopias: Speculative Life and the Music of Other Worlds* (2021), for example, is part of a wave of scholarship on Black and Indigenous anti-state decolonialism and visionary utopianism; their work represents a vital study of histories and imaginations excluded from Eurocentric anarchist history. Brown models utopia as a form of spiritual surrender, rooting freedom in the cosmos beyond the human. Tracing the art of Sun Ra, Alice Coltrane, and Samuel Delany, while drawing from Ernst Bloch and Octavia Butler, Brown writes: "Utopia is a part of a continual becoming, an embrace of change itself."[148] Ultimately,

Brown asks, "What does it mean to be ethical, if ethics is not predicated on the model of responsibility?"[149]

Theorization of responsibility lies at the heart of anarchist diasporism: it posits freedom as the beginning of relations of moral alterity, not their dissolution. The poet Abba Gordin wrote *Yidishe etik* (Jewish Ethics, 1937), which seeks to synthesize rather than sever the ethical systems of classical anarchism and Jewish philosophy. In "Anarchist Morality" (1897), Kropotkin calls for a militant mutuality and reciprocity: "By proclaiming ourselves anarchists, we proclaim beforehand that we disavow any way of treating others in which we should not like them to treat us.... Because we ourselves should ask to be killed like venomous beasts if we went to invade Burmese or Zulus who have done us no harm. We should say to our son or our friend: 'Kill me, if I ever take part in the invasion!'"[150] Kropotkin's ethics make militant the reciprocity of the Golden Rule: rather than "Do unto others as you would have them do unto you," he pleads to be killed if he ever takes part in another's dispossession.

Inspired in part by Kropotkin, Grace Paley's poetry lays out the ethical concerns of anarchist poetics. Paley identified as a "somewhat combative pacifist and cooperative anarchist"—although the Federal Bureau of Investigation categorized her as a communist and kept her file open for thirty years.[151] Paley had studied with W. H. Auden, who described himself as "a confirmed anarchist individualist."[152] In "Some Notes on Teaching: Probably Spoken," Paley advises all her students to read anarchist and Black radical memoir:

don't go through life without reading the autobiographies of Emma Goldman
    Prince Kropotkin
        Malcolm X[153]

In *Ethics,* his final and unfinished work, Kropotkin models "poetical" forms as capable of heightening readers' ethical commitments: "And when the poet has found the proper expression for his sense of communion with the Cosmos and his unity with his fellow-men, he becomes capable of inspiring millions of men with his high enthusiasm. He makes them feel what is best in them and awakens their desire to become better still. He produces in them those very ecstasies which were formerly considered as belonging exclusively to the province of religion."[154]

The last stanza of Paley's poem "Therefore" returns Kropotkin's ethical-poetic fervor. The poetic speaker recounts what she has "learned in politics and / dream from William Blake / and that beloved Prince Kropotkin." She reads them with Robert Nichols, the name of Paley's partner, in the living room and in bed, "before we loved and sometimes afterwards."[155] The poem names Blake and Kropotkin in the same breath and then sweeps out the window, gazing over a lush pastoral scene and up to the moon, looking with awe at the night sky. Reading Kropotkin and Blake together suffused domestic life with pleasure; poetry and ethics commune with moonlight and love.

Beyond the naming of anarchist philosophers, Paley's poetry thematizes anarchist ethics straightforwardly: "Why not speak the truth directly? Just speak out! Speak up! Speak to! Why not?"[156] Yet the power in one's voice is realized in community, through the mutuality of speaker and listener. In "A Poem About Storytelling," Paley balances these roles: "The first person may be the child who / says Listen! Guess what happened! / The important listener is the mother / The mother says What?"[157] It is an origin parable about the mutuality of speech, couched not in abstract philosophy but through the dialogue of children, mothers, neighbors, fathers, and villagers.

Indeed, Paley's texts were deeply vernacular in their process of composition, often moving between prose, poetry, and "speaking directly." In an interview with Joann Gardner, Paley recalled the spoken roots of what grew into the poem titled "Responsibility." She lays out the poet's responsibility in thirty-two lines and charges poets to move between social classes, refuse to pay war taxes, and speak truthfully:

> It is the responsibility of society to let the poet be a poet
> It is the responsibility of the poet to be a woman
> It is the responsibility of the poet to stand on street corners
>   giving out poems and beautifully written leaflets
>   also leaflets you can hardly bear to look at
>   because of the screaming rhetoric
> It is the responsibility of the poet to be lazy   to hang out and
>   prophesy
> It is the responsibility of the poet not to pay war taxes
> It is the responsibility of the poet to go in and out of ivory
>   towers and two-room apartments on Avenue C
>   and buckwheat fields and army camps
> It is the responsibility of the male poet to be a woman
> It is the responsibility of the female poet to be a woman
> It is the poet's responsibility to speak truth to power as the
>   Quakers say
> It is the poet's responsibility to learn the truth from the
>   powerless

It is the responsibility of the poet to say many times: there is no
>   freedom without justice and this means economic
>   justice and love justice
It is the responsibility of the poet to sing this in all the original
>   and traditional tunes of singing and telling poems
It is the responsibility of the poet to listen to gossip and pass it
>   on in the way storytellers decant the story of life
There is no freedom without fear and bravery   there is no
>   freedom unless
>   earth and air and water continue and children
>   also continue
It is the responsibility of the poet to be a woman   to keep an eye on
>   this world and cry out like Cassandra, but be
>   listened to this time[158]

The poem originated from her address to an *American Poetry Review* conference around 1990, where she was the sole woman presenter:

> JG: You wrote in the poem "Responsibility" that it's the poet's duty to be a woman, and then you wrote that it's the male poet's duty to be a woman.
> PALEY: Yeah, that gets a lot of men mad, or at least, annoyed.
> JG: What does it mean?
> PALEY: Well, first I said, it is the responsibility of the male poet to be a woman. So people thought that I would then say, it's the responsibility of the woman poet to be a man. No. It's not the responsibility of a black person to be a white person.
> JG: Well, also, the oppressed have already learned a great deal about the oppressor, trying to survive within that dominance.
> PALEY: They know it. Yeah.
> JG: Why does that make men angry?
> PALEY: People think that everything has to be equalized. Also guys may feel deprived of their progressive generosity. Actually many men do understand what I'm talking about.[159]

In this exchange, Paley explains how the subversion of poetic parallel structure lays bare the reader's expectations. The poem's opening also reverses communist expectations of "responsibility" in declaring (as she spoke): "it is the responsibility of the male poet to be a woman," not the responsibility of the poet to serve a party line. This approach diverges from Yiddish socialists such as the Trotsky-sympathetic Aaron Glanz-Leyeles, who maintained that poetry must be a "helping tool (not to mention maidservant) of the [labor] movements" and that even labor leaders with no literary background considered it "part of socialist duty to compose poems."[160] Paley's next line provokes the question of what it means to be a woman—is it an ethical condition, a category that anyone can and must become?

Paley repeats the incantatory formula "it is the responsibility of the poet to be . . . ," puncturing its sloganistic prescriptiveness by hailing the genres of gossip, folk art, and femininity: "It is the responsibility of the poet to sing this in all the original / and traditional tunes of singing and telling poems." Ultimately to hear Cassandra, Paley insists, we must be attuned to mundane spaces like "two-room apartments on Avenue C" as much as to classrooms, buckwheat fields, and army camps.

Paley's speaker demands both "beautifully written leaflets" and those unbearable to look at. Here she thematizes the question of anarchist aesthetics: beauty and screaming-ness, what the avant-garde Soviet Yiddish writer Peretz Markish called "shudderingness," a credo of *shoyderlekhkeyt*. She does not privilege novelty over "traditional tunes of singing and telling poems" but embraces everyday speech and ephemera alongside crafted text. Paley plays with the idea of prescriptiveness itself: How can a poet have a duty? How can she not? "Responsibility" suggests one way of reading anarchist aesthetics: attunement to the vernacular, allegiance to marginalized femininity, simultaneous investigation of ethical prescription and subversion of formulaic language, and the naming of affect (fear and bravery), refusing "freedom" as a philosophical abstraction. The poem lives in the long duration between uprisings: not the moments of drama and liminality, when life and law unthaw, but a slow wave before the surge, and the time in its wake. The poem specifies no era or generation; it is what Kenneth Rexroth has termed, in a poem saluting the Haymarket generation, "the permanent emergency."[161] Paley uses no final punctuation, leaving the future unwritten—a frequent gesture in her work.

Paley roots her literary expression of anarchism in the vernacular, attuned to women's speech, open to communion with ancestors and strangers. As one of her characters remarks, "I digressed and was free."[162] Yet within the digressions of anarchist poetics, an attention to ethics against power remains. There is no solitary, stationary anarchist theory of literature, but the questions of ethics and prefiguration are centered. As Jesse Cohn writes, "Since an anarchist ethical stance means both a refusal to dominate and a refusal to be dominated, an ethical approach to the text cannot simply mean a receptive or empathetic reading, in which we merely submit to its terms, nor can it mean a purely active reading, reading as the 'use' or violent 'appropriation' of the text; instead of positing ourselves as the slaves or the masters of texts, we ought to place ourselves into a dynamic relation with them, to see each encounter with them as a dialogue fraught with risk and promise."[163] Roger Dadoun writes that anarchist literary theory is "not simply a matter of cataloging 'anarchist elements in literature,' whether works by anarchist authors, addressing anarchist topics, or purporting to be stylistically anarchic. Nor is a coherent body of anarchist theorization on literature a mere hypothesis; it exists, albeit almost completely consigned to official oblivion, in the historical archives. Like other forms of literary theory which draw on the traditions of oppositional political movements, e.g., ecocriticism, postcolonialism, Marxism, feminism, queer theory, etc., anarchist literary theory draws its inspiration from the body of thought and practices which have historically comprised the anarchist movement."[164] Another distinctive quality of anarchist historiography is its centering of individual lives, rather than Marxist separation of "economics" and "politics." The titles of Paul Avrich's books reveal this biographical tendency: *Anarchist Voices, Anarchist Portraits.*

Among the few Yiddish literary critics who wrote with an explicitly anarchist lens was Borekh Rivkin (1883–1945). Though Rivkin is best known today for coining the term *yidishland* (Yiddishland), his iconoclastic contributions to anarchist literary theory range beyond that keyword. After joining the Bund in 1903, he quickly turned toward anarchism. Around 1908, Rivkin published in Russian anarchist journals in Geneva under the name B. Sp-a (Baruch Spinoza), claiming the Sephardic philosopher admired by so many anarchists. In 1911, his first Yiddish work appeared in London's *Zherminal* and *Arbeter fraynd,* papers later edited by Rudolf Rocker and Rabbi Yankev Meyer Zalkind.[165] In New York he published prolifically, studying *landsmanshaften* (mutual aid societies organized by Jewish immigrants' hometowns). Rivkin's *A gloybn far umgloybike* (Belief for Unbelievers), a book of anarchist literary criticism, was edited by Abba Gordin.[166] Aaron Glanz-Leyeles and Yankev Glatshteyn hailed his work: "Everything that Rivkin wrote was hot, and his coolest thoughts and analyses were also heated to glowing. . . . He believed that a writer's work resembled an arena for which he first had to create a show. . . . When Rivkin turned to take up the ideas of Yiddish writers, he set out on a route that rescued him, that afforded him broad possibilities for expression, but that was not a blessing for literature."[167] Like Zalkind, Rivkin's radicalism emerged from religious fervor; in Rivkin's case, he wrote with an ecstatic urgency. Avrom-Ber Tabatshnik called him a "maximalist."[168]

Rivkin envisioned Yiddish literature as *kmoy-teritorye,* a "pseudo-territory" which hovers glistening above the page, replacing both geographic territory and classical Judaism.[169] In "A Pseudo-Territory—In Place of Religion," Rivkin breaks from Marxist frameworks of Jewish history and situates the emergence of *kmoy-teritorye* when Jews were no longer economic "middle-men" of Europe:

> They sought to shape Jewish literature to serve as the most suitable tool, like religion, to establish a relationship with civilization. This is built on the principle that humans are not dependent on God, but free agents and creators. Literature has the merit that it both communicates with civilization and nourishes the folk's soul, as religion does. Both these functions are crucial. From religious pseudo-territory, literature takes upon itself the Jews' responsibility—their role in the future, the higher justification and purpose for existence—and translates it into modern worldliness.
>
> This is what I identify as pseudo-territory within literature.[170]

Community ethics—for Rivkin, as for Paley—transferred from the realm of religion to literature.

The Yiddish anarchist archive can be seen as *kmoy-teritorye:* a place summoned by the page, unmapped, expansive in genre—poems and plays, ballads and elegies—and ephemera: love letters, telegrams, eulogies, speeches, editorials, vignettes, handwritten memoirs, headlines, prison notes, melodies. As A. Litvak wrote, "Singing agitation spoke more to the heart of the primitive worker" than did pamphlets.[171] Casting such a capacious net around "Yiddish anarchist literature" allows for a richer portrait of the movement and writing produced in the course of workers' daily lives. Although anarchist characters appear within Yiddish novels, rarely did anarchists themselves compose extended prose fiction. This lack of novels underlines how the possibilities of radical life and literature were cut short by deportation, repression, and prison. Consider ephemera itself as an anarchist form, reflecting the precarity of refugee, migrant, and worker life, and divesting from chronological novelistic structures. Beyond the material evidence of its literary and historical archives, Yiddish anarchism offers a pedagogy of reading and translating techniques that seek to recognize the immanence of solidarity and mutual aid.

PART ONE

Elegy

CHAPTER I

"Subterranean Fire"

HAYMARKET'S GENERATIONS

In 1885, after arriving in Cincinnati from Kaluga, Russia, a young garment worker and poet named Dovid Edelshtat witnessed a rousing talk by the anarchist organizer Albert Parsons. Despite still learning English, Edelshtat was spurred on by Parsons's oration to join the *Yidisher arbeter fareyn* (Jewish Workers Union). Barely one year after delivering that speech in Cincinnati, Parsons would become a central figure in what was called (depending upon one's position) the Haymarket Affair, the Haymarket Riot, or the Haymarket Tragedy—and the martyred hero of elegies by Edelshtat and countless others radicalized by these events.

On May 4, 1886, following the last speeches at a strikers' demonstration for the eight-hour workday, a dynamite bomb was lobbed at police dispersing the crowd. Several officers and at least four civilians were killed by the bomb and the policemen's gunfire. German immigrants, who composed one-fifth of Chicago's population at the time, were rounded up across the city in droves. Parsons and seven other anarchists were convicted of conspiracy, though none were charged with throwing the bomb. On November 11, 1887, four of the defendants were hanged; one defiantly died by suicide, "robbing the executioner"; and the remaining defendants served prison sentences until Governor John Peter Altgeld pardoned them in 1887. All the defendants were members of the anarchist International Working People's Association (IWPA), which had grown to five thousand members, triple the membership of its main leftist rival, the Socialist Labor Party (SLP).[1] The Haymarket defendants delivered incendiary speeches from the courtroom to the gallows, their words ripe for translation and adaptation by songwriters and literary radicals.[2] As labor historians Karen Avrich and Paul Avrich note wryly, "By giving the anarchists their first martyrs, the Haymarket executions stimulated the growth of the movement, especially among recently arrived immigrants who were finding their new country indifferent and the authorities undependable."[3] The Haymarket executions opened the floodgates of critical elegy, journalism, and music as artists and protesters confronted the public with their riotous mourning. After Haymarket, noted Edelshtat's biographer Kalman Marmor, the poet and his motifs were "no longer the same."[4]

"THE GRAVES OF THE FIGHTERS ARE A HOLY LADDER": DOVID EDELSHTAT'S HAYMARKET SUITE

Haymarket accelerated the burgeoning labor movement's demands beyond shortening the workday. Radicalized further by Parsons's execution, Edelshtat joined the more militant *Pionere der frayheyt* (Pioneers of Freedom).[5] Many Jewish immigrants felt driven to radicalization by the "conversion experience" of Haymarket.[6] One observer recounted that when the physician and editor Michael Cohen "cried out at a New York anarchist meeting, 'It was the 11th of November, 1887, that made me an Anarchist,' he almost made audible the voice of the audience, as they too exclaimed: 'And us too.' "[7] Saul Yanovsky, the influential editor of *Fraye arbeter shtime* (Free Voice of Labor), recalled weeping all night and turning from an onlooker to a fighter the next morning. The Catholic-raised, Yiddish-speaking poet and organizer Voltairine de Cleyre sensed "a surge of comradeship sweeping over the earth this night" as anarchists gathered internationally in their comrades' memory.[8] Emma Goldman, too, dated her life as an anarchist from the origin point of Haymarket.[9]

The legacy of Haymarket profoundly affected literary and labor culture in Chicago and transnationally.[10] Nelson Algren writes of the "big dark grudge cast by the four standing in white muslin robes, hands cuffed behind, at the gallows' head. For the hope of the eight-hour day."[11] Walking tours and statues reinscribe the memory of Haymarket into the city; poems proliferate and circulate that memory beyond Chicago. Haymarket functioned as a *diasporic* circuit of memory production: protests in the name of the martyrs tended to be much larger in countries other than the United States. Shelley Streeby vividly documents Haymarket as an international event.[12] November 11 remained vivid in the memory of transnational labor in Argentina, Chile, Cuba, Uruguay, and Mexico, "where exiled Spanish and Italian anarchists organized the first labor unions and led militant strikes and May Day marches in the decades after Haymarket."[13] Chicago comrades to come focused on building alliances with Mexican revolutionaries, as the "Haymarket memorialists seemed especially ardent to reach, make, perhaps call into being a public that might galvanize itself into a movement poised to avenge martyrs like the Haymarket anarchists through a new revolution aimed at multiple economic oppressions."[14] Haymarket anarchists cited the militant abolitionist John Brown as a key figure in their genealogy. Parsons in particular had been inspired by Brown to organize a group of African Americans in Texas to attempt to free a Reconstruction-supporting judge from prison.[15] One major organizer for their defense, a German-born doctor named Ernst Schmidt, had worked with the Underground Railroad and met with John Brown in 1858, the year before the raid at Harpers Ferry.[16] Editors of labor papers in Kansas, Brown's state, frequently compared the executions of Brown and the Haymarket defendants.[17]

In addition to becoming a symbol for transnational and multiracial commitments, Haymarket unfolded within a profoundly multilingual city. Chicago was home to at least thirty-seven anarchist papers in several languages between 1879 and 1930.[18] Parsons edited the English-language newspaper *The Alarm*, "which wobbled between weekly and fortnightly, for economic reasons."[19] *The Alarm* was a rare radical English-language paper in the multilingual Midwestern context, and it was later restarted by Parsons's widow, the militant woman of color Lucy Parsons, who had previously edited *Freedom* (1890–1892). Chicago also hosted four anarchist newspapers in Italian, five in Lithuanian, five in Czech, two in Russian, one each in French, Japanese, Danish, and Swedish, plus six in German, including the *Arbeiter-Zeitung* on weekdays, the *Vorbote* on Saturday, and the *Fackel* on Sunday.[20] These papers collaborated across languages, with *Alarm* and *Arbeiter-Zeitung* sharing an office.[21] Indeed, the German word *Ruhe* (rest, quiet) was the code call-to-arms printed in the *Arbeiter-Zeitung*.[22] There does not seem to have been a Yiddish-language anarchist newspaper published in Chicago during this period.

If the plot of the Haymarket Affair was class war, its subplot was citizenship. Defendants were primarily immigrants, with five born in Germany: August Spies, Adolph Fischer, George Engel, Louis Lingg, and Michael Schwab. Oscar Neebe, born in the United States, had German parents. Parsons was the sole convicted man born and raised in the United States. Like them, Edelshtat's trajectory of radicalization was transnational, arcing from Kaluga, Russia, through London, where he encountered other Proletarian poets who distilled their visionary message into simple, forceful rhymes and lyrics. Having survived injury from the pogroms of 1880, Edelshtat emigrated with hopes of establishing a farm colony in the United States and learned to speak Yiddish to communicate with fellow workers in an Ohio sweatshop. He died of tuberculosis at age twenty-six at a sanatorium in Denver, Colorado, in 1892.

A prolific writer and editor, Edelshtat published poems in radical papers nearly every week from 1889 to 1892, helping originate the genre of the Yiddish "newspaper poem."[23] In 1890, leading up to the third anniversary of the Haymarket executions, Edelshtat published a series of poems in *Fraye arbeter shtime* (Free Voice of Labor) titled "August Spies," "Louis Lingg," *"Der 11-ter November,"* and "Albert Parsons." These four poems were printed in two-week intervals in the newspapers, inscribing Haymarket into memorial time. Ori Kritz describes the group of poems as a "didactic tool" whose publication alongside the portraits of the martyrs "function[s] as a kind of ritual preparation of the reader for the memorial event, which then takes on something of the character of non-festival calendar markers in Jewish and other traditions. In these as in other groups of poems, such as the poems about the French Commune, Edelshtat used the cyclical nature of traditional Jewish observance to fix the events as ritual markers in a civil religion of communist anarchism."[24]

Elegy is an anarchist pedagogy. The ritual repetition of songs, speeches, and poetry leading up to the anniversaries of the Haymarket executions teach an alternate calendar, countering nationalist temporality. The Book of Lamentations (*Eikhah*) is read in synagogue annually on the ninth day of the month of Av, the anniversary of the destruction of the First and Second Temples in Jerusalem. The ritual re-reading of *Eikhah* is accompanied by fasting and sitting upon the floor, practices that embody diasporic remembrance. Studies of English-language Haymarket elegies have explored their religious dimensions.[25] In her study of these elegies, Kristin Boudreau notes, "these poets wrote in order to keep the blades keen. . . . In writing poems that were meant to be read, recited, sung, and circulated, the Haymarket elegists followed the anarchists themselves in seeking to transform official legal, political, and labor culture."[26] While Boudreau centers the "functional" aspect above their "enduring literary status," Yiddish Proletarian poems went beyond serving as "scripture" for a new ritual calendar. The poems' internal temporality imagines a way out from capitalist and carceral time. As Re'ee Hagay notes, Jewish mourning "challenges secular homogenous time."²⁷ Dubbing the condemned men martyrs (*martirers*) folded them into Jewish messianic time and made them symbols of the masses of unnamed, exploited, and exhausted workers. As loss disordered the world, the elegists sought to re-order it, seizing public grief as the raw material for collective action. Esther Schor characterizes this process as "an ideal of revolutionary sympathy, in which feeling flowers into action and action is nourished by feeling."²⁸

Edelshtat and the Proletarian poets envisioned walking through the door of grief into revolution. Their work anticipated the broader twentieth-century turn toward critical elegy, as Jahan Ramazani argues: "the modern elegist tends not to achieve but to resist consolation, not to override but to sustain anger, not to heal but to reopen the wounds of loss."²⁹ Elegy remains a potent genre of protest, as Claudia Rankine writes: "National mourning, as advocated by Black Lives Matter, is a mode of intervention and interruption that might itself be assimilated into the category of public annoyance. This is altogether possible; but also possible is the recognition that it's a lack of feeling for another that is our problem. Grief, then, for these deceased others might align some of us, for the first time, with the living."³⁰

As grief breaks apart linear time, the ritual temporality of mourning structures elegiac forms. Classical Greek elegies move through three stages: lament for loss, praise for the dead, and consolation for the bereaved. Jewish rituals of mourning have a five-stage temporal cycle: first are intense periods of pre-burial mourning (*aninut*) and *shiva* for one week, when the bereaved are visited by congregants known and unknown, bearing food; then a month of mourning (*sheloshim*) for all but a parent; after one year, the deepest mourning ritual for a parent is complete (*yud-bet chodesh*); and for every year after comes the *yortsayt*, or the annual memorial for the dead, marked by prayer and candle. In Jewish tradition, the ethics of *hesped* (eulogy) are set out. The Shulchan Aruch, a 16th-century legal code, guards against excessive eloquence for the speaker's self-aggrandizement, but exaggeration for the merit of the deceased is permitted.³¹ As Moshe Halbertal notes in a study of *Eikhah* (Lamentations): "In lamentation, language operates in full gear, reality doesn't make sense anymore, everyone has betrayed, but language has stayed intact; it is the only weapon left. The posture of bewildered, isolated protest sharpens the expressive capacities; over generations of lamentation liturgy, poetry unfortunately has reached an insurmountable height."³² The elegist must navigate the genre to increase the spiritual merit of the deceased as well as to move the listener. Grief is a practice of labor, devotion, and mutual aid in comforting the bereaved.

Edelshtat's elegies imbue religious cycles of mourning with radical content.

His Haymarket suite is a form of docupoetics, translating and dramatizing historical speeches, the men's last words, and other ephemera. Edelshtat draws from Lingg, Parsons, and Spies's courtroom speeches, amplifying or blurring their militancy for dramatic effect. These speeches were translated into Yiddish decades later by A. Frumkin in 1933 as *Barimte redes fun di shikago'er martirer* (Famous Speeches of the Chicago Martyrs), introduced by Alexander Berkman, continuing the process of Yiddish memorialization.[33] Edelshtat's poem "Albert Parsons" compares him to Marat and Spartacus, emphasizing not citizenship but race: Parsons was "a kemfer, a frayheyts profet / fun di vayse un shvartse shklafen!" (A fighter, a prophet of freedom / to white and Black slaves!) The historian Paul Avrich centers Parsons's identity as a descendant of *Mayflower* settlers: "Anarchism in the United States has often been dismissed as an alien phenomenon, a doctrine imported from Europe with few native roots or adherents. There was nothing alien, however, about the protagonist of our story."[34] Parsons himself constructs a genealogy of American radicalism extending from the Revolutionary War to a projected anarchist revolution. Parsons's political identity varied throughout his life, from his early years as a soldier for the Confederacy to his multiple runs for office, including an 1879 nomination for president from the Socialistic Labor Party. In 1881, after Chicago election officials attempted fraud to unseat a socialist alderman, Parsons and others lost faith in state democracy.[35]

Most of the Haymarket defendants were German by birth or heritage except for the English-born Samuel Fielden and Parsons, who turned himself in to police with faith in the prospect of a fair trial. He was alone among the Haymarket martyrs in turning himself in, as Avrich notes: "He did not believe that the state of Illinois would strangle him and his comrades in defiance of all the evidence in their favor. His love of humanity and justice, his faith in the ultimate honesty of mankind . . . led him to walk into the jaws of death."[36] Parsons wrote in September 1887, "Knowing myself innocent of crime, I came forward and gave myself up for trial. I felt that it was my duty to take my chances with the rest of my comrades. I sought a fair and impartial trial before a jury of my peers, and knew that before any fair-minded jury I could with little difficulty be cleared. I preferred to be tried and take the chances of an acquittal with my friends [rather than] to be hunted as a felon."[37] Parsons's courtroom speech appealed to the Constitution: "They have violated free speech. They have violated and denounced the right of self-defense. . . . These great blood-bought rights, for which our forefathers spent centuries of struggle, it is attempted to run them like rats into a hole by the prosecution in this case."[38] Here Parsons casts anarchism as the natural extension of "free speech, of free press, of public assemblage," appealing to the Constitution—a rhetorical turn markedly different from those of his

European-born immigrant co-defendants, and a tactic which largely subsided post-1890s.[39] Once a child soldier in Texas during the Civil War, Parsons had migrated to Chicago, transformed himself into an advocate for Black and Indigenous rights, and became editor of the English-language anarchist paper *The Alarm.* Parsons's wife, Lucy Gonzales Parsons, was most likely born enslaved and identified as the daughter of Mexican and Native American parents, rather than as Black. While more strident than her husband, Lucy Parsons likewise appealed to the liberties promised by the Constitution and the right to bear arms.[40]

"Albert Parsons" uses as epigraph the translation of his famous last words *"Loz di shtime fun folk gehert vern!—A. Parsons"* (May the voice of the people be heard!).

Er hot tsum folk in zayn shprakh geredt,
Banutst fir im fershtendike vofn.
Er var a kemfer, a frayheyts profet
Fun di vayse un shvartse shklafen!

Er hot di shklafen-velt barayzt
Un mit trern benetst ire keyten!
Iberal flegt zayn frayer geyst
Di shtoltse fligl farshpreytn!—

Tsvishn shteynbrekher, shmiden un veber,
In yeder shklafen-getselt—
Er hot in di mayns fun koyln-greber
Zayn fraye tribune geshtelt!

Untern ofenem himel, in regen un frest
Hot er di frayheyt gepredikt!
Un mit zayn dunernden protest
Di laydnde shklafen ferteydikt![41]

He spoke to the people in their dialect,
his words like weapons: lucid, direct.
He was freedom's prophet, one who fights
for the enslaved, both Black and white!

He wept upon their shackles
traversing the slave-world
near and far, the proud wings
of his spirit unfurl!

Among stone-breakers, blacksmiths, and weavers,
in every slave abode—
deep in coal mining tunnels
orations he bestowed!

Freedom he would preach
in rain, in frost, beneath skies' open vaults!
For suffering slaves he'd beseech
and protest like thunderbolts![42]

The final verses use the language of sacredness:

Zayn herts var an ofener heyliker bukh
Fun a ernsten kemfer un denker—
Vi biter, vi groyzam darf zayn undzer flukh
Tsu zayne farfolger un henker!

His heart is an open holy text
by a genuine thinker and fighter—
how bitter, how cruel must be our hex
upon his despot and noose-tier!

Without naming the Confederate origins of Parsons's biography, Edelshtat emphasizes his redemptive arc toward abolitionism. Edelshtat often uses images of slavery in reference to wage exploitation, the enslavement of Africans, and the biblical Pharoah (*"In Dem Land Fun Piramidn";* In the Land of Pyramids). Metaphoric usage of slavery was common in anglophone anarchist discourse of his day; these images' resonance with the Passover story, however, was intertextual for Yiddish audiences.

Louis Lingg was the antithesis of Parsons: a German-born immigrant and bomb-maker who testified that *his* bombs were a different diameter than those thrown at Haymarket. In contrast to Parsons's appeal to Constitutional law, Lingg delivered a fiery courtroom speech: "I despise your order—hang me for it!" Edelshtat's fifty-six-line poem "Louis Lingg," which appeared in *Fraye arbeter shtime* on October 24, 1890, transplants Lingg's speech from the courtroom to "the world's blood-stained stage." The poem opens with a vision of Lingg as classical warrior appearing before the poet, then moves to a dramatic rendition of his courtroom speech, and ends with a call to revolution and assertion of the hero's immortality.

Er shtet far mir in a shtrom fun likht
Oyf der velt's farblutikter bine,
Es rut oyf zeyn vunder-shenem gezikht
Der freyheyt's heylike shkhine.

Yung un kreftik, in shvartse loken,
Mit a shtarken odler-blik;
Vi Brutus shtolts un unershroken
Va er in frayheyts krig!

A leyb in kamf—zayn heldishe brust
Var mit a blumen-harts geshlogen;
Vos hot mit der heyligster libe gevust
Tsu liben dos, vos iz sheyn un erhaben!

In a stream of light before me, he stands
on the blood-stained stage of the world.
Upon his splendid countenance
the holy Presence of freedom unfurled.

Young, dark-tressed, vigorous,
with the strong gaze of an eagle.
Like brave and fearless Brutus
he stood for freedom's struggle!

A lion in battle—in his hero's chest
there beats a heart of blossoms!
It knows well that the love most blessed
is love for beauty and the Awesome.[43]

Lingg appears before the speaker like a divine apparition, calling the poet to become a witness. This portrait casts the dynamite-militant as a noble figure who, though not Jewish himself, has the Divine Presence alighted upon his face (*der frayheyt heylike shkhine*). Lingg's hair appears rather light in photographs, which makes his "dark locks" (*shvartse loken*) seem coded as a Jewish typology. Edelshtat re-narrates Lingg's courtroom speech and adapts the actual text into six rhymed stanzas:

Ikh zog aykh ofen: ikh gloyb in kraft,
in kraft fun di arbeter-reyen!

Gevalt hot undzer velt fershklaft
Un gevalt vet zi bafrayen!
"Oyf ayere blutike mord kanonen
Mir veln farnikhten di keytn un tronen
Mit undzer gigantisher shrit!
Ir lakht—ir denk: "Vart, bruder, vart,
Mir velen dayn shtime dershtiken, tsershtern."
Merder! Dershtikt mikh! A tsveyter vet bald
Oyf mayn heyliken postn zikh shtelen!

I tell you directly: in force I believe,
the force of workers' authority
Power has enslaved our world
and power will set it free!
Your cannon of bloody gravestones
We will answer with dynamite
We will demolish all chains and thrones
with our tremendous stride!
You laugh—you think, "Just wait, brother,
We'll suppress and strangle your cry."
So choke me! For after my murder
another arises to my holy duty.

Edelshtat adapts the militancy of Lingg's oration and leaves the conditions of his suicide unspoken. Regardless, in Edelshtat's world martyrs cannot die: "Lingg is not dead . . . Above the battle-barricades / Still hovers his spirit!"

Edelshtat folds Lingg into Jewish messianic temporality without disrupting the taboos against speaking of the dead. Edelshtat calls down the Shekhinah to alight upon Lingg: "On his beautiful face rests / Freedom's holy Divine Presence." This image echoes Dyer D. Lum's account of another Haymarket martyr's sublime moment of death: "Those who saw [Adolph Fischer's] face say that it shone with a white light on the scaffold."[44] Lingg was strikingly handsome, but this image of an anointed beauty erases his actual final act, writing *"Hoch die anarchie!"* (Up with anarchy!) in his own blood upon the cell walls as he died from a gun-wound to the jaw. In Edelshtat's poem he appears radiant, redeemed, beautiful again—his injury repaired by poetic prosthesis, if not the coming of the messianic age. Though Haymarket was rarely a topic of German-language literature, at least one poem on Lingg similarly evades representation of his suicide. H. Lippold writes, "He held the flag of the future high, / His courage was untamed, / He knew even in death how to shame the executioners." Lippold presents Lingg in a similarly hagiographic manner: not the fiery militant, but "a man of a rare kind, / completely without fear or blame, / a prodigy of the present, / a man of true nobility."[45] Edelshtat transforms Lingg into a specifically Jewish martyr, as Ori Kritz explains: "[The] Shekhinah is used to designate God's nearness to men in moments of extraordinary holiness. For example, the Shekhinah is held to be present when men study the Torah (Pirkei Avot 3:3). When the speaker tells us that freedom's Shekhinah is resting upon Lingg's face, this implies that he is in a moment of exceptional holiness. In the poem, this moment occurs when Lingg is delivering his final speech. The parallel is clear: the speech is equivalent to an exegesis of the Torah."[46] The poetic speaker calls out, "Murderers! Choke me! A second will soon / Take my place on the holy post!" These lines echo Edelshtat's earlier poem *"In kamf"* (In Struggle), which became a popular song.[47] The call proclaims that other fighters will take the place of the martyred on the front lines, replacing them and continuing to struggle against *tiranen,* on into the radiant future. "Louis Lingg" ends with the blazing light of a new century, as though heralding jubilee: "And the sun of the twentieth century / Shines on his proud face." The final lines invoke Gregorian time, rather than the Hebrew year, converging secular and religious temporalities.

Newspaper reportage of the time reveled in dramatic and graphic accounts of Lingg's suicide. One article, subtitled "The Dynamite-Maker Kills Himself in Jail," writes from the perspective of guards and deputies and paints a gruesome, theatrical picture, sympathizing with the horrified policemen who discovered Lingg's body.[48] The journalist emphasizes the deputy's fear of the prisoners and "affrighted" response to encountering Lingg's corpse. The reporter then devotes paragraphs to detailing the "rags and strings of flesh which decorated [Lingg's] head," painting a gothic portrait of the anarchist's demise. Against such gory journalism, Edelshtat, Lippold, and other poets sought to restore Lingg's body to wholeness. They look away from the scene of mourning, as a mourner would, rather than gawk as might an enemy. "Louis Lingg" declares that death leads to ascension: "The graves of the fighters are a holy ladder, / Which leads us to freedom and happiness!"

Edelshtat's revolutionary messianism characterizes "August Spies," the first poem published in his Haymarket suite. Spies's courtroom orations quote Goethe and Victor Hugo:

If you think that by hanging us, you can stamp out the labor movement—
the movement from which the downtrodden millions, the millions who

toil and live in want and misery—the wage slaves, who expect salvation—
if this is your opinion, then hang us! Here we will tread upon a spark, but
there, and there, and behind you and in front of you, and everywhere,
flames will blaze up. It is a subterranean fire. You cannot put it out. The
ground is on fire upon which you stand. You can't understand it. You
don't believe in magical arts, as your grandfathers did, who burned
witches at the stake, but you do believe in conspiracies; you believe that
all these occurrences of late are the work of conspirators! You resemble
the child that is looking for his picture behind the mirror. What you see,
and what you try to grasp is nothing but the deceptive reflex of the stings
of your bad conscience.[49]

Edelshtat's tribute calls Spies *a begaysterter profet* (an inspiring prophet) who
committed a *heylike tat* (holy deed). The poem ends with a vision of coming
revolution, building upon the image of Spies as holy prophet. Spies's last words
prophesy the resurrection of hanged men: "The time will come, when from our
coffins / Will rise a powerful voice / Stronger than that which you want now
to choke / A thousand times stronger, more striking!"[50] These echo Spies's last
words bellowed from the gallows: "The day will come when our silence will
be more powerful than the voices you strangle today!" Edelshtat's version adds
"when from our coffins" and the "powerful voice" (*a mekhtiger kol*). Diasporic
diction informs the meaning of the line: for "voice," Edelshtat uses the word *kol*
from the Aramaic (*loshn-koydesh,* or "holy tongue") linguistic component of
Yiddish, rather than *shtime* (from the Germanic component); this signals pro-
phetic intertextuality with Jewish texts, rather than with Spies's own German.

The final poem of the cycle is "11th of November," named for the Haymarket
martyrs' common *yortsayt* (death anniversary). Edelshtat repeats themes, images, and phrases from the earlier three poems, ending with a vision of November 11th transformed from a day of mourning to "announce to the slaves of all
the world, / That that very day would be the day of liberation!"[51] The Haymarket convicts will return as spirits to goad workers on to revolution: "Five spirits
stained with blood will hover/over the people's-tribune among suffering slaves."
This poem is the most forward-looking and least specific to Haymarket, referencing the men who died only obliquely as "five spirits." Edelshtat chooses the
Germanic word *shtime* rather than the loshn-koydesh *kol,* as he did in the earlier
verse, though he repeats the image of "freedom's holy voice" (*der frayheyts heylike shtim*). Edelshtat heralds a religious vision of the world to come, an anarchist revolution encompassing this world and the next, spanning secular and

religious time. The Haymarket suite is marked by spiritual rhetoric, repairing the bodies and constructing a lineage of "martyrs" stretching back to Socrates' time. Edelshtat's poems fold the Haymarket martyrs into mythic time, weaving extraordinarily religious iconography around them like the halo of an illuminated portrait. These are poems of grief: they look away from the scene of violence; they exalt the fallen; and they envision walking through the door of grief into revolution.

Edelshtat in turn became a muse of elegy and Proletarian hagiography. His death at a young age from tuberculosis inspired great public mourning, with at least fifteen commemorative poems published. Saul Yanovsky recalled the impact of his poetry upon workers who spoke at a memorial service:

> Among the comrades there was one Shteynberg, a cabinetmaker by trade, one of the most devoted and stoic comrades that I knew. Not only had he never contributed a word in any discussion whatever, but rarely even a word from him in a business-meeting, so that we all expected that this person can not utter two words publicly. Today, to everyone's astonishment, suddenly we saw this same Shteynberg ascend the platform, start a recitation of Edelshtat's "Testament," and then begin speaking and explaining with the simplest words, what meaning Edelshtat's works had for him in his drab worker's life. He spoke and tears flowed from his eyes, and together with him the entire assembly wept.[52]

Edelshtat's friend, the charismatic and volatile Proletarian poet Yosef Bovshover, inscribes their intimacy in "To the Memory of David Edelshtat—Written the day of his death (October 17, 1892)." Goldman described Bovshover in her memoirs as "a high-strung and impulsive man of exceptional poetic gifts."[53] Bovshover mourns his loss and consoles himself with the "holiness" and urgency of Edelshtat's call for liberation. Bovshover's poem has been translated by Rose Freeman-Ishill in the collection *To the Toilers,* published under Bovshover's alias Basil Dahl and introduced by Benjamin Tucker. Freeman-Ishill's version enters the female translator into the *goldene keyt* of anarchist elegy, as her translational voice adheres to Bovshover's. The paratext by Bovshover's contemporaries forms a kind of elegiac archive for the poet who, like Edelshtat, suffered deep poverty during his lifetime. As his translator Aaron Kramer notes, the sixteen years of silence during Bovshover's mental collapse were a great loss to Yiddish literature. Bovshover's final stanza foretells a time of freedom, which will necessitate recognition of his comrade-poet: "And in freedom's fullest glory / The time will come for which I crave / When the world will pause to place / A wreath of flowers upon your grave."[54] Like Edelshtat, Bovshover teaches his audience how to mourn and urges fellow labor poets to write not melancholy laments but "strong, fiery verses."[55] Within his family, Edelshtat remained a force of memory.[56]

Elegy is a pedagogical form that teaches solidarities. Transforming Parsons and Lingg, hailing Parsons's abolitionism and Lingg's militancy but recasting both through a spiritual lens, Edelshtat adapts the liturgical forms of lamentation into revolutionary poetics suitable for public culture. In the late twentieth century, Russian Israeli poet Yosef Luden continues this anarchist tradition of saluting Edelshtat. Luden cites Edelshtat's futurity in poems such as *"In yam fun blut"* (In the Sea of Blood), in which he summons "you, my people, arise from your graves!"[57] In the poem "Dovid Edelshtat," Luden writes:

> No song can die
> when it bursts forth from a fiery spirit
> lighting hopes,
> bearing solace.
>
> "O good friend, when I have died,"
> He sang before he passed.—
> Who was drunk with dreams,
> who dreamed in drunk colors?
> Today the flag is tinted a shameful red.[58]

Luden begins two verses with lines directly citing Edelshtat, from the famous poems *"Vi lang"* (How Long) and *"O guter fraynd"* (Oh Dear Friend). Luden extends Edelshtat's lines into the present, making elegy dialogic.

"MY SHOP MATE": MALKA HEIFETZ TUSSMAN AND WOMEN'S LABOR AFTER HAYMARKET

In 1912, twenty-five years after the Haymarket trial, Malka Heifetz Tussman (1893–1987) arrived in Chicago. Before she became a renowned Yiddish feminist poet, her early work was embedded historically into the Proletarian legacy of Haymarket and appeared in the paper edited by Lucy Parsons. Heifetz Tussman was born in the Ukrainian province of Volhynia, then part of the Russian Empire, second of eight children, and published six volumes of Yiddish poetry between 1949 and 1977. As a child, Heifetz Tussman wrote Russian-language poems about the impoverished lives of neighboring peasants.[59] Though teachers mocked her poems in class, she managed to read "certain books I'm not allowed to read yet," like Tolstoy. She wrote of herself, "Under terrible conditions she pursued her learning."[60] Two years after arriving in the United States, she gave birth to her first child with the cantor Shloyme Tussman. She soon began publishing, first brief pieces for the English-language anarchist paper *The Alarm*, then her first Yiddish short story in 1918, followed by a Yiddish poem in 1919. Her early affiliation with anarchism has been forgotten, though in her later years in Berkeley, California, she recalled how all the young anarchist men were once in love with her.

Upon immigrating to the United States, Heifetz Tussman recalled, "A young man gives me a gift—*Leaves of Grass* by Walt Whitman. I read, I discover a new America, a new poetry." Like many other young Yiddish anarchists, Heifetz Tussman found that Whitman's vision opened a portal to the possibility of American comradeship. Rimbaud also "open[ed] me up to Myself, g[a]ve me freedom of movement within the rhythm of my own being, my own breathing."[61] Her autobiographical writing longs for love, nature, fidelity to one's own creativity, the freedom to publish in Yiddish, to invent new words, to harmonize with the sounds of the wind in the stalks and one's own breath. Kathryn Hellerstein asserts that Heifetz Tussman "served as a bridge between the generations of Yiddish poets who emigrated from Eastern Europe and of those American-born Jewish poets who have taken up the task of making Yiddish poetry known to a readership that knows little Yiddish."[62] She built another bridge, between the Yiddish and English anarchist poets.

The Alarm was initially published by Albert Parsons and was then restarted by his widow, Lucy Parsons, and her co-editor V. Dolen in November 1915.[63] Among the new *Alarm*'s prominent contributors was Nina van Zandt Spies, widow of August Spies. A socialite and heiress, Van Zandt Spies had initially attended the Haymarket trial for entertainment but became moved by Spies and visited him in prison; they drew attention, she recalled, from "a mob of newspapermen . . . who howled and raved when our proposed marriage became known."[64] Van Zandt Spies organized closely with the Industrial Workers of the World (IWW) until the end of her life and bequeathed her small remaining fortune to animal welfare, to the consternation of her comrades.[65] The new *Alarm* was a memorial edited by Haymarket widows of different social standing from one another—a white heiress and a Southern woman of color—who worked with the legacy of Haymarket for the rest of their lives. Their militancy resisted the role sentimental English-language elegy cast them in. One such poem recounts the martyrs' graves "bedewed with our fair women's tears." The anonymous "Price of Freedom" was written to the tune of "Annie Laurie"—which Albert Parsons was thought to have sung before his execution—and laments:

"To-night my babes are crouching / By their weeping mother's side, / For this country's sake their father / Leaves his children and his bride."[66] Against this maudlin caricature of the widow, the actual Haymarket widows refused to retreat from public view.

The year 1914 was especially prolific for anarchist women at the helm of English-language newspapers in the United States. Although Karen Rosenberg emphasizes the "silence" of anarchist men with regard to their wives' labor and domestic sphere, the Haymarket widows organized and propagandized widely and militantly.[67] The same year that Lucy Parsons's new *Alarm* appeared, another woman founded an anarchist paper in Chicago: Margaret Anderson and the *Little Review*. Housed in the Fine Arts Building with art nouveau murals and panoramic views of Lake Michigan, Anderson's office still retains the gold lettering from her time. That same year in New York City, Margaret Sanger founded *The Woman Rebel* to circulate information on birth control, which was quickly suppressed under the Comstock Laws.[68] The English-language papers of Parsons, Anderson, and Sanger joined Emma Goldman's *Mother Earth* as popular militant media.[69]

Celebrated with a re-opening ball in October 1915, the new *Alarm*'s first issues paid tribute to Haymarket, publishing portraits of the condemned men alongside their speeches. Under the heading "The Martyrs of 1886," Parsons and Dolen write: "28 years have passed. 'The Alarm,' once edited by Albert R. Parsons, is alive again. As our comrades in 1885, the new 'Alarm' is spreading the discontent in all parts of the country, uniting the workers in the task of overthrowing the capitalist system. Comrades! Teachers! Martyrs! Your brave death and noble lives will inspire us in the propaganda."[70] *Alarm* published poems by Mary Carolyn Davies and quotations from Kropotkin and others. Beside the masthead, each issue defines "OUR PRINCIPLES." *Alarm* announced the creation of other new papers—such as *Revolt* (edited by Hippolyte Havel, the artist Robert Minor, Elizabeth Gurley Flynn, and others) and Alexander Berkman's *The Blast*—in a show of comradely non-competition, promoting anarchist papers in Italian, Yiddish, and Chinese. Its interest is international, signified by Lucy Parsons's report on Mexico. Its coverage of the lives of poor children (such as "A Worker's Child" by Van Zandt Spies) was written by women.

In contrast to Edelshtat's martyrology, Heifetz Tussman thematizes the mundane hours of factory labor, inhabiting not messianic time but the homogeneous duration of reproductive labor. Heifetz Tussman's pieces for *The Alarm* confess the pain and exploitation of factory work. Her contributions share the urgency and militant fire of her co-contributors yet stand out for their poetic ear. Heifetz

Tussman signed her name as the English version "Mollie T—." Her vignettes appear alongside Lucy Parsons's militant call to arms. In the first issue of the reconstituted *Alarm,* Heifetz Tussman writes with a highly intimate voice:

"A YOUNG MOTHER'S REFLECTIONS."

Yes, it is pleasant to study a little child; to love it, and feel its loving caresses. Every time mine puts her hands upon my breast, my heart leaps with joy! But when I look, long, long into her expressive eyes, some questions already seem to be crowded into the coming years. I fear they may be these.

"Mother, did you ever stop to consider that perhaps I, your child, too, may suffer and starve in the midst of plenty, that has been created by the working class, of whom I am one?"

"Did you, mother, ever picture to yourself your child, tramping the streets of a great, rich city, in misery and despair? Oh! Why, a thousand times why, did you bring me into such a world, mother?"

Such are the questions I am reading in my little child's eyes.

MOLLIE.[71]

The child foretells the future, not as a sign of hope but portent of pain. The labor of the mother is physical, emotional, and moral, as she confronts her responsibility for creating life alone. Silvia Federici argues that "in the new capitalist regime *women themselves became the commons,* as their work was defined as a natural resource, laying outside the sphere of market relations."[72] To question love as the source of labor, as Tussman does in this piece, unsettles ideas of "naturalness" of reproductive labor. Her vignette "EXTRA!" appears in the new *Alarm*'s second issue:

"E-x-t-r-y-a!" I heard the newsboys shouting.

As I was much interested in the strike of the clothing workers which is in progress now in Chicago, I sped out into the street, got a paper and having no patience to get back into my room I stopped at the corner to see the extra strike news.

"Extra! President Wilson is engaged to a rich widow, who was a famous beauty in her youth. She weighs 140 lbs; during the eight years of her widowhood she wore only black dresses; she changed them now for bright."

When I began to look anxiously for some strike news, I found in a corner printed in small type: "Another striker shot by a policeman today."

A little further it read: "A young man committed suicide; reason—hunger."
Still further: "A young girl ended life: out of work."

I read and read, but it was all NON-EXTRA news.

Mollie T.

Heifetz Tussman's "EXTRA!" was printed beside an ad for Emma Goldman's lecture series, whose titles reflect the themes of the vignette:

ATTENTION!

EMMA GOLDMAN of New York will lecture in Chicago at the FINE ARTS THEATER 410 S. Michigan AVE from November 21st to 28th 1915.

The subjects will be:

Preparedness, the Road to War and Disaster; The Right of the Child not to be born; The Message of Anarchism; Sex, the Great Element of Creative Art; the Philosophy of Atheism.

Miss Goldman will also deliver 5 lectures in Yiddish at Workingmen's Hall cor. 12th and Miller Sts. Starting Friday Nov. 19 8 P.M.[73]

Did Heifetz Tussman attend Goldman's lectures in Chicago in 1914 and 1915, and would she have chosen English or Yiddish? Margaret Anderson swooned for Goldman's presence during her Chicago lectures on drama in English, which she reported rapturously for the *Little Review*.[74] Goldman gave more than 320 lectures that year, some with audiences of over 1,000 attendees in Chicago. Their well-promoted and piercing titles—"The Right of the Child not to be born," "The Mother Strike," and "The Birth Strike"—are dramatized in Heifetz Tussman's struggle with the ethics of motherhood.[75]

While writing for *The Alarm*, Tussman also lectured on the north side of Chicago on Yiddish literature. An announcement for the "Pioneer Women's Club of the North Side" at the Folks Institute invites readers: "Mrs. Mollie Tussman will review the 'Goilem' by Laiwik [H. Leivick]. Everybody is invited to attend this meeting. No charge for admission. This meeting will be very interesting as Mrs. Tussman has made a thorough study of the drama of Mr. Laiwik, it will be followed by a discussion of all present." Leivick's version recasts the golem tale as one of a child's longing for his father's love and affection.

In the third issue of the new *Alarm*, Heifetz Tussman published "My Shop Mate":

At the factory where I was working there were many old maids. I was very anxious to know what did they think after spending their youth and

health in the place. But I dared not start a conversation for fear of hurting their feelings.

One morning when I came to work [I] found my neighbor Anna, a
girl of about forty, sitting stooping at her machine. Her large gray eyes
were fixed upon the work. It was a calm look which expressed neither
[*ink blot, illegible*] nor hopes. The glow of her cheeks was gone long ago
and had given place to yellow spots that witnessed to her oldness and
weariness.

She looked at the clock and at the calendar.

On that morning she looked different than any other morning and
that made me think something was the matter with her. In reply to my
question whether she does not feel [well] she raised her head and looked
at me a little while mutely then said:

"Today is twenty-six years since I am working in this factory. I am
old and weary and will soon be unable to work. What will then become
of me?"

She lowered her voice and continued swallowing her tears: "My machine was changed twice during the time and I . . . I am still working . . ."
she bent her head over the machine.

"Get to work! To work! Conversations on Sunday!" I heard the foreman shouting.

Anna gave a hateful look at her work and started in for the twenty-
seventh year.

  Mollie T—[76]

"My Shop Mate" is Proletarian realist prose, naming the oppression of labor
and factory temporality, an entire life eaten up by menial labor, the toll a machine takes on the body, and the social bonds formed between workers. Here
Anna speaks through a narrator who respects her interiority ("I dared not start
a conversation for fear of hurting their feelings"). The relation between body and
machine is one of endurance; this woman has outlived two machines. Whereas
Edelshtat exalts "working women" to "help us" (and who is "us"?), Heifetz Tussman's *arbeter-froy* is portrayed by her fellow female worker without romance or
valor, in the shared misery of constant male supervision.[77] Anna is literally si-
lenced by a male voice, shouting "Conversations on Sunday!," perhaps identifying the factory as a shop not run by Jews. The English prose further reveals the
traces of Yiddish syntax ("Today is twenty-six years since I am working in this
factory," "I was very anxious to know what did they think").

Heifetz Tussman's vignettes elaborate the phenomenology of laboring bodies under capitalist time through the first-person voice, which is at the core of Proletarian verse. Hers, however, does not make the male body its protagonist. The voice of the foreman appears as an intrusion into working women's space, as in Morris Rosenfeld's lines about the personification of a clock: "I hear in its tone all the boss's wild anger, / His dark, gloomy look in the pointers that show."[78] The poet Chaim Plotkin (born 1910) portrays the machine alternately as a hungry child, a wild animal, and a surrealistically anthropomorphized creature in "I and the Sewing Machine," which Aaron Kramer translated:

> Machine—a common sewing machine:
> wheels and bolts, all ice, all steel.
> But when I spur it, make it sing,
> it's like a wind through a grassy dale.
> I often see the machine as a horse:
> I—a galloper—bent low—
> Though it stands still, I keep my course—
> on, on I go.
>
> I've known its language very long,
> understand its laugh and song,
> hear the hours struck and sped:
> Quick, give silk! Quick, draw thread!
> Give a squirt of oil;
> give, give!
> To the mouth that swallows whatever it's fed.
>
> The needle flies, "foot" jigs at its sewing;
> the "tongue" laps at the damp uproar:
> Not only oil—blood should be flowing!
> And you, operator,
> zhoom!—and give more![79]

The vignettes represent factory temporality, the common theme of Proletarian poetry with its corpus of images of the clock against the body. Elizabeth Freeman writes of the process by which social time imposes itself upon the human body, making the "timed" body analogous to the "racialized" or "gendered" body. Freeman begins where Michel Foucault's model of temporal discipline left off: "Time penetrates the body and with it all the meticulous controls of power."[80] As Edelshtat sings of immortality in extraordinary defiance of the state, Heifetz

Tussman documents the duration of factory's control over working women's time.

Within the context of *The Alarm,* Heifetz Tussman stands out for her sensitivity, lack of bombast, and attentiveness to women's labor. She records the sensuality of caring for a child and her concern for older women who work alongside her. "A Young Mother's Reflections," "EXTRA!," and "My Shop Mate" each portray the lives of working women with urgency and pathos. She takes care to represent others' voices, as well as her own fears. Hers is the most affecting and original text in the paper, striking for its attentiveness to the texture of working women's lives.

At the center of Proletarian poetry is the phenomenology of laboring bodies in relation to time and the mechanical. The philosopher Elaine Scarry writes that people in pain metaphorize physical agony as an external instrument acting upon them: hammering pain, striking pain, and the like. Scarry's own language becomes lyrical to approach that near-cosmic alterity: "When one hears about another person's physical pain, the events happening within the interior of that person's body may seem to have the remote character of some deep subterranean fact, belonging to an invisible geography that, however portentous, has no reality because it has not yet manifested itself on the visible surface of the earth. . . . The pains occurring in other people's bodies flicker before the mind, then disappear."[81] Scarry argues that the invisibility of physical pain confounds our ability to speak of it or recognize the suffering of others. The Sweatshop poets' oeuvre makes workers' pain visible, not through machine metaphor but through the mechanization of the body.

Morris Rosenfeld structured "The Sweatshop" as a schedule of the working day. The poetic speaker describes his loss of self in the din of the shop: "Mayn ikh vert dort botl, ikh ver a mashin" (literally, My self becomes null and void, I become a machine). Rosenfeld uses the less common loshn-koydesh word *botl,* a halakhic legal term that amplifies the particularity of selfhood in contrast to the repetitive sounds of the machines, mimicked by vocabulary from the Germanic component of the language. The speaker's sense of self wanes as meaningful time is erased, moments passing like ship's sails. The clock's hands become a pointy tongue, prodding the laborers to work harder and faster: "I hear in its tone all the boss's wild anger, / His dark, gloomy look in the pointers that show . . . "[82] Finally the clock calls the worker "Machine!," inverting their animacy. The clock loses its object-ness as he loses his humanness. It anthropomorphizes into a boss with a grotesquely human body; it grows a tongue in place of a "hand" or "face," the conventional vocabulary for the body of a clock.

Rosenfeld's poem exemplifies how the Romantic insistence on the lyrical "I" acts as a stylistic counterpoint to the erasure of self, described thematically. The speaker describes his body phenomenologically, beginning with the loss of sensation and attendant loss of self; at noon, when "the master goes off for his lunch," feeling returns to the work-numbed limbs, and the speaker begins to weep. The workroom, now empty, appears as a battleground. In the workers' hour of freedom "the dead come to life"—a strongly messianic phrase, evoking religious visions of the world to come, when all will be resurrected. For three verses, the speaker is filled with a visceral need to fight. The clock now rouses him, urges him to rebel, and returns to him feeling and thought, the hours like "a stream with no dam." Time itself is liberated and flows beyond the clock's regulation, the lunch hour becoming an "island in time," mobilizing the religious metaphor of the sabbath. But just as the speaker begins to awaken from the stupor of labor, an alarm sounds to mark the end of lunch and the boss's return. The felt sense of liberation from time subsides: "I forget who I am in this deafening scene— / I'm losing my reason, I'm losing my self— / I don't know, I don't mind, for I am a machine." Rosenfeld captures the ebb and flow of the felt self over the course of the workday; this is no less "individualistic" for vividly illustrating the erasure of self, identity, and bodily autonomy. In Heifetz Tussman's prose, the loss of self is experienced through womanhood and motherhood.

Heifetz Tussman's vignettes represent both the duration of Haymarket memory and the temporality of motherhood. Who will raise the "new generations of fighters" heralded by Edelshtat? Is it moral to bring new life into a suffering world? Heifetz Tussman engages the ethics of motherhood and gendered temporalities, pointing to the long shadow of Haymarket as a structure of time. Haymarket's afterlife persists, but factory women outlive machine after machine. Locating Heifetz Tussman's work within Haymarket genealogies and the anarchist literary milieu of Chicago reveals Yiddish literature's extended conversation with Proletarian poets across languages and genre.

HAYMARKET'S LEGACY IN SPACE AND SOUND

The Haymarket tragedy remains a centripetal force in anarchist collective memory. On May Day in Waldheim Cemetery, Chicago, visitors still place flowers by the graves of Emma Goldman, Lucy Parsons, Voltairine de Cleyre, Elizabeth Gurley Flynn, and their Chicago comrades. In material culture, the engraving of the Haymarket men arrayed around a Maypole circulates on printed blankets, tea towels, and other consumer goods. Teko Sāso's *November 11* draws its lyrics from Haymarket court speeches, and the French punk band Louis Lingg and the Bombs snarl Lingg's words verbatim: "I despise your order, your laws, your force-propped authority—hang me for it!"[83] Devin Hoff's instrumental "The Alarm" bows the bass with grandeur and groan, growing ragged at the end of the piece, chewing it up, kicking new space into the name.[84]

Haymarket's temporality is thematized in "Again at Waldheim" by Kenneth Rexroth (a non-Jew, though assumed to be so by Ezra Pound, whom he declined to correct).[85] "Again at Waldheim" converses with de Cleyre's poem "Light upon Waldheim" and apostrophizes to that generation:

> You knew that nothing could ever be
> More desperate than truth; and when every voice
> Was cowed, you spoke against the coalitions
> For the duration of the emergency—
> In the permanent emergency
> You spoke for the irrefutable
> Coalition of the blood of men.[86]

To be an anarchist is to live disjointed with one's own era, Rexroth suggests. He calls across half a century to Voltairine de Cleyre, citing her elegy for Haymarket "Light upon Waldheim," itself written ten years after the executions. Jesse Cohn calls Rexroth's poem an "artifact of anarchist resistance culture, summoning the forces of memory and example . . . against the hopelessness of 'permanent emergency.' "[87] Like Luden, Rexroth chafes against his times, belatedly dwelling within tropes of labor romanticism. Rexroth's "irrefutable coalition of the blood of men" echoes Edelshtat's call for "the slaves of all the nations" to extend "in friendship a brother-hand" and lives within Heifetz Tussman's enduring temporality of the "permanent emergency" post-Haymarket.[88]

CHAPTER II

"A Great Cleaver Cut Through America"

SACCO AND VANZETTI

In 1920, thirty-four years after the Haymarket trial, the Italian immigrant anarchists Nicola Sacco and Bartolomeo Vanzetti were tried and convicted for the shooting of two payroll guards during a robbery in South Braintree, Massachusetts. Followers of the militant Luigi Galleani, they served seven years in prison before their execution on August 23, 1927. Despite a biased trial process, all seven of Sacco and Vanzetti's appeals were rejected by Judge Webster Thayer, who sentenced them to death after seven years in prison. The case unfolded in a time of heightened prejudice against southern and eastern European immigrants and widespread fear of anarchism and communism. As with Haymarket, the trial was riddled with inconsistencies of evidence and ethnic bias, and immigrant workers recognized citizenship and statelessness as the subplot in these courtroom spectacles. The executions drew a passionate transnational response: Latin America saw mass walkouts of workers; in Geneva movie theaters showing Hollywood films were ransacked; and in Paris tanks were needed to protect the U.S. embassy from mobs.[1] The IWW's agitation set off major Colorado coal strikes. Many feared that the Sacco-Vanzetti execution would trigger international revolution.

Seven months after the men were executed, news of their deaths finally reached anarchist prisoners in a Russian gulag. The secret report, typed on petal-thin paper, remained anonymous "in order not to expose [the correspondent] to further Bolshevik persecution":

12 other Anarchist comrades, workingmen, were sentenced to 3 years in Solovietsky for demonstrating against the execution of Sacco and Vanzetti and at the same time protesting against the persecution of Anarchists in Soviet Russia. . . . When the Anarchists in the Upper Uralsk prison heard of the execution of Sacco and Vanzetti they declared a one-day hunger strike as a protest against the outrage.[2]

The prisoners' hunger strike testifies to international anarchists' extraordinary affective and intellectual connection to Sacco and Vanzetti. This smuggled letter links Bolshevik and U.S. federal incarceration systems and expresses the prisoners' fellow-feeling, no less intense for its belatedness.

The Left was united in mourning or performing lamentation for Sacco and Vanzetti. While the defendants had inhabited a multilingual milieu, English-language newspaper coverage of the trials carried the anarchists' voices further than their own propaganda could reach. Poets across the Left poured out a great torrent of literature damning the trial. At least 144 English poems were published by such writers as William Carlos Williams and Edna St. Vincent Millay; there were a few German poems and one French novel.[3] There was little Italian-language literary response. In the United States, celebrities like Dorothy Parker were arrested demonstrating for a retrial. In 1927, Henry Harrison edited the *Sacco-Vanzetti Anthology of Verse* with poems by Ralph Cheyney, Siegfried Sassoon, and Louis Ginsberg, the father of Allen Ginsberg, who himself wrote in the mid-1950s: "America Sacco & Vanzetti must not die."[4] A second poetry anthology, *America Arraigned!*, appeared in 1928. The sheer volume of literature on the theme of the Sacco-Vanzetti case demonstrates the ongoing engagement with anarchist history and thought among writers across the Left.

English-language literature largely discussed the Sacco-Vanzetti executions as a national loss of innocence. Edna St. Vincent Millay's poem "Justice Denied in Massachusetts" describes America as a once fertile landscape, scarred by the verdict: "Shall the larkspur blossom or the corn grow under this cloud? . . . we have marched upon but cannot conquer; / We have bent the blades of our hoes against the stalks of them." On the picket line Millay carried this sign: "If these men are executed, justice is dead in Massachusetts," a phrase mourning the loss of American exceptionalism along the lines of Parsons's courtroom speech. John Dos Passos's novel *The Big Money* (1936) follows a character's loss of naïveté as she campaigns for the two Italian anarchists. She exclaims: "If the State of Massachusetts can kill these two innocent men in the face of the protest of the whole world it'll mean that there never will be any justice in America ever again." The

jaded journalist replies, "When was there any to begin with?"[5] George Woodcock remarks on the "still elegiac" tone of the poet Kenneth Rexroth's *Autobiographical Novel:* "it is the tragic presence of Sacco and Vanzetti that most
haunts the book. Rexroth sees their fate as in some fundamental way marking
the end of the strange innocence which accompanied the vitality and even the
brutality of the world he had been describing." Rexroth's mundane experience
of time is traumatized by the execution: "At that time, during the third week of
our stay in San Francisco, Sacco and Vanzetti were executed. A great cleaver cut
through all the intellectual life of America. The world in which [my wife] An-
drée and I had grown up came for ever to an end."[6]

Unlike the exclamations of shock from Rexroth, Millay, and others at the
execution, the poetry in Yiddish about Sacco and Vanzetti oriented primarily
toward their seven years in prison.[7] The poetic structures of this work, through
repetition and kaleidoscopic montage, embody alternative temporalities beyond
the linear and punitive temporality of the state. Like Edelshtat and Heifetz
Tussman, Yiddish modernists in the United States used the elegiac form to critique state power. As Luden and Bovshover bound their voices to Edelshtat and
extended the genealogy of Haymarket, modernists drew from Haymarket-era
poetics in their responses to Sacco and Vanzetti's trial, incarceration, and execution. The prodigious genre of Sacco-Vanzetti poetry in Yiddish attests to
the strong presence of anarchism in North American culture, with which poets
across the Left needed to contend in the late 1920s. With two dozen anarchist
newspapers and popular song culture, compared with a more circumscribed
monolingual-English radical culture, it was nearly a social mandate for Yiddish
poets to address the case. Tracing the modernists' unfinished conversation with
Haymarket, this chapter situates Sacco-Vanzetti poems within a broader trajectory of anarchist poetics, listening for the echoes of 1887 within 1927.[8] The two
trials were widely linked by anarchist writers; in her letter to an organizer of the
Sacco-Vanzetti Defense Committee, for example, Goldman connected "the Chicago murder of our people with impending murder of Sacco and Vanzetti."[9]

While English-language Sacco-Vanzetti poems largely rehearsed the trial as
a loss of American innocence, Yiddish poets thematized an *anarchist diasporic
temporality* that resists carceral time and disrupts nationalist time. The political
valence of temporality is central to Yankev Glatshteyn's *"Sako un vanzetis montik"* (Sacco and Vanzetti's Monday) and Moyshe-Leyb Halpern's "Sacco-Vanzetti."
The tragedy of Sacco and Vanzetti lies in its everydayness; the unsingular agony
of incarceration is refracted in the masses' agony of daily drudgery. Sacco and
Vanzetti's execution reiterates the uncompleted aspirations of the Haymarket

militants. Yiddish Sacco-Vanzetti literature is largely focused on the men's incarceration, unlike its English-language counterpart, which casts the day of execution as a sudden loss of American innocence. The Yiddish poems critique
broader U.S. anarchist movements' tendencies to reproduce American exceptionalism and settler temporalities. The poets fold these historical events into
Jewish temporalities, spiritual and revolutionary. These poems reflect the emphasis of contemporaneous anarchists such as Joseph (Yosef) Cohen, who centered the prison sentence rather than the execution: "Seven years of torture,
how can one forget this?"[10] This focus on Sacco and Vanzetti's seven years in
prison—rather than their execution—reveals an orientation toward state violence of endurance, not surprise. Yiddish translations of Sacco and Vanzetti referred to them as "the two martyrs," reinscribing a Haymarket lineage.[11]

Jahan Ramazani notes "the persistence of the traditional elegy within the
modern," arguing that "within this heightened resistance" to sentimental elegy,
modernists "achieve[d] a unique balance between the elegiac and anti-elegiac,
between the consolatory and melancholic mourning."[12] The form of Proletarian
elegy persists within Sacco-Vanzetti literature. Whereas Edelshtat wrote for the
factory floor and the funeral parade, Halpern and Glatshteyn's Sacco-Vanzetti
verses are too complex to serve the movement as protest songs. Halpern decon-
structs the idealized brotherhood of workers, and Glatshteyn's long poema weaves
surreal and mythic imagery throughout documentary of Sacco and Vanzetti's case.
The poetic structures of their work, through repetition and kaleidoscopic montage,
embody alternative temporalities beyond the linear and punitive temporality of
the state. In both Halpern and Glatshteyn's poems, Sacco and Vanzetti barely register as individuals—a sharp divergence from Edelshtat's hagiography. Nor do the
two Galleanists appear as pacifists, as English-language poets polish away their
militancy.[13] Unlike the Haymarket elegies, modernist Sacco-Vanzetti poems de-
center the "martyrs" and turn away from the hagiographic mode to interrogate the
perpetrators. The primary subjects of modernist Sacco-Vanzetti verse are power,
time, punishment, the frailty of comradeship, and the ease of complicity. Halpern
and Glatshteyn's entries in the genre of anarchist elegy grew cynical and scathing
because the luminous aspirations of Edelshtat's generation were left unfinished.

"TWINNED ARE YESTERDAY AND TODAY": GLATSHTEYN'S SACCO-VANZETTI POEMA

The modernist poet and critic Yankev Glatshteyn (Jacob Glatstein) published the 270-line poema *"Sako un vanzetis montik"* (Sacco and Vanzetti's Mon-

day) in 1929, two years after the execution, when Glatshteyn was thirty-three—
the same age as Vanzetti at his death.[14] The title of the poem establishes its unusual
temporality. Is this the Monday before their execution? The title sets the poem
in mundane, expectant time during their prison sentence: neither the day of the
execution (a Saturday), nor the day before or after. In the opening verse, blue
dawn fog wraps a city (unmarked as Boston). The city is returning to rhythms of
mass industry, as people emerge from the privacy of the weekend into collective
working life: "everyone solitary while together, / everyone together while solitary, / tens hundreds thousands millions—/ millions walking, walking, walking / (solitary while together) / . . . gates shut and sealed like coffins, / deafened
are the ears of the city. / Nothing, nothing will happen."[15] Glatshteyn's opening
echoes the first line of Vanzetti's memoir, *Story of a Proletarian Life* (1923):
"Nameless, in the crowd of nameless ones, I have merely caught and reflected a
little of the light from that dynamic thought or ideal which is drawing humanity towards better destinies."[16] Even in the format of a memoir, expected to be
an account of the individualistic self, Vanzetti writes himself as apiece with the
masses, entering subject-hood as mere refraction of "the Ideal." Glatshteyn's
opening verse draws from archetypal images of labor poetry, such as Bovshover's
image of the city as teeming factory.[17] Glatshteyn here echoes Bovshover's cu-
mulative structure in "A Song to the People," which describes factory work
through the precise accumulation of repetitive gesture, mimicking the repetition of labor itself: "The mute ordinary (*der shtumer geveynlekh*) knocks swiftly
and in haste in every gate, / in the houses alarm clocks are ringing, / coffee
grumbling in blackened pots, / fresh rolls waiting. / A heavy cover of holiness
winds above the city, / Is it the train of Sunday's dress, or a dream clinging / To
the city's marrow? / Was there something or will something happen?" The translator, Lawrence Rosenwald, writes: "[Glatshteyn] is more interested in the relation between the two prisoners' calendar and the regular calendar of the week
than he is in either by itself. . . . We might sum up that exquisite balance [of
chronos and *kairos*] by looking at an apparently simple line: *di frishe zeml vartn,*
'the fresh rolls are waiting.' What are they waiting for? On the one hand they
wait to be picked up, brought inside, buttered, and eaten; they await their ordinary fate. But they and the other beings and objects in the scene are also waiting
for something extraordinary to happen, some unique event in the non-cyclical
story of Sacco and Vanzetti."[18]

Glatshteyn alternates biblical intertextuality and mock-epic register: "A
heavy cover of holiness winds above the city, / Is it the train of Sunday's dress,

or a dream clinging / To the city's sleepy marrow?" ("Iber der shtot viklt zikh a shvere hil fun heylikayt, / Iz es nokh di shlep fun zuntik, oder a kholem vos klept zikh/Tsum farshlofenem markh fun der shtot?") The specter of a divine presence covering the city is feminized: here it is not the Shkhine hovering over the city, but "the train of Sunday's dress." Rather than *havdole,* the ritual marking sabbath's departure, the workers feel Sunday's dress sweep past as the workweek begins. This religious image is deflated and ironized by Glatshteyn's orthography, which phoneticizes loshn-koydesh, severing the visual relationship between Hebrew/Aramaic and modern Yiddish. The line "Deafened are the ears of the city" has shades of Jeremiah: the destruction of Jerusalem converges with the grinding banality of U.S. state violence. The socialist Aaron Glanz-Leyeles's Sacco-Vanzetti poem also employs biblical intertextuality: "Sing me a song of that which must come. / Sing me the song of payment. / How can I sing when every night I turn on and off electric lights."[19] Leyeles parodies a verse from Psalm 137: "Sing us a song of Zion. / How shall we sing the Lord's song in a strange land?" Not exile but the American electric chair mutes the singer's tongue.

Glatshteyn's rhythm twists and turns back on itself, repeating the verbal prefix sounds of *tse-* (emphasizing fracture or dispersion) and *tsu-* (together), as in the sonically complex line "Klor in der tsetumlenish hot er a tsetumlter klorn gezen":

Fartsvilingt hot zikh der nekhtn un der haynt
Un zikh tsuzamengevaksn un zikh tsuzamengehorbet
In ayn klorn plonter.
Klor in der tsetumlenish hot er a tsetumlter klorn gezen
Vi vaynik treyst es brengt der roz fun a fartog
Ven der tog aleyn ligt shoyn a basheydter
Fun nekhtn un fun eyernekhtn,
Ven di sho'en zaynen bloyz shvindltrep aroyf tsu yener sho fun yenem tog,
Vu er iz aleyn vi a ganef bahaltnerheyt shoyn geven
Un areyngeshtekt dort a meser.

Twinned are yesterday and today
and grown together and bent together
in a single clear tangle.
Clear in the bewilderment did he bewildered see clearly
how little comfort the dawn's rose pink can bring
when the day is already determined

by yesterday and the day before,
when the hours are only a spiral staircase leading up to that hour of that day,
where he himself in secret, like a thief, has already been
and has stuck in a knife.[20]

A reader would assume, based upon the title and mood of existential monotony,
that this stunned figure is Sacco or Vanzetti awaiting execution at dawn, but this
expectation is soon upended: "Because from yesterday till today the Governor /
has paced on the bridge of a sleepless night." The governor, self-appointed
"guard . . . of the consciences of the world," paces with a gun on his shoulders.
The poem centers the governor's dark night of the soul, not Sacco and Vanzetti's
suffering. Glatshteyn describes the governor's nocturnal musings with mythic
invention: "Midnight. Joyous demons have danced his own thoughts around
him / and laughed away, mocked away from him the fear in his eyes." This refusal to neither dehumanize the governor nor naturalize his power recalls the
language of appeals from the International Anarchist Group helmed by Warren Starr Van Valkenburgh, an editor of the anarchist paper *Road to Freedom*:

> Governor Fuller should be given every opportunity to prove himself a
> fair and just man, an able and humane executive but he lives in a world
> apart from the workers and he may be unconsciously swayed by the pow-
> erful forces which have so far won their case by deceit and cunning, by
> threat and chicanery.
>   SHOW YOUR SOLIDARITY THAT YOU STAND ON THE
> SIDE OF HUMAN RIGHTS / JOIN THE MIGHTY MOVEMENT
> TO FORCE JUSTICE FROM THOSE WHO SIT IN HIGH
> PLACES. PRESERVE YOUR OWN LIBERTY BY INSISTING
> UPON THE LIBERATION OF SACCO AND VANZETTI.[21]

This verse is also reminiscent of the visitation from ghosts of history in Yosl
Grinshpan's poem "Vanzetti's Ghost" (1929). As Judge Webster Thayer lies "in
his palace / on his golden bed," he envisions Vanzetti as an incinerated skeleton,
pacing the floorboards, bringing with him ghosts of the American past: "And
behind the red Satan stands, / the Yankee Klan . . . and the anthem swarms with
slaves."[22] In Grinshpan's poem, Thayer's mind generates historical hauntings long
before the Vanzetti case. Compare Grinshpan's and Glatshteyn's mythic temporality to, for example, John Dos Passos's 1927 poem, where prison regulates time
("Do you know how many hours there are in a day / when a day is twenty-three
hours on a cot in a cell . . . ?").[23] In the world of Dos Passos's poem, the machin-

ery of prison time has no hold on the outside. In contrast to Dos Passos's flat ideological stereotypes of wardens, judges, and statesmen as "black automatons," Glatshteyn richly imagines the governor's haunted nights:

> Di nakht iz gelegn vi ayn shtik fun shvartse tsayt,
> Un nit er hot gehert vi es ankern op di minutn,
> Un nit er hot gehert dem plyesk fun a gefalener sho in vaser.
> Nor vi a shvere dumpike vog hot di nakht gehoyert iber im
> Un farshtelt dem toyer tsu a morgn.
> Vet morgn keynmol nit kumen?
> (Zol morgn keynmol nit kumen)
> Di fis vern mid fun hin-tsurik,
> Shpan avek fun zikh,
> ariber yener zeyt fun farglivertn fintster.

> The night lay there like a piece of black time,
> and he hasn't heard how the minutes weigh anchor,
> and he hasn't heard the splash of a fallen hour in the water,
> but only how a heavy, musty wave hangs in the night above him
> and blocks the gate to a new day.
> Will tomorrow never come?
> (Let tomorrow never come.)
> The feet grow weary of back-and-forth,
> stride away from themselves,
> beyond the far side of the curdled darkness.

Time appears at once material and fluid, with the heaviness of an anchor and the mystery of a suspended wave. The repetitive movements of the governor, pacing back and forth in his room at midnight, recall the movements of workers walking to work on Monday morning at the opening of the poem. Everyone faces the same horizon of dread, eroding the difference between powerful and powerless. This restless portrait echoes the famed IWW poet Arturo Giovannitti's "The Walker" (1914):

> I hear footsteps over my head all night.
> They come and they go. Again they come and they go all night.
> They come one eternity in four paces and they go one eternity in
> four paces, and between the coming and the going there is
> silence and the Night and the Infinite.

For infinite are the nine feet of a prison cell, endless is the march
of him who walks between the yellow brick wall and the red
iron gate, thinking things that cannot be chained and cannot
be locked, but that wander far away in the sunlit world, each
in a wild pilgrimage after a destined goal.[24]

Only in the third section of Glatshteyn's poema are Sacco and Vanzetti finally alluded to, appearing in a hallucinatory flight of imagery—storming the
Bastille (they were sentenced on Bastille Day), leaping flames, and children re-
joicing at the prisoners' liberation, all times unfurling simultaneously: "Someone has reshuffled the cards. / Reversed what's to come and what's been." These
lines embody the spiraling of time: "Twinned are yesterday and today/and
grown together and bent together." The Yiddish syntax grants agency to time:
Glatshteyn coins the word for literally "twinning themselves." In Glatshteyn's
vision, Sacco and Vanzetti experience liberation of time, while the temporality
of the state constrains the governor to live like "a prisoner in the State House"
peering from a tiny window. This inversion evokes Morris Rosenfeld's poem
"The Sweatshop," which is set during lunch hour, an island in time during which
the worker can imagine beyond the oppressions of the present. The fluid temporality lived by Sacco and Vanzetti allows for moments of possibility unknowable
to the governor.

This "chaotic, kaleidoscopic" mode undoes the stringencies of nationalist
time, interrupting the notions of history espoused by the governor, who says:
"the cloak of method can never be stripped away, / and revolutions happen only
in history. / And history is what is taught by old grandfathers with no teeth /
and it always begins with Once—once upon a time." The governor's ambivalence
toward his role in history is revealed in his imagined monologue to the singing
protesters calling for clemency:

Ver hot oysgezungen inmitn nakht?
Oyf der brik zitst eyner un tsitert fun kelt.
Di fis aruntergehangen in vaser,
Zitst er un zingt shtil:
Ratevet! Ratevet!
Gut. Zing biz veytok.
Shtekh mikh durkh mit dem gezang vi mit goldene shpilkes,
Ober ze, hoyb oyf dem kop tsu mir un farshtey:
Ikh bin nit ersht un bin nit tsveyt un bin nit sof.
Ikh bin a flater in dem bliask fun shneln farbrikn baveg,

Ikh trog mit shrek an opgetrogenem guf,
Ver bin ikh tsu vern mer vi ikh bin?

Who sang out in the night?
Someone sits on the bridge and trembles with cold.
His feet hanging down in the water,
he quietly sits and sings:
Clemency! Clemency!
Good. Sing till you break.
Run me through with your song like a golden needle,
but look, lift your head up to me and understand:
I am not first and not second and not the end.
I am a fluttering in the brightness of quick, colorful motion,
I carry in fear a worn-out body,
who am I to become more than I am?

The protesters call out for clemency, but what would it have meant to pardon Sacco and Vanzetti, as the last Haymarket defendants escaped their sentence? Can the poets acknowledge that martyrdom was more galvanizing than clemency? Elias Canetti theorizes that state power is reified *more* powerfully through the act of pardon, which seems to restore a man back to life—more powerful than execution.[25] And in comparison to state resurrection, what power lies in Vanzetti's forgiveness of his executioner? Sacco and Vanzetti were often portrayed as Christ-like despite their non-pacifism, as in Vincent G. Burns's poem: "Cruel men, beware! The Christs you kill / Will walk in power with us still!"[26] Glatshteyn reverses the trope of the alpha and omega, placing it in the mouth of the governor: "I am not the first and not the end, / before me and after me a chain of people / cynically immortalizing themselves, / fastening themselves to the neck of a world-memory / and the waters will never erode their names." Glatshteyn's sardonic, mock-epic reference to Song of Songs 8:7 is juxtaposed with Christ-like imagery of alpha and omega. This passage further judaizes the judge as one to whom they lift their eyes for help. The governor knows his immortality will be granted not in history books but through the protest songs of his opponents:

Vey iz mir. Vey un vey un vey.
In mayn oyern klingen tsvey nemen
Un mit zey vet mitklingen mayn nomen.
Un du vos zingst inmitn der shverer nakht

zing mikh oykh areyn in dayn gezang,
un veb mikh oykh areyn in di fedim [fodem] fun dayn lid
Her du mikh un mayn shtim vi zi shneydt durkh di velt:
Ratevet!

Woe is me, woe and woe and woe.
In my ears two names are sounding
and my name will resound with theirs.
And you singing amid the heavy night
sing me too into your song,
weave me too into the threads of your song
hear me and my voice as it cuts through the world:
Clemency!

Sweatshop poetry tropes of labor converge in this image of song: threads of music, weaving, and the remarkable "Run me through with your song like golden needles."[27] "Shtekh mikh durkh mit dem gezang vi mit goldene shpilkes" transforms the humble instrument of garment workers—or perhaps the shoemaker Sacco's leather-working tool—into gold. The pin and needle are the paradigmatic image-objects of Sweatshop poetry, with intertextual echoes in proverbs, fables, and scripture. The repetition of a single gesture over long hours of work renders the movement of the worker an extension of the machine's automation: the staccato of an electric sewing machine marks time like the ticking of a clock. Morris Rosenfeld's "To My Beloved" represents these gestures of labor: "Here rules the struggle harsh for bread, / And I must tremble when I sew."[28] Imagery of needles is found in many popular Yiddish labor songs, such as *"Mit a nodl, on a nodl,"* which exalt the nobility of work, combining pious traditions with labor consciousness.[29] This needle passage is among the most direct of Glatshteyn's reinventions of Sweatshop poetry. In his signature poem "The Millionaire of Tears" from "Songs from the Ghetto," Rosenfeld channels a worker's lament. It was published in 1913 in Emma Goldman's *Mother Earth,* in a translation by Florence Kiper:

> 'Tis not a golden tuning fork
>   Attunes my voice to song,
> Nor at a beckon from the stars
>   Do silver fancies throng.
> A child's sad whimper in the night,
>   A wearied worker's moan,

O these alone awake my heart
    Its music to intone,
And with a flame my song takes life
    From my poor brother's grief;
Therefore I die before my time,
    With meagre days and brief.
What will they give me as reward—
    In wretchedness my peers?
A millionaire of tears am I;
    With tears they pay for tears.[30]

Rosenfeld's sweatshop worker laments that his creativity is circumscribed by poverty, as he hopes to awaken his enslaved fellow-workers with the fire of his song ("O, nit keyn goldener kamerton / shtimt on meyn kol tsum zingen, / es ken der vunk fun oybn on / mayn shtim nit makhn klingen; / dem shklaf's a krekhts ven er iz mid / nor vekt in mir di lider,— / un mit a flam lebt oyf meyn lid, / Fir meyne or'me brider").[31] Glatshteyn's image of "golden needles of song" represents the art of proletarian singers holding the governor accountable—a tribute, perhaps, from the modernist to the Proletarian poet.

Modernist reinvention of images of domestic labor is not unique to the Yiddish context. Nina Gurianova notes that while Italian futurist artists tended to embrace images of new machinery and momentum, Russian modernist artists tended to depict hand tools of traditional trades: "While Italians chose to be the utopians in their purely futuristic ambitions, Russians never rejected the past, and indeed 'internalized' and deconstructed archaic myth, making a clear argument in their poetics for primitivism against all the attractions of civilized modernity."[32] As Russian futurists experimented with imagery of the humble hand tool, so did the Yiddish anarchist modernists refuse to give up labor symbology. This represents not a rejection of the previous generation but a retention and reinvention. Like Harry Houdini, the magician (and rabbi's son) who primarily used common household objects like needles and locks in his stage act, this is an image of transcendence via the tools of the mundane. One of Houdini's signature acts was called the "East Indian Needle Trick," described as a "yogie masterpiece." Despite its being dressed up with an orientalizing name, that stage image was read by Jewish audiences as the cunning transcendence of a man over drudgery and labor.[33] Houdini would have his mouth inspected by a committee of men on stage, then swallow fifty to one hundred needles and twenty yards of thread, and drink a glass of water to "wash them down." He would then

pull out the thread, with all the needles threaded upon it. Although earlier magi-
cians had performed this feat using a few dozen needles, Houdini used enough
needles and thread to stretch across the length of the stage. Like Houdini fabri-
cating his stunning stagecraft from domestic tools, Glatshteyn takes the signature vocabulary of the Sweatshop poets—needles, workers' songs as resistance—
and creates a modernist image from it. By re-combining the components of an
older style, he threads the needle anew. Like Houdini's transcending tools of hand
labor, Glatshteyn takes the signature vocabulary of the earlier anarchist poets—
needles, workers' songs of resistance, the possibility of time liberated—and re-
invents them in magical, modernist images. Rather than mystifying power, their
modernist sleight of hand works to make the perpetrators' hands visible.

MOYSHE-LEYB HALPERN'S "SACCO-VANZETTI" AND THE CRITIQUE OF COMRADESHIP

Like Glatshteyn, Moyshe-Leyb Halpern satirizes the social forces that con-
spired for Sacco and Vanzetti's execution and avoids canonizing the men themselves. Halpern (1886–1932) was born in eastern Galicia and came to the United
States in 1908, after studying painting and German literature in Vienna for
about a decade. He was closely affiliated with *Di yunge* (the Youngsters), a poetic school known for privileging *shtimung* (mood) over the perceived didacti-
cism of the earlier Proletarian poets. Chana Kronfeld theorizes his more complex iconoclastic standing as "the deviant paragon among his contemporaries, *di
yunge,* and as a proleptic paragon for the introspectivists, who reacted against
them."[34] Benjamin Harshav described Halpern's approach as "an existentialist-
anarchist slashing at life in general and at American capitalism in particular."[35]
Halpern's forty-line poem "Sacco and Vanzetti" (1927) is explicitly connected to
those men only through its title and date, de-exceptionalizing their execution:

> Men ken zikh oysraysn a groye hor fun kop,
> Vos kumt tsu fri amol fun tsar, vos iz tsu shver;
> Nor vemen in dayn tsar es dakht zikh oys,
> Az s'iz im shver der kop zayner mit hoyt un hor,
> Vi epes, vos er ken nit trogn mer,
> Oyf ot di knokhn di tsvey orime, vos heysn aksl,—
> Bay dem mentsn—
> Zol er nit blaybn shteyn demolt mit moyl un oygn ofene,
> Vi in a dulhoyz ergets;

Un oykh der shteyn fun vant iz harter fun zayn kop
Un shlogn zikh on im vet brengen bloyz a bayl,
Nit greser fun an epl oyf a boym, vos dart
Un hot nit ver es zol im opraysn in tsayt.
Un s'iz dokh do an oysveg haynt a gringerer
Far dem, vos zukht im:
Men darf nor ruik zayn a vayl,
Un vi a tifus-kranker tsuboygn dem kop tsu dem, vos golt.
A bruder iz er dokh,
Un men darf nit broygez dayn oyf im,
Far vos er nemt di hoyt nit mit.
Er tut nor vos men heyst un ven men tsolt derfar.
Un oykh dos toytnkleyd,—
Dos oykh—hot oyfgeneyt a bruder, vos iz hungerik.

Un az a kind—dos orimste,
ven men tut es on a beged in a tom-tov,
Geyt bam hant, vuhin men nemt es mit:
Meg men oykh zikh lozn firn tsu der toytnshtul, vos vart
Vi alt men zol nit zayn.
Un az es blankt shoyn oykh dos toytndike kuper oyfen kop
Vos ken nokh shver zayn demolt?
A kinig—ven dos gantse folk afile veynt arum zayn tron—
darf shvaygn, ven men kroynt im.
Un az fun fayer iz di kroyn oyf im dem oysderveyltn
Iz dos a vunder-kroyn in ot der vister velt.
Un bloyz der volf, vos eybik loyert er, vayl er iz vild
Un bloyz der royber in der fintster—
Shrek zikh far fayer.
Kinder shtume, nokh
mit oygn ofene, os zeen gornisht nokh,
shtrekn zikh tsum fayer.
Un bloyz der shmeterling, vos gart nokh likht
In khoyshekh fun der nakht,
Bagengt mit tseshreyte fligl eybik—
Dem toyt in fayer.[36]

You can tear a gray hair from your head
that grew from grief, too heavy and too soon;

but if you think in your grief
that your head with its skin and hair
is too heavy to carry any longer
on the two poor bones
called, in humans, "shoulders"—
then don't hang around with mouth and eyes agape,
as in some madhouse;
for the stone in a wall is harder than your head
and striking it will only raise a lump
no bigger than an apple on the tree, withered
with nobody to pluck it in time.
There's an easier way out now
if you're searching:
Be calm a while,
like a man sick from typhus bends his head to be shaved.
He is your brother, after all—
don't get angry with him
for not scraping up your skin along with it.
He does what he's told and gets paid in return.
And the death-clothes—
a brother made those too, a hungry brother.
And if the poorest child
will follow you anywhere
when you deck him out for a holiday
and lead him by the hand,
you too will follow anyone
to the death-chair
that's waiting,
no matter your years.
And as the fatal copper gleams around your head,
what's heavy then?
A king—though all the nation weeps around his throne—
must keep mute when he's crowned.
And if the crown laid upon the elect
should be made from fire,
it's a wonder-crown amid this wasteland world.
Only the wolf—always crouching, waiting, wild—
and only the bandit in the dark

fear fire.
Children still unspeaking
with open eyes unseeing
reach out their hands towards fire.
And only the butterfly, pining for light,
meets eternity with open wing—
death by fire.[37]

The poem's self-interrupting rhythm beats an anarchist hurly-burly melody. "Sacco and Vanzetti" is structured by a series of macabre twinned object-images: the crowning of a king doubles with the copper execution band "coronating" the heads of the doomed; a child is dressed up for a religious holiday, and an adult is wrapped in a death shroud; a baby reaches toward fire, and a moth circles the flame that will consume it. Halpern pairs the kingly head bowed for coronation and the head bowed for execution, collapsing the hierarchy signified by each gesture. The repeated generic phrase *men ken* (one can) points toward the universal experience of aging. There is an almost liturgical cast to the harrowing image of the child dressed for holiday, as though perhaps led toward sacrifice on the mountain. Rather than centering the single moment of execution at the apex of the poem, this stagnant, iterative temporality evokes Sacco and Vanzetti's seven prison years. Halpern "rhymes" the prisoner with a typhus patient, the convict with a king, and your own walk toward death with the trusting child led toward celebration.

As traditional with elegies, Halpern records the day of composition, "September 4, 1927," dating it shortly after the execution on August 23, 1927.[38] But there the similarities end, as Halpern radically defamiliarizes the genre of lament. First he dismantles the human body into animal parts: *Di knokhn di tsvey oreme, vos heysn aksl, / bay dem mentshn,* "the two poor bones / called, in humans, 'shoulders'"; *knokhn* more literally means knob or knuckle, making the body nearly inanimate. Yiddish has several verbs differentiating human activity from that of an animal, but few nouns, which makes *knokhn* all the stranger. Halpern's word choice reminds us of the proximity of the animal, separated from the human not by essential biological difference but through language. Mel Chen notes "how objectification and dehumanization are positioned in relation to animacy."[39] Thrown against the presence of the animal world, the absurdity of hierarchy is brought into relief: thieves and kings, forest wolf and butterfly (*shmeterling*) all face the same fiery horizon.

These animals populate Halpern's recurring menagerie in "My Restlessness

Is of a Wolf," "The Bird," and others. Halpern repeatedly contrasts the image of a lonely king shaking upon his throne with the freedom of nonhuman animals, as in *"Der gasnpoyker"* (The Street-Drummer):

> Zingt der foygl fray un freylekh,
> tsitern oyf zayn tron der meylekh,
> tsitert iz nit keday,
> zing ikh, vi der foygl, fray,
> un geshvind,
> vi der vint . . .
>
> The bird so free and joyful sings.
> On his throne trembles the king.
> Trembling is folly:
> I sing like the bird, so free,
> and just as fast
> as wind's bombast . . . [40]

The persistent presence of animals within the sphere of human parable—and the poet's identification with the unbounded animal realm—reveals the insult of caste. In the second long section of "Sacco-Vanzetti," Halpern shifts register. *"Un az a kind—dos orimste, / ven men tut es on a beged in a tom-tov"* uses the loshn-koydesh word *beged* to make clear that the poor child is all dressed up for a Jewish ceremony, probably wearing loaned garments. This is the only phrase marking Jewish particularity, and it stamps the child with poverty.

Studies of the Yiddish Sacco-Vanzetti genre often focus on questions of ethnic identification and representation. Jordan Finkin writes, for example, that the "Yiddish Sacco-Vanzetti poets went beyond their English-language contemporaries to develop a distinctive thematology, one that claims a stake in American identity politics."[41] Alternatively, the genre is portrayed as a de-fanged "commemorative" form. Khone Shmeruk, Irving Howe, and Ruth Wisse introduce Halpern's "Sacco-Vanzetti" thus: "Liberals protested that they had been sentenced for their anarchist beliefs rather than for any crime they had committed, and radicals used the case to attack the American system of justice. Many Yiddish poets and writers wrote commemorative works on this subject."[42] These approaches extend the tendency to reduce literature with proletarian themes to its social and participatory function or to cite it as first and foremost an archive of immigrant life. In a more recent article, Lawrence Rosenwald reads Halpern's poem as "an invitation to identify with the oppressed": "[he] directs sympathy most explicitly, not to Sacco and Vanzetti, but to the ordinary people one might at first think of as their oppressors. Halpern's man who sews the 'death-smock' ... is complicit with the state. ... But to treat him as an oppressor would be to be in accord with the dominant ideology of the period, ... by warding off the threat of general working-class solidarity."[43] Jordan Finkin similarly understands these lines as sounding a "sympathetic note" to the executioner and the workers who made the prison uniform: "This passage offers yet another image of acquiescence at the heart of the poem, this time with a note of sympathy for the executioner and the functionaries of execution. They are 'brothers,' after all, not to be condemned by misdirected contempt or even scorn. The poem describes them as part of a larger apparatus against which appeals are futile."[44]

In her study of H. Leivick's *"A yor Sako Vanzeti"* ("A Sacco Vanzetti Year"), Amelia Glaser emphasizes the poetic identification between Jewish and Italian pain: "Leivick's attention to non-Jewish victims is a call to his American Yiddish readers to stand up on behalf of others."[45] Glaser comments on the significance of Leivick's loshn-koydesh word choice *kateyger,* accuser: "By commemorating the *yortsayt* of the convicted Italian anarchists ('Fuller's bite / hasn't even been covered / with a scab'), Leivick calls Jews to action on behalf of one of their own."[46] Glaser's reading emphasizes Yiddish empathy and identification with the non-Jewish defendants. Leivick's poem, however, ends with a horrifying image of Vanzetti upon the electric chair (*"Un vi zikh Vanzeti zidt"* / "And how Vanzetti sizzles").[47] These graphically imagined death scenes *unsettle* identification with the condemned men: even within ostensibly empathetic poems, graphic representations of the suffering body signal difference and dehumanization rather than fellow-feeling—as with many extremely graphic Yiddish anti-lynching poems, which undercut their political aspirations to anti-racism through caricatured imagery. Leivick's gory image of the anarchist's "sizzling" body recalls the sensationalistic journalist's gaze upon Lingg's death, not the mournful averting of a comrade's eyes. Who but the executioner would watch this scene of execution? Who but the coroner could write the death report? Where Edelshtat looks away, Leivick stares.

The act of witnessing was never left to chance. For three days, Sacco and Vanzetti lay in state; thousands filed past their bodies to pay their respects or participate in the spectacle of their death. Their choice of cremation was a final declaration of anarchist atheism; they were the first to be executed in Massachusetts without last rites, and the Catholic Church considered cremation a scandal. Only Sacco and Vanzetti's most treasured comrades were permitted to enter the crematorium. After their cremation, the labor leader Rose Pesotta—a close friend of Vanzetti's—was among the few to be ushered into the sanctum of the state crematorium.[48] Sunday, August 28, 1927, was the day of their funeral; as many as twenty thousand mourners followed the twin hearses on an eight-mile march, bearing flowers, as for charismatic saints.[49] The authorities forbade a band to play, and the undertaker wore a tuxedo. Many mourning protesters were clubbed by mounted police along the way. Newsreel footage reveals few women or people of color in the crowd. Little footage survives, however: Hollywood producers were coerced into destroying a large amount of film; the remaining clips were commissioned and saved by the Sacco-Vanzetti Defense Committee.[50]

Compare the disidentification of Leivick with the grief and ferocious urgency of anarchist writing and public ritual as the day of execution approached. A telegram from the Sacco-Vanzetti Student Committee in the United States, for example, summoned protesters with the hot precision of a found poem: COME ARMED WITH BLACK BAND ON YOUR SLEEVES / COME ARMED WITH INEXTINGUISHABLE FAITH / SACCO AND VANZETTI MUST AND SHALL LIVE.[51] In a letter to her friend Warren Starr Van Valkenburgh, an organizer of the Sacco-Vanzetti Defense Committee, Emma Goldman requested a copy of the *Chicago Law Journal* for reference to compose an article connecting "the Chicago murder of our people with impending murder of Sacco and Vanzetti."[52] She writes: "You are certainly doing devoted work for Sacco and Vanzetti, if only it will bring results. It makes me shiver when I think how dreadful it must be the days now for the two splendid men. I get a sinking of the heart when I think of the possible outcome. I can not tell you how rotten I feel that I could have no share in the campaign."[53] Van Valkenburgh's response demonstrates the depth of identification with the two Italian anarchists and concern over communist co-optation or liberal dilution of their "Ideal":

> [Vanzetti] has a wonderful soul, a heroic spirit and audacity beyond compare—please write him. Tomorrow a one hour "General Strike" is to be called—we'll see what happens. The Communists are running so we can only hang on. The idea is so stupid—like tickling a rhinocerous [*sic*] with a feather. Every day in New York the local lefts and rights are double crossing and slugging one another. The man on the street thinks Sacco and Vanzetti is a new dance or breakfast food—so a "General Strike" is called to add insult to injury and yet we must line up with these bloody throat cutting politicians! The irony of it. Yes, write both Sacco and Van-

zetti, but be tender with Sacco, he is a crushed and broken man. Vanzetti is a philosopher, this ordeal has made him a halo bearer.[54]

Valkenburgh's letter vividly illustrates their frustrations with communists and emotional identification with the condemned men, which was borne out further in Goldman's increasingly desperate letters as the date of execution approached. Halpern expresses no such outpouring of ache or shock.

When read with Halpern's broader work, "Sacco-Vanzetti" makes unmistakable the satire of unearned brotherhood throughout the poem. His early writing included the scathing "Open Letter to Morris Rosenfeld" in *Der kibitzer,* which likened the popular Proletarian poet to a rusty mechanical clown in an amusement park, performing for spare change.[55] His poem *"Salyut"* ("Salute") indicts the Yiddish genre of anti-lynching poems for its solipsism. First published in *Di Vokh* on January 24, 1930, "Salute" was anthologized in 1934, two years after Halpern's death, when the lynching of Leo Frank in Atlanta may have intensified its meaning to Jewish readership.[56] Like "Sacco-Vanzetti," "Salute" has been studied and anthologized primarily as a protest poem. Julian Levinson, for example, describes it as "a meditation on the phenomenon of lynching" with a "note of strident protest."[57] Yet the poem's brutal cynicism and ultimate self-indictment precludes straightforward protest against external society alone. Nor is it an elegy for an individual: despite its denunciation of violence, the victim is portrayed as an anonymous flayed young body, under the gaze of the poetic speaker. The second half of the poem is saturated with self-contempt and intimations of sexual shame. In the penultimate stanza, even as rhyme and meter hold their regularity, the speaker dissociates from the scene of lynching:

> Un ikh zog dir—s'iz nit der krekhts fun tsvaygn,
> nit der shtrik, mitn gantsn klapergetsayg,
> nit dos federl in vintgetrayb
> vos hot farzamt zikh tsu klepn tsum layb,
> nor du—dos troyer-geshtank fun der velt,
> vos hot zikh fun vaytn anidergeshtelt,
> mit di hent, durkh di keshenes, baym dikh,
> fartrakhtn a lid far der velt un far zikh.

> And I'm telling you—it's not the grunt of the bough,
> not the rope with all its rigging,
> not the feathers windblown
> too late to stick to the body,

> no—it's you! The sorrow-stench of this world,
> standing there apart
> with hands through your pockets, stroking yourself,
> thinking up a poem for the world and for you.[58]

Halpern's poetic speaker hovers somehow, split between implicated witness and shaming accuser. The confusion or conflation of "you" and "I" extends the opening lines ("There are things in this country too"), in which the witness identifies as a migrant but does not name the "something" (*epes*) among us as a pogrom. The poem's tortured fury condemns both the perpetrators of the lynching and those masturbatory poet-idealists who imbue art with redemption. In some contemporaneous anti-lynching poems by Black poets such as Countee Cullen, the victim was portrayed as a modern-day Jesus on the cross, suggesting the possibility of salvation.[59] Halpern mocks a corrupt Christianity: "If blackness, [the priest] says, is a blunder of God, / Then it's sinful to mix black and white."[60] There is no hope here of a redemptive theology, let alone flickers of human solidarity. Julian Levinson claims to discern in Halpern a "sense of comradery with the subjugated Negro."[61] Yet despite this liberal reading, Halpern's descriptions of the dying boy challenge the possibility of comradeship between two such degraded figures as this self-pleasuring observer and victim. As Ruth Wisse observes, "For Halpern, the pretense of brotherliness where none existed was a particularly corrupting form of self-deception."[62]

"Sacco-Vanzetti" echoes "Salute" as a manifesto simultaneously against brutality and the simplistic pieties of "social justice" poetry. In his critique of the artist's exceptionalizing gaze, Halpern was prescient. The use of graphic visuals of death has been widely debated in recent years, particularly in opposition to Dana Schutz's painting *Open Casket* (2016), which depicts the mangled, abstracted body of Emmett Till. Protests at the Whitney Biennial by Black artists included Parker Bright, who blocked the painting from gallery view and wore a shirt with the words "Black Death Spectacle."[63] Graphic representation of racialized state execution or mob violence will never produce comradely identification with victims, these activists argued.

Considering his bitterly satiric oeuvre, notes of socialist piety and utopian internationalism from Halpern would only sound off-key. Instead, an anarchist reading of "Sacco-Vanzetti" reveals Halpern's critique of cross-ethnic identification as a mere claim to bystander innocence. The Italians understood their persecution as the result of their "race," as in Vanzetti's letter to Justice Thayer: "I am an Italian, a stranger in a foreign country, and my witnesses are the same kind of people. I am accused and convicted on the testimony of mostly American witnesses. Everything is against me—my race, my opinions, and my humble occupation."[64] Euro-American writers' broad support and identification with Sacco and Vanzetti cast into relief their silence around contemporaneous struggles for Black liberation. In the poem "Scottsboro, Too, Is Worth Its Song" (1934), which appeared the same year as Halpern's posthumous collection, Countee Cullen chastises those who hailed Sacco and Vanzetti but not the "Scottsboro Boys."[65] Cullen does not extol any possibility of solidarity across race and immigration status; beside the inequity between Black and white citizens in the United States, Sacco and Vanzetti's status as immigrants collapses into whiteness. Cullen indicts the literary establishment as turning away from anti-Black violence and merely singing "sharp and pretty tunes." Likewise, rather than positing any exculpatory or unifying "brotherhood," Halpern describes a world without workers' innocence. Lest we mistake these lines for sincerity, he caustically implores the reader not to be cross with the barber "for not scraping up the scalp as well"! "A bruder iz er dokh, / Un men darf nit broygez dayn oyf im, / Far vos er nemt di hoyt nit mit. / Er tut nor vos men heyst un ven men tsolt derfar": He is after all a brother, who does it for the money. Halpern's sarcasm interrogates any rhetoric of solidarity that does not acknowledge mutual injury. His long poem "A Nakht" (A Night) similarly dismantles the rhetoric of war-brotherhood through gallows humor:

> Ongevirn hot dayn bruder
> Nebekh, beyde hent in shlakht.
> Ken er zikh shoyn mer nit kratsn
> Nemt im nit keyn shlof baynakht.
>
> Your own brother, poor thing,
> lost both his hands in the war.
> Now he doesn't sleep at night—
> since he can't scratch himself anymore.[66]

Even the possibility of finding private peace in sleep is revoked by war. This soldier, granted a sarcastic *nebekh* (pobrecito, poor thing), could be the brother of the tailor sewing shrouds for Sacco and Vanzetti: he is no less implicated in violence for having suffered himself, no less immune from pillory. Halpern's poem "Abie Curley, Hero of the War" deflates military grandeur as readily as he pierces the sanctity of Sacco and Vanzetti: "Abie Curley dare not reminisce about delight / for he shrieks / and then, in a coughing fit, he'll spit out blood. //

However, Abie Curley's not an angry fellow; all he closes is his left eye / when he weeps / with medals flashing on his chest and with his crutches."[67] Heraldry is a useless prosthetic for the injury of war.

In "Sacco-Vanzetti" and these poems, Halpern's anarchist analysis lies not in avowing identification but in exposing complicity. The image of a poor tailor sewing a prisoner's death-garb analogizes debates surrounding labor and World War I, when mainstream unions advocated to expand jobs in arms manufacture. Radical labor groups such as the IWW lambasted the creation of jobs in the weapons industry as harmful to the internationalism of workers and soldiers; instead, they urged workers to remember the transnational kinship of workers. "And the death-clothes too / These too were tailored by your brother who was hungry" models a world where, if all are brothers, all must be complicit. Halpern critiques the socialist valorization of labor for the war effort and instrumentalization of comradeship. Halpern himself immigrated to the United States to avoid the military draft in Germany, but biography is not necessary to explicate these lines. "Sacco-Vanzetti" demonstrates how power circulates between workers, unconfined to the warden. Prison as a structure extends into the hospital and barracks, even into nature. As in "Salute," with its indictment of lynchings and the non-Black poets who appropriate imagery of Black death, Halpern implicates the reader: the narrative lens is so wide that it becomes convex, reflecting those in the periphery and himself. The laboring body is affected by time, deteriorating and vulnerable, inverting Edelshtat's restorative gesture toward Lingg's maimed body.

Though Halpern pillories the *fantasy* of solidarity, Sacco and Vanzetti's own ethos was poignantly comradely. In the moment before his execution, "Vanzetti shook the warden's hand and thanked him for caring for him, a display of composure that reportedly affected many of the witnesses very deeply. He declared that he wished to forgive [those] putting him to death."[68] Little of Sacco and Vanzetti's faces or voices appear through Halpern and Glatshteyn. Visual art representing the trials of 1886 and 1920 reflect this difference in poetic gaze: the Haymarket martyrs are wreathed in glory, whereas Sacco and Vanzetti's judges are caricatured as skeletons and grim reapers. Widely reproduced Haymarket iconography revels in Victorian tropes of memorialization, such as circular compositions to be clipped for a locket. In contrast, the artist William Gropper turns from Sacco and Vanzetti's faces altogether, save for their trademark moustaches; he removes the faces from the judge and executioner, reducing them to specters of death. In Ben Shahn's suite of twenty-three paintings, *The Passion of Sacco and Vanzetti* (1931–1932), their gray dead faces are barely visible above the coffins' rim.

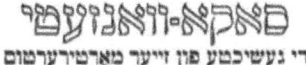

"The true terror" (Der emeser terer). Illustrations by William Gropper
in Melech Epstein, *Sako-Vanzeti: di geshikhṭe fun zeyer martirertum* (Sacco-Vanzetti:
The History of Their Martyrdom), distributed by the Yidisher sektsye vorkers
(komunistishe) partey (New York, 1927).

Facing the viewer are morosely colored portraits of Judge Webster Thayer and
two legal commissioners who proffer lilies, symbols of martyrdom, above the
cement-gray corpses. Like Glatshteyn and Halpern, Shahn makes the faces of
executioners and prosecutors grimly visible.

Whereas Edelshtat cites Lingg, Parsons, and others to carry their voices into
Yiddish, Sacco and Vanzetti do not sing through Glatshteyn and Halpern. The
Italian anarchists were extraordinarily prolific, and their courtroom statements,
letters, and memoirs were widely disseminated. Vanzetti was rapturously attuned
to nature, and he recounted the "unspeakably beautiful" garden and countryside
of his youth in Villafalletto, Italy: "You ought to see the king wasps, big, velvety,
lucid, ravishingly forcefully on these flowers' calices, and the virtuous honey-
bees—the wasp, the white, the yellow, the forget-me-nots, the hedge's butterflies
and the variated armies of several genuses of grass eaters, the red conconcinas,

the meadows gri-gri. Each of your step [sic] would arise from the ground a rainbow cloud of these creatures, with a multiphoned vibration of wings."[69] Vanzetti writes with the lyrical capaciousness of Kropotkin's litanies of the wild. Letters to both of their sons were put to music by Woody Guthrie and, later, Pete Seeger, in one of the first concept albums; Seeger adapts Sacco's letter of August 27, 1927, from Charlestown State Prison to Dante, "My dear Son and companion."[70] Written five days before his execution, just after he ended his hunger strike, Sacco's letter describes his experience of prison temporality to the twelve-year-old boy: "Much have we suffered during this long Calvary. We protest today as we have yesterday. We protest always for our freedom. . . . So Son, today life begins to revive slow and calm, but yet without horizon and always with sadness and visions of death."[71] His reference to Calvary, site of Jesus's crucifixion, is the sole religious image, yet love of nature is exhorted: "take [your mother] for a long walk in the quiet country, gathering wild flowers here and there, resting under the shade of trees, between the harmony of the vivid stream and the gentle tranquility of the mothernature, and I am sure that she will enjoy this very much, as you surely would be happy for it."[72] The letter evokes the landscapes of Italy, a deterritorialized vision as utopian as the dreamlike reprieve from factory work in Rosenfeld's *"Mayn rue plats"* (My Resting Place).

Woody Guthrie's album *Ballads of Sacco and Vanzetti* (recorded 1945–1946) paints their portrait, as in "Two Good Men": "Vanzetti was a dreamin' man/A book was always in his hands."[73] The ballad ends in the personal voice: "But I'll remember these two good men / That died to show me how to live." Pete Seeger adapts those lines in the song "Sacco's Letter to His Son," a profoundly affecting ballad, in an album commissioned by the Smithsonian Folkways director Moe Asch, relative of Sholem Asch. Sacco's letter to his twelve-year-old son, Dante, poignantly dramatizes the call to the future—not to become an anarchist, but to be an ethical person, to become "the beloved boy I had always dreamed":

> If they should kill us, you must not forget to look at your friends and comrades with the smiling gaze of gratitude as you look at your beloved ones, because they love you as they love every one of the fallen persecuted comrades. . . . [It] is the struggle and fight between the rich and the poor for safety and freedom, Son, which you will understand in the future of your years to come, of this unrest and struggle of life's death.[74]

In his memoir *The Story of a Proletarian Life* (1923), Vanzetti writes, "I know that only in liberty can man rise, become noble, and complete."[75] This individualism, expressed through the insistent first-person voice, posits that liberty, impossible in the sweatshops, is a prerequisite for the development of identity. Similarly, Rosenfeld's speaker, addressed by the metonymic object of a clock, cannot achieve the horizon of being within capitalism's temporal regulation. Leivick's image of the clock echoes Rosenfeld's, in Glaser's translation: "oh, we won't forget how the clock hands / dripped with blood that August night."[76] Here he evokes the Proletarian anthropomorphization of time: "I fear that, relentless, the clock drives me on /And calls to me: 'Machine!' / And screams to me: 'Sew!'"[77]

The anarchist anthropologist David Graeber recently remarked, "In Germanic languages, including English, the word 'free' derives from 'friend,' because the idea is that a slave can't have friends. . . . One common theme [of divine kingship] is that there is a hidden affinity, even kinship, between kings and slaves, because they are the only kinds of people who have no social relations other than relations of domination."[78] This anarchist motif of the loneliness of the powerful manifests in Halpern's and Glatshteyn's focus on the judges and governors, imagining their inner worlds as barren, in contrast to the comradeship swelling up for Sacco and Vanzetti outside their prisons. Their Sacco-Vanzetti poems take up the aesthetics and strategies of anarchist poetry: exploding carceral time, extending anarchist motifs from the Proletarian poets, and making visible those state actors and complicit workers who perpetuated suffering. Halpern's critique of liberal unionism takes an "anarchist turn" in deriding the instrumentalization of comradeship and rhetoric of solidarity that colludes with militarism. Glatshteyn's imagery and temporality draw deeply from earlier anarchist Yiddish poets to address the Sacco-Vanzetti trial. Reminding us of the transience of hierarchy and lonesomeness of the powerful, Halpern's king is uncrowned and Glatshteyn's Judge Thayer endures haunted nights. Both poets give tribute not by canonizing immigrant "martyrs" but by defamiliarizing state violence.[79] Although the Sweatshop poets were marginalized in literary historiography and anthologization, their political imaginations extend through the verse-worlds of Yiddish modernists. Their poetic critique of temporality and the state is not expressed as a loss of innocence but through historical analogy and radical genealogy.

MARTÍN ESPADA'S SACCO-VANZETTI

Martín Espada offers a new entry in radical Jewish poets' enduring fascination with Sacco and Vanzetti. In 2017, to commemorate the ninetieth anniversary of their execution, the Puerto Rican poet published "I Now Pronounce You

Dead," subtitled "For Sacco and Vanzetti, executed August 23, 1927." Espada's work draws often from labor history, as in his sonnet sequence about the Paterson Silk Strike of 1912, *Vivas to Those Who Have Failed,* whose title cites Whitman. He takes up the tropes of canonical Sacco-Vanzetti poetry: the dramatic retelling of the execution, the timestamp of their death, the elegiac honoring of Vanzetti's unearthly virtue toward his executioner, and the rejection of linear time. Like Glatshteyn and Halpern, Espada turns his gaze to follow the warden and executioner rather than Sacco and Vanzetti:

> On the night of his execution, Bartolomeo Vanzetti, immigrant
> from Italia, fishmonger, anarchist, shook the hand of Warden Hendry
> and thanked him for everything. *I wish to forgive some people for what*
> *they are now doing to me,* said Vanzetti, blindfolded, strapped down
> to the chair that would shoot two thousand volts through his body.
>
> The warden's eyes were wet. The warden's mouth was dry. The warden
> heard his own voice croak: *Under the law I now pronounce you dead.*
> No one could hear him. With the same hand that shook the hand
> of Bartolomeo Vanzetti, Warden Hendry of Charlestown Prison
> waved at the executioner, who gripped the switch to yank it down.
>
> The walls of Charlestown Prison are gone, to ruin, to dust, to mist.
> Where the prison stood there is a school; in the hallways, tongues
> speak the Spanish of the Dominican, the Portuguese of Cabo Verde,
> the Creole of Haiti. No one can hear the last words of Vanzetti,
> or the howl of thousands on Boston Common when they knew.
>
> After midnight, at the hour of the execution, Warden Hendry
> sits in the cafeteria, his hand shaking as if shocked, rice flying off
> his fork, so he cannot eat no matter how the hunger feeds on him,
> babbling the words that only he can hear: *I now pronounce you dead.*[80]

Espada's decolonial move appeals to the transience of empire through the fall of this prison, succumbing "to ruin, to dust, to mist" within continental space. Espada notes the significance of place in the poem: "I wanted to draw a connection between the repression of immigrants past and present. This is nothing new, and it doesn't work. It so happens that the former site of Charlestown Prison, where Sacco and Vanzetti were executed, is the current site of Bunker Hill Community College—a school with a sizeable immigrant population, speaking in many tongues. As the saying goes: *Aquí estamos y no nos vamos.* Here we are and here we stay. The poem is also about the paradox of a good man in a bad system—the warden at the prison, in this case—and the compromise with lethal injustice that will haunt him for the rest of his days."[81]

Like Halpern and Glatshteyn, Espada makes visible the ambivalent hands of power and focuses not on martyrs but perpetrators. The poem jumps in time from stanza three to stanza four, back to a suspended moment when the haunted warden remains unable to eat. The poem's temporality seems at first bound up with an eternal mourning for the two men, but then it widens to take in the multiplicity of immigrant languages of Boston—Spanish, Portuguese, Creole—as though rhyming with Vanzetti's tongue from "Italia," his own words lost to ether. The prison has eroded, its inmates replaced by free children, rhyming with Vanzetti's own longing for the future; this turn toward a reproductive futurity evokes Vanzetti's own address to his son and and Heifetz Tussman's description of a child's accusatory gaze toward the corrupt world. But Espada gives the last word to the warden's pronouncement, perhaps putting the lie to Spies's defiant shout from the gallows: "The day will come when our silence will be more powerful than the voices you strangle today."[82] Haymarket and Sacco and Vanzetti remain unfinished.

Part II turns from the memorialization of contemporaneous trials toward the construction of anarchist genealogies rooted in Jewish religiosity, scripture, and deep time.

PART TWO

Genealogy

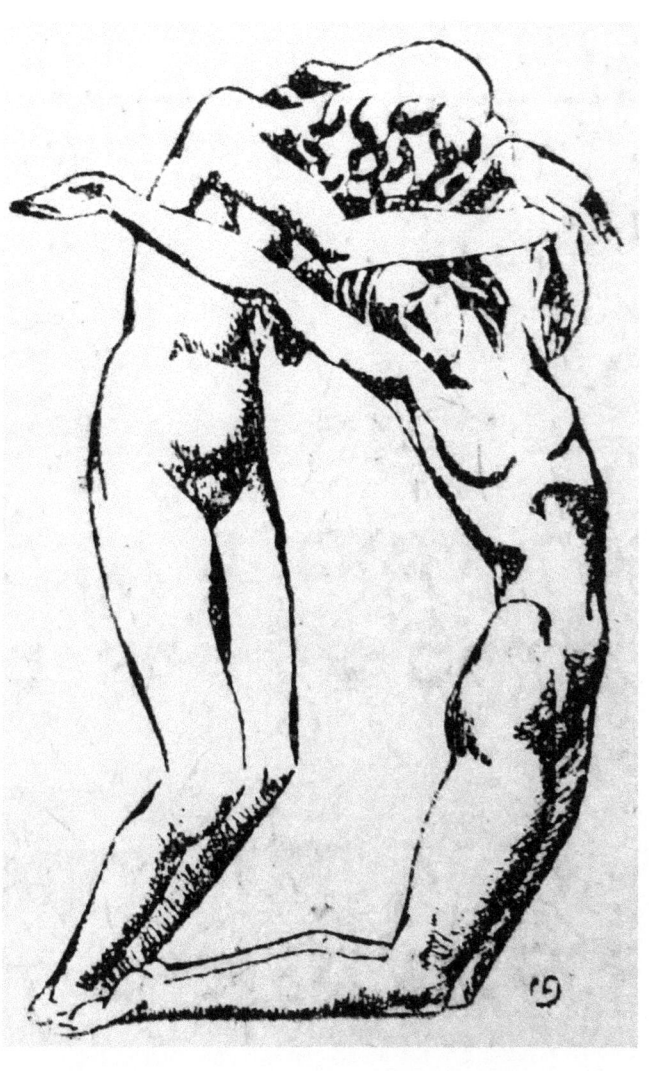

CHAPTER III

"Anarchism by Our Grandmothers"

FEMINIST GENEALOGIES

We consider incomplete any history
which is based on non-perishable traces.

—*Rivolta femminile*

Anarchist genealogy recounts history as a reparative form. The Jewish and Puerto Rican poet Aurora Levins Morales models "medicinal uses of history" and the historian as a *"curandera"* (a traditional, often Indigenous healer). Levins Morales—whose work has been framed as anarcha-feminist[1]—writes: "The role of a socially committed historian is to use history, not so much to document the past as to restore to the de-historicized a sense of identity and possibility. Such 'medicinal' histories seek to re-establish the connections between peoples and their histories, to reveal the mechanisms of power, the steps by which their current condition of oppression was achieved, through a series of decisions made by real people to dispossess them; but also to reveal the multiplicity, creativity and persistence of resistance among the oppressed."[2] Like the *curandera*-historian, Yiddish anarchist feminist genealogists sought to reveal the contingency of oppression and illuminate historical practices of mutual aid.

Historical and literary genealogies co-produce one another through citation, reference, allusion. This chapter examines the feminist genealogies of three women who contributed to the Yiddish anarchist press in the United States: the poet Malka Heifetz Tussman; the journalist, anthropologist, and gynecologist Katherina Yevzerov Merison; and the poet and journalist Rosa Lebensboym, who primarily wrote literature as "Anna Margolin." Margolin and Yevzerov Merison were linked to prominent anarchist men but scarcely recognized for their own political methods. Margolin, Heifetz Tussman, and Yevzerov represent the

interaction between feminist literary imagination and anarchist historical genealogies that foreground the experiences of women.

Yiddish anarchists sought an archive of life without state authority. In search
of a lineage, they turned to the Hebrew Bible and Talmud, diasporic memory and
philosophy, and accounts of Indigenous politics as prooftexts for the fallacy of
domination. Their genealogies link the liminal moments when state power could
have dissolved, before executions, deportations, or newspaper office bombings;
and their readings of the Hebrew Bible hail its heroes—in particular the prophets, Judith, Deborah, and Gideon—as proto-anarchists. Unlike postmodernist
genealogy, which emphasizes rupture and discontinuity, these Yiddish anarchists
extended Jewish models of history as an unbroken golden chain (*goldene keyt*).[3]
They sought to root their credo within the natural and ancestral worlds, producing lines of comradeship across deep time. This genealogical tendency mirrors
the values and conventions of *yikhes,* which, as ChaeRan Freeze notes, evolved
in Eastern Europe "from a narrow biological meaning of lineage or genealogy to
a prestigious trait that could be acquired through marriage based on scholarly
merit, wealth, or political status."[4] Freeze dates the concept of *yikhes* from the
Polish Middle Ages, when Hasidic pietists "sought to create 'pure family units'
in protest" against the merely rich, rather than the spiritually meritorious. Similarly working against a model of prestige based on accumulation, anarchist
yikhes establishes radical thought as a tradition of critiquing power, bolstered by
scriptural interpretation, sentimental martyrology, and the familial relations of
movement figures. Anarchist *yikhes* is a literary strategy across genres of poetry,
courtroom speeches, memoir, correspondence, historical monographs, and journalism.[5] Tracing the poetics of genealogy across heterogeneous forms resists the
production of a singular canon of Jewish anarchism. For poets, intertextuality is
a form of genealogy that makes texts into comrades; for historians, establishing
a (Jewish) history for anarchism was paramount for legitimizing the movement.

How did Jewish anarchists view historical statelessness? Did experiencing
immigration and deportation inform their theories, in comparison to European
Christian anarchists with citizenship? What historical moment did they identify as the root of anarchist genealogies? And why were their eyes trained so
keenly on the past, rather than "utopian" futures? While individual genealogies
differ depending on which singular starry events they link into a meaningful
constellation, three of their aims converge: to create ideological *yikhes,* legitimizing ancestral lineage; to move beyond the *temporality* of the nation-state,
toward diaspora enduring through the transience of empire; and to cultivate *affective kinship,* reaching beyond familial or ethnic relation.

Whereas Michel Foucault emphasizes rupture and discontinuity, these anarchist genealogists interrupt teleology but claim connection among themselves, multiplying the numbers of their adherents and creating kinship and intimacy with anarchist ancestors. Unlike messianic models of a time to come, Jewish anarchist models of time were formed by attachments to scripture and ritual practices. In this sense, Jewish anarchists became auto-ethnographers, leading expeditions into their own sacred texts, memories, and folkways. Yet in their search to document the realities of non-hierarchical living, they often reproduced colonial temporalities of progress and evolution by invoking a figural Native outside of time—a tendency that continues to be critiqued in contemporary anarchism.[6] Kropotkin likewise betrays his aspirations by displacing "the Mutual Aid of Savages" to the past, rather than building comradeship with their Native contemporaries.[7]

Part II examines the multiplicity of Yiddish anarchist lineages, particularly religious and feminist formations.[8] Chapter 3 considers the tensions within suffragist-anarchist feminism and theorizations of female citizenship. Chapter 4 turns to claims of the Hebrew Bible as proto-anarchist in Yosef Luden's poetry and anarchist histories and Sholem Shvartsbard's speeches and writings. Luden, Shvartsbard, Yosef (Joseph) Cohen, and Saul (Shoel) Yanovsky constructed an illustrious history for Jewish anarchism, while feminist genealogies demanded other modes of theorizing temporality altogether. For anarcha-feminists of the late nineteenth and early twentieth centuries, at stake was not only the establishment of legitimacy for a radical school of thought, but proof of women's intellectual participation in all realms of life. Their gaze was accordingly focused less on patriarchal Jewish history than creating a women's history of the whole world. The relation of Euro-American women to the state in this period fundamentally differed from that of men: democratic representation was an impossibility, regardless of any desire to vote, own property, or marry. While male anarchists renounced participation in state processes, women's non-participation remained involuntary, and anarchist women experienced statelessness more intimately than their male comrades. At the same time, European Jewish immigrant men had greater opportunity to become enfranchised than other ethnicities subjected to legal obstacles (such as the Chinese Exclusion Act of 1882, only repealed in 1943). These women at once navigated anarchist ideals and participated in the suffrage movement, a complex positionality criticized by fellow anarchists of all genders. They frame mutual aid not only as an anthropological genealogy but as a tactic to make feminized labor visible. Cohen, Luden, and Yanovsky aimed to document a movement that had been ignored or minimized by North American labor historians. Anarcha-feminists, in contrast, sought to establish women's history. Some women stood simultaneously among the ranks of anarchists and suffragists, troubling the boundary between anti-statism and citizenship advocacy.

The relation of Euro-American women to the state in this period fundamentally differed from that of men: democratic representation was not possible for them, whether or not they *wanted* to vote. While male anarchists renounced all engagement with the state, women's political "statelessness" remained involuntary. Settler suffragists searched for a "usable past," often drawing from the political formations of their Indigenous contemporaries, in particular the political life of Haudenosaunee (Iroquois) women.[9] As Brandon Benallie notes, had New England suffragists conversed with other Native communities such as the Diné and Hopi, their model might have been decentralized rather than bureaucratic representative democracy. Yet even though they drew from Native political formations, some suffragists responded furiously to federal granting of property and citizenship rights to Native peoples. The suffrage movement remained invested in the settler state, even as suffragists drew inspiration for their own inclusion from Indigenous societies. The writing of women involved in both anarchist and suffragist movements reveals an ambivalence about female citizenship and the exploitation of women's labor recast as mutual aid.

KATHERINA YEVZEROV MERISON: ANARCHIST, SUFFRAGIST, GYNECOLOGIST

Katherina Yevzerov (later Yevzerov Merison) was one of the few women who contributed to the Yiddish anarchist press as an author.[10] Born in Nevel, Vitebsk, in 1870, she mastered Hebrew and Aramaic by age ten and encountered nihilism through her own reading. The archivist Moshe Goncharok claims that Isaac Bashevis Singer's character Yentl is inspired by Yevzerov's childhood, though his short story "Yentl the Yeshiva Boy" ends before its protagonist arrives in the United States. Yevzerov and her family emigrated to the United States in 1888, and she earned a medical degree at New York University in 1893 or 1895. Upon graduating medical school, she became involved in both the labor and suffrage movements. As a doctor, Yevzerov Merison served poor families in New York City.[11] She merged advocacy and medicine, serving as secretary of the "aid organization for Russian prisoners of war in Germany and Austria" during World War I and representing them as a delegate to the International Red Cross.[12]

Yevzerov's articles appeared in an array of leftist newspapers, including *Fraye arbeter shtime, Tsukunft, Der Tog, Forverts,* and *Zherminal* under the pseudo-nyms Rosa Ziserman and, grandly, Ezra Sofer, a reference to the biblical scribe and priest who returned from Babylonian exile and reintroduced the Torah in Jerusalem (Ezra 7–10, Nehemiah 8). She frequently covered children's health, child factory labor, and women's rights. Yevzerov provides a combination of his-tory lessons, reflections on personal experience (here, being barred from apply-ing to Columbia University's medical school in 1890), and analysis of the inter-sections of abolition, militarism, and class in the struggle for women's rights.

Yevzerov befriended Emma Goldman and, with her husband, became an honored member of anarchist and socialist circles.[13] She wrote anarchist "con-fessional prayers" for "Kol Nidre Balls," the infamous carnivals held in the streets in front of synagogues on Yom Kippur to spite and provoke their pious neigh-bors between 1889 and 1893 in New York.[14] Yevzerov's husband, Y. A. Merison (Yankev-Avrom Yerukhimovitsh), was a fixture of New York City's anarchist milieu. Goncharok claims that he "descended from a famous rabbinical family, whose *yikhes* descended from the medieval commentator Rashi. Studied in the Slobodker Yeshiva under the tutelage of Hirsh Khayes, one of the most impor-tant developers of Musar Hasidism."[15] Merison translated widely: Darwin, Wilde, Malatesta, Marx, Stirner. In his afterword to the translation of *Das Kap-ital,* he thanks Yevzerov for her help with the translation; it is likely that she contributed to his other translations, women's health guides, and physiology textbooks as well, considering her linguistic skills and degree in gynecology. Upon Merison's death, a grand parade was held in his honor, snaking through the Lower East Side to Seward Park and the building of the socialist newspaper the *Forverts.* In contrast to the recognition for Merison, I have been unable even to locate Yevzerov's papers and found few references to her in her husband's archive. Evidence of her public life is primarily documented through her lecture advertisements in the *Forverts.*

Yevzerov advocated for women's suffrage in multiple leftist newspapers. In the winter of 1900, she published articles in *Fraye gezelshaft* (Free Society) that "searched history to explain the social standing of women."[16] In a series on "the burning Woman Question" in the *Forverts* in February 1900, she wittily debated issues of women's class status and financial dependence with Dr. Ida Badanes, who wrote in response to her *Fraye gezelshaft* essay.[17] In an article titled "The American Women's Movement and the Victory for Women in the Last Elec-tions," she responded to the *New York Times*'s opposition to the amendment that granted New York women the vote in 1917. *Times* editors had claimed that "in a time of national peril strong men must make the decisions that control policies" and that "judging the feminine suffragists by their leaders, they have been, as a class, pacifists and enemies of preparedness."[18] She writes:

> Since the terrible war began in 1914, women in every country have become active in all areas: taking up collections, attending to the wounded, entering all the occupations and industries. They are taking the place of men who are away on the battlefield: they are employees in banks and offices, they drive trolleys, make ammunitions, and, in many cases, are under fire. . . . All this has certainly had an impact on men, and the old claims against voting rights have fallen like a cause with no substance. Woman suffrage is a fruit of the war that the diplomats of Wilhelmstrasse and Guildhall did not foresee in their plans.[19]

Yevzerov and the *New York Times* both invoked the war as justification for or against women's suffrage. Yevzerov opposed militancy in protest tactics: "The participants are no doubt convinced they are carrying out a sacred task, but this seems to me a useless expense of energy." She characterizes both the British suffragists' struggles ("they stole into Parliament through the roof, they tied themselves to the railing of the gallery, they beseiged the House of Commons") and their government's repression as "overstep[ping] the bounds of reason and justice."[20] Other feminist anarchists set aside their reservations to celebrate the British suffragists' militancy. In *Mother Earth,* for example, Rebecca Edelshon praised their "methods of warfare."[21]

Strikingly, in Yevzerov's argument for suffrage, she cites the Proletarian poet Winchevsky familiarly: "The socialists have naturally always believed that women should have equal rights with men. Grandpa M. Winchevsky sang about this long ago in his 'Spirit of Freedom': 'I come to entrust / To women / Every right to help build / Freedom's great throne.'" Claiming the poet as "Grandpa Winchevsky" and referencing his song of 1899 ("Equality's Great Throne") places her in a family of Yiddish socialism, which she further elaborates through Jewish affect: "Women, however, are impatient and want to have their rights immediately (just as the Jews do not want to wait for the Messiah to come)."[22]

Yevzerov Merison's goal of full citizenship and property rights for women was condemned by writers at *Fraye arbeter shtime,* who called her and Merison's ideas "revisionist." Emma Goldman opposed women's suffrage on the grounds that its supporters essentialized women's characters: "To assume [a woman] would succeed in purifying something which is not susceptible of purification, is to credit her with supernatural powers. Since woman's greatest misfortune has been that she was looked upon as either angel or devil, her true salvation lies in being placed on earth."[23] While Goldman's objections were shared by other feminist anarchists, the Yiddish-speaking Catholic writer Voltairine de Cleyre grew anxious that debates on women's suffrage would internally split the anarchist movement. Her letter to the editor Joseph Cohen reveals her concern: "I read your letter in the 'Free Word' [*Dos fraye vort*]. I also read Yanovsky's comment on the articles therein. And while I did not read the articles (for want of time) it seems to me from Livshis's account of them that Yanovsky was rather justified in his observation that the articles would have been in place in the Forwards. 'The Anarchistic Party!'—After a while we shall have 'Votes for Women' in the 'platform.' Your suggestion that we find out what anarchism is, and what activity is consistent with it, is all right. But it's a bad thing to exhibit all our perplexities to the enemy."[24] De Cleyre mocks the idea of a representative "Anarchistic Party" for which women might someday be able to vote, and she displaces advocacy for universal suffrage to the *Forverts,* the socialist newspaper.

Despite her involvement with anti-suffrage anarchist circles, Yevzerov took another tack, writing, "If one cannot introduce socialism in its entirety all at once, one should introduce as many pieces of it as possible."[25] Steven Cassedy notes that for those familiar with the women's movement of the later twentieth century, Yevzerov's contributions "are likely to appear rather tame. There are no calls for militant action and no comprehensive program for a women's rights movement."[26] Although her advocacy was considered mild by both anarchists of her day and later feminists, Yevzerov consistently addressed issues largely ignored by the male writers of the Yiddish anarchist press and brought a strong historical perspective to her work.

Yevzerov compiled her articles for the anarchist newspaper *Fraye gezelshaft* (Free Society) into the book *Di froy in der gezelshaft* (Woman in Society). It was published in 1907, thirteen years before the Nineteenth Amendment passed, which extended voting rights primarily to settler women. Her volume was published as part of a series on world history by *Fraye gezelshaft* and its *"genosn oysgebers"* (comrade-publishers). The introduction notes that while these editions are risky "from a business standpoint," they are necessary for "general progress" and "the enlightenment of the Jewish masses."[27] *Woman in Society* spans the genres of polemics, anthropology, and gender and racial analysis, decades before an academic turn to feminist anthropology. She references several anthropological texts, including Lewis Henry Morgan's kinship study *Ancient Society* (1877), to emphasize the differences in gender roles across cultures.[28] She also draws from the work of the Finnish sociologist Edward Westermarck and the Russian populist Petr Lavrov.[29] Kropotkin's *Mutual Aid: A Factor of Evolution* appeared as a book two years earlier, but it is likely that she encountered his Russian ethnography earlier. Neither Kropotkin nor Yevzerov uses the vocabulary of socialism or anarchism in their studies; instead, they foreground the soundness of their scientific research.

Yevzerov aimed to disprove claims of women's biological and cultural inferiority. Yevzerov constructs an eternal figure of liberated womanhood across centuries and territories, placing Indigenous women's history at the center of her genealogy. Theresa Warburton identifies this paradox:

> In attempting to illustrate a far-reaching tradition of anarchist feminist thought, this [genealogical] approach ignores the specificity of the US settler context and the unique challenges that it presents not only for imagining an anti-state position on stolen land but for understanding the relationship between the social and political institutions through which settlement is structured. Put another way, the focus on the long arc of anarchist feminist history neglects what Joanne Barker (Lenape) has called "the polity of the Indigenous," which she defines as "the unique governance, territory, and culture of Indigenous peoples in unique and related systems of (non)human relationships and responsibilities to one another." The result is an elision of the question of settlement within the establishment of an anarchist feminist tradition.[30]

One may read the presence of Native women's political histories as an intervention into sexist colonial systems, though such "inspiration" rarely benefited their sovereignty.[31]

Chapters in Yevzerov's *Woman in Society* include "The Woman of Wild and Primitive Peoples," "The Woman in Ancient Greece," "The Woman in Ancient Rome," "The Medieval Woman," and "The Woman of the New Age." Anthropological engravings depict a naked woman surrounded by men with spears, attacking her head and limbs, labeled "A Marriage Ceremony of the Ancient Australians"; another illustration portrays a Turk grabbing "his so-called fleeing bride" (*kloymersht antloyfener kale*).[32] Yevzerov attributes her information on Turkish marriages to Elisee Réclus, the French anarchist translated by Yiddish linguist Alexander Harkavy. Although describing "exotic" marriage rites, Yevzerov uses specific terminology familiar to a Jewish readership, such as *badekt zikh di kale mit langn shlayer* (the bride covers herself with a long veil).[33] In the midst of this passage, Yevzerov describes the wife as "truly a slave to her husband" due to dowry (*nadn*) convention.[34] Although she ostensibly refers to non-Jewish

Turkish tradition, her usage of loshn-koydesh ritual terms suggests an internal critique of Jewish marriage rites. Less focused on Jewish history than any of the other genealogies cited here, Yevzerov nonetheless articulates a subtle critique, similar to Freud's use of Jewish terminology in his discussion of "African fetish" and circumcision. As in Cohen's *Jewish Anarchist Movement in America,* Yevzerov narrates progression from "the primitive" toward the "civilized," with anarchism a common thread.[35] Yevzerov, however, uses the vocabulary of "primitivism" to question the "civilized" status of modern Westerners, in the same rhetorical strategy as Kropotkin's—which nonetheless reproduces a eugenic temporality.[36]

Such feminist genealogy was a major rhetorical strategy of U.S. suffragists. In 1876, Susan B. Anthony and her colleagues initiated work on a six-volume *History of Woman Suffrage.* A major political inspiration for settler suffragists was the political life of Haudenosaunee (Iroquois) women.[37] Elizabeth Cady Stanton wrote in 1891, "In the councils of the Iroquois every adult male or female had a voice upon all questions brought before it. The American aborigines were essentially democratic in their government. . . . The women were the great power among the clan." Stanton discussed how clan mothers could nominate and remove chiefs from power: "They did not hesitate, when occasion required, 'to knock off the horns,' as it was technically called, from the head of a chief and send him back to the ranks of the warriors."[38] Cady Stanton cited these "essentially democratic" models in her vision of women's political power. Yet although suffragists grounded their argument in Native political formations, some vehemently opposed property rights and citizenship for Native peoples. Haudenosaunee society was particularly hierarchical and matriarchal, as Brandon Benallie notes.[39] For a Haudenosaunee woman to become "equal" with men, then, would be "a step down." Claiming the expansion of citizenship as the path to gender liberation—rather than abolition of the state—might have been a different vision if settler feminists were informed by Indigenous societies that were less hierarchical or non-matriarchal. Warburton emphasizes the importance of Indigenous non-state genealogies that may converge with anarchist conclusions, through their own lineages of thought and culture: "Compelling alternatives to the nation-state exist throughout hundreds of Native tribes and nations on this land, who demonstrate alternative modes of social organization prior to the establishment of the US nation-state in particular, as well as the nation-state structure in general—modes which continue to this day, as Native peoples enact and fight for sovereignty and self-determination. [Thus] any approach to anarchism and feminism should affirm these differing genealogies."[40] Cady Stanton and Susan B. Anthony simultaneously supported U.S. imperialism in the Philippines during the Spanish American War and enfranchisement of female citizens.[41] The suffrage movement remained invested in the settler state, while drawing political inspiration for women's personal inclusion from Indigenous societies.

Yevzerov's genealogy considers alternative forms of kinship and attachment. She critiques polygamy as "unfavorable for the woman,"[42] whereas "polyandry (one woman has many men) brought about the celebrated period of mothers' rights (matriarchy) and a golden age for women's status in society. In Greece, the *heterizmus*[43] ('friendly' houses of women, who were devoted to beauty and love) [advanced] the status of women, eliciting respect through their education and boldness."[44] Yevzerov asserts, "In brief, the woman is no pest to man; she is no better and no worse than him."[45] Her portrayal of ancient Greece does not glory in the early days of democracy but instead appraises Plato and portrays women's struggle for freedom within a patriarchal system. Proto-feminist triumphs are attributed to women alone:

> The women of Greece fought for freedom and equality, and as we have
> seen, they triumphed through mass unity. A change occurred in the idea
> of womanhood: instead of before, when people maintained that the soul
> of a woman is inferior to a man's soul, Plato taught in the *Republic* that
> women's character is equal to the character of men, and that women are
> thus capable of spiritual and civic activity comparable to men. One must
> also not exclude them from the creation of knowledge, nor from taking
> part in state matters. Naturally, since Plato was a child of his time, he
> likewise taught that the individual must submit oneself to the state. Even
> today, many teach that one must be submissive to the state or to the family or to some higher Being. Not only did the women of ancient Greece
> suffer through this, but men and women of today and always have suffered on account of these ideas, in all parts of the globe.[46]

Yevzerov critiques Plato's valorization of the state above the autonomy of the individual as a flaw in philosophical reasoning. She attributes Plato's belief in the equality of male and female souls (though not bodies) to the voices of unnamed women of his time. Anticipating David Graeber's *Fragments of an Anarchist Anthropology* (2004), Yevzerov de-centers ancient Greece and Rome as originating democracy, taking their philosophers to task and highlighting instead those who lived at the margins of the ancient world.[47]

Yevzerov frames segregation as a gender issue, an analysis rarely expressed by

a non-Black feminist in the early twentieth century. She surveys historical figures such as Elizabeth Blackwell (1821–1910), the first woman to earn a medical
degree in both the United States and the United Kingdom. Yevzerov explicitly
criticizes segregation as an obstacle to women's education, analyzing the confluence of racism and sexism that forbid women's full participation in schools and
universities. She notes that in 1832, when the Quaker educator Prudence Crandall admitted an African American girl to her school, thereby creating the United
States' first integrated school until white students dropped out in protest, and
Crandall was arrested twice. Crandall soon reopened the school exclusively for
African American girls, refusing to educate white students. Yevzerov concludes
with a positive assessment of women's educational and international progress—
"thanks solely to energetic women"—that includes the right to own property,
make a will, and speak publicly. She reserves special praise for "extraordinary"
Finland, where nineteen women were elected to Parliament.[48]

Yevzerov admiringly described the work of the Jewish suffragist and abolitionist Ernestine Rose, a *firerke* (female leader) who circulated a petition in 1836
for married women's right to own property—and succeeded in gathering only
five signatures.[49] Nonetheless, Rose presented her petition to the legislature, and
in 1848 she and her comrades Paulina Davis and Elizabeth Cady Stanton succeeded in amending the law. Yevzerov expounds on the reasons that some women
opposed suffrage:

> Some women responded that they fear men would laugh at them; other
> women said that they have enough rights, and many men complain that
> women already have too many rights. But these women leaders were not
> intimidated by such foolish obstinacy [*akshones*], and Ernestine deliv-
> ered a public speech about women's rights and the legislature in Michi-
> gan. Now we must understand how much strength it took for a woman
> to give a public speech: the "oratoress" was likely to wind up [covered]
> with rotten onions, spoiled eggs, etc. Youngsters often chased them down
> in the streets and wagged a finger at women who possessed character
> strong enough to stand against public opinion, and they endured all
> kinds of persecutions.[50]

Ernestine Rose endured censure for her free thinking, such as that of one Rev-
erend G. B. Little in 1855: "We know of no object more deserving of contempt,
loathing, and abhorrence than a female atheist. We hold the vilest strumpet
from the stews to be by comparison respectable."[51] The anxiety he expressed,
linking atheism with women's suffrage and sex work, was widespread; indeed,

after women's suffrage was achieved in four western states, sex workers' voting did succeed in unseating many of the police officials who had intimidated them.[52] Though Yevzerov names racism as a form of oppression, she does not remark on antisemitism, nor does she mention that the suffragist, atheist, and abolitionist Ernestine Rose was the Russian-born daughter of a rabbi.

Yevzerov sought to prove the existence of matriarchal and pre-state societies and thus undermine the apparent inevitability of patriarchy. *Woman in Society* rousingly concludes with a feminist recasting of the sovereign individual: "One must take notice that women are capable of producing and contributing to all branches of human endeavor, if they merely have the inclination and strong will. One must expose the false idea lying at the root of women's enslavement, and say to women themselves: Think independently, rely on yourself alone, be free!"[53] She directly addresses the reader, building not universal comradeship but autonomous sisterhood as a factor of survival, earned through thousands of years of political formation. Yevzerov's suffragist anarchism provides another entry in the complexities of what J. Richards terms "female citizenship." *Di froy in der gezelshaft* both maps possible solidarities and reveals the limitations of settler imagination as issues of suffrage, citizenship, and democratic representation still remain contested.

"TO LIE AT THE ROOT": MARGOLIN'S SUBTERRANEAN GENEALOGIES

Like Yevzerov, the writer widely known as Anna Margolin moved in both anarchist and suffragist worlds.[54] Born Rosa Lebensboym (or Lebensbaum) in Brisk, Lithuania, in 1887, she immigrated in 1906 at the age of nineteen to New York, where she worked within the circles of a predominantly male literary intelligentsia. Margolin's work for the press was wide-ranging: she translated Russian and French literature (largely without attribution), reported from Europe on women's suffrage, edited the anarchist paper *Fraye arbeter shtime* for six months, and contributed the column "In the Women's World" to *Der tog* (The Day), a daily paper she co-edited. The historian Ayelet Brinn notes that Margolin frequently "used her columns to question the boundaries of women's writing, to explore political issues, to question stereotypes about inherent female traits, and to argue that writing by or for women should not be seen as inherently frivolous."[55] In later years Margolin fell silent as a poet and became a recluse. Her last published poem appeared in 1932, twenty years before her death in New York City.

Margolin's voice burst into print in 1920. Her earliest short story appeared in the *Fraye arbeter shtime* under the pseudonym Khave Gros, though accounts vary on the questioning of her gender by male editors prior to publication.[56] Margolin's second husband, the poet Reuben Iceland (Eisland), writes that *Fraye arbeter shtime*'s editor Yanovsky invited her to join the editorial staff as secretary (*sekretarin fun di redaktsye*)[57] on the strength of her prose: "She gladly accepted, though he paid very little, because she had no other prospects of earning money. She held the job about six months. But she didn't like the work and also didn't like the environment in which she found herself in New York; without [the cultural writer Chaim] Zhitlovski's brilliance, all of New York seemed banal and gray. She grew restless and began to dream of returning to Europe."[58] Iceland's account lingers on her difficulty with the journalistic sphere, which she disdained, though she was materially compelled to work in the press's orbit for much of her life.[59]

Margolin participated in multiple iterations of leftist movements throughout the arc of her intellectual life. Norma Fain Pratt minimizes the extent of her political commitments but notes that "as an adolescent in Warsaw she belonged to a Jewish anarchist populist group called the Socialist Territorialists."[60] Yet Margolin ardently advocated for women's suffrage in her columns, informed by her travels where women became enfranchised earlier than in the United States. Like Yevzerov, her political imagination was sparked by European suffragists; like Goldman, she rejected the idea of womanhood as essentially pacifist. In a discussion of "Women in World War I," Margolin remarked that "woman is no gentle, peaceful person that trembles before the slaughtering knife and craves a quiet nest"; rather, most women are "less of a dove than an eagle."[61] Another article castigates Woodrow Wilson's five-volume *A History of the American People* (1902)—serialized in the same paper—for its erasure of women's history, recommending instead the work of the historian Mary Ritter Beard.[62] She termed women "the silent partners of progress," which resonated with Yevzerov's scholarship.[63]

Around 1910, between travels to Warsaw and Tel Aviv, Margolin visited Kropotkin at the villa in a London suburb where he lived in exile.[64] Kropotkin's health was ailing then, and at sixty-eight, he suffered from the English climate. She was about twenty-three and had arrived bearing a letter of introduction from Yanovsky. Many in London radical circles perceived her relationship with the elder anarchist to be romantic. "If so," remarks Faith Jones, "Kropotkin, who was forty-five years her senior, was another in Lebensbaum's series of older intellectual paramours."[65] Iceland instead emphasized her significance to Kropotkin's intellectual development and praises the elder anarchist as "eynem fun di

shenste un eydlste mentshn un groyse geyster fun yener tsayt" (one of the most
beautiful and noble people and greatest spirits of that era).[66] Iceland describes
the intensity of their connection as devoted, if brief:

> She spent four weeks in London. And during those four weeks, at Kropot-
> kin's request, she went to him every day. The old anarchist-theoretician
> had chosen a young Russian, a devoted follower of his, to bring her to
> him every day. And he came every day at exactly the same time and took
> her to Kropotkin. In letters to various people, Kropotkin mentioned her
> name several times, praising her highly [zi shtark geloybt]; in one letter,
> he even wrote that she was the only person who had made him think
> about the Jewish question.[67]

What did Margolin and Kropotkin speak about every day for a month during
their punctual meetings? How often did he think of her after her departure?
Did they talk as they wrote, in great gushes? Did they speak more honestly in
Russian, Yiddish, or English? Her archive includes letters from Kropotkin's family after his death, but their exchanges seem polite, mundane, in comparison to
that abbreviated intensity. Beyond observers' gossip about their intense connection, one can only seek to discern the ripples of that encounter in their respective work.

Following her month with Kropotkin, Margolin traveled to Paris, where
she continued to cultivate social relations with Russian revolutionaries. Iceland
recalls her connection to Vladimir Burtsev (1862–1942), an exiled publisher renowned for unmasking agents provocateurs: "Burvez [sic] gave her enough material about the secrets of the Russian Revolution that she could send frequent
correspondence to the Forverts in New York. This was her source of income the
whole time she was in Paris."[68] Though her contributions to the *Forverts* in this
time do not appear to directly reflect this connection, their collaboration places
Margolin firmly within the circle of exiled Russian anarchists active in those
cities.

Recent scholarship contextualizes Margolin primarily as a woman writer.
Avrom Novershtern "illuminate[s] the bonds connecting Anna Margolin's poems
to that body of work known as 'women's poetry in Yiddish,'" and Zohar Weiman Kelman compellingly queers Margolin's verse.[69] Margolin may also be located within a lineage of anti-statist poets. Like Yevzerov, Margolin interrogates
the narrative of a noble male and European genealogy of liberalism and democracy, and she defamiliarizes the singular, stable Western self.

In a letter, Margolin describes her complex political and spiritual convictions:

"I haven't ever been able to be secular even though when I was young I was a flaming anarchist. I have always talked to God, and in times of sorrow, I admit I have given God hell."[70] This tension—her simultaneous yearning upward and calling divinity down to account—structures Margolin's *Lider*. The anarchist identification stated so plainly in the letter is only intimated in her verse, sub-merged within a death-haunted eros. "Epitaph," the poem engraved in part on her headstone, ends with a phrase closely echoing the letter, defiant through abjection:

> Un vi in shoen fun ibermut
> hot zi mit got zikh shver gevert,
> Vi tif gezungen hot dos blut,
> Vi tsvergn hobn zi tseshtert.
>
> And how in hours of exultation
> she took God to task,
> how her blood sang deeply
> as dwarfs destroyed her.[71]

This desire toward and castigation of God resounds through *Lider*. In *"In gasn"* (In the Streets), the image of Golgotha gives way to an avowal of belief in a ter-rifying divinity at the end of life:

> Geven gebet, un tsorn geven, kharote.
> Un itst shrayt oyf di letste shrekn-fule note
> fun lebn, zinkendik in shtoyb.
> Un dokh, o got, o payniker, ikh gloyb:
> ikh vel mit finger goyses nokh onrirn a shtern
> un an umendlekh tif, umendlekh tsertlekh vort derhern.
>
> Pleading, raging, regretting,
> now the last terrible note of life
> blares forth, sinking into the dust.
> And yet, O God, O tormentor, I do believe:
> With dying fingers, I will yet touch a star,
> and I will hear an eternally profound,
> an infinitely tender word.[72]

The word translated by Shirley Kumove as "regret" is *kharote,* higher-register loshn-koydesh suggesting not only remorse but repentance. Her use of loshn-koydesh follows with *goyses,* a person at death's door. On the brink of death, this person still raises his or her finger to avow: "I will yet touch a star." This theo-logical *vort* (word) circulates: in the poem *"Toyt-mid fun der last fun a kholem"* ("Dead-Tired from the Burden of a Dream"), Margolin's speaker insists upon the persistence of a transcendent word:

> Epes vet muzn, muzn blaybn oyf der erd:
> A glants fun keynem nit gezen,
> a vort fun keynem nit gehert.
>
> Something must remain upon the earth:
> an unseen radiance,
> an unheard word.[73]

The Yiddish line repeats, keening: "Epes vet muzn, muzn blaybn oyf der erd" (Something *must, must* remain upon the earth). Light and sound transcend human perception, no less vibrant for being bodiless.

Margolin throws her voice into a host of rough figures: gangsters, beggars, madwomen, sinister foremothers. She also takes up Christian motifs that are taboo for a Jewish writer of any gender to treat sympathetically. "Mary Wants to Be a Beggar Woman" (*"Mari vil zayn a betlerin"*), one of her earliest published poems, appears as the sixth poem of her seven-poem "Mary" suite:

> Zeyn a betlerin.
> Vi fun a shif, vos zinkt,
> varfn ale oytsres oyfn vint:
> di last fun dayn libe un last fun di freydn,
> un az ikh aleyn zol mer zikh nit derkonen—
> oykh mayn gutn tsi mayn shlekhtn nomen.
>
> Zeyn a betlerin.
> Shtum zikh sharn iber groye trotuarn,
> vi der shvartser shotn fun ale hele lebns,
> un far geshenkte groshns
> koyfn zikh tsum shpiln
> a vanzinikn kholem un a shtiln,
> vos knoylt zikh zilberik in roykh fun opyum.
> Aynshlofn in gas unter der zun,
> vi in feld a mider zang,
> vi a tseflikte blum,
> vos iz farvelkt un umreyn,

un dokh getlakh,
un hot nokh alts a por sheyne zeydene bletlakh.
Un oyfloykhtn mit krankn likht fun a lamtern,
zikh oysviklen fun der shtumer groyer nakht,
vi a nepl fun nepl, vi a nakht fun der nakht.
Vern a gebet un vern a flam.
Zikh avekshenken tsertlakh, brenendik un groyzam.
Un zayn eynzam,
vi nor kenige un betler zaynen eynzam.
Un umgliklakh.
Un geyn azoy mit farvunderte oygn
durkh groyse soydesdike teg un nekht
tsum hoykhn gerikht,
tsum shmertslakhn likht,
tsu zikh.

To be a beggarwoman.
To hurl all your treasures to the wind
as from a sinking ship:
the weight of your love and the weight of bliss,
so I recognize myself no more—
neither my good nor my evil names.

To be a beggarwoman.
Trudge silently down gray sidewalks
like the dark shadow of each bright life
and trade groschens
to play with a calm and foolish dream
that swirls into silvery plumes of opium smoke.
To doze in the street beneath the sun
like a weary song in a field,
like a tattered bloom,
faded and unclean
and yet divine
with a few silken petals, still, despite it all.
And to shine with sickly lantern light,
taking shape in the speechless gray night
like the fog of fog, like the night of night.
To become a prayer and become a flame.

To give myself away tenderly, ardent and pitiless.
And to be alone
as only a king and a beggar are alone.
Abandoned.
And so to walk with wounded eyes
through great hidden days and nights
to the high court,
to the stinging light,
to the self.[74]

The Yiddish is saturated with sibilants, a sonic hissing throughline as the meter and rhyme pattern disappears and resurfaces. It opens with a jagged and indeterminate phrase: *zayn a betlerin,* which avoids the common declaration of identity at the start of a poem (not "*I am* a beggarwoman"). At first the poetic speaker longs to toss away riches, seeking freedom through abjection. The poem's forms and images are coded as feminine: a beggar lady, a wilting silken flower. Yet the figures of metaphoric comparison are masculine or abstract: a king, a (male) beggar, a prayer, a flame. Gender flickers across the poem, as light changes through fog and twilight. The poetic speaker longs for submission to the wind, flinging away oneself, entering destitution, and so to enter oneself at last. Robert Wolf translates these lines in a more colloquial register: "To give myself away, tender, burning, cruel. / And to be alone / As only kings and beggars are alone. / And unhappy."[75] I chose "abandoned" for *umgliklakh* to heighten Margolin's startling parallel between beggar and king: two men unseen as themselves.

The poem is structured by images of rule and value, woven through the natural world of blooms and fog: kings, the high court, treasure, a groschen. Its speaker longs to relinquish power in every quarter, to replace the "high court" with her own secret consciousness. The word *zikh* (self, both as noun and reflexive verbal complement) is repeated six times, leading up to a crescendo of identity. This self *moves,* pulled between the will toward self-abnegation and the return to a psyche that cannot be jettisoned. Class identity is mere ballast dropped to sail toward a truth beyond morality, beyond "both my good and evil names." As the literary scholar Melissa Weininger notes, Margolin's "Mary" is never fully identified with the virgin mother of Jesus: "This ambiguity itself is part of Mary's usefulness to Margolin: in Mary, Margolin finds a persona with which to evoke a marginal female self who, through her own concealment, can expose the masks forced on women, and particularly on the Yiddish woman poet."[76] But does the beggarwoman beg in "Mary Wants to Be a Beggar Woman"? Margolin twice repeats the word *shtum,* silent or mute. This would be a beggar who implores with the gaze, not the voice.

Lider opens with *"Ikh bin geven a mol a yingling"* (1929), perhaps the most-studied modern Yiddish poem by a woman. Kathryn Hellerstein translates it as "I Was Once a Boy":

> Ikh bin geven a mol a yingling
> gehert in portikos sokratn
> es hot mayn buzem-fraynt, mayn libling,
> gehat dem shenstn tors in aten.
> Gevezn tsezar. Un a hele velt geboyt fun marmor,
> ikh der letster, un far a vayb mir oysderveylt
> mayn shtoltse shvester.
> In royznkrants baym vayn biz shpet
> gehert in hoykhmutikn fridn
> vegn shvakhling fun nazaret
> un vilde mayses vegn yidn.

> I was once a boy, a stripling
> Listening in Socrates' portico,
> My bosom-buddy, my sweet darling,
> Had Athens' most beautiful torso.
> Was Caesar. And from marble constructed
> A glistening world, I the last there,
> And for my own wife selected
> My stately sister.
> Rose-garlanded, nursing wine all night
> In high spirits, hear tell the news
> About the weakling from Nazareth
> And wild tales about Jews.[77]

Like Virginia Woolf's character Orlando, who traverses centuries and genders, Margolin's poetic speaker overflows time and territory, roaming from the Greek halls of Socrates to the marble world of incestuous Roman emperors to the outskirts of Christendom's dawn. The poem opens with a deceptively simple line: "Ikh bin geven a mol a yingling." Although its grammatical structure is straightforward, the plurality of possible meanings demands a close reading. *Yingling* presses at the edges of both gender and language: it is a yiddishization of the German word for boy (*jüngling*), rather than a Yiddish word from the Germanic component of the language, such as *yingl* or the diminutive *yingele*. Margolin uses a term not properly located within Yiddish *deutschmarish* vocabulary and Judaizes a term belonging to German, deflating it as a signifier of high culture. Its indeterminacy raises questions of difference between the identity of the speaker then and now: were they once male, and are no longer? Were they once a gentile, and are no longer? Or does it point to a trajectory altogether different? Even the simple adverb *a mol* (once), which clearly modifies *bin geven* (I was), describes an uncertain degree of change from the past: when did this transformation occur?

The linguistic boundaries questioned by that intriguing first line are pushed even further by Margolin's play with component awareness (*komponentn-visikayt*), drawing from Yiddish's "international" vocabulary. The lover's body is suggestively compared to classical architecture: he was possessed of *dem shenstn tors in aten*, "the finest torso in Athens." *Tors*, as with the English *torso*, conventionally describes a marble bust or Greek statue. Margolin puns with *buzem fraynd* (bosom buddy) and *tors*, emphasizing the speaker's admiration for this classical physique. The comparative compliment "finest torso in Athens" implies competition, perhaps the tradition of Greek sport. Architecture is emphasized in the lines "Gevezn tsezar. Un a hele velt / geboyt fun marmor, ikh der letster" (the world built from marble promises to endure), but the speaker is aware of his impermanence: "ikh der letster" (I the last one) is a masculine form, the only word that genders the speaker, and contrasts the fluidity of time, transience of the body, and marble of monuments. Weiman Kelman notes, "Gender fluidity is not the only indeterminacy at play here, for the speaker imagines themself not only in the privileged position of a man, but also in that of a non-Jew, who looks down on the Jews of the 'wild tales.' Margolin aligns Jesus (the 'weakling from Nazareth') and early Christianity in general with the weak effeminate Jewish males of her present, for 'weakling' was the dominant stereotype of diasporic Jewish masculinity of the time. . . . Instead of investing in dominant power and looking forward to the future, Margolin shows these powers as destined to fall, by weaving a queer history that resists heteronormative futurity."[78] Making visible the transience of empire is a key anarchist genealogical tactic, from Luden to Shvartsbard and on. The alignment of Margolin's poetic voice with paganism echoes Yevzerov and others' identification with precolonial societies.

Margolin queers the genre of heroic anarchist elegy exemplified by Edelshtat, Rosenfeld, and Luden, who place non-Jewish "martyrs" within Jewish temporality. Yevzerov wrote for the same papers and moved in the same circles as Margolin, and *"Ikh bin geven a mol a yingling"* shares the impish disruptiveness of Yevzerov's critique of Plato, written from the position of (imagined) bordellos of Athens. Margolin thematizes the diasporic aspect of Yiddish by strategically placing loshn-koydesh components against *daytshmerishizms* and internationalisms. Through the language itself, Margolin plots the lines of a queer diasporism, bending the rigidity of German masculine forms into *yingling* and rhyming it with *shvakhling* to produce a new relation between languages.

The use of "diaspora" in contemporary queer theory parallels nineteenth-century usage in its refusal to reify territorial origins. Queer theorist David Eng suggests "what might be gained politically by reconceptualizing diaspora not in conventional terms of ethnic dispersion, filiation, and biological traceability, but rather in terms of queerness, affiliation, and social contingency."[79] Eng's model of diaspora as a generative political affiliation, rather than the passive result of catastrophe, describes the communities of readers created through poetry in a minor language. The diasporic texture of Margolin's poem marks rupture and trauma within itself. It starts and stops; the subjects of sentences are left unstated: *gevezn tsezar; zayn a betlerin.* Weiman Kelman notes that this poem stops one couplet short of a full sonnet, as though bitten off at the end: "The lack of couplet leads to a heightened emphasis on the closing line, which ominously links the rise of Christianity and the history of anti-Semitism. By 1946 the meaning of the closing line had changed dramatically, so much so that Margolin requested that Leyb Feinberg, who was translating this poem into Russian, change its order: 'I only ask that in the final stanza you transpose the order of the last two lines, because I wrote the poem so that its entire weight should rest on the last line ('And strange stories about Jews'). A line which I could not lift my hand to write in the present era of our great catastrophe.' And yet the rise of catastrophe seems to me to be already written into the poem itself, where Margolin's own art constructs a cyclical image of history, repeatedly striking a celebratory tone that holds the seeds of downfall yet to come."[80]

This awareness of historical backshadowing in Yiddish literature places the poem within a specifically Jewish twentieth-century temporality, unreconcilable with hegemonic Christian temporality. Prominent theorists of queer temporality such as Carolyn Dinshaw extrapolate from medieval Christian models of monastic time.[81] Further attention is needed to queer Jewish (and Muslim, Santería, and other) religious temporalities, which may not run parallel to the foundational models of queer theory. Across that difference, however, there are possibilities for connection. Dinshaw describes her work as dealing "directly with such desire—a queer desire for history. . . . I focused on the possibility of touching across time, collapsing time through affective contact between marginalized people now and then, and I suggested that with such queer historical touches we could form communities across time." Dinshaw's model is not to straightforwardly recover lost archives, but rather, to alter affective relations to history.[82] Margolin's queer desire for comradeship and ancestry across time resonates also with Jafari Allen's discussion of diaspora as variously "a genealogical matrix of the present moment" and "dynamic, unsettled," emphasizing human networks of connection rather than territorial space or "origins."[83] In this usage, "diaspora" describes a non-essentialist identity that remains connected with the transnational movement of one's ancestors. Allen casts the social, even erotic, aspect of diaspora as resistance and asks "how many friends can we wrap ourselves around . . . how many dunes to cross, our bodies aching with desire?"[84] Allen's queer internationalism is neither the same as the earlier European paradigm of statelessness nor is it theologically saturated, as with *goles* discourse. Allen valorizes diaspora as a mobile alternative to nationalism, which Margolin thematizes through the unsettlement of language itself.

Following "Once I Was a Lad" in *Lider* is *"Muter erd, fil getrotene, zungevashene"* ("Mother Earth, Well-Trodden, Sun-Washed"). Like the opening poem, "Mother Earth" projects the poet's voice deep into inchoate space. Aaron Kramer translates:

> Muter erd, fil getrotene, zun-gevashene,
> tunkele shklafin un harin
> bin ikh, gelibter.
> Fun mir der nidriker un der batribter
> vakstu aroys—a mekhtiker shtam.
> Un vi di eybike shtern, un vi fun zun der flam,
> krayz ikh langn un blindn shveygn
> in dayne vortslen, in dayne tsveygn,
> un halb in vakh, un halb in driml
> zukh ikh durkh dir dem hoykhn himl.[85]

> Mother Earth—trodden, sun-bathed,
> dark slave and mistress
> am I, O dear one.
> From me, the lowly, the drear one,
> you flourish forth: a mighty stem . . .
> and like the sun's flame, like the sky's eternal diadem,

among your roots, your boughs I wind
in a silence long and blind.
Half waking, half asleep I lie—
and seek, through you, the lofty sky.[86]

Engulfing the root of a great tree, the poem speaks from beneath the surface of
the earth, half-conscious. Silent, dark, and nurturing, at once enslaved and em-
powered, the yearning soil gazes up at what it has birthed. The poem's genealogical motif is established in the line: "Fun mir der nidriker un der batribter /
vakstu aroys—a mekhtiker shtam." Joseph Leftwich translates these lines: "Out
of me, the humbled and dejected, out of me / You grow a mighty tree."[87] *Shtam*
signifies both tree and origin, race, lineage, or tribe; here Margolin avoids un-
ambiguously botanical words (such as *boym*). The poetic speaker represents the
earth's own proto-consciousness, from whose abjection comes mighty yearning
for the heights.

Commentary on *"Muter erd"* has tended to focus on its treatment of gender.
Reuben Iceland, the poet's partner, characterizes it as "built on the well-known
and, if you will, even banal idea that a woman does not live her own life, but
rather lives through the life of the man she loves, and that the man is what he is
only thanks to her. . . . Tone, rhythm, and image, everything here is harmonious,
as if one grew out of another, and all three together express in ten lines, so beautifully and profoundly, what woman in every generation has felt in her blood for
man."[88] Iceland's interpretation is at once universalizing and essentializing, as
he celebrates the "harmony" of the poem's components. The feminist scholar
Norma Fain Pratt, on the other hand, characterizes the poetic speaker as "a more
androgynous Self, one in which male and female are inextricably bound together."[89] The first person is grammatically feminine, however; the identities
tunkele shklafin un harin (dark slave and mistress) all have feminine adjectival
endings. Read with an anarchist lens, *"Muter erd"* reveals an identification with
the literal underground. Its poetics claim the under-territory as a primordial
body; all is born from underground, Margolin reminds us. Mother Earth eroti-
cally encircles (*krayz*) the roots of the great tree to its hilt, absorbing and releas-
ing the potentiality of the world. Aaron Kramer translates the poem with greater
emphasis on images of sovereignty, such as "the sky's eternal diadem."[90] "Mother
Earth" may be read as a parable of anarchist genealogy. Its speaker writes from
within the grave, a kind of womb.

"Muter Erd" burrows more deeply than "Once I Was a Youth." The trope of
roots (*vortslen*) winds throughout *Lider,* whose first section is even titled thus.

In the poem *"Der maskarad iz oys"* ("The Masquerade is Over"), Margolin's poetic speaker plainly states:

> *Un ikh lig bay di vortslen fun zakhn.*
> I lie at the root of things.[91]

What does it mean to identify with and lie at the root, to lay one's body onto the ground and look up? This is the primary gesture of *Lider:* to lie down, weary, death-haunted, and gaze up. "The Masquerade is Over" opens, however, with an erotic and racialized image: "Di nakht, a yunger neger mit a royz, / hot lakhndik geneygt zikh zikh iber mir" ("Tonight, a young black with a rose / bent over me, laughing").[92] This Black male figure laughs without words, a strange echo of the repeated phrase in Gertrude Stein's *Three Lives* (1909): "Rose laughed when she was happy but she had not the wide, abandoned laughter that makes the warm broad glow of negro sunshine."[93] Sonically, *neygn* (to arch over) echoes *neger* (a Black person); visually, his racialized body appears as a set dressing, unelaborated and apiece with the collections litany of oriental modernist images such as Chinese lanterns. The sonic pairing of *neger/neygn* follows Margolin's aesthetic preference for echoes and imperfect rhymes, often referred to as "feminine rhymes" in English. She explains this in a letter to Iceland (Eisland) on January 17, 1921:

> Not rhyme—harmony. I use bad rhymes, because *I don't want* good ones. Don't think I'm making excuses for a mistake. . . . Why not rhyme the vowels, using the most hostile, furthest consonants. For example, "redn-fekher" [talk-fan]; "laydn-rayfer" [suffer-ripe]; "shtarbn-leopard" [die-leopard]. In English this is called *assonance.*[94]

It is not only her use of the set piece of a laughing Black lover but the specific music of her word choice that takes part in Euro-modernist exoticization. Throughout *Lider,* the speaker's pale white hands enter and linger in her poems' frame. To renounce both "good" (masculine) rhyme and "good" (non-miscegenated) sex comprised two aspects of her female modernist transgression.

Margolin sustains an attention to bodily posture, the one who lies down at the root versus the one who bends over her. In *"Mayne teg vortslen in shteyner"* ("My Days Take Root in Stones"), the poetic speaker may even be dead and buried, watching nonhuman temporalities of growth from below:

> Vi mit dine farkriplte tsvaygn,
> zay voltn a himl geshpint

iber mir, iber mayn shvaygn,
vos veyltn do a veyl un farshvindt.

As with slender, gnarled branches
which tarries a while and is gone
they would weave a heaven
over me, and over my silence.[95]

The boughs are anthropomorphized as *farkriplte* (disabled), likening the tree's form to the speaker's unseen body beneath, honoring her silence under heaven. Again and again, Margolin's poetic speaker renounces the posture of uprightness, whether in erotic submission or in becoming animal or tree, like the fugitive Daphne before Apollo. To become the root is an early abdication from the human.

The motif of bodily identification with un-nationed, pre-linguistic earth recurs in the "Mary" cycle. In its opening poem, *"Vos vilstu, mari?"* (What Do You Want, Mary?), the poetic speaker declares, "Ikh volt gevolt di fis farvortslt in der erd" (I would have wanted my feet to be rooted in the earth). This Mary, perhaps mother of the Christian god, commingles with "mother earth": "Bin ikh a mentsh, a blits, di umru fun di vegn, / oder di shvartse krekhstndike erd?" ("Am I a human, a bolt of lightning, the unrest of the roads, / or the dark moaning earth?")[96] Where does motherhood, earthiness, ancestry, humanness begin and end? *Shtam,* the pivot-term of *"Muter erd,"* returns as keyword in *"Mayn shtam redt."* This poem's title has been alternately translated as "My Ancestors Speak" (Shirley Kumove) and "My Roots Speak" (Faith Jones). Its poetic speaker is held captive to a litany of forebears, whose "impurity" of heritage, pride, and shame are all accounted for:

> My ancestors:
>> Men in satin and velvet,
>> faces long and silky pale,
>> Faintly glowing lips
>> and thin hands caressing faded folios.
>> Deep into the night they speak with God.
>
>> Merchants from Leipzig and Danzig
>> with clean cuffs, smoking fine cigars.
>> Talmudic wit. German niceties.
>> Their look is clever and lacklustre,

clever and self-satisfied.
Don Juans, dealers and seekers of God.

A drunkard,
a pair of converts in Kiev.[97]

Avrom Novershtern characterizes "My Ancestors Speak" as a poem of ruptured
genealogy: "Both the poem's title and its position near the beginning of *Lider*
prompt the reader's expectation that the subject here is the poet's family tree.
However, the ambivalent ending contradicts this expectation. Anna Margolin is
very far from 'forging' a 'golden chain' that will stretch from 'them' to 'me.' Neither does she fall into the obvious alternative of a clichéd break with tradition."[98]
Read through the context of anarchist temporality, the final stanza overturns
the expectation of a confessional, single self separate from the memorialized
masses:

> All of them, my ancestors,
> blood of my blood,
> flame of my flame,
> dead and living mixed together,
> sad, grotesque, immense.
> They trample through me as through a dark house.
> Trampling with prayers, and curses, and wailing,
> rattling my heart like a copper bell,
> my tongue quivers,
> I don't know my own voice—
> My ancestors speak.[99]

Ikh denken nit mayn kol— / mayn shtam redt: Margolin chooses the word *denken,* to reason, and *kol,* the loshn-koydesh word for "voice" without the political
valence of the Germanic *shtime.* Ancestral masses overwhelm the speaker's rational facilities with their clamor, making themselves impossible to forget or
displace.

Margolin writes up from beneath the soil. Hers is a poetics of displaced origins, preferring dirt, Don Juans, ruins. Margolin embraces an anarchist orientation toward unvalorized and overgrown spaces, which remain present beside
the marble architecture centered in Novershtern's and Barbara Mann's reading
of classical statuesque forms in her verse.[100] Reading Margolin in conversation
with formal and historical Yiddish anarchist genealogies invites new compari-

sons of the lines and breaks across Proletarian and modernist poetry. Her lavish imagistic pleasures coexist with an ethos of anti-heroism. She plays the "major" civilizations in a minor key, revealing their contingency rather than rehearsing the liminal triumphs of anarchist history. The only martyrdom her poetic speakers long for is internal and erotic abdication. As Rexroth calls to Goldman and de Cleyre in "Again at Waldheim": "In the permanent emergency / You spoke for the irrefutable / Coalition of the blood of men." Margolin thematizes the anarchist consciousness of civilization as "permanent emergency" and speaks for the inchoate coalitions of still-unknown kin.

Reading Margolin alongside Yevzerov, Heifetz Tussman, and other women writers with deep anarchist ties reveals genealogical poetics as a feminist and anti-statist strategy. An anarchist reading of Margolin includes her participation in historical movement circles and traces her anarchist images of abdication and *vortslen-estetik* (roots-aesthetics). Still I wonder: what did Margolin and Kropotkin talk about all day long?

ALL ROOTS PROBE DARKNESS: MALKA HEIFETZ TUSSMAN

Long after Malka Heifetz Tussman composed English-language realist vignettes for the post-Haymarket journal *Alarm,* an anarchist pulse still ran through her Yiddish poetry, together with her feminist commitments and spiritual delight in ecology.[101] *Am I Also You?* (1977) collected poems from six Yiddish books from 1949 to 1977, translated by her protégée Marcia Falk. In a letter to Falk, Heifetz Tussman describes her childhood feeling of kinship with the natural world, such that human language must be bent to approximate its sounds: "I would hide in the tall stalks of wheat and listen as they made words. The breeze talked to the stalks, 'Ziv-Ziv,' and I would say 'Viz-Viz.' " When her father discovered her early poems composed of such sounds, "[He] smiled and said, 'Leave her alone. These are her own words. We don't understand.' (My father was also looking for hidden words in Kabbalah.)"[102] Heifetz Tussman thus connects her childhood linguistic experimentalism with her father's own mystical practices.

Heifetz Tussman's later writing revels in sensory life: nature, the body, the world outside factory walls. Poems such as *"Erd-tsiternish"* ("Earthquake") speak of a "Mama-god" (*mame-gots*), and *"Duner mayn bruder"* ("Thunder My Brother") hails a fearsome kinship: "My powerful brother, / Stones rolling on stones—your voice."[103] In "Like the Root," Heifetz Tussman speaks—like Margolin's "Mother Earth"—to the radical:

> You've grown
> but not
> grown up
>
> You're ripe as
> earth is
> raw
> where roots probe
> deep
>
> Like all roots
> you probe
> in deep darkness[104]

"Like the Root" establishes Heifetz Tussman's voice as spare, conversational, and impishly ironic, often summoning up a particular interlocutor or character through her regard.

The penultimate poem in Heifetz Tussman's *Lider* (Poems, 1949) is *"Ikh bin froy"* ("I Am Woman"), which concludes the cycle *Froyen* (Women).[105] "I Am Woman" speaks through a multitude of feminine identities, all marked as Jewish, in Marcia Falk's translation:

> I am the exalted Rachel
> whose love lit the way for Rabbi Akiva.
>
> I am the small, bashful village girl
> who grew up among the tall poplars
> and blushed at the "good morning" of her brother's tutor.
>
> I am the pious girl
> who paled as her mother raised her hands to her eyes
> for the blessing over the Sabbath candles.
>
> I am the obedient bride
> who humbly bent her head beneath the shears
> the night before the wedding.
>
> I am the rabbi's daughter
> who offered her chaste body to save a Jewish town
> and afterwards set fire to herself.

I am the woman of valor
who bore and fed children
to earn herself a little place in paradise.

I am the mother
who, in great hardship,
raised sons to be righteous men.

I am the Hasid's daughter,
infused with her father's fervor,
who went out defiant, with her hair cropped,
to educate the people.

I am the barrier-breaker
who distributed *Bread and Freedom*
and freed love from the wedding canopy.

I am the pampered girl
who set herself behind a plow
to force the gray desert into green life.

I am the one whose fingers
tightened around the hoe,
on guard for the steps of the enemy.

I am the one who stubbornly
carries around a strange alphabet
to implant in children's ears.

I am all these and many more.

And everywhere, always, I am woman.[106]

The observational vernacular of Heifetz Tussman's early realist vignettes gives way to an "I" expansive enough to subsume contradictory political identities. The poetic speaker declaims her transcendent womanhood without privileging secularism or religiosity, defiance or submission, Zionist "pampered girl" or Kropotkinite brandishing *Broyt un frayheyt* (the Yiddish translation of *Conquest of Bread*). The unifying image across this women's genealogy is the shearing of hair. The first woman to speak is "exalted Rachel / whose love lit the way for Rabbi Akiva," that is, the wife of the Talmudic sage. Rachel (as she came to be known only in later sources) sold her hair to support Akiva's study; later she is rewarded for her sacrifice with the gift of a golden headdress.[107] Next the "obedient bride / who humbly bent her head beneath / the shears / the night before the wedding" twins her piety with another woman's politics: "I am the Hasid's daughter, / infused with her father's fervor, / who went out defiant, with her hair / cropped, / to educate the people" ("Ikh bin di khasidishe tokhter vos hot mitn tatns hislayves / Getrogn dos geshoyrn kepl in folk areyn"). The hair of the "Hasidic daughter" is self-shorn, referencing the style of Russian nihilist women; her fervor is not the rejection but the transmigration of her father's spiritual passion (*hislayves*). The same gesture of hair-cutting tracks across time to signify women's relations to husbands, fathers, sages, and philosophers. The repetitive first-person form of "I Am Woman" lends itself to verbal performance. Heifetz Tussman refuses to prescribe a single essence of womanhood; the free-loving anarchist is no less Jewish than her self-sacrificing sisters. Identities of Jewish womanhood are iterative and equal, Heifetz Tussman maintains: change is not loss. Still, if read teleologically, there is a progression from the Talmudic help-mate to the hoe-hefting fighter.

Marcia Falk's translation, which appeared in 1977, inevitably resonates with feminist writers in English who affirmed personal voice, and readers may have been surprised to learn that the poem was first written in Yiddish nearly three decades earlier. Falk shortens the lines to clipped pronouncements, whereas Heifetz Tussman's original is closer to a prose poem with each stanza a single long sentence. In Yiddish the line breaks seem dictated by the size of the page until the final stanza, which tapers to the final single-word line *froy*. As in the work of Irena Klepfisz, which was informed by the Chicana bilingualism of Gloria Anzaldúa, there are English echoes of Nikki Giovanni and the swaggering cadences of the U.S. Second Wave in Falk's forceful, brief lines. Giovanni's "Ego Tripping (there may be a reason why)" opens: "I was born in the Congo / I walked to the fertile crescent and built / the sphinx," the speaker striding like Margolin's "lad" or Heifetz Tussman's Rebbetzin Rachel across the ancestral world. But Heifetz Tussman appeals to the power of valor and piety, where Giovanni's speaker announces her own divinity: "I am so perfect so divine so ethereal so surreal / I cannot be comprehended / except by my permission."[108] Heifetz Tussman's poem was celebrated in multiple articles in the Jewish feminist magazine *Lilith,* one of which explains her activism to readers of a younger generation: "*Bread and Freedom* is a reference to Heifetz Tussman's work in Chicago's anarchist-socialist political scene of the 1920s, where she advocated for economic justice and Marxism at the risk of deportation and arrest."[109] In English, in the context of a popular magazine, Heifetz Tussman's clipped, declamatory voice sounds like a native speaker of feminist vernacular.

"I Am Woman" places anarchist women squarely within a Jewish feminist genealogy. The poem does not hold a singular image of resistance closest to its heart, but regards oppositional identities as un-estranged. The same gesture of embodiment—women's shorn heads—is imbued with contradictory meanings over time, a commonality she regards with warmth rather than irony. As with Yevzerov's *Woman in Society,* which builds to a crescendo of direct address, Heifetz Tussman's poetic speaker swears allegiance to no static credo but the multiplicities of (Jewish) womanhood and the act of making kin.

Reading Yevzerov, Heifetz Tussman, and Margolin together illuminates genealogy as a major aspect of Yiddish anarchist feminist poetics. Rather than severing the past to build a new world, they sought to draw out the feminist possibilities latent and liminal within history. They were informed by Jewish models of temporality and made a distinct departure from antisemitic anarchist movements. This confluence of deep cultural models leads to a distinct articulation of "curative" history, in which anarchism was immanent and germinal. Yevzerov claims presence within transnational history, whereas Margolin calls us to recognize women's absence. Yevzerov calls galvanizingly, directly, to the reader; Margolin leaves us on the cusp of recognition; Heifetz Tussman speaks with the voice of nature, evoking primeval sounds outside the human. Margolin and Heifetz Tussman thematize a feminist genealogy across deep time, name archetypes, and construct a chain between generations. Where Margolin bends linear gender itself, Heifetz Tussman celebrates varied manifestations of feminine identity. Theirs are not the linear anarchist genealogies of Luden, Cohen, and Yanovsky, but instigations and disruptions of respectability. Their genealogies resonate with the motto of the contemporary Bolivian group Mujeres Creando: "We're not anarchists by Bakunin or the CNT [Confederación Nacional del Trabajo], but rather by our grandmothers, and that's a beautiful school of anarchism."[110]

CHAPTER IV

"The Prophets Were Socialists"

RELIGIOUS GENEALOGIES

In the best seller *The Dawn of Everything: A New History of Humanity* (2021), the anarchist anthropologist David Graeber and the archaeologist David Wengrow aim to revise grand narratives of the past 30,000 years. Wengrow and Graeber posit that the "ultimate question of human history" is not one of material access but "our equal capacity to contribute to decisions about how to live together."[1] The book appeared shortly after Graeber, the son of a Yiddish stage actress, had passed away. The authors center the "Indigenous critique," ascribing authorship of ideals of freedom to both Native social life and individuals such as the Wendat leader Kandiaronk. Their narration of 30,000 years of human history, as Carolyn Nakamura notes, "curate[s] episodes to lead readers to specific ideas about human nature and future possibilities orbiting around a particular project of freedom."[2]

The scope and aims of *The Dawn of Everything* were anticipated by mid-twentieth-century Yiddish anarchist accounts of history. These projects aimed to both record the history of a nascent anti-statist movement and reveal the embeddedness of anarchist social organization within deep history. Although they draw at times from instances of Indigenous lifeways, these Yiddish anarchists were particularly invested in locating a genealogy of anti-statism within Jewish history.

Considering their aesthetic investment in written history, anarchists lamented all the more other leftists' erasure and minimization of their movement.

Three editors of major Yiddish anarchist newspapers—Joseph (Yosef) Cohen, Saul Yanovsky, and Yosef Luden—each wrote histories of anarchism in their later years. None of these have yet been published in English, though the tome *Di yidish anarkhistishe-bavegung in amerike* (The Jewish Anarchist Movement in America, 1945) by Joseph Cohen (1878–1953) was translated by Esther Dolgoff.[3] In 1948, Saul Yanovsky, editor of *Fraye arbeter shtime,* published *Ershte yorn fun yidishn frayheytlekhn sotsializm: oytobiografishe zikhroynes fun a pyoner un boyer fun der yidisher anarkhistisher bavegung in England un Amerike* (Early Years of Jewish Liberationist Socialism: Autobiographical Memoirs by a Pioneer and Builder of the Jewish Anarchist Movement in England and America), filled with personal reminiscences and accounts of the Yiddish anarchist press.[4] Yosef Luden's *Kurtse geshikhte fun anarkhistishe gedank* (Brief History of Anarchist Thought, 1984) traces a lineage of anarchist philosophy from the Bible to the Essenes to the Austrian-born philosopher Martin Buber.[5] The Białystok-born Herman Frank, who edited *Fraye arbeter shtime* for eleven years, also produced a valuable history of the Jewish anarchist movement—one of the few that included Buenos Aires organizers.[6] In the foreword to his massive work *The Jewish Anarchist Movement in America,* Cohen claims that "even those Jews who did not remain long in the ranks of the proletariat and somehow gained professional and middle class status—even those who became outright American bourgeois—could hardly have escaped in their youth or their first years as immigrants in this country being touched and influenced by the broad network of cultural and social activities of our movement."[7] Cohen emphasizes its cultural centrality: "Our movement played a preeminent role in the development of the Jewish labor movement and the cultural, educational, and social life of the Jewish immigrant communities, not only in this country but also in the wide world wherever circumstances had cast our Jewish wanderers.... We have sent our newspapers, our journals, our books, our pamphlets, the inspired songs of struggle by Edelshtat and Bovshover everywhere. Where have the crystal-clear words of Peter Kropotkin translated into our own mother tongue not reached!"[8] Cohen was troubled by the absence of written histories of anarchism: "Our comrades did not write history, they *made* history. They left the systematic recording of events to others. Often these 'others' were fiendish and ignored anarchist contributions; sometimes, they maliciously misrepresented the facts. They tried to give the impression that we disrupted the work, that like Don Quixote we fought windmills, that we made no constructive contributions! The history of the Jewish immigrants in this country is as yet virgin territory."[9] Cohen uses the phrase *nit keyn ba'arbet feld,* an uncultivated field—a metaphor whose Talmudic over-

tones (laws regarding untilled fields) return in Rabbi Yankev Meyer Zalkind
and Yosef Luden's histories of anarchism.[10]

FROM GIDEON TO EDELSHTAT:
LUDEN'S GENEALOGIES

Even secular radicals were invested in a narrative of anti-statism grounded
in Jewish history and religiosity. In *Di yidish anarkhistishe-bavegung in amerike*
(*The Jewish Anarchist Movement in America,* 1945), Joseph Cohen locates the
origins of radical philosophy with "primitive man." The work is clearly informed
by "classical" anarchist genealogies: Cohen shared Bakunin's belief that humans
possess an inherent, almost animal "desire to rebel,"[11] and his emphasis on evolution echoes Kropotkin.[12] Yet unlike the European "classical" anarchists, Cohen
identifies seeds of radicalism in the Hebrew Bible: "Anarchism has a proud and
long history. In the Bible and in other writings of other ancient peoples, we find
clear evidence against the evils of sovereignty, injustice and exploitation. The
prophets continually exhorted the oppressors of the people and foretold of a time
when violence and injustice will disappear from the world."[13] Cohen lays claim
to an ancient, dormant anarchism that, he asserted, later re-surfaced through
struggles against the church and colonialism.

This genealogical impulse animates the historical and poetic work of Yosef
Luden. Born in Warsaw in 1905 or 1907, Luden moved to the Soviet Union and
organized as a communist until the Moscow show trials of the late 1930s. Accounts of his emigration to Tel Aviv differ. In one oral history, he recounts
smuggling Jewish children into Mandatory Palestine and settling there himself
during the Second Aliyah, briefly living on the kibbutz Kedma. Another biography claims that he arrived in 1948 and became a soldier.[14] In Tel Aviv, Luden
operated an anarchist press from his home and turned to writing poetry. In 1971
he became editor of *Problemen,* and he remained at the paper until it folded
twenty-one years later, the last Yiddish anarchist newspaper published anywhere
in the world. Founded by Abba Gordin in 1958, *Problemen* was initially a bilingual Yiddish-Hebrew project called *Problemen/Problemot.*[15] Luden published
sixteen novels and poetry collections and contributed to papers as far-flung as
Parizer bleter (Parisian Pages), *Dorem-afrike* (South Africa), *Oyfgang* (Arise) in
Holon, and *Fraye arbeter shtime.* He was affiliated with the Jerusalem-based group
Agudat Shokhrey Khofesh, Association of Advocates of Freedom (AShUAKh,
an acronym spelling "fir tree" or, cheekily for a Jewish group, "Christmas tree"
in Hebrew). His younger brother, Itzhak Luden, edited the Bundist newspaper

Lebns-fragn (Life Questions) from 1971 onward—the last Israeli Yiddish news-paper to fold, in April 2014.

Luden's *A kurtse geshikhte fun anarkhistishe gedank* (A Brief History of An-archist Thought) was published by *Problemen* Farlag in Yiddish in 1984, appear-ing also in Hebrew translation. Its title page identifies it as "a gift for readers of *Problemen,*" suggesting that it was sent to subscribers and tied to an existing community. The book's epigram announces: "Anarchism—ideological alterna-tive to all societal doctrines [*toyres*] which have disappointed." Luden announces his aims: "History is not merely the collection of facts from human theory and not only a sum of memories of peoples. It is also the result of constant social conflict between powers. . . . The aspiration for freedom, equality and justice is as ancient as human consciousness."[16] His genealogy of anarchism begins with the Bible and ends with Buber; contra Bakunin, Luden reads biblical narratives as proto-anarchist texts. He claimed that many other ancient cultures contained anarchistic elements, particularly Persian and Chinese thought,[17] and discusses Lao Tzu as the "Chinese Stirner."[18] Luden emphasizes the communitarian as-pects of early Jewish society:

> In ancient times the idea of freedom and justice, in opposition to force, was drawn from religion. For the oppressed, God became the symbol of justice. The Tanakh describes how Gideon rejected the people's demands for him to be their ruler, with the words: "Not I but God will rule over you."[19] In the times of the Judges, the Jews lived without the framework of government, and they safeguarded social justice. The twelve wander-ing Hebrew tribes likewise settled in Canaan without any knowledge of private property: the earth was their inheritance, the entire tribe's pos-session. At that time, the Hebrew word *ba'al* [master] meant "husband," before the wars fought by the tribes to defend their existence. These wars troubled their contented lives, when "each sat below under his grapevine and fig-tree in peace and forgiveness."[20] From these tribal wars was born the notion of a centralized regime and a king, which would organize the people both to defend themselves and to conquer. Force and private property introduced class binaries between rich and poor, ruler and ruled. Thus were corruption, greed, and private quarrels introduced. The gov-ernment created limitless laws over humanity, and man was no longer as happy as before. Their primary hope became a return to the earlier society of living together with equality and mutual aid—back to the old tribal order, to the lost "golden age."

This also became the call of the Prophets. The Prophets were men of great spirit who clearly saw that world governments compete between themselves, fight against each other, and struggle for might and mastery; they saw, too, that the strong were broken, and they foretold a coming reign of righteousness and justice. The Prophets became protectors of the oppressed. . . . They warned the rich and mighty: "You plowed evil and harvested rage, you ate the fruit of falsehood."[21] The Prophets held up the ideal of righteousness, bound up with the vision of eternal peace and brotherhood of the people, "when wolves will live together with lambs." And not by might nor by glory but through spirit will the kingdom of God be built.[22]

Luden claims the Essenes as "the first anarchists among the Jews": "In their time, they had aroused great admiration among the learned, such as Philo and Josephus Flavius. They numbered around four thousand men and were occupied with agriculture; their kingdom did not collect gold nor silver nor territory, but just enough to provide necessities for the needy. They did not own any property, nor aspire to riches, and they lived in communities with collective ownership. They designed no weapons to murder or enslave through war. They esteemed freedom highly. They did not possess any slaves and lived in equality, like blood-brothers. They were bound by three principles: love for God, for human beings, and for morality. They lived unmarried lives but were not forbidden to marry. They had a strong revulsion to any powerful military organization. According to them, domination was a sin. The Jews' negative attitude in that era toward militarism is best illustrated by the Talmudic aphorism: 'No one is pious down here [on earth] if he is going to be branded an evil-doer [*menuvl*] in the next world.' "[23] The Essenes were also claimed as anarchist forefathers by the Californian poet Kenneth Rexroth, who cites them in *Communalism: From Its Origins to the Twentieth Century* (1974). Luden cites the Prophets as proto-anarchists as well: "Faith was a purely individual matter, when the call of the Prophets abolished the difference between brothers. . . . 'Hear this word upon the mountain of Samaria: Those that rob the poor oppress the pauper' [a reference to Amos 4.1]. With these words, the Prophets' rage warned against the oppressor. The Prophets stood up for social justice and integrity. According to the Torah, the worker is of foremost importance. . . . The soil of *Erets-Yisroel* ought not to be bought, because it is God's land, which he gave to all types of people. 'And the land was given to Adam.' "[24] Luden contrasts the Essenes' egalitarian brotherhood with the Roman idea of the godly king. He favors the Es-

senes' "anti-consumerism" over Spartan commerce, militarism, and devaluation of
the sick.[25] The "war-spirit" of Sparta defined its society, and he criticizes Athens's
class system and use of slavery and the "continual war between the patricians
and plebeians in Rome." Luden includes early Christians, or "Jewish-Christians,"
among the first anarchists, reading the Essenes' holding of land in common as
anti-capitalist practice.[26]

For Luden, Gideon's rejection of monarchism comprises what Jonathan Boyarin and Daniel Boyarin call "the internal critique within the Tanakh (Hebrew
Bible) itself, the dissident voice that is nearly always present."[27] In "Diaspora:
Generation and the Ground of Jewish Identity" (1993), they write: "Zionism itself is predicated on a myth of autochthony. We will suggest that a Jewish subject-
position founded on generational connection and its attendant anamnestic re-
sponsibilities and pleasures affords the possibility of a flexible and nonhermetic
critical Jewish identity."[28] By "autochthony," the Boyarins refer to a specific sort
of indigeneity, born from the earth. (They do not cite Native scholars nor engage with Indigenous thought but refer to the Greek usage of the term.) Like
Luden, the Boyarins identify a Jewish textual lineage recast in twentieth-century
radical vocabulary that counters imperialist interpretations of scripture. The
Boyarins seek to recuperate "the genealogical" as a Jewish term, contra Pauline
critiques. While Boyarin and Boyarin read the biblical land promise as a critique
of autochthony, Luden reads that story as an ethical guard against land ownership: "The soil of *Erets-Yisroyl* ought not to be bought, because it is God's land,
which he gave to all types of people. 'And the land was given to Adam.' "[29] Lud-
en's reading favors communalism and disavowal of property logics, rather than
postcolonial analysis. Luden's anarchist genealogy concludes with a discussion
of the Jewish Austrian religious philosopher Martin Buber (1878–1965), whose
Paths in Utopia (1949) considers radical theories of community in Proudhon,
Kropotkin, and Landauer. Bookended by Buber and the Essenes, Luden frames
anarchism as the very foundation of Jewish radical political imagination.

Luden's poetry thematizes anarchist genealogy, particularly its espousal of
kinship with heroes and poets of generations past. His verse is heavily informed
by the style and content of the Proletarian poets, first among them Dovid Edelshtat, whose verses appear as epigrams to Luden's *Collected Works,* volume 2
(1994). Luden writes in regular rhyme and meter, extending Russian verse
preferences—themselves imported from French—across languages. His love
of couplets creates a sense of romantic belatedness, jovially out of joint with the
literary hegemony of his own time and antagonistic to the avant-gardes of fifty

years earlier. In *"Dikhtung"* (Poetry), Luden references Mayakovsky's daring "cloud in trousers" only to disavow the futurist's style: "Poetry should not wear a modern dress." Instead, Luden's final couplet prescribes: "Into flames your poems of freedom should burst, / Rhyme *storm* and *dreams* together in verse."[30] His poems are populated by traditional Ashkenazi tropes like the golden peacock, wanderers, dreamers, and biblical figures, as in "Rachel and Leah," "Yizkor" (Remembrance Prayer), *"Goldene keyt"* (Golden Chain of Generations). The poem *"Mayn shtot"* (My City) similarly draws out the Sweatshop poets' aspirations, envisioning rest after labor. Unlike the urban Proletarians, Luden maps European diasporic memory onto Mediterranean landscapes and factory labor onto open-air markets in an anarcho-Zionist poetics:

> Street tangles with street, here hot life churns,
> wings spread. A market bustles and burns.
> Labyrinthine alleys toward the wide sea turn
> Through these man-made narrows, alive with love—I thrum.
> Over machines' swirl of speech,
> traversing boulevards, dreams reach.
> The sun seeks a place to hide
> under shuffling clouds, ominous, cold-eyed.
> Who strolls, two-footed legends colossal,
> who strides, these living novels?
> The city's heart sings, a day quenched still,
> an end to sirocco, to clamorous jostle.
> A sweet fresh summer wind from the sea
> arouses love in a city asleep.
> Awake, fantasy—how wonderful the sensation
> Awake and crave night's hot imagination.
> City of my sweet joy and melancholy,
> play Haydn's music upon my soul.
> Why here did fate carry me?
> To dream and love in summer-dusk's honey.
> Toward the houses I cast a smoldering glance
> beneath their windows lies my joy, perchance?
> Not in lavish shops nor houses high
> but faces that shine, lightning eyes.
> Go far, old years weary with grieving!
> Now I serve the god of love in the city of spring.

Traipsing these streets with unsatisfied hunger—
a yearning Yiddish singer.[31]

Gazing at Tel Aviv ("the city of spring") of the 1980s, Luden speaks in the decadent voice of a flâneur from the 1890s. The repeated opening phrase of the line
"vakht oyf der dimyen—a vunderlekh gefil" riffs on the call of Edelshtat's poem
"Vakht oyf!" (Awake!), extending his elegiac relation with Edelshtat. Luden
projects the yearning tropes of labor romanticism onto a Mediterranean city,
using the Hebrew word *khamsin* for specific wind, which I translated as "si-
rocco" to mark it as a term of foreign origin. The poetic speaker walks over
streets and rooftops like a flying figure in a Chagall painting (a pun on *"iber-
gangn,"* to beg door to door or, literally, walk over the houses). He marvels at the
improbable presence of Yiddish there—who are these two-footed legends, these
living novels, who walk Israeli streets? In the closing phrase, the poetic speaker
declares himself to be what we suspected: "A *farbenkter* Yiddish singer." *Farbenkter* means yearning or homesick, and how we read that final adjective deter-
mines the key of the poem. Is he homesick for another place or another time?
Has lust grown entangled with nostalgia, where the youth of the movement and
his young years converged? He wants to see strange faces, not the rich shops and
markets, although those too are described in the vocabulary of a factory worker,
who hears voices whir like machines. Luden's genealogical approach seeks kinship with radicals from the Essenes to the Proletarians.

"CALL ME VENGEANCE!": SHOLEM SHVARTSBARD AND THE POETICS OF RETRIBUTION

While Luden claimed the gentle Essenes and pious Gideon as anarchist
ancestors, Sholem Shvartsbard invoked far bloodier passages: Jacob's sons in
Genesis 3:4, Judith the avenger, and the unnamed Levite concubine at Gibeah.
Shvartsbard was a poet, watchmaker, soldier, and assassin who gained fame and
adulation for assassinating the Ukrainian Cossack Symon Petliura, an act which
informed Jewish philosophy through Hannah Arendt.[32] Born in Izmail, Bessa-
rabia, in 1886, Shvartsbard served in the Russian army and the French Foreign
Legion. A socialist from a young age, he turned toward anarchism while studying Kropotkin in Western Europe. He framed his anarchism as the synthesis of
loyalty to God and workers, as he writes in a memoir:

One time I met with a cell of revolutionary agitators and discussed
whether there is a God in the world or not. I tried to prove that socialism

has nothing to do with religion. A rude young man named Idel the Carpenter stood up and demanded of me: "What, you believe in God?"

"Yes, I believe."

"Go to hell." He spat in my face. "A socialist that believes in God?! I have nothing more to say to you . . . " I found myself a little let down by the conviction that there is no God . . . but secretly I was sure the opposite was true: "God is with us socialists" and that the "Prophets were socialists before Karl Marx and Ferdinand Lassalle and they spoke with God."[33]

Shvartsbard's testimony that "the Prophets were socialists before Karl Marx" echoes Luden's and Goldman's Jewish genealogies. His poetry of the 1910s likewise employs biblical and rabbinic intertextuality to represent modern life, comparing the horrors of the Western Front to "the bones of Ephraim's Tribe / that were scattered in the Valley of Jezreel."[34]

In 1919, Shvartsbard witnessed brutal anti-Jewish pogroms in Kiev and lost fifteen family members in Odessa to antisemitic violence.[35] Shortly after this experience he returned to Paris, and he became a French citizen in 1925, remaining haunted by loss and the violence he had seen. In 1920, he befriended the anarchist philologist and rabbi Yankev Meyer Zalkind, a Yiddish translator of the Talmud and editor of the paper *Arbeter fraynd* (Worker's Friend). Shvartsbard published a Yiddish verse play for children in its pages.[36] Shvartsbard's early poetic temporality was a romantic utopianism, which later turned toward biblical justifications for assassination and vengeance, likely informed by his relationship with an iconoclastic rabbi. Zalkind became his intellectual mentor and father-figure; he offered Shvartsbard new platforms in the London papers *Arbeter fraynd* and *Der yunger dor* (The Young Generation). Shvartsbard published under the name *Baal-khaloymes*, the Dreamer (Master of Dreams), reflecting the romantic spirit of his verse. In 1923, Zalkind published Shvartsbard's four-scene play in *Der yunger dor*, staged by the Paris Jewish Children's Troupe. Titled *"Farn yungn dor"* (To the Young Generation), the play begins with a choir of children in animal masks singing in a garden. The play unfolds like a ballad: a wanderer with a bindle arrives, singing of a village where swamp frogs croak, puppies bark, and the smithy's hammer resounds. Another child, "disguised as a teacher in spectacles," asks a series of political riddles: "Who has treasures, who has money? / Who has orchards, who has fields? / Who owns all, who lacks nothing? / Who is the happiest in the world?" Children march out and unroll a flag, emblazoned with the slogan "Undzer moto iz dos lebn / Undz geher dos un der tsukunft"

("Our motto is life / It belongs to us and the future"). The play ends with a girl dressed as a flower-seller, strewing blooms:

> Go forth from school,
> out from the cramped houses,
> into the perfumed world
> where silver shouts resound,
> carrying through the air.
> Children, here's my gift,
> my splendid-smelling flowers
> kissed by the sun and dew,
> just picked from the garden bed.[37]

Shvartsbard's verse play aligns with Zalkind's pedagogical ideals: liberation from cramped and narrow village schools, attention to the rights of laborers and migrants, cultural pride in Yiddish, unity with nature, and effulgent rest for Jewish workers. The play presented Jewish workers with the sight of their children dressed as flowers, prefiguring a "perfumed world" far from the sweatshops of the East End.

When Symon Petliura arrived in Paris, Shvartsbard swore to avenge his family and the 50,000 to 100,000 Jews whose deaths he held Petliura responsible for in the pogroms of 1919–1920. In a grandiose memoir, Shvartsbard recounts his father visiting him in dreams and demanding vengeance. Shvartsbard carried a photo of Petliura's face torn from an encyclopedia page and, on May 25, 1926, he found Petliura walking in the street. Shvartsbard shot him five times and announced, "I have killed a great assassin." He was immediately arrested and stood trial in October 1927. His attorney was the charismatic Henri Torrès, who previously defended the Spanish anarcho-syndicalist Buenaventura Durruti and represented the Soviet consulate. For Shvartsbard's case, Torrès used Parisian Yiddish papers to locate survivors of Ukrainian pogroms who could provide testimony. Zalkind was invited by Shvartsbard's defense committee to travel to Paris as a consultant from London, and they remained in contact throughout the trial. The case effectively served as a referendum on French antisemitism, and Shvartsbard delivered a performance from the stand to his audience, excoriating French guilt. More than a thousand French spectators attended, as well as five hundred journalists from as far away as China, Birobidzhan, Australia, and Latin America.[38] Perhaps due in part to the French court's hesitance to create more anarchist martyrs, Shvartsbard was acquitted of all charges by the jury. The packed courtroom erupted in chants of "Vive la France!"[39]

"L'endroit où Petliura fut tué" (site where Petliura was killed).
YIVO Archives, Center for Jewish History, "Trial of Shalom
Schwarzbard [Shvartsbard]" (Folder 648A) Mizrakh
Yidisher Historisher Arkhiv, RG 80.

Grand parties with the Yiddish literati were held in his honor, and memora-
bilia with his portrait honored him.[40] One photograph documents the occasion: Shvartsbard sits at the center, flanked by huge bouquets, attended by the
novelist and party host Sholem Asch, no stranger to controversy himself.[41] Asch
befriended Shvartsbard's wife, Anna Shvartsbard, during the trial and composed
a fictionalized biography, *Ver iz der "merder"?* (Who Is the "Assassin"?). Despite
Shvartsbard's status as celebrity assassin, however, the literati did not hold his
poetry in the same high esteem as his five shots. Shvartsbard's poetry in *Dreams
and Reality* was poorly reviewed by the critic Shmuel Charney who, as Kelly
Johnson notes, "traces the impotence of Schwarzbard's muse back to this dis-
connect between dream (desire) and reality (effective writing)": "He lacks the
ability to sing himself out in poems, but he wants, he wishes, he is dying to sing
himself out. He's seeking the lost melody of his soul. Without it he cannot
live. . . . He carries himself around with his muteness, with his stuttering, like the
poet does—with his word."[42] Anna Shvartsbard composed poetry in the 1930s,
publishing one piece in *Fraye arbeter shtime* titled *"Di neyterin"* ("The Seamstress").[43] Like her husband's work, Anna Shvartsbard's poetry treats the themes
of Jewish heroism and the harm to workers' bodies from the toil of labor.
    Despite the ambivalent critical reception of his style, Shvartsbard employed

Party celebrating Shvartsbard's acquittal in Paris, with Sholem Asch
and other literati. Beinecke Rare Book and Manuscript Library,
Yale University, Sholem Asch Papers, GEN MSS 115 Box 15 f. 185.

high-flown poetic rhetoric in his court defense to dramatic effect. Shvartsbard
justified assassination Talmudically, placing himself in a lineage of Jewish heroes. Yosef Hayim Yerushalmi writes of "those Jews who are still within the enchanted circle of tradition, or those who have returned to it." These Jews, he
continues, "find the work of the historian irrelevant[;] they seek, not the his-
toricity of the past, but its internal contemporaneity. Addressed directly by the
text, the question of how it evolved must seem to them subsidiary, if not mean-
ingless."[44] This affective identification with biblical figures occurs cyclically, such
as on Passover, when Jews follow the imperative to regard themselves as having
personally left Egypt. Thus, Yerushalmi argues, "the historical events of the biblical period remain unique and irreversible," while psychologically "those events
are experienced cyclically, repetitively, and to that extent at least, atemporally."[45]
Shvartsbard's rhetorical defense strategy emphasized his position within such
an "enchanted circle of tradition." As Kelly Johnson notes: "Schwarzbard's
penchant for typologizing and drawing historical parallels ... knew no limits. In
another example from his trial, he even compared Petliura to the Roman Em-
peror Titus—the ancient destroyer of the Temple in Jerusalem. Whatever other
factors may have informed the assassination, on the level of Schwarzbard's philosophy of history, anger engendered by two thousand years of persecution rang
out in the five shots fired that day. . . . After Schwarzbard had made yet another
similar historical reference on the first day of the trial, chief prosecutor César

Anna Shvartsbard, Sholem Shvartsbard, and the lawyer
Henri Torrès. YIVO Institute for Jewish Research,
YIVO Archives, Center for Jewish History, "Trial of
Shalom Schwarzbard" (Folder 648A) Mizrakh Yidisher
Historisher Arkhiv, RG 80.

Campinchi asked sarcastically: 'You do understand, gentlemen of the jury, that
we are dealing with a biblical story here, and not Petliura?' "[46]

Letters between Shvartsbard and Zalkind shed light on Shvartsbard's theology—or perhaps the religious rhetoric deployed to justify his act. One letter
to Zalkind written from Prison de la Santé in Montmartre during the trial expresses admiration for Judith, the biblical assassin of Holofernes. Shvartsbard
had been long fascinated with Judith, Deborah, and female warrior figures in
general, since his time at the front.[47] Johnson observes that many of his "love
poems reveal a Delilah-complex and fear of emasculation."[48] Emma Goldman
also claimed Judith as a Jewish anarchist icon: "At the age of eight I used to dream
of becoming a Judith and visioned myself in the act of cutting off Holofernes'
head to avenge the wrongs of my people. But since I had become aware that social injustice is not confined to my own race, I had decided that there were too
many heads for one Judith to cut off."[49]

Shvartsbard's prison letter opens with a declaration of desire for vengeance:
"My dear Dr Zalkind! The voice of my insulted people[,] the lives of the thousand martyrs [and] the cripple, helpless and weak, cry out—I am here! I have
answered. In me has long burned the decree.... That sadist [Petliura] has bathed
in Jewish blood, and the persecutions cast upon the Jewish people have torn at
my heart." Shvartsbard describes reading Israel Zangwill's *Dreams of the Ghetto*

and George Bernard Shaw's play *Saint Joan,* which moved him to tears. He addresses Zalkind intimately, considering him a conduit to the world outside prison: "I turn to you, my dear Zalkind, and through you, to all human hearts and deep souls." The letter concludes with the dramatic lines: "I am with you *semper idem,* yet my name has changed: instead of Sholem [Peace], call me Nekome [Vengeance]!"[50]

In a letter from his prison cell to the editors of *Fraye arbeter shtime,* Shvartsbard withheld the religious sentiment he had poured out to Zalkind. "Enough of slavery, enough outpouring of tears, an end to imploring, crying, bribing," he writes in the gerund-heavy style of Edelshtat. "I was too kind to this murderer under whose command thousands, tens of thousands of Jews, infants at the breast, old white-haired men, women and men, were exterminated. . . . . Well, I didn't spare any bullets for this murderer. I fired five shots into his ugly body!" These two prison letters show how Shvartsbard crafted a more controlled and studious persona to communicate with his role model Zalkind. Yet his letters also gesture toward nonviolence, as in his references to Kropotkin as "that noble Russian heart" and "the Buddha of our time."[51]

The spectacle of Shvartsbard's case put questions of citizenship, republican universalism, antisemitism, and political violence on trial. Torrès argued that Shvartsbard's act was the natural, liberated consequence of a Jew becoming a Frenchman, deploying the rhetoric of citizenship: "A Jew who would lift a stick to defend himself was an unknown phenomenon. Well! I say that when one becomes a French citizen as did Shvartsbard, when one experiences the freedom, full of life, among the Parisians, when a French soldier in a trench has held a hot steel in his hand, a new soul, ardent and trembling with excitement, then is awakened within him that one strikes out for the sake of justice."[52] While ultimately persuasive to a French court, Torrès's rhetoric translates the religious current of Shvartsbard's own writing into a secular testament to the transformative quality of citizenship.[53]

Shvartsbard adored Zalkind. The frontispiece illustration in his memoir, depicting a bare-chested man wrapped in *tallis* and *tfilin,* idealizes the whirling vision of Orthodox anarchism embodied by Zalkind. In 1929, Shvartsbard reminisced about visiting the monument to the Paris Commune together:

> Once, walking with Dr. Zalkind around Père Lachaise in Paris, we paused at the monument to the Commune with its fiery inscription by Victor Hugo: "That, which we want, that, which we demand in the future—is not vengeance—merely justice."
>
> "Indeed, the words of the great poet are fitting for us," Zalkind re-

plied. "The entire world, which remains so guilty and ungrateful to us, will now demand justice from us."[54]

Shvartsbard portrays himself and Zalkind as radical cosmopolitans, conversant with French literature and history. Viewing the non-Jewish Western world as both intellectually indebted to Judaism and neglectful of its Jewish people, they share a revenge fantasy in which individual Jews arise to mete out justice when France, Russia, and other empires fail to act. Such rhetoric bears the hallmarks of Zalkind's grandiose thought: collapsing contemporary political events into biblical temporal schemas, identifying proudly with the "insulted Jewish people," and defying the state justice system to instead align with transcendent Talmudic law. Shvartsbard held Zalkind in high regard as a figure of everyday resistance, as well. In one article, Shvartsbard related how the scholar attacked a group of Nazi brown-shirts with his walking stick: "Just a short while ago, he was riding in a car in Berlin. A pair of swastika-toting young men [*haknkroytser*] walked by ridiculing Jews. My Zalkind wasn't lazy—and shattered his cane on them."[55]

Shvartsbard shared Zalkind's dream of forming an anarchist Jewish society in Palestine, but when he attempted to sail there in 1928 without a visa, he was turned away through the coordinated efforts of anxious colonial officials. Johnson notes, "French authorities in Beirut turned him back with a 'wink' to the British. The paper *Israël* in Cairo reported that the reason behind the refusal was the fear of the colonial authorities that 'the arrival of Schwarzbard might provoke disturbances in the country.' They preferred to wait 'until the Jewish sentiment excited by the Schwarzbard trial calmed down a bit.'"[56] Following his attempted entry, Shvartsbard returned to journalism, published his two-volume memoir, and embarked on an international speaking tour in the early 1930s. Yet the public image Shvartsbard projected of himself as a religious avenger is complicated by his contemporaries' accounts. Isidore Wisotzky recounts his time on the "defense gang" in a remote village in France, protecting Shvartsbard in hiding. Wisotzky's unpublished manuscript is worth citing at length:

> After he had gained his freedom, the Petlura gang were looking for revenge and Shvartzbard had to go into hiding. He lived under constant surveillance. I volunteered to be in that group of friends and comrades who spent as much time as possible in that watch. However, just like the others I had to be approved by Shvartzbard himself as to whether I was trustworthy. I got in touch with the right people and told him of my qualifications.

On a beautiful sunny Parisian morning, I was met by two comrades at a cafe. I knew one of them. We took a train to I don't know where even to this day. After riding for about an hour, we stopped at a station in a small medieval village and met three men on bicycles (all three looked alike to me). They rode slowly along as we walked. All carried revolvers. After the formal introductions, one of the three asked questions of a very close nature about comrades in the United States. Since I knew the correct answers he told me with a broad smile that he was Sholom. Here I was, face to face, with a man who had fought in two revolutions, first against the Tzar, then again the Bolsheviks, who also had fought in the First World War as a soldier in the French Army, and who had killed a man outright. Now there were hundreds of bandits looking for a chance to kill him.

Full of smiles, this middle-aged restless, soft-spoken fellow, short in size, blond, with determined eyes, and a keen sense of humor, greeted me. "The first thing to do while you are here," he said, "is to learn to shoot and shoot straight. You see this bird flying? I will aim at it and shoot it down. That's the way all Jews should learn to shoot, so they don't become the victims of every kind of drunken hooligan."

We soon reached an iron gate attached to a red brick wall which surrounded the house in which Sholom lived. Two men on the inside opened the gate. As we came into the house, we were met by a most motherly woman, Anna Shvartzbard, the wife of Sholom. She had a head of dark hair, and black, clever but sorrowful eyes, radiating all the agonizing troubles she went through with her husband. Since they had no children, Sholom was both her child and her spouse. The entire place looked like a small fortress. Before we could even take a good look, we were served hot borsht and potatoes and wurst and herring which Jews from all over the world sent to him in gratitude. I learned that they also received cheeses and other edibles. Besides food items, they also got Torahs, and large and small prayer shawls in spite of the fact that Sholom was an atheist. Some even sent cash, which was most appreciated.

We started our vigilance. There were eight of us. Four were on guard one night and the other four the next. The guard changed frequently. The nights went and days disappeared. We sang, drank, reminisced, discussed, solved the problems of the world. Thus I spent two weeks at the fort of Sholom Shvartzbard, the man of nerve, bold and brazen, and a darn good shot.[57]

Wisotzky describes Shvartsbard as an atheist, despite his memoir's account of his religiosity and the image he presented to Rabbi Zalkind. Surely, if fans sent him Torah scrolls in gratitude, Shvartsbard had succeeded in placing himself into a religious genealogy.

Rejected from the shores of Palestine, Shvartsbard moved to South Africa to raise funds for the Russian historian and diaspora nationalist Simon Dubnov's Yiddish *Encyclopedia*. There he passed away from a heart attack in 1938. In 1967, following the wishes expressed in his will, Shvartsbard's remains were exhumed and repatriated to the soldiers' cemetery at Moshav Avihayil near Netanya, Israel, close to Zalkind's home, which he could not visit in life. Today, two streets are named for *Ha'nokem* (The Avenger) in Jerusalem and Beersheva; meanwhile, Ukrainian streets are named for Petliura, and his statue still decorates plazas. Thus Shvartsbard, once an anarchist refugee rejected at Palestine's shore, was reburied in Israel as a military hero. He did not become a reciprocal hero to non-Jewish radicals; his insistence on Jewish pride, religious rhetoric, and personal eccentricity perhaps made him unassimilable. Yet he appeared as a spectacular figure in France, with widespread reporting on the case and a triumphant courtroom display. His unlikely trajectory disrupts any linear narrative about Jewish anarchist relations to history and territory.

Luden and Shvartsbard constructed genealogies of Jewish anarchism rooted in biblical and gnostic narrative. Shvartsbard's memoir, poetry, and courtroom testimony re-inscribed him within an "enchanted circle" of Jewish memory centered on revenge to expunge pogrom trauma. His poems and letters cite Judith and Deborah to justify vengeance, constructing a lattice of intertextuality around assassination. Despite his dramatic persona as an avenger of Jewish pain, Shvartsbard is represented by Yiddish modernists as an ambivalent symbol of a crooked revolutionary psyche. For Luden, the Prophets and Essenes offer a Jewish "usable past" of mutual aid and anti-militarism, and his poetry cites Edelshtat and Proletarian forms as links in Jewish anarchist history. While neither cultivated what Hayyim Rothman terms "anarcho-Judaism," they claimed heterogeneous forms of religious memory as the grounds for political action.

PART THREE

Markish's Modernism

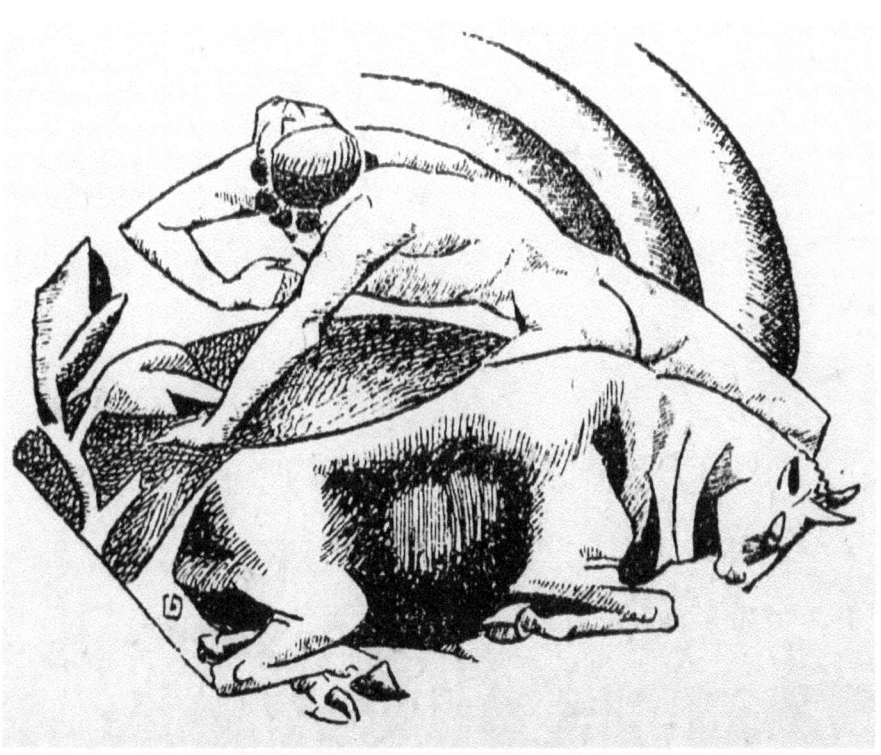

CHAPTER V

"My Heart Has No Roof"

MASCULINITY, ANIMALITY, AND ECOLOGY IN MARKISH'S POETRY AND MANIFESTOS

In his wild Warsaw years in the early 1920s, the poet Peretz Markish (1895–1952) wrote a long poem titled *"Tsu keynem nit"* (To Nobody), which includes this stanza:

> Dos harts iz on a dakh!
> Un vint libn zikh mit dem
> un regns khezhvndike veykn es
> vi fleysh a shtikl in a veytkop
> un nekht anumltike shlofn dort
> un vign toyte zumers bay a kanets . . .

> My heart has no roof!
> Winds make love to it
> and rains of Kheshvan soak it
> like a piece of meat in a soaking pot
> and recent nights sleep there
> and dead summers swing near as a lantern . . . [1]

This audacious movement of an image from romanticism to expressionism is paradigmatically Markish. The unsheltered human heart descends swiftly from the wind's lover to meat in a pot, slashing the loftiness of the opening image. Biblical intertextuality is another hallmark of Markish's poetic technique: the

Jewish lunar month Kheshvan is known for its bitterness, when Noah's ark floated over the flood. The speaker's "heart with no roof" evokes a sukkah, the temporary dwelling set up on the holiday of Sukkot through which celebrants gaze at the stars. In this single stanza, Markish compresses Jewish temporality and ritual into a flight of expressionism—or, it could equally be said, makes expressionism Jewish.

Markish was hailed by Russian translators for introducing to Jewish poetics "the dynamics of new rhythms, the colloquial speech of the revolutionary street, images fresh to the point of insolence. . . . It seems that there is no area in poetry where he would not leave a trace: ballads, odes, elegies, sonnets, free verse, folk tunes, oratory, political invective."[2] While the presence and persistence of anarchism has been almost wholly unconsidered in the study of Yiddish modernism, it hovers and surfaces throughout Markish's multi-genre work. Anarchist diasporism in Yiddish poetry stems from an antiteleological worldview, as found in Markish's literary practices of bending time and imagining history before, after, and beyond the state. His epic orientation took on heroic proportions with the novel *Trot fun doyres* (March of the Generations), a saga of the Warsaw Ghetto smuggled out and published in 1966, and the 20,000-line poem *Milkhome* (War, 1948). Yet even within a work that praises Stalin, the final pages of *Milkhome* plead for a demilitarized world: "Is the mind cut by the border?"[3] The capaciousness of his verse allows for communist and anarchist readings, sometimes internally dissonant, sometimes converging.

Markish expands the realm of artistic and social possibility destroyed by Bolshevik persecution and antisemitism, and the profound erasure of Jewish anarchist history has further obscured the antitotalitarian aspects of Markish's writing. Elie Wiesel wrote about Markish in tones of betrayal: "How could a poet as gifted as Markish defer to the law of a Stalin? How can a real Jew—that is, someone who seeks self-definition by and through his Jewish condition—succumb to the communist faith, which, at the extreme, preaches total assimilation?"[4] Adding to this critique of communism as anti-modernism, Astrid Deuber-Mankowsky claims: "Markish stopped being modern only when he became embedded in a Soviet state literary system. Perhaps it was in the establishment of socialist realism, of an aesthetics tied to a state political structure, that marked the beginning of the end of Markish as a modern."[5] Recent works by David Shneer, Chana Kronfeld, and others have critiqued the "backshadowing" that would blame Soviet Jewish writers for their fates. For a poet who plumbed the pleasures of the present and raged for antifascism, the process of backshadowing obscures the complexity of his art.

Anarchist diasporism describes the convergence of Jewish diasporic experience and visionary anti-statism in Markish's work. Alongside and after writing poems hailing Lenin and Stalin, his work remained suffused with anarchist aesthetics and poetics, from his early poetry and manifestos to his final, posthumously published poema *Der fertsikyeriker man* (*The Man of Forty*). I read Markish with an anarchist lens and historicize anarchist thought in his work. This lens further brings into focus the political valences of temporality in his poetry and manifestos, where euphoric embodiment of the present escapes the strictures of capitalist hourly wage systems and the state temporality of Soviet Communism. Without eliding Markish's communist activity, this chapter documents his poetic affinity with anarchism, beginning with his early manifestos that explicitly identify with anarchist forms and social praxis. The following chapter traces the themes of this book—elegy, critique of the border, genealogy and temporality, and language politics—in Markish's epic poema *Der fertsikyeriker man*. The study of Markish's forgotten masterpiece *Der fertsikyeriker man* illuminates the prefigurative anarchist aspects of Yiddish modernist poetry—visions and verses long overshadowed by what followed.

"TUML-TUML OF REVOLUTION": ANARCHISM IN MARKISH'S LIFE AND CRITICAL RECEPTION

Born in 1895 in Polonnoye, a town in Volhynia in northwestern Ukraine, Peretz Markish in his youth attended *kheyder* (religious Jewish elementary school) and sang in a synagogue choir. Drafted during World War I and discharged after the February Revolution, he then settled in the city of Ekaterinoslav, which had suffered extensive pogroms in 1882 and 1905. Here he may have encountered anarchists of the Revolutionary Insurrectionist Army, also called the anarchist "Black Army" (not to be confused with the ultranationalist Black Hundreds), which considered Ekaterinoslav a strategic site. The commander of the Black Army cavalry and guerillas was Nestor Makhno, who sought to build a stateless communist society during the Ukrainian revolution and dissolved Bolshevik "revolutionary committees" (*revkomy*) in Ekaterinoslav. Makhno's relation to Jewish communities remains controversial, marked by the antisemitism of his followers. The historian Elye (Elias) Tsherikover compiled witness testimony of pogroms carried out by Makhno's army.[6] Jewish anarchists often countered charges of antisemitism against him as an individual. The Kronstadt historian Ida Mett recorded her positive memories of Makhno: "When accused of anti-semitism, he took grievous offense and was saddened by it, as he was too closely connected in his past with internationalist ideology not to be sensible of the significance of such a charge. He was proud of having had the ataman Grigoriev shot and reckoned that all the rumors of pogroms supposedly carried out by the Makhnovists were just odious inventions."[7] In 1939, Max Nomad wrote: "For years he had worn the unenviable halo of a bloodthirsty ruffian, a leader of counterrevolutionary cutthroats and the most dreaded organizer of anti-Semitic pogroms. Yet anyone who was anxious to see him could meet him every Saturday night in the Russian-Jewish Anarchist Workers' Club of Paris."[8] Makhno visited with the Jewish anarchist brothers Abba and Ze'ev (Wolf) Gordin, editors of *Anarkhiia*.[9] His arrival in Markish's town instigated a proliferation of the press, as Paul Avrich writes: "[His] first act on entering a large town [was] throwing open the prisons. . . . Free speech, press, and assembly were proclaimed, and in Ekaterinoslav half a dozen newspapers, representing a wide range of political opinion, sprang up overnight."[10]

Makhno's presence in Ekaterinoslav led to significant encounters with the Markish family. In her memoir, *The Long Return,* Esther Markish writes that her father was threatened one night by a mob of antisemitic Black Army volunteers. She claims that he was saved by a man on horseback—Makhno himself. After rescuing him, Makhno turned back and called after her father to put on galoshes, lest he catch cold.[11] Esther Markish's son David Markish wrote a novel, *Poliushko-pole* (Dear Little Field, 1989), in which Makhno plays a central role. The novel traces the involvement of three Jewish brothers in three movements: the Bolshevik army, Makhno's army, and the White Army. Only the Makhnovist brother survives, sent by Makhno to a commune in Palestine akin to the one he had aimed to build in Ukraine. Shimon Markish and Maria Rubins note, "[David] Markish's depiction of Makhno's attitude to the Jews was innovative for the time, since Soviet historiography portrayed the anarchist leader as an organizer of pogroms."[12] Perhaps the family story of Makhno saving his grandfather's life informed this plotline.

Peretz Markish left Ekaterinoslav for Kiev in 1918 and went on to Warsaw in 1921, where he remained until returning to Moscow in 1926. During these years he traveled to Berlin, Paris, London, and Palestine and cultivated a charismatic persona as performer of his own poems. He published prolifically across genres, with futurist-liturgical long poems at the heart of his project. His poetry in this era declared an ecstatic felt sense of the world across the collections *Shveln* (Thresholds, 1919) and *Stam* (Just So, 1921–1922); the long poems *Nokhn telerl fun himl* (After a Saucer in the Sky, 1919), *Volin* (Volhynia, 1921), and an unfinished long poem titled *Veyland* (Sorrow-land, 1920–1922); a volume of poetry and poetic prose, *Inmitn veg* (Midway, 1919); a volume of literary criticism and essays, *Farbaygeyendik* (In Passing, 1921); and the children's poetry collection *Shtiferish* (Pranks, 1919). In these Warsaw years he also worked with literary collectives and co-founded journals, notably *Khalyastre* (Gang, 1922), co-edited with I. J. Singer, and *Literarishe bleter* (Literary Pages, 1924). Although his work circulates in Russian and Hebrew translation, little has appeared in English.[13]

Markish returned to the Soviet Union during a period when the state supported Yiddish arts. Markish served on the Jewish Anti-Fascist Committee, broadcasting exhortations for world Jewry to join in the struggle against fascism. Markish was the only Yiddish writer to be awarded the Order of Lenin; seven years later, in 1946, he was awarded the Stalin Prize as well. These awards were not benign plaudits, but tools of control: the poet Avrom Sutzkever recalled that Markish "turned gray" when informed about the prize and remarked, "Even in the 'good years,' they wanted to liquidate him."[14] Witnesses recalled Markish's refusal to applaud at cultural events honoring Stalin—a great risk that few in the massive crowd took. The turning point came in January 1948, when Stalin ordered the assassination of Markish's best friend, the actor Shlomo Mikhoels, and presented the murder as a car accident.[15] Immediately upon hearing the news of his friend's death, Markish wrote *Sh. Mikhoels—A ner tomed baym orn* (S. Mikhoels—An eternal flame at his coffin). The liquidation campaign against Soviet Jewish culture thundered on, as the Moscow State Yiddish theater where Mikhoels had performed was shut down and mass arrests of Yiddish writers began. On August 12, 1952, after three years in prison, Markish was executed, one of thirteen prominent Soviet Jews, including five Yiddish writers, on the "Night of the Murdered Poets." His family was exiled for ten years as "family members of a traitor of the Motherland." Markish was formally rehabilitated, after Stalin's death, in the Union of Soviet Socialist Republics (USSR) in 1955, and collections of his poetry appeared in Russian in 1957, 1960, and 1968; some of his work was translated into Russian by Anna Akhmatova and by his son, David Markish, using an intermediary literal translation.[16] Even the flamboyant poet Yevgeny Yevtushenko declared that Markish's poetry was "too overpowering for me to do justice to a translation."[17]

Contemporary readers and critics recognized the anarchist character of Markish's writing. In 1923, the London newspaper *Arbeter fraynd* (Worker's Friend) reviewed Markish's poetry performance, claiming "Markish the Jew, the anarchist, walking with the heavy baggage of his people, a bleeding and wounded vagabond like Shimon, amongst refugees and ruined ones. . . . Markish's depth of being-together with comrades is also apparent. Here, he is more comrade than poet. Here, he is 'ours.'" Ahrne Goldberg describes Markish as an anti-nationalist "storming the Yiddish Bastille" and "sing[ing] with wind and hurricanes, with the creative unrest of a furious world . . . carrying within himself the strengths of Prometheus to hasten and scorch worlds and build other, more beautiful worlds in their place."[18] Goldberg liberally borrows the poet's keywords: *umru* (restless), *shoym* (foam), *shturem* (storm), *huragan* (huricane), and profligate use of the "Modernist *tse*—," a verbal prefix that emphasizes the action of dispersion. Goldberg names Markish an *apikores* (intellectual heretic) and compares him to a "young, complicated Stirner," the German anarchist-individualist philosopher. Goldberg lambasts the assumption by Jewish "nationalist" readers that a radical's art would inherently seek "to destroy classical, traditional ethics and aesthetics of beauty":

> Just one brief characteristic lays down the difference between us and "them": A year ago I read an article by our deceased Dovid Frishman,[19] in which he marveled "that such destructive and revolutionary nature as that of the socialist Rosa Luxembourg also possessed a spring-source of poetic music [*negine*], of poetic songs and love for every creature." Markish will perhaps remain a marvel to them as well, but not to us.[20]

While Markish might "remain a marvel" to those readers who imagine an impenetrable division between complex artistry and a "revolutionary nature," Goldberg recognizes a deep affinity between the two.

Although Goldberg hailed Markish's anarchist tendencies, communist critics recoiled from this element of his work, even as they celebrated his odes to Soviet power and the Red Army. In the early 1940s, the communist critic Alexander Pomerantz (1901–1965) called Markish's poetry "a splendid weapon": "Markish was no common pen-warrior, but a Pavlichenko-sniper," comparing his virtuosity to famed Red Army sniper Lyudmila Pavlichenko's three hundred confirmed kills.[21] Pomerantz, who had lived in the Soviet Union from 1933 to 1935 and remained a member of the American Communist Party until 1950, praises Markish's range, referencing his collection *A toyt di kanibaln!* (Death to the Cannibals! Moscow, 1941): "The theme, the ideas, the content and style of the poems is—death to the cannibals! Intensify the hatred, awaken the fury against the cannibals and strengthen the love for the Red Army, . . . for Moscow, for wounded Red Army fighters, for the Soviet land, for the Polish partisan, for all antifascist fighters. For such aims, Markish used all the colors of his palette, his full image-, feeling-, and thought-riches: pathos, satire and humor, lyric, folklore, the ballad, the poema, the ode,—all forms and media of his poetic arsenal. The unusual theme he embodied in strange, strong, and impression-filled images of hate and love, of 'holy fury' and 'quivering love.' . . . Despite the heaven-wailing, shuddering description of the fascistic cannibal, Markish does not despair."[22]

Like Goldberg, Pomerantz also mimics Markish's own prose style in his critique: "Markish's hatred for the cannibals is borderless, and so his love for the antifascist fighter is also without border. . . . With borderless love for the 'winged' antifascist fighters, his courage is higher than the stars. Even nature struggles against the cannibals, Markish shows us!"[23] Pomerantz declares that "Markish sees future-visions" and praises his "social explosion-stuff and sniper style-turns."[24]

After bestowing high praise on Markish's heroic verses, Pomerantz disdains his anarchism as a regrettable phase. Pomerantz writes that during his Kiev years, Markish composes a "whole line of rebellious abstract poems" and "arrives with wandering-motifs and cosmic-motifs and expresses the *'tuml-tuml'* (religious Jewish elementary school) of revolution."[25] "Here they come to express the atmosphere of the petit-bourgeois stratum, that have reacted to the revolution with an anarchist-individualist manner. Certainly in the book *Stam* [Ordinary], Markish tried to touch directly on the October Revolution, but here as well he remains further from any abstract—truly, inspired—praise-song. He had not grasped the strengths and the aims of the Revolution at that time."[26] Pomerantz is dismayed by the first-person voice of Markish's early work: "Carefree, aimless: this is Markish's slogan." He finds Markish's early work too abstract and undisciplined, which poses a threat to the collective. Though Pomerantz hails Markish's later work praising the Red Army, he casts the Kiev years as an unfortunate individualist period. However, in later assessments of Markish and the legacy of Soviet writers, written in the early 1960s, Pomerantz shifted from disciplining their ideology toward a more reverential tone.[27] Although both Goldberg and Pomerantz recognized the significance of anarchism for Markish, Goldberg hailed Markish as an anarchist "comrade" and Pomerantz disdained his "anarchist-individualism." Markish's brash style and signature keywords were so contagious that both writers mimic his style, even while critiquing it.

"SMASHING TERAH'S IDOLS": JEWISH ANARCHISM IN MARKISH'S ESSAYS AND MANIFESTOS

Markish's manifestos and theoretical essays of the 1920s are charged with the anarchist impulses of his era, before the artistic hegemony of socialist realism and Bolshevik repression of the Kronstadt uprising. Like Sweatshop poets of the previous generation, Markish's avant-garde cohort theorized poetry as a social form. During his Warsaw years, Markish cultivated radical artistic sociality through literary collectives. He contributed to the journal *Albatros* (Albatross) and founded *Khalyastre* (Gang) with Uri Tsvi Grinberg and Melekh Ravitch.

Khalyastre quickly became both a literary almanac and a social space from 1922 to 1924. As Elazar Elhanan observes, "These poets created utopian Yiddish cultural autonomies wherever they dwelled: Kiev, Warsaw, Paris, Berlin, as well as New York and Palestine. In publishing houses and P.E.N. clubs they created models of national culture for a stateless people. In Warsaw, the Khalyastre was one avant-garde group among others, vying for its own version of the future utopian community."[28] *Khalyastre*'s name (meaning band, bunch, or gang) reappropriated a critical remark made by Hillel Tsaytlin, the influential editor of *Moment,* regarding the writers' scandalous behavior.[29] Ravitch claims that the idea for the journal emerged after he exclaimed, "Guys! Let's publish a journal—a journal of the present-day—no, of tomorrow—no, of the day after tomorrow!" This anecdote that emphasizes the dizzy temporality of their literary project.[30] The editors illustrated their literary identity as boisterous, free-roaming men: placed above a poem by Moyshe Broderzon, one engraving depicts three men in marching formation, arms aloft and akimbo in the stylized shape of the letter aleph: "We, the young, a happy, boisterous gang [*khalyastre*], / We're trodding on an unknown path / through deeply melancholic days / through nights of fright. / Per aspera ad astra!"[31] The journal's title proclaims its contributors' identity as a band, roaming like a medieval guild of troubadours (*shpilmener*) beyond the frontiers of accepted taste, linking radical artistic collectivity with anarchist sociality.

Markish opens the first edition of *Khalyastre* with a ferocious manifesto evoking the horrors of the twentieth century. Its inaugural image is an "electrohead": "On der shteynerner vant fun eybikayt klapt zikh un blutikt zikh der ayzerner un oysgedroteveter elektri-kop funm tsvantsikstn fayer-geshmidtn yorhundert. Zayne vey-geshreyen shoydern, vi der fal-geshray fun opraysndike zikh bergishe lavines, vos trogn zikh in opgrunt" (Outside the stone wall of eternity, the iron and wire electro-head of the fire-forged twentieth century beats and bleeds. Its woe-cries shudder, like the falling-cries of torn-off mountain avalanches tumbling into the abyss). Markish's manifesto continues: "Un azoy geyen mir: tsevarfn, eyntsikvayz un ineynem—in anarkhistishe khalyastres bandes un federatsyes" (And so we go: scattered, one by one and all together—in anarchist bands and federations). The *Khalyastre* manifesto anticipates Judith Butler's definition of anarchism as "an ethos of sociability," making the social bonds between poets a literary aim in itself.[32]

Markish's poetic praxis reached far beyond the urban literati. In a recent Yiddish oral history, Frida Zak recounts the day in 1939 when Markish returned to his hometown of Polonnoye, a town in Volhynia, in the borderlands of the Russian Empire. He visited her high school and danced and recited poetry with students around their New Year tree until five o'clock in the morning.[33] These accounts demonstrate the embeddedness of his poetry within multiple social spheres.

Markish's essay collection *Farbaygeyendik* (1921) declares, as Paley might say, the right of a poet to be a poet. Its title means ephemeral, temporary, or passing by, related to *farbaygeyer,* wanderer or passerby—a diffident banner for the bold claims within.[34] These essays argue that there is a higher standard of art than beauty: estrangement.[35] Markish considers the identity of the Yiddish poet and the creative process in a brash, baroque style laden with metaphor and propulsive, churning address, as though elaborating his thoughts extemporaneously to an audience:

> We fear no word—whether that word is "God" or that word is "Revolution." We feel them, we live them, we breathe them. But revere them— no, not these. The artist does not create out of obligation, with a schedule, or because he is required to. . . . If he is not satisfied, he destroys and makes anew.
>
> . . . The true schedule of the artist is the unrest of his heart, its mood. The true orchestral conductor is the artistic sense of vigilant attention that flows through one movement, and also one gesture without weight and without measure—the conductor's intuition. The musical score is the great, eternal, unending world. Let one call it art, God, revolution— that's not important; once again, that is—Life!
>
> . . . The human spirit of creativity is so intertwined with the spirit of revolution that it's hard to say which fertilized which, or which produces the other. They inspire one another; they make one another complete [*memale*]; and they aspire to merge harmoniously to generate a third— into eternal movement, into eternal unrest, into the infinite. Thus it is not right to say "revolutionary artist" or "revolutionary poet," just as it's redundant to say "a running wind." Only say "wind!" and we already know that the forests and the seas are—awake!

Farbaygeyendik synthesizes the futurist and nihilist spirit of the European avant-garde with a specifically Jewish corpus of imagery and metaphor:

> The elemental force of destruction, like the force of creation, is eternal.
>
> That which has been created must be destroyed—because destruction is the eternal driving power and might of creation. Without destruction, there cannot be creation. A human "being" [*zayn*] is a ring, a triple chain of striving and achievements. Then, once we observe the celebration

[*yontif*] of a success, we become seized, besieged and besotted with a
new aspiration. We destroy one "custom" [*"shteyger"*] and make a new
one, then the forthcoming one will hinder the creation of yet another
new one—and so on. That is the law of living and dying, that is the law
of constant movement. We destroy the traditions of the past. They were
created for this end. Our father Avraham chopped up Terah's wooden
idols; we chop up Avraham's wood; those still to come will chop up ours;
and so on. That is the perpetual unrest and dissatisfaction of spirit.[36]

Such interpenetration of destruction and creation echoes Mikhail Bakunin's
manifesto of 1842, which concludes: "Let us therefore trust the eternal Spirit
which destroys and annihilates only because it is the unfathomable and eternally
creative source of all life. The passion for destruction is a creative passion, too."[37]
This strain of thought resurfaced in the Anarcho-Futurist Manifesto, composed
in Kharkov in 1919, which calls: "Extinguish the old!" The Russian anarcho-
futurists' pounding rhetoric mimics the Italian futurists, particularly Filippo
Tommaso Marinetti, as they wage war against the past: "We are uninhibited!
Not for us the wailing sentimentality of the humanists. . . . Raising the black flag
of rebellion, we summon all living men who have not been dehumanized, who
have not been benumbed by the poisonous breath of Civilization! All to the
streets! . . . Death to world Civilization!"[38] Though he evokes Bakunin's maxim,
Markish's lineage of creative-spiritual destruction is traced to the midrash of
Avrom avinu (our father Abraham) destroying the idols in his father's wood shop.
Rather than manifesting the anxiety of influence or Russian nihilism, Markish
roots the "elemental force of creative destruction" in Genesis Rabba. *Farbaygeyendik* departs from the nihilism of the Russian anarcho-futurists, who wage war
against the past. For a Yiddish writer to call to destroy the past would represent
self-erasure. Markish's *Farbaygeyendik* and his *Khalyastre* manifesto announce
an impassioned voice, formed by engagements with Russian anarchist thought,
Bakunin, and the social forms of the avant-garde, with metaphors rooted in Jewish intertextuality and history, rather than the nihilist will to obliterate memory.

"HAPPY IS THE BAREFOOT ONE":
MARKISH'S EARLY COLLECTION SHVELN

In 1919, Markish published the collection *Shveln* (Thresholds) in Kiev. Its
cover and frontispiece were designed by Yosef Chaikov (1888–1979), who later
illustrated the second cover of Markish's poema *Di kupe* (The Heap). One year

before Paul Klee's "Angelus Novus" (Angel of History), Chaikov's figure descends from a cloud or perhaps ascends from the angular shtetl rooftops below. Framed by an arch, this figure gestures with delicate hand to forehead and a beam of light refracted from the other palm. Its grimacing face is flanked by long, dark sidelocks (*payes*); its narrow chest, slim hips, and muscular thighs emerge from a cloud, feet dancing. Is this an angel descending, woe-stricken by the humanity it finds? Or an androgynous Jew, rising up to heaven from a humble village? The interplay of Markish's poetic voice across futurist, romantic, and folkloric forms is reflected in the illustrations by Chaikov, which alternate between tensely drawn-up figures and languorous lovers bent together in the fields, arch-backed horses, and gestural blooms. The mysterious landscape of its cover reflects *Shveln*'s saturation with images of time, fields, horses, and the cosmos. The opening suite of thirteen numbered, untitled poems is *"Erd"* (Earth), and the rhyme *ferd/erd* (horse/earth) repeats across the poetic sequence. Smell, the most ephemeral sense, is central to its sensorium. Confluent with Yiddish modernist convention, the first poem is a declaration of self:

Oyf erd, oyf erd, oyf hoyler erd!
Borfis, vayt ibern faykhtn feld . . .
Hert!
Vi s'viderkult mir op arum di gantse velt!

Tsebrekh, tsevalger dayn gebayd
un kum mit mir, un freg mikh nit vuhin,
oyf erd, oyf erd, oyf hoyler erd,
di gantse velt un ikh, un ale blien!

Oyf erd, oyf erd, oyf hoyler erd,
kayor, banakht, batog,—
kh'bin a ben-yokhed ba dir, erd,
ikh bin an aynunayntsiker oyf dayn farmog!

Mit fis mit borfis tsu akern
Dayn vaykh un varem leyb
Un varfn zikh oyf dir un flakern . . .

Hey mentshn, friling, zun un nekht—
Oyf erd, oyf erd, oyf hoyler erd . . . !

On earth, on earth, on bare earth!
Barefoot, far across damp field . . .

Listen!
We echo around the whole world!

Smash your house, demolish it
and come with me, don't ask where
on earth, on earth, on bare earth,
the whole world and I, and all that blooms!

On earth, on earth, on bare earth,
dawn, night, day,—
I'm your only son, Earth,
I am the only one you own!

My feet, bare feet plow
your soft and warm body
trembling and blazing upon you . . .

Hey people, spring, sun, and nights—
earth, earth, bare earth . . . ![39]

Like Margolin's *"Ikh bin geven a mol a yingling"* and Glatshteyn's "1919," Markish's opening verse announces the poet's genealogy. He claims no human lineage, only the soil and his bare feet upon it. His kinship with earth is complete and solitary, as its only son, though he calls out *"Hey mentshn"* as though passing at a distance. *"Erd"* continues:

Kum aroys mit mir in feld, mayn bruder,
eyn aleyn . . .
Tu zikh borfis oys,
di erd mit dayne fis tsegrob
un loz oyf dir a regn geyen . . .

Trink zikh on mit regn zat
un fal tsu dr'erd—a faykhte, frishe blat . . .

Khraste oyf dayn hemd
un loz dayn layb tsu erdn-layb
un mit ir blayb . . .

Kum mit mir aroys in droysn, bruder,
farkhline zikh mit sheyn,
mit heysn tog, mit frisher nakht,
valger zikh avek in mitn velt

un shray:
in breytn feld, in breytn feld! . . .

Come with me to the field, my brother,
alone
strip barefoot
dig the earth with your feet
let it thrill you

Drink rain to satisfaction
and fall to the earth—a moist, fresh leaf

Undo your shirt
drop your body to the body of the earth
and remain with her

Come out with me, brother,
gleam with beauty
in hot midday, wander in fresh night
wallow in the world
and holler:
wide field, wide field![40]

The poetic speaker invites a brother-reader to join in and dally in fields, to grow dissolute in spring. The word calling to dishevel your garments (*khraste*) has the sonic echo of a non-fused Polish word (*chwasty*) for weeds, which furthers the image of organic disintegration. The invocation of a wide field is a set Slavic phrase, mimicking the cadence of popular song and recirculating this folk style into modernist forms. The speaker declares the unity of self, art, and the world:

I am the earth myself,
I am the field myself,
I am the song myself,
and I descend in a cloudburst
of myself alone . . .

I burst
And I bury . . . [41]

This descent (*arop gey*) in a cloudburst is perhaps represented by Chaikov's liminal figure on the cover, feet dancing on earth, hands beaming light, a cloud preserving its modesty.

I run after rascals watering their horses,
half-naked on horseback, rattling the river;
I sit beside all the shiksas of this earth
singing songs with them as one.

I smell of field-nights, of day-song,
of river-body, of wild moss
a song travels in my sleeve
and tickles me,—what more do I need?

I throw stones to the heights—ho, ho!
Run after me, seek me across the great world,—
What do you need of me? I am gone,
I am beside the river, I am in the field.

I run after rascals watering their horses,
half-naked on horseback, rattling the river;
I sit beside all the shiksas of this earth
singing songs with them as one.[42]

Like Whitman casting in his lot with rough company, Markish uses the gendered, derogatory terms for non-Jewish young men and women (*shkotsem* and *shikses*), affiliating wildness with ethnic difference. The sense of smell defines this speaker's body, rather than its appearance, age, or gender; its most ephemeral attributes link the body to the earth's sensorium. This section rhymes (ABAB) and repeats its refrain, taking on the structure of a ballad and departing from the shorter, looser lines of earlier poems, blending futurist and folkloric forms, high modernist and popular country tropes.

The heterogeneous forms of Markish's "Earth" sequence reach a climax in a poem often studied on its own, *"Veys ikh nit tsi kh'bin in d'reym"* (I Don't Know If I'm at Home). This final poem may be read as a revealing anarchist moment in Markish's early work.[43] It bears the hallmarks of European futurism, while innovating a uniquely Jewish and diasporic sense of time and space contracted to a single ecstatic moment-space. Crucially, there is no valorization of speed, machines, or the metropolis; the singular speaker exists in unformed, natural space. The speaker's voice links temporality and embodiment, declaring *"Mayn nomen iz: Atsind"* (My name is: Now). *Atsind* is the abstract noun for the present, the continuing now. Time is no longer sequential; history does not move through predetermined economic stages, but all thrums in simultaneity. This ravenous hyper-presence demands indeterminacy: "I don't know if I have a home, /

Or have a-far, / If I'm a beginning, or an end." Exemplifying Yiddish anarchist diasporism, Markish's unending whirlwind of the present obliterates the duality of before and after, here and there. These lines also mark a departure from aesthetic movements that championed *do'ikayt*—the sense of hereness and being loyal to the soil, associated with Bundism—and *dortikayt*—thereness, or Zionist longing for a deferred homeland.[44] The duality of *do'ikayt* and *dortikayt* is dissolved by Markish's ecstatic embodiment of the present, both and neither here nor there. The speaker is a field, a burst of cloud, dissolved in sea foam, the lover of the world. The speaker's androgynous body is at home in the world, the only child of *erd* alone, citizen of no country.

"WITH AN UNDONE SHIRT": MAYAKOVSKY AND MASCULINITY

Markish's presentation of masculinity was crucial for both his poetic voice and social presence. This interpretation of masculinity synthesized Jewish spiritual and European futurist tropes, particularly modeled after the charismatic poet Vladimir Mayakovsky.[45] Like Markish's work, Mayakovsky's verse contained both anarchist and communist elements; his relation to Soviet nationalism was similarly tumultuous, alternately confrontational and patriotic. In March 1918, Mayakovsky declared in the *Futurist Newspaper* that "Futurism was the aesthetic equivalent of 'anarchist socialism.'" With his poet-comrades, he took over a restaurant and briefly converted it into a club for "individual-anarchist creativity."[46] Mayakovsky's affiliations with Russian anarchism do not seem to have formally continued after April 12, 1918, the day when the Soviet secret police (Cheka) murdered forty anarchists and arrested some five hundred more.[47]

Markish adored and emulated Mayakovsky. Esther Markish recounts how her husband retold the Hasidic tale of the pure-hearted boy who pours out his prayers through a flute, re-casting Mayakovsky as its hero: "Why, there you have the history of art. . . . Only today it isn't a penny flute that's needed, but the trumpet of a Mayakovsky!"[48] The Yiddish Soviet critic Nokhem Oyslender recalls how Mayakovsky figured in the "oedipal" triangle against Bialik, as recounted by Roy Greenwald: "Recalling the occasion on which he gave Markish a copy of Vladimir Mayakovsky's '*Oblako v shtanakh*' [The Cloud in Trousers, 1914–15], Oyslender describes Markish's turning to him and exclaiming: 'If I had enough money, I would have bought a train ticket to Odessa and visited Bialik, given him this book, and said: Here, genius. Take this book and enjoy it.' Oyslender seems to interpret this as a kind of oedipal plot in which Markish, upon reading 'Oblako v shtanakh,' recognized in Mayakovsky a poetic brother capable of freeing him from the authority of Bialik, the father."[49] Mayakovsky begins his epoch-making poema "A Cloud in Trousers" with a self-portrait of the poetic speaker striding through space: "The might of my voice shakes up the world / as I walk, a beautiful twenty-two-year-old." Mayakovsky proclaims in the foreword: "'Out with your love,' 'Out with your art,' 'Out with your regime,' 'Out with your religion'—[such are my] four cries."[50]

Clothing was crucial for both men's poetic and social identity. Mayakovsky was known for his flamboyant taste, notably one "androgynous yellow blouse that frequently attracted satirical derision from his contemporaries."[51] Amelia Glaser notes that "in his self-presentation, as well as his verse, Markish was striving to become a Mayakovskian nihilist-prophet. And he was increasingly successful."[52] Ilya Ehrenbourg recalls in his memoir: "As I passed *La Rotonde,* I saw a familiar face on the terrace. It was the poet Peretz Markish I had known in Vienna. It was hard not to notice him, because his beautiful, inspired face stood out in any environment. Boris Lavrenev assured that Markish looked like Byron. Perhaps, but perhaps it only resembled that image of the romantic poet that emerges from hundreds of canvases or drawings, poems, the air of another era. Markish was not only romantic in his poetry. His hair buckled in a romantic way, his head wear was romantic (he did not wear a tie and his collar was always open) [*il ne portait pas de cravate et son col était toujours ouvert*]. And this adolescent air, which he kept until death, was also romantic."[53] Ehrenbourg portrays Markish as a self-conscious pastiche of sartorial romanticism.

Their attention to how shirts fall around the torso made Mayakovsky and Markish careful interpreters of the dandy, a paradigmatic figure across European romantic and modernist poetry. Connor Doak argues that Mayakovsky's poetic speaker portrays himself as the desired object: "Maiakovskii is arguably adopting the coquettish role traditionally associated with women: like the Romantic *belle dame sans merci* or Symbolist Beautiful Lady, he rests confident in his own sexual allure. He will accept smiles from women to sew onto his blouse, but remains at a tantalizing distance from them. In placing himself on a pedestal as an object of erotic contemplation, he offers a defiant challenge to the prevailing assumptions about love and sexuality in Russian literary culture. Rather than the poet using the lyric as an instrument to seduce women by praising their beauty, as in the Romantic tradition, or as a means of spiritual inspiration, as in Symbolism, Maiakovskii uses the lyric to construct a self who will prove attractive to women."[54] Doak describes how "the young Maiakovskii fashioned a gendered public persona, which could appear either androgynous or hypermasculine. On one hand, Maiakovskii sported an androgynous yellow blouse that frequently attracted satirical derision from his contemporaries. On the other hand, his impressive stature, operatic bass voice and manly swagger led fellow poet Benedikt Livshits to compare him to a 'Sicilian *Mafioso,* transported to St. Petersburg by some twist of fate,' a 'robber bandit' and an 'anarchist bomb-thrower.'" [55] Mayakovsky's poetic performance of gender transformed the poet—rather than politician or bureaucrat—into the new ideal for Russian revolutionary masculinity.

Whereas Mayakovsky's masculinity was a strategy for redefining Russian revolutionary manhood, Markish's sartorial poetics negotiated a specifically Jewish masculinity. In an untitled poem from *Shveln,* Markish re-codes the *tallis* (fringed prayer shawl), a paradigmatically male, Jewish religious garment:

> tu ikh on af zikh di finsternish
> ibern kop, iber di fis, iber di hent . . .
> ikh gey arum, vi in a groysn shvartsn tales,
> mit poles ongerisene fun ale zaytn,
> un drape zikh af shvartse vent . . .
>
> I don the darkness
> over my head, over my feet, over my hands . . .
> I walk around as though in a large black *tallis,*
> coat-tails ripped on all sides,
> scrabbling at the black walls . . . [56]

Yael Chaver interprets the blackened *tallis* as a pointed rejection of the purity symbolized by its usual whiteness: "the image of the speaker wrapped in a black *tallis* serves to create an abrupt defamiliarization that foreshadows the vision of a world gone awry. . . . In early twentieth-century European culture black was also a major symbol of Anarchism. . . . As an artist closely attuned to modern trends, Markish would have been aware of the political symbolism attached to that color." [57] The tattered coattails, emblem of European tailoring, visually rhyme with the fringes of a *tales-kosn,* the religious undergarment with split seams and four tassels. Markish's black *tallis* expresses masculinity, religious and ethnic identity, and abandonment in a single symbolic image, as iconic as Mayakovsky's yellow blouse. The black anarchist *tallis* echoes the frontispiece in Shvartsbard's memoir, with the slender, bare-chested man wrapped in a billowing prayer shawl.

Clothing offers symbolism but no protection for the human body in Markish's poems, whose subjects walk barefoot in disheveled shirts. His poetic speak-

ers exhort us to walk barefoot on the earth beside them: "Happy is the barefoot one upon your unknown path . . . !"[58] In "I Don't Know If I'm at Home,"
he declares the body to be as ephemeral as sea foam, "mayn guf iz shoym, un
s'shmekt mit im fun vind" (My body is sea foam and reeks of wind), clothed in
an "undone shirt" (*tseshpilyet hemd*). The (male) body dissolving into foam is at
once highly erotic and spiritually coded, as though only his soul has persisted to
write after the body has dissolved into the sea and ether. Markish's futurist line
more discreetly echoes the association between ejaculation and the creative process in Whitman's *Song of Myself:* "Something I cannot see puts upward libidi-
nal prongs, / Seas of bright juice suffuse heaven."[59] This is among the more sexually explicit lines in Markish's oeuvre; for all the gestures of undressing, the
naked body is rarely regarded directly. As Seth Wolitz remarks, "[*Khalyastre*]
were modernist in art, but not in sex."[60]

The defenseless, barefoot, suggestive presentation of a modernist body refutes the armored bodies of Italian futurist art. Umberto Boccioni's brass sculp-
ture "Unique Forms of Continuity in Space" (1913), for example, wears a hel-
met, its face replaced with a tilted crucifix; the human body is subsumed into
a tank and cross with currents of air like tail-fins in its wake. Where Boccioni
thematized the motion of the human body in space as weaponry, Markish's
sense of motion and temporality floats to the other extreme. As Jordan Finkin
notes in a study of *"Shtot"* (City), Markish designates the poema's "I" through
"the dust he kicks up in walking," the body in movement as dissipated as "the
smoke of my passing-by" (*dem roykh fun mayn 'farbey'*).[61]

This state of embodiment is characterized as *hefker,* a key term that circulates throughout Markish's oeuvre. The poetic speaker evinces at once a swaggering inviolability of spirit and a total permeability of the physical body. Whereas
Mayakovsky's Russian futurism severed the genealogy of religion, Markish's
loshn-koydesh claims a linguistic *yikhes* extending from Talmudic thought to
the present, evident in the terms *hefker* and *sof.* Markish expresses gendered embodiment through the vocabulary of religious and ethnic identity. Markish describes embodiment through Jewishly marked vocabulary: "There are no reins
on me, / I'm nobody's, I'm unclaimed [*hefker*], / Without a beginning, without an end." This is a judaized wandering, with echoes of the *luftmensch* trope, a
drifter or "man of air"—here, a man shaped by wind. This Yiddish folk figure is
fused with the modernist troubadour through the key word *hefker,* which signifies both wild abandon and abject desertion; its abstract noun (*hefkeyres*) means
"anarchy," and its verbal form *zikh mafker zayn* means to behave altruistically or
self-sacrificially.[62] Kronfeld considers *hefker* to be "a central marker of the young

modernist's early engagement with the echo-chamber of traditional Jewish intertextuality. . . . Beyond slang collocations, and the impoverished anarchist they
portray, the idea of *hefker* is central to rabbinic law (Tractate Shkalim and Yeva-
mot, for example), one of the most ambivalent *Halakhic* concepts."[63] Because
hefker demands the redistribution of wealth and land, defines one's duty to the
poor, and sets the parameters of community legislative authority, *hefker* is ripe
for anarchist reclamation.

Hefker must be contextualized as a category of Jewish law and poetics. The
(male) body is *hefker:* unsheltered, undone, and wild. It melts and merges with
the forces of nature; skin offers no armor. It may be disabled; it pushes itself past
the norms of health. It is not self-sufficient, but porous, about to burst into
oblivion at any moment. Markish's embodiment of masculinity vacillates between superhuman intensity and complete bodily evanescence. His poetic voice
rarely defines masculinity in opposition to or domination over femininity or
the natural world but instead embodies a state of ephemerality, about to burn
away and disappear. *Hefker* appears in a key phrase in the closing of Markish's
"Maestoso Patetico" (1922):

A hefker-brodyage vet haynt bay dir, got,
zayn in likhtikn heykhl,
me ruft mikh tsu zun oyf mit ershter aliye,
mayn brokhe kh'zol makhn oyf ir—oyf der toyre fun ale planetn un veltn!
ikh vil nit, ikh vil nit farshpetikn, mame,
kh'bin aliye lkhamo . . .

A wanton-vagabond comes to you today, God,
in the bright Temple
I am called to the sun with the first rising,
my prayer upon you—on the Torah of all planets and worlds!
No, Mama, I do not want to be late
I rise to the sun . . . [64]

In "Maestoso Patetico," Markish's compound noun (*hefker-brodyage,* wanton-
vagabond) links the Hebraic component with the Slavic folk trope of the tramp
(*brodyage*), hero of ballads; it ends with non-fused Hebrew. As with *Shveln,*
Markish synthesizes vocal personas from across high- and low-register folk and
religious vernaculars. To read a genealogy of *hefker* in the present day accumu-
lates another intertextuality: its highly charged usage in contemporary Israeli
Hebrew. The contested space of East Jerusalem has been described as *hefker,*

meaning *terra nullius,* vacant land that can be claimed and settled. The element of wantonness remains in its conjugated form as a chauvinistic slur (*mufkeres, bimbo*). The Hebrew graffiti *dam Yehudi eynu hefker* (Jewish blood is not cheap) has functioned as a threat of retaliation against antisemitic violence. The space between Yiddish modernist *hefker* and Israeli Hebrew *hefker* is itself a political open field.

The intense bodily states thematized in Markish's poems and manifestos were matched by his visceral performances: "The poet spits out a poem like a blood clot."[65] The poet Melech Ravitch describes Markish's stage presence as a self-sacrificial offering: "He was sweating so much that steam, as if from a big kettle, rose off of him up to the high wings of the stage, as if he were burning on some kind of altar."[66] Others recall his presence in hagiographically erotic terms: in an oral history, Frida Zak and her husband enter a reverie as both recall the night they met Markish, dwelling on his electric charisma and the softness of his hands, whose touch felt like down (*pukhik*).[67] Markish's presence bore out his Warsaw-era credo of *shoyderlikhkayt* (shuddering-ness): poet and audience were both left shaken.

Where the (masculine) body stops and starts is indeterminate: a poet's presence expands to fill a hall or contracts to a droplet of sea foam. Markish's performances embodied this condition of shuddering as generative vulnerability. Markish's shuddering calls to mind Édouard Glissant's *tremblement*, "trembling thinking": "An instinct, an intuition of the world that we can't achieve with imperial thoughts, with thoughts of domination, thoughts of a systematic path toward a truth that we've posited in advance. . . . We need trembling thinking— because the world trembles, and our sensibility, our affect trembles."[68] The constellation of *hefker* and *shoyderlekhkeyt* may be yoked in *tremblement*: a poetics of trembling.

"THE INVISIBLE BETWEEN": ELEGY AND ANIMALITY IN DI KUPE AND YERUSHE

Markish's *Di kupe, a poeme* (The Heap, A Poema) laments the Horoditch pogrom of two hundred and sixteen Jews during the Ukrainian Civil War in a blood-curdling expressionist howl. Markish indicts God, modernity, and the world, expressed through the forms and vocabularies of Jewish lamentation— whose practice he indicts as well. Earlier anarchist elegies produced martyrs—as Edelshtat and Bovshover linked loss with imminent revolution—or forced readers to engage the psyches of perpetrators, as Glatshteyn and Halpern did. Markish refuses both the production of martyrs and the naming or typologizing of perpetrators. *The Heap* overturns the entire human order, stripping the possibility of human justice, leaving beauty only to the animals.

The covers of each edition of *Di kupe* placed it within a different artistic genealogy. The first edition was published in 1921, shortly after Markish's arrival in Warsaw, followed by a revised edition in 1922 in Kiev. The Warsaw edition resembles an oversized, stapled broadside. Its cover was designed by the Polish constructivist artist Henryk Berlewi (1894–1967), who abstracted the Hebrew letters in the title into an arrangement of flames above a landscape of pyramidic heaps. Three years later Berlewi designed the cover of Markish's *Radyo* (Radio), whose lightning bolt–shaped letters pushed calligraphic abstraction even further.[69] The Kiev edition of *Di kupe* is much smaller, the size of a hand, with a cover by Yosef Chaikov, who had illustrated *Shveln* a couple of years earlier. Chaikov's cover mimics the composition of El Lissitzky's iconic constructivist lithograph "Beat the Whites with the Red Wedge" (1919). Within a circle penetrated by a triangular wedge, Chaikov encloses two living figures bearing a corpse upon a vertiginously tilted landscape. To read the title, one must rotate the book, turning the world upside-down again. Greenwald interprets the compositional parallel between Chaikov and Lissitzky as representing Markish's "dialectical concept of Jewish history":

> Whereas Lissitzky's wedge stands for the Reds in opposition to the circle that symbolizes the Whites, Tchaikov's illustration does not offer such a binary opposition in that both the circle and the pyramid represent the same thing: Jewish history as an endless repetition and as a mound of corpses, respectively. [The] pyramid of corpses in Horoditch is not just the most recent repetition of catastrophe but also the last one. The civil war during which the corpses of Horoditch had piled up is the historical event that, by ushering in the triumph of the Revolution, will once and for all interrupt the cyclically catastrophic course of Jewish history.[70]

Chaikov's illustration introduces sky, circular text, and three figures—two bearing the fallen one. Greenwald reads Chaikov's illustration as representative of Jewish cyclical time, following Simon Dubnov, as well as a "dialectical" model of time "that claims to see progress and change precisely at the moment when Jewish history appears to continue in its cyclical repetition. Within such a reading of history, the 'circle' that 'leaps' would suggest that the closed loop of the circle was broken and that history has taken a new direction. If the word 'leap' indicates that the direction of the movement is also upward, then Markish's circle has opened up a third dimension and becomes a spiral."[71] Barnett Zumoff's English translation of *The Heap* (2015) is illustrated with the series of etchings *Disasters of War* (1810–1820) by Francisco Goya and "Folly in Sacks" (1815–1819) from Goya's *Disparates*. The three covers locate *Di kupe* within a genealogy of Western art history: Chaikov speaks to Lissitzky; Berlewi riffs on calligraphic tradition and novel constructivist typography; and the twenty-first-century selection of Goya relates the Spanish and Russian artists' respective subjection to state censorship and posthumous publication. Like Goya's *proverbios,* the language of *Di kupe* is at once baroque, nightmarish, and vernacular.

An elegy has the potential to serve as an ethical witness and make public the act of mourning. *Di kupe* challenges Hayim Nahman Bialik's canonical Hebrew poem on the Kishinev pogrom, *"Be'ir ha-haregah"* (In the City of Slaughter, 1903). Bialik had been sent to Kishinev to write a report on the pogrom, after which he composed "City of Slaughter." Markish, in contrast, rejected the idea of visiting Horoditch in person, refusing to follow in Bialik's footsteps. After reading sections of *Di kupe,* the Soviet Yiddish critic Nokhem Oyslender inquired whether Markish had considered visiting Horoditch. According to Oyslender, Markish responded, "What for? I see the mound from here." To this, Oyslender replied, "Yes, you see the mound from here, but you might see more from there."[72] Their exchange posits "the mound" as unfixed to a single ethnographic site, but present in any space, towering over the poet. Addressing the heap, Markish's poetic speaker exclaims: "Hey, spread out you flanks of the world! / You extend from the Nile to the Dnieper now."[73]

What does it mean for a poet to refuse the ethnographic stance of "seeing more from there"? Even without traveling to the site itself, photographs of the devastation caused by the pogroms were widely circulated through postcards, newspapers, and a Soviet exhibition, some of which Markish must have viewed.[74] Between 1919 and 1921, a group of Jewish activists in Kiev was organized by the historian Elye Tsherikover to document pogroms in the Ukraine, including one surviving photo of Horoditch.[75] This group was called Redaktsions Kolegiye Oyf Zamlen Un Oysforshn Di Materialn Vegn Di Pogromen in Ukraine (Editorial Committee for Collection and Investigation of Materials Relating to the Pogroms in the Ukraine), and Tsherikover published two Yiddish books on the pogroms as well.[76] The photograph of Horoditch in Tsherikover's archive has no photographer listed, and its caption is in French: "Victimes du pogrome d'Horoditch, organisé par la bande des partisans commandé par Goly" (1920).

One woman in dark clothing lies, cheek to the earth, at the center; around and upon her lie small children curled against several women, their hands and feet aloft in rigor mortis. The photographer would have stood over the corpses to record their expressions in close-up. Though Markish declined to place ethnographic witness above poetic witness as a form of accessing truth, photographs and eyewitness accounts such as those collected by Tsherikover likely informed his poetic composition.

The liturgical, prosodic, and revolutionary aspects of *Di kupe* have received great scholarly attention from Amelia Glaser, Seth Wolitz, David Roskies, Elazar Elhanan, Roy Greenwald, and other scholars.[77] Glaser observes that Markish "uses the marketplace as a metaphor for death" and "develops a poetics that conflates human bodies with merchandise."[78] Greenwald analyzes its religious intertextuality: "Indeed, the linearity of the discourse in *Di kupe* is interrupted by citations from Jewish liturgy that are themselves part of the poem's collage, because the act of citing, in this context, means both quoting and summoning before a court. The speaker is not merely quoting these verses but also summoning them just after Yom Kippur, the Day of Judgment, to bear witness to a past that has expired or to face his own blasphemous accusation."[79] Elhanan focuses on the poema's "revolutionary function" and claims that "Markish created an Expressionist model of utopian community with the poem *Di kupe,* a community that was elaborated and developed through the activities of the Khalyastre."[80] Elhanan reads the poema as the toppling of authority, "the new world disorder":

> In the hyperbolic over-the-top conclusion of the poem, God, who was exiled by the speaker to roam the world, is crucified on the Heap, which is then crowned as queen of all mountains and spits the Ten Commandments in Mount Sinai's face before settling back, stinking and malcontent, with the same obstinate refusal that opened the poem. . . . The Heap's world dominance does not translate here into authority but rather into the negation of it. As the third-person singular that appeared in the opening sonnet is transformed into the first-person plural in the conclusion, the Heap becomes a symbol of the new world disorder, a collective reservoir of ressentiment that poisons and stinks up the old world. For those who shared this ressentiment, *Di kupe* offered a radical negation of the political order that established itself after the war. . . . [The] poem and its aesthetics function as a rallying point for the Yiddish modernists' *khalyastres* and anarchist federations, turning Horoditche's desecrated market square into a pilgrimage site.[81]

Elhanan interprets *Di kupe* as ultimately "a call for communal action, to storm the establishment and take its sacred spaces, replacing its authority with that of the revolutionary poets, who compose their scripture from ruined traditions. For him the long poem is a performative gesture, changing reality as it is performed. It is utopian projection of the place poets ought to occupy in the new world."[82]

An anarchist reading of *Di kupe* begins with its critique of domination and additionally engages radical elegy and animality. Animal motifs have long been used to undo human hierarchies and boundedness throughout Yiddish literature, as in Halpern's poems. Anarchist poets figure animals as a sort of memento mori, a reminder that humans are not masters of the world. Animality is a particularly fraught leitmotif in Jewish literature; Jay Geller's *Bestiarium Judaicum* documents the animalization of Jews in Western literature and examines the "Jew-animal figure" as a defining trope of antisemitic discourse.[83] For Markish, the natural landscape is animated by the human desire for intimacy with the animal world. Dehumanization can only be forced by the human world; animals cannot be agents of dehumanization. Jack Halberstam writes of "the experience of becoming feral" as a longing to join "this world of wild things . . . not as visitors, but as part of it."[84] Halberstam contrasts this desire for wildness with "the white male romance of masculine self-sufficiency and rugged individualism."[85] For Jewish writers always already classed with animals, or for whom such "rugged individualism" is unattainable, desiring one's caste-assigned proximity to animality requires poetic negotiation.

Markish's animals appear in sharp flashes of beauty, beyond the horrors wrought by humanity. The *nekro-velt* of *Di kupe* is a nihilist ecology that contains both the dehumanization of Jews and anthropomorphization of animals as mourners. Animals appear as portents and wait to feast upon the murdered Jews of Horoditch. The animal metaphor aligns with Glaser's frame of the heap as desecrated marketplace, where meat is bought and sold. *Di kupe* is rife with domestic and exotic fauna: crows, camels, deer, sparrow-hawks, black cats. Some are metaphorically determined, and others are a surreal presence without clear symbolism. Deer and camels appear as creatures of lament. Deer are crepuscular animals, active in the liminal hours of daybreak and sunset, and Markish dubs them *hirshn-kayor*, deer of daybreak. Barnett Zumoff translates these passages:

> And the deers of dawn, with hymns of praise
> engraved on their horns of pure smoke,

with sunset in their mouths like snowy storks,
anoint the moonrise.

Into the evening heights go the camels,
with turned-up mouths, on the snow-white desert,
like old priests with smoke-impregnated cloaks,
and drag the murdered corpses
across the Dnieper on wooden wagons.

They've just come from having a warm heart,
are full of blood and still warm,
and tremble arm-in-arm with the heights of the evening.

Why, camels, are you walking to the Dnieper,
concealed like thieves by clay and wood and fire?
Why, camels, are you going to the water like potters?
Oh potsherds—the Dnieper loves potsherds!

And the corpses have purified themselves
and have laid themselves down on wooden rafts.
And the camels walk with heads held high.
Their mouths turn upward, they weep in the desert.[86]

Markish maps biblical landscapes and fauna upon the European palimpsest site of the pogrom. Camels walk incongruously to drink from the Dnieper River, which flows through Belarus and Ukraine to the Black Sea; a "wind from the desert" blows.[87] The loshn-koydesh word *shire* (song of praise) emphasizes the biblical intertextuality. The poetic speaker addresses the camels directly, as the heap is addressed. The final stanza underscores the fluidity of agency between animals and the dead, who have purified themselves and laid themselves down ("un zeynen di—aleyn zikh—, / un leygn aleyn zikh oyf hiltserne vogns, / un geyen verblyudn di helzer gehorbet, / di meyler farrisn un veynen oyf mid-ber").[88] The stanza "And the deers of dawn, with hymns of praise . . . " repeats, laden with unabashed and hyperbolic beauty: the deer commune with liminal temporality (moonrise and daybreak at once) and other animals ("snowy storks"). The inventiveness of this passage is unashamed, splicing lament with shocks of beauty. Temporality and animality commingle: "And sunsets chewing their cuds on trampled grass, / as if on little bones from little children's hands—/ will a miracle not happen already?"[89]

The animals of *Di kupe* are not immune to catastrophe, and they lament along with the heap. There is slippage between species and ethnicities, as *Di kupe* animalizes Romani people as crows, "black Gypsies" beside the corpses:

> You'll feel more cheerful, Heap, with the old crows—
> children, guests, and acquaintances (no Evil Eye!).
> And the crows will live here satisfied, without complaints,
> with entire families, like black Gypsies.
> And their little eggs are warmed by the corpses.
> God help you to be fruitful and multiply.[90]

Greenwald reads the collapse of God into the realm of the animal as part of the poem's complete nihilism: "The divine being is represented as a dog ('Caress them, lick them, as a dog / Licks its scabby, suppurating hide'). Within a few lines, the monotheistic deity is subjected to a materialistic realization and is reduced to a mere animal—a hungry mammal that takes its place within the ecological system."[91] Animality in *Di kupe* contains the only traces of transcendence beyond perpetration, after God and the whole world are shattered. The deer of dawn with their smoky horns lament destruction, which no human remains to voice within *Di kupe*'s cosmos.

Markish's writing before and after *Di kupe* revels in desire to enter the realm of the animal and escape the human world. This distinguished him from his poetic cohort, as Seth Wolitz notes, "Except for Markish, the *Khalyastre* movement was uncomfortable with nature."[92] Markish writes in *In droysn* (Outdoors, 1919): "Arumkhapn mir vilt zikh ale ki / un leygn zikh mit zay oyf dr'erd / un reven glaykh mit zay" (I will embrace all the cows / and lay with them upon the earth / and bellow along with them).[93] The poet speaks no more artfully than barnyard animals and embraces the cows and the earth together. During his years in the mountains of the Caucasus, Markish composed the ecologically detailed collection *Yerushe* (Inheritance), published in 1948—long after critics considered him "no longer modern" due to his Communist affiliation.[94] *Yerushe* includes only one explicitly party-aligned poem, "Lenin's Bas Relief." The collection is animated by exquisitely tender regard for the animal realm. In the poem "Evening Walk," Markish's radical ecological vision emerges. The poetic speaker goes strolling, when a butterfly alights upon his heart:

> On an evening stroll, amid the noises of the street,
> A butterfly flies toward me, lands upon my heart;
> —From where comes such a pleasant, such a welcome guest?
> —And why so late? See, the night's already falling . . .

The darkness all around us spreads its borders
And the stars light up one another and then fall;
Only I with my welcome guest—beside me
Go strolling in the street, as with a bride.

A trolley, passing by, waves to us a hurrah,
An omnibus sends us—a rain of fireworks.
—Where do you order me to go, my guest, for this short while?
—Perhaps, my guest, you'll rest just for a moment?

As if spellbound, we two continue strolling,
but we don't let ourselves be lulled to sleep—
Then with the slightest buzz, as if through tissue paper,
My guest—ready to take flight, spreads out its wings

And through their transparency shows me:—what's beyond,
Where the heavens are melting—golden-hued, and clear,
For all the summer songbirds are already there,
Only you, my guest, are missing from the choir.[95]

The poem is a romance: together they walk, dazzled, like a groom with his bride ("banand / shpatsirn loz ikh zikh in gas, vi mit a kale"). The speaker reaches a Blakean revelation of infinity through contemplation of a butterfly's wings upon his heart. He serves his "guest" hospitably, speaking to the butterfly as her submitting companion ("Where do you order [bafelstu] me to go, my guest, for this short while?"). The inventions of humanity hail them: street cars, fireworks. The poetic speaker is the groom of nature; their proud union, ephemeral (farbaygeyendik) as it is, brings revelation. The poetic speaker enters the world of the butterfly in mystical passing and looks back at the human world through its veil. Like Margolin's gaze from up beneath the soil, reaching through the roots, Markish's alignment with the animal anoints him.

Markish's poetic speaker encounters and regards animality throughout Yerushe. In "Zelbstfargesung" ("Self-Oblivion"), he sings of the orchestra of animals: cicadas playing the cymbals, cuckoo birds and nightingales, the smith-worm hammering. Amid this cacophony of joy, he asks: "Why then should not a man give up his bounty, / When every living thing gives of itself with bliss" (Iz vi-zhe zol der mentsh nit opgebn zayn gob, / vi yetvider bal-khay mit khedve git zikh op).[96] Markish chooses loshn-koydesh terms to link bal-kha (animal) and khedve (joy), underscoring the connection between delight and creation. The voices of all beings "fill to brimming / the entire world with sound, the entire world with gold." No messianic future is summoned when the present is Edenic. "Self-Oblivion" ends with verbatim repetition of its opening lines, casting animals as our spiritual teachers. In the following effervescent poem, "Figaro," the nightingales and flower-stalks incline their ears and applaud the sound of opera from a radio: "The mountains grow taller and still deeper the sea / When heard is the voice of man from its source,— / It's here. It's there. Everywhere—celebration. / —*Bravo, bravissimo,—Figaro, Figaro.*"[97] Now Markish centers the human voice, as it enchants the world. "The Bat" (*Di fledermoyz*) is the most anthropomorphic portrait, following the bat through her flight, "wrapping herself in her weekday shawl— / That she pulled up over her head," as though her wings were garments.[98] The poem traces her dwelling in the liminal hour:

> S'iz shoyn nit nakht, s'iz nokh nit tog
> der sof un onheyb zikh farmishn;
> a fledermoyz git zikh a trog
> in dem nit-onzeevdikn tsvishn.

> It's no longer night, nor yet the day,
> The end and the beginning come together;
> Suddenly a bat darts swiftly out
> In that indefinite in-betweenness . . .

This creature dwells in the *nit-onzeevdikn tsvishn* (literally the "invisible between") and flees from the white light of dawn. Given its context in a collection of poetry written in 1948, it may be tempting to interpret this as political metaphor. The desire to escape through becoming-animal persists, from *Di kupe* to his late ecological work, reaching for entrance to a realm outside the human.

Markish's manifestos, futurist poetry, expressionist lamentations, and ecological visions reveal a depth of anarchist formations throughout his oeuvre. His metaphoric imagination visualizes the overturning of authority without a singular prefigured future. In the twentieth-century ruins of *Di kupe,* intimacy with the beyond-human opens an escape portal from genocidal modernity. The anarchist urge to abolish borders rings throughout Markish's work, from *Shveln* to his epic poema *Der fertsikyeriker man* (*The Man of Forty*), which he began the same year as *Di kupe* and which shares a poetic root.

CHAPTER VI

⊷——◄⦿►——⊷

"The Border, a Wound"

MARKISH'S SMUGGLED POEMA

THE MAN OF FORTY

Hours before his arrest at Stalin's order on January 27, 1949, Peretz Markish gave his wife, Esther Markish, several manuscripts. Among these was *Der fertsikyeriker man* (*The Man of Forty*), a virtuosic and densely enigmatic eighty-page poem. As he handed her the documents, Markish told his wife: "[*The Man of Forty*] is the best thing I've ever done. I want you to take special care of it."[1] Esther Markish arranged for a cousin to smuggle the manuscripts out in a potato sack. In 1954, when she returned from exile, Esther Markish reclaimed the manuscript from its hiding place in Baku. The poet's son David Markish (born 1938) published a full Russian translation in rhyme and meter "without abbreviations or censorship revisions" with a Leningrad press in 1968.[2] Once Esther Markish and her family settled in Tel Aviv, the Yiddish poem was finally published in 1978, accompanied by pen and ink drawings by the Soviet Israeli muralist Lev Syrkin.[3]

Markish began to write *The Man of Forty* in 1922, a year after composing *Di kupe* and the same year he assumed co-editorship of *Khalyastre* and *Albatros*. Esther Markish notes that the publication fulfills her late husband's last will and testament. The first half of the poema was composed while he was "in other lands," between 1922 and 1926; the second half was written "in different ink" largely between 1929 and 1930, and he continued to work it over for decades. Esther Markish recalls often asking him why, if the book was *der hekhster dergreykhung fun zayn dikhtung,* the supreme achievement of his poetry, did he refrain from completing it? He responded "in a joking voice": "When we grow

179

old, raise children, free ourselves from all worries and obligations—then I will finish it."[4] This is the same requirement for those who wish to study Kabbalah: only men over forty who have fulfilled their family and worldly obligations may turn to the mystical sphere. Markish's wife laments, "But he was not destined to grow old." *Fertsikyeriker man* represents a single throughline of his life's thought, extending from his youthful futurist experimentalism through his years of displacement and projected into the future as the opus of his old age.

An anarchist reading of *The Man of Forty* recovers the presence of a more complex poetics than the "party-line propaganda" with which critics have long characterized his later work. The poema moves between expressionist scenes of war and revolution to visions of borderless space, radical temporality, and erotic liberation. The poem is divided into two books with a total of eighty poems in twelve couplets each. The first book searchingly addresses a cryptic, absent man of forty years; the second book hurtles through abstract industrial landscapes towards an unnamed destination. Its regular rhyme and dominant amphibrachic tetrameter stabilizes Markish's extravagant metaphors and abstractions within a tightly corseted form, shaped by Russian-language prosody. As with *Di kupe* and other works of the 1920s, Markish's text is characterized by the simultaneity of liturgical and biblical intertextuality beside and through futurist and expressionist bare shock.

For decades, Markish had kept the manuscript of *The Man of Forty* hidden deep in the drawer of his writing desk and refused to show it to anyone, including his wife.[5] Chana Kronfeld writes, "[*The Man of Forty* is] at once his most Jewish and his most anarchist book, and I believe it is the key to his life's work."[6] The anarchism of Markish's poema may be located in its poetic defiance of authoritarianism, its exuberant subversion of state communist iconography, and its central concern with the figure of the refugee.

In the introduction to the Russian translation of *The Man of Forty*, published after Markish's death and before the original Yiddish edition appeared, Sergei Narovchatov writes:

> At long last, he set to composing a vast canvas of profound and complex design. . . . [*The Man of Forty*] poema is full of reflections on the Jewish people's historical destiny, on their hard road to happiness.[7] Naturally, Biblical symbolism weaves itself into the very fabric of the work: History, here, exists not on a scale of years, but of centuries. That seemingly obscure figure, the "Man of Forty," becomes less opaque when we remember the Biblical story of the Jews wandering for forty years in a "great and terrible" desert. This image embodies the idea of attaining the "promised land," attaining happiness for all Jewish people. The poema's insistent re-

frain emphasizes the significance of this common idea for each separate individual: "[*A esli ty vyduman, net tebia–pust' / Ostanetsia mnoiu pro-lozhennyi put'*] The search for the "promised" land—the Jewish people's [*narodnogo*] happiness—does not lead us down smooth or easy roads. In poetry, many phantoms arise; phantoms that people, in their longing, mistake for the land they seek. But the poet does not make that mistake: He can tell copper from gold in these false lands [*lzhezemli*]; he sees clearly, he sees something altogether different and beautiful, something within an attainable distance. . . . The poema was many years in the making. Echoes of Exodus and Deuteronomy reverberate with current events. Philosophical meditations alternate with international news. In Germany, fascists came to power. The Soviet Union stood as the last bastion against fascism, against the regime destroying Markish's people. And his poema concludes with the apotheosis of [a] socialist society.[8]

Narovchatov captures the texture of Markish's poema, thick with biblical inter-textuality and historical parallel. An anarchist reading of *The Man of Forty*, however, centers the contingency of its final vision and seeks to lift the Soviet teleology imposed upon its unbordered cosmos, in contrast to what his rehabil-itative Russian editors cast as the completed "apotheosis of socialist society." That Markish continued to actively revise a project begun in his fiery 1920s—and that he held it so close to his heart as his "opus," throughout the 1940s—counters historiography of his engulfment within propagandistic forms. A. Novershtern, for example, characterized Markish's return to the Soviet Union as marking the end of his experimentalism, writing that "this decision closed the modernist pe-riod of his writing."[9] Yet after his return to Russia, *The Man of Forty* still pulses with the sounds and images of unfinished insurgency:

> Tsebrokhn di zeygers fun kroynshtot un shtet,
> Tsebrokhn der seyder fun sho'en un teg!
>
> Un ibergekert oyf der anderer zayt
> Shoyn hengt kalender un er dart un er tayet.
>
> Es lign di teg in gevalger fun brokh—
> Un vu iz do shabes, un vu iz do vokh?
>
> Oysgemisht ale vi zangen in shnit—
> Iz velkher den zuntik, un velkher—nit?[10]
>
> Smashed are the clocks of capital and cities,
> Smashed is the order of hours and days!

Overturned, the calendar hangs
backwards, withering, melting.

Days wallow amid rupture—
where is the sabbath, where is the week?

All tangled like sheaves at harvest
Which then is Sunday, which is not?[11]

As in Markish's other works, the number forty is of great significance: "*To a Jewish Dancer*" is composed of forty verses, and in *Brider* (Brothers, 1929), the armored train infected with typhus has forty cars, a number that he repeats in rapid succession. The highly symbolic number forty evokes both liminality and catastrophe: the number of years that the Israelites endured in the desert, the number of days Elijah spent in the wilderness, and the Jewish age of (male) spiritual maturity.

The Man of Forty opens with the poetic speaker calling to a mysterious figure: "Man of Forty! In your pain, you are hailed!" This mythic man is joined on the side of the road by a nameless *hefkerdik* child, found on the path to a mountain. The poetic speaker is fatherless, lamenting like Rachel on the road, evoking a classical trope of exile. A strange refrain extends across these opening verses: "If you do not exist, if you cannot be / May my path point toward you, Man of Forty!" Is the Man of Forty a desert mirage of exile? *Hefkerdik* here summons not the fierce possibility of bohemian adult life, but the abjection of an abandoned child, begging for a bed and linens. An unnamed speaker, orphaned in a strange landscape, recognizes the child's need, but will the speaker shoulder the burden? In "Jewish Responses to Violence: Necropolitics, *Hefker*, and Yiddish Literature of the 1920s," Harriet Murav states, "To declare something *hefker* is to disavow it, remove it from the realm of care and responsibility."[12] Who is neglected, and who is the abandoner? They seem to be an eternal unassimilable refugee, the "pure man in himself" who stands impossibly, permanently outside the political order, and, as noted earlier, was theorized by Giorgio Agamben: "the status of the refugee is always considered a temporary condition that should lead either to naturalization or to repatriation. A permanent status of man in himself is inconceivable for the law of the nation-state."[13] The poetic speaker is the subject of political abandonment and perhaps an abandoner as well.

Markish's corpus of key terms thematize this borderland figure of bare life. Along with *hefker*, the words *umru* (unrest), *shturem* (storm), *heymlozikayt* (homelessness), and *brodyage* (vagabond) circulate throughout Markish's vocabulary, from *Shveln* through *Fertsikyeriker man*.[14] In an early manifesto, Markish characterizes *umru* as "that anxious wandering and seeking, incarnated in sounds, movements, melodies and plastic colours . . . called 'art.'"[15] Exilic unrest forms the substratum of Markish's world; his style is structured with tropes of anarchist diasporism. Like Arendt's claim that refugees are the avant-garde of their people, Markish's incantation of *hefker* and *umru* thematizes the conditions of unrest he experienced.

"RED MONKS": CENSORSHIP AND TRANSLATION

Markish's poetics were shaped by forces of censorship. His writing is textured with loshn-koydesh, the Hebrew and Aramaic linguistic component of Yiddish rendered taboo by Soviet language reform programs.[16] A recently declassified report to Stalin from 1949 urged the dismantling of Jewish writing associations and cited Markish for expressing "nationalist tendencies."[17] Yet Markish continued defiantly using loshn-koydesh, religious themes, even claiming the very word *Jew,* as Esther Markish reveals: "In 1969, I saw something that the ordinary Soviet citizen is never permitted to see: the censor's corrections on the galley proofs of the last book of Markish to be published in the USSR. The censor had red-penciled the word Jew wherever it appeared—as it did frequently—in the volume, and he suggested that the editor replace this 'unacceptable' term by words such as man, citizen, or passer-by. The word Jew was taboo."[18] Soviet censorship of the vocabulary of Jewish identity functioned as a kind of cynical translation, as Max Weinreich remarks on this edition of Mani Leyb's poetry:

> When Mani Leyb, in his *Yingl-tsingl khvat* (New York, 1920?), wrote, *"Un di goyim un di yidn / hobn zikh gelebt tsufridn"* "and the gentiles and the Jews / lived happily," he surely used a mere linguistic fact, without putting any emotions into the use of the word *goyim*. But the Soviet reprinters of the poem reintroduced the full negative meaning into the contrast and deemed it their duty to introduce a negation of a negation; so they changed the text: *"Un di yidn un nit-yidn* ['non-Jews'] */ hobn zikh gelebt tsufridn."*[19]

When Soviet publishers removed any traces of a derogatory shadow-meaning, they sought to resolve the tension between their espoused internationalism and *lehavdl-loshn* (language of separation). Within several years, however, the Communist regime sought to "resolve" that tension not only by internal erasure of the language of difference but by banning Yiddish and Hebrew, as it did during

World War I.[20] A haunting photograph of Esther Markish (Esfir Lozebnikova-Markish) illustrates this censorship: she stands in a group of four people, one of whose faces has been excised, another's body completely cut out.[21]

Markish's subversively ornate style was informed by the need to elude censorship. Referring to a brief published excerpt of *The Man of Forty*, Esther Markish recalls, "The only thing we could count on was the abysmal ignorance and stupidity of the censors. . . . They couldn't make head nor tail of this difficult poem, and they gave their okay."[22] She notes that censors "let slip by" a section containing furiously anti-communist passages, coded as a critique of religion. Markish depicts "red monks" (*monakhn*) as self-castrated bureaucrats: "Bay nakht in di heyln. In heyl mit a lekht. / Zey shnaydn far frumkayt zikh oys dos geshlekht" ("Night in the caverns. In a cave with a piercer / Piously, they excise their sex"). The pettiness of these red monks "with stars on their sleeves" is inhuman: "With relish they take vengeance / On men for their laughter, on a flea for its bite." The world is suffused with the red of ideology, upturning natural order: "Di nakht iz avek, nor der khoyshekh iz do / Un tshadyet mit roytlekhn veyroykh in tol" ("Night is gone, only darkness is here / filled with fumes of reddish incense in the valley"). Yet the poetic speaker prophesies that the red monks will be obliterated: "Nor yung iz der tog un frish iz der tog, / Un s'brot zey di zun oys vi flekn fun tol" ("But young is the day and fresh is the day, / And the sun will scorch them to stains on the valley").[23] The censors could not recognize the trifling, doomed red monks as portraits of themselves.

This edition was framed by the political pedagogy normative for Soviet publications, which needed to negotiate Markish's "Jewish nationalism." In the introduction to David Markish's translation, Sergei Narovchatov writes: "Markish's significance as a writer goes beyond the bounds of Jewish literature. While remaining a deeply national poet, with an outstanding knowledge of his people's psychology, character, and language, Peretz Markish became an all-Soviet [*obshchesovetskii*] poet, familiar to many millions of *our* readers [italics added]. His art [*tvorchestvo*] is international: the idea of a brotherhood of peoples in Lenin defined its content and its direction."[24] As he did not know Yiddish, David Markish worked with an interlinear prose translation, which he transformed into verse.[25] His Russian hebraizes the opening poem:

> fertsikyeriker man! zay bagrist in dayn payn!
> s'vet dikh keyner nit maydn, s'vet dikh keyner farbay
>
> Man of forty! Be greeted in your pain!
> Nobody will shun you, none pass with disdain

Privet tebe, sorokaletnii! shalom!
k tebe my stremimsya, k tebe my idiom

Hello to you, man of forty, shalom!
It's you that we're seeking, we're coming to you.[26]

The poema opens with a mysterious apostrophe. In preparing translations to English, I chose to alternate between rhymed and unrhymed renditions from the consistently rhymed Yiddish, evoking the variety of voices within the poema, the temporal duration during which it was written, and its range of registers. David Markish removes this couplet's recognition of pain and introduces the Hebrew word *shalom* as a greeting, marking it irrefutably as a Jewish poem: "Greetings, Man of Forty! Shalom! / It's to you we aspire, it's toward you we go."[27] One of the poema's frequent refrains first appears at the end of the opening page: "Tomer bistu nito, oyb du bist nit faran, / Zol mayn veg tsu dir zayn, fertsikyeriker man!" ("If there is no you, if you don't exist / My path to you, Man of Forty, persists!") David Markish writes: "Repeatedly using the refrain in the final couplets of chapters, the hero turns to the forty-year-old who has outlived slavery, to perfect freedom, to God: 'And if you are invented, you are not there, let the path paved by me remain!' . . . 'If you are invented' is not a declaration of faith, it is a rustle of hope. A hope that is unlikely to come true."[28] The political situatedness of translation and its publication history adheres multiple temporalities upon *Fertsikyeriker man*'s complex internal temporality.

Sergei Narovchatov claims that *The Man of Forty* ends with the apotheosis of socialist society. Framed as a completed utopia in Soviet literary spheres, Markish's own resounding, restless critique is erased. The translation functions as a communist prosthetic, armoring "weak" images—a barefoot world, wounded bodies, impossible longing to make kin with the cosmos. Raya Shapiro notes, "The Russian translation's triumphant tone is belied by its violent, extractive images, all introduced into the poem by the translator: The workers' hands are lumber to be felled; the people are raw ore, smelted into the country's prosthetic legs."[29] In Markish's Yiddish, the final chord is left unresolved. Reading the poema with an anarchist lens attunes us to Markish's own critiques. While David Markish's Russian rendition emphasizes the vision of a "completed" utopia, his father's prosody undoes its own political pre-determinacy. The Yiddish edition of *Fertsikyeriker man* printed facsimiles of Peretz Markish's handwritten manuscript opposite typeset pages. The presence of the facsimiles emphasizes the intimate materiality of the manusript; in comparison to the typeset poems, it reveals Markish's phonetic orthography (for example, he writes *makhnes* with an aleph and ayin). The Israeli typesetter standardized this Soviet orthography, unmarking the text's geographic and historical origins, which are reinscribed through the inclusion of Markish's handwriting. The Russian edition dates *The Man of Forty* to "1920–1930," though the Yiddish edition suggests he continued to work on the poema in later years.

"THE BORDER A WOUND AND THE BORDER A BROTHER": UNBINDING SPACE

From his first published Russian poem as a teenager ("*Granitsa*," Border) to his last Yiddish work, Markish's writing critiques the border as political formation and prefigures its dissolution. This enthrallment is striking for a poet in a country with the world's longest border and a heavy history of curtailing citizens' movements. In 1882, the minister of the interior had announced that "emigration does not exist for Russian citizens," and the very idea of mass Jewish movement was "incitement to sedition."[30] Free movement was again made illegal barely two months after the Russian Revolution, though Jews' freedom of movement was restricted long before the border closure. Against such constraints, in 1935 Markish published a poem titled "Moscow" in the almanac *Sovetish*, imagining that city as the site from which redemption bursts into the world: "Es tut zikh on di vayt mit blit, / es efenen zikh oyf di roymen, / es mekt shoyn op zikh yeder grenets" ("The horizon is putting on blossom, / the realms are opening, / the borders are vanishing").[31] *Man of Forty* uses a varied vocabulary of the borderlands: geo-political (*grenets*), spatial (*kant* and *rand*), material (*shter*, obstacle, and *ayntsam*, fence), and territorial (*zoym, kant*).

Against the USSR's policy of closed borders, the poem abolishes all borders of time and territory, proliferating visions of mass movement across vast space: "Tsebrokhn der shter un tsevolgert di tsam— / Mir konen shoyn geyen iber luft, iber yam. // Nito iz keyn eygns, nito iz keyn fremd, / Vel ikh oyston dem troyer vi kh'tu oys a hemd" ("The obstacle's smashed and the border's demolished / We can pass now through air, over sea. // Property is no more, there's no ours, no theirs / I take off my grief as I take off my shirt.")[32] The phrase *Nito iz keyn eygns, nito iz keyn fremd* links the abolition of personal property ("there's no ours") with border dissolution, as *fremd* signifies both ownership and foreign territory or otherness. As with other verses about clothing, affect is not essential but external, easily doffed or donned. In Poem 9 of Part 2, Markish hails modes of human kinship with land beyond property and ownership:

> Is this not spring heaped and multiplied upon spring?
> When children gather, they flock together . . .

And what is a border and what is a limit
When children are springing from land to land?

And what could be forbidden to them, after all,
If the earth rushes to meet them?[33]

Spatial relation becomes kinship relation. Sometimes the brim of space appears as a brother or a child. Elsewhere the shore becomes a sensual extension of the mother's body, cradling the poet like a sail:

The sea grows feverish before night's arrival
distance ponders, distance mulls.

Blue stillness, such stillness.
Somewhere a sailboat tarries.

A sail—cradle of childlike sleep,
suspended calm as a crescent moon

Swaying and swinging between
silvery border and silvery seam.

Dozing off in silver slumber
there trembles within its cradle—a star.

The sea is made like a silver bed
and stars lay down enchanted.

When the new moon spreads its path
across the still sea, its mirrored swath

Conjures, enchants, rouses and summons—
Who isn't stirred? Who isn't sloshed?

Who will wake so late, this silver guard,
to skate with stars?

Skate to the mirrored boundary
with stars beside you, stars for company

A silver one appears, reaching to the bowed moon
and latches a thirsty mouth to the cradle

When such light drips between lust and sunrise,
who could prevent me from being a child?[34]

Markish ends with a question as though overcome by feeling. This passage reworks images from both *Yerushe* (1940) and *Di kupe* (1921). Here, the edges and extremes of the world shimmer, making kin with the silver heights, whereas in previous iterations, the image of nursing from the sky is claustrophobic and doomed. In *Di kupe,* Markish makes the sky a dried-out mother:

> Vi zangn tsien meyler zikh tsu dare dikes
> Fun hoykhn,—khmaredik far,
> Vet khotsh a trif der himl ton?
>
> Un himlen, gleykh vi bloye blekhene tsheynikes,
> Tseboygn, boygn zikh tsu bakn nakete,
> —vet khotsh eyn mol a kape ton?

> Mouths like stalks stretch out to skinny teats
> from the heights, sealed with clouds.
>   Will the sky at least give a drip?
>
> And the skies, like blue tin teapots,
>   Bent over, bend to the naked cheeks-
>   Will they at least once drip a drop?[35]

The Man of Forty reworks this image from the pogrom poem *Di kupe,* making the sky's "skinny teats" grow voluptuous. The heights nurture or deny. *The Man of Forty*'s luscious moon-cradle appeared earlier as a withered coffin in *Di kupe:*

> Night has unbuttoned her black mouth,
>   with its teeth of sparkling stars.
> go row the silver rowboat of the new moon,
>   you lonely ones.
>
> Whoever gets no rest on a bed,
> whoever gets no healing from the night hours,
>   go row it naked, without a coffin—
>   row the silver sailboat of the new moon.
>
> Load it with food to stuff yourself, new moon—
>   lay a couple of corpses in it,
>   and quiet crows, like clouds,
> will wander around in the silver sailboat of the new moon.[36]

These similarities reveal how the visual world of *The Man of Forty* was elaborated in and through his unhidden work.

Markish renders the border as a space of violence, *farvundn randn,* a wound on the edges of the earth.[37] The anarchist philosopher Thomas Nail writes, "The common mental image many people have of borders as static walls is neither conceptually nor practically accurate. If anything, borders are more like motors: the mobile cutting blades of society. Just like any other motor, border technologies must be maintained, reproduced, refueled, defended, started up, paid for, repaired."[38] In *The Man of Forty,* the border is a wound that can be healed through poetry's reparations. Poem 33 of Part 1 envisions the healing of rupture:

> Es trift der kayor vi a goldener zalb
> Oyf shpitsn fun berg un oyf shpitsn fun vald.
>
> Mit a tsitrikn vint un mit likhtikn shorkh
> Leygt zikh tsu, rirt zikh on un vekt oyf der kayor.
>
> S'pruvt di kleyninke fligelekh—tsum fliyen a shvalb
> Un der klung fun kayorikn shmid vekt dem vald.
>
> A gefokh, a gefli, a getsvitsher bafalt
> Un es filt zikh mit freyd un gezang on der vald.
>
> Ot-ot gist zikh shoyn iber di velt bizn rand
> Mit zalbung fun shayn un mit goldn getrank.
>
> Nor a shtrek ton di hant un a tsi ton dos moyl
> Funem hoylinkn layb, fun der hoylinker hoyt—
>
> Un es git zikh der vald in di heykhn a trog,
> Un mit hent—dem kayor, un mit grables—dem tog.
>
> Un ikh bin do oykh, un oykh mir iz bashert
> Tsu zayn oyf a freyd fun kayor oyf der erd.[39]

> Daybreak drips like a golden salve
> Upon mountain peaks and forest peaks.
>
> With quivery wind and bright rustle
> Dawn dozes, stirs, and wakes up.
>
> A swallow tries to soar on tiny wings
> Dawn's blacksmith thunder-peals rouse the woods.
>
> A waving, a winging, a twittering strikes
> The forest fills with joy, replenished by song.

Any minute now the world streams over its border
Anointing with shine and golden drink.

Reach out a hand, just tug at the mouth
of the bare body, of bare skin—

And the forest lifts itself up high and fast
And with hands, lifts the dawn and with shovels—the day.

And I am here too, I'm also fated
To be upon earth at joy of daybreak.

Ot-ot gist zikh shoyn iber di velt bizn rand, "Any minute now the *world* overflows to its border." *Rand* is the rim or circumference of a container, not the geopolitical border (*grenets*), which Markish uses repeatedly elsewhere in the poem, along with the border terms *zoym* and *kant.* Markish shakes normative temporality with the literal phrasing "any moment now already": this is not the postmodernist "always already" but the modernist merging of past, present, and future into a single, urgent moment. *Ibergisn* means to decant or overflow, evoking the sumptuousness of wine pouring out of a vessel, which sets up the second half of the rhyme's messianic imagery. *Zalbung* is a noun coined from the verb *zalbn,* to anoint or consecrate. Biblical anointing is performed with oil, performed with hedonistic "shine and golden drink." The poetic speaker's presence at the joy of daybreak is fated, apiece with the world, in the realm of the animals and birds also fated to be there, singing. Markish's daybreak is an undetermined, ambivalent moment of possibility, before birds even know how to fly, as he judaizes and hedonizes the image of the Revolution as a new dawn. In the Russian translation, David Markish changes "golden salve" to a communist red and makes the landscape more explicitly sexual: "Dawn flows out like red anointing oil / onto the mountain top's breasts and the fields' thighs."[40] This unresolved unity of multitudes and fierce embodiment of nature streams into the third poem of Part 2:

Ot do iz a barg, un ot dort iz a taykh,
Nor der veg iz mit ale, mit yedn baglaykh!

Ot do iz a grenets, ot dort iz der rand,
Nor iber dem rand iz a hant mit a hant.

An opbeyg fun rekhts un fun links—a gefar,
Nor onkumen vet men farvundikt un dar.

Gegangen a tog un gegangen a yor,
S'bagleyt der farnakht un es vart der kayor.

Es benken di trit nokh a veg un nokh geyn,
Un shtendik far eynem tseviklen zikh tsvey.

Un di tsvey zikh geport, un di tsvey zikh gemert,
Un ot viklen zey oyf shoyn di gantsinke erd.

Un dos moyl iz in dorsht un in fiber farzoymt.
Vel ikh oyfgeyn tsu dir un dir zogn azoy:

Fun undz—iber rand, fun undz—unter rand,
Tsegeyen zikh vegn tsu yetvidn land,

Tsu yetvidn mentsh un tsu yetvidn kind—
Un epes fargeyt, un epes bagint.

Keyn eynem—farteylt, keyn eynem—farzen,
Un oyf yetvidn trot zikh tseglekern tsen,

Un hundert un toyznt fun gor fun der erd—
Un s'stayet keyn otem, un s'klekt nit keyn trer.

Iz vos iz a barg un vos iz a taykh,
Az der veg iz tsu ale—mit yedn baglaykh . . .

Right here is a mountain, right there is a stream
But the path is for all, for all as equals!

Right here is a border, right there is the edge
Yet over the edge is a hand with a hand.

From the right, disparity. From the left—danger,
Yet they will arrive wounded and wan.

They walked a day, they walked a year
The dusk accompanies and the dawn awaits.

Footsteps yearn for a path, yearn to walk
Two are rolling up the whole world as one.

The two mated, the two multiplied,
And there at once enfolded the entire world.

And the mouth thirsts, stitched closed in fever.
I'll come to you and tell you this:

From us—over the border, from us—under the border,
Roads dissolve away toward every land

To each person, to every child
Something sets and something dawns.

Nobody passed over, not one overlooked
Each footstep chiming out ten chimes

Hundreds and thousands from over the earth
No breath is enough, no tear suffices.

Then what is a mountain and what is a stream
When the road is for all—all as equals . . .[41]

Markish unsettles the categories, not only of human borders but of natural difference ("What is a mountain and what is a stream"). Images of dissolved duality reference the Platonic creation story, in which one being is separated into
two, and Genesis, with its injunction to be fruitful and multiply. "Beyond the
edge is a hand with a hand" calls up the icon of union badges and internationalist banners, while retaining the texture of an experimental line rather than a
slogan. The choice of *rand* (rim, edge) rather than *grenets* (geopolitical border)
evokes a hand helping another person from over the edge of an overflowing,
deluged world. In the line "Un dos moyl iz in dorsht un in fiber farzoymt" ("And
the mouth thirsts, stitched closed in fever"), the word *farzoymt* evokes border
imagery: *zoym* is a seam, hem, or border, so the throat could be seamed shut or
bordered in fever, closing up with illness.[42]

Several opening poems of Part 2 delight in the explosions of time and distance, echoing the poetics of destruction elaborated in Markish's 1921 manifesto.
These images of infinite space and time are laced through with the constraints
of respiratory illness and the limitations of a singular body, its throat sewn up
in pain and fever (*un dos moyl iz in dorsht un in fiber farzoymt*). This repetition
embodies the iterativeness of chronic illness, making the speaker cough over and
over. There is no expectation of a healed body or end to physical suffering; images of liberation are expressed only collectively, through the anticipated arrival
of new masses marching across vast distances. In Poem 6, Markish's poetic speaker
incants lines of pain and lack ("My mouth's seamed in fever and hunger ache")
amid the golden cosmos:

Sieve this day with a golden sifter
the molten sun festers, its sieve blisters.

With radiant yellow and sun-gold plume
he waters and sprays the valley's bloom.

Whether a day or an hour it appears
night lulls sleep with silvery conjure.

From far within far, from border to unbanked shore,
a silver path throws open the sea's door.

Such radiant Far, such silvered route
urges on to ride the crescent moon.

My mouth's seamed in fever and hunger ache.
I rise to you and to you I will say:

—Smash the hurdle, demolish the boundary—
We already know how to walk in air, over sea.

Nothing is foreign, nothing is ours
I'll dress in sorrow like I put on a blouse

Dash down the silver road of the globe
you the sun has ignored, light never enrobed

I'll call them hither, I'll bring them here,
I'll call and gather them from over the earth.

Come to us, brothers, and come to us, guests
who we are, whence we came—Forget.

For each, for all, the valley's prepared—
Vivas to you, may joy come and be shared![43]

Further in Part 2, Markish diverges from this pattern of splicing rapture and rupture. Poem 30 offers lush border-freedom without the interjection of pain and constraint:

S'shmekt der tog oyf di vegn mit zunzaft geshmak
Un der yam hengt in vayt, vi a bloyer hamak.

Ven es git a tsefokh zikh a vel nokh a vel,
Iz tsetantst zikh der yam, iz der yam—karosel.

Beygt di khvalyes vi kemlen di hoykers oyf frakht,
Un oyf freydike rayters un makhnes er vart.

Iz durkh bergn-gevelb iber yamikn breg,
Geyen makhnes arayn, geyen makhnes avek.

S'bagegnen zikh makhnes un shnaydn zikh ayn,
Un gezang baym avek, un gezang bayn arayn.

S'zaynen tsugn aroys funem gantsn farband
Un: "—di zun un dem yam un dem opru derlang!"

Nor oyf eynemens ru veln zibn zayn vakh,
Un oyf zibn mol tog—zol nor eyn mol zayn nakht!

Az di hoykh hot farvigt un der vint—nit geshtert,
Lign berg mit di bergike brust tsu di shtern.

Un kvaln fun vaynzaftn kvalndik kvelt—
Iz der yam biz di kni, un di gantsinke velt!

Es shlayfn zikh shteyndlekh fun layber getsundn
Un der breg iz gebet mit geshlifener zun.

N'az dos harts trinkt zikh on mit a tog oyfn yam,
Mit a tog oyf der zun, un di zun hot gezamt,

Vert farshikert dos layb, un tsu kukn vert shver
Vi es lign di berg mit di brust tsu di shtern . . .

Upon the roads, day fills with savory sun-sap
the sea hangs like a blue hammock in the distance.

When wave lands a blow upon wave
the sea bursts into dance, the sea's a carousel.

The sea bends the waves' back like camels' humps
Laden with cargo, awaiting joyful riders and hordes.

Through vaulted mountains over marine borders
Multitudes come, multitudes leave.

Masses collide, cut through each other
A song as they leave, a song as they come.

Trains depart from the whole union
Saying: "Strike sun and sea and rest!"

For every single rest, seven will keep watch
And for sevenfold day, let only one be night!

When the heights are lulled and the wind unhindered
Mountains repose, mountainous breast to the stars.

Springs of wine-juices spring, springing
The sea, the whole world—they reach to your knee!

Flint polished by kindling bodies
The shoreline beds down with sharp-polished sun.

When the heart gets soused on a day at sea
From a day of sun, and the sun lingered

When the body's drunk, it's hard to see
How mountains lie, breast to the stars . . .[44]

Mass movement extends over the ocean shores: "Iz durkh bergn-gevelb iber yamikn breg, / Geyn makhnes arayn, geyn makhnes avek" ("Through vaulted mountains over marine borders / Multitudes come, multitudes leave"). Markish summons a Mayakovskian giant figure: "The sea, the whole world—they reach to your knee!" Matching this geographic expansiveness, the poem uses more "international" vocabulary, such as "hammock" (originally from Taíno) and "carousel" (French). Its irreligious imagery is reflected in the near-total lack of loshn-koydesh, except for *makhnes,* hordes. Yet the poem also has a psalm-like quality, animating the natural world lustily: hills do not skip like lambs but repose like breasts toward the stars, and the sea dances with abandon. As Jordan Finkin notes, mapping the landscape onto the human body is a favorite device of Markish's, creating an "ersatz intimacy" between place and stateless poetic speaker.[45] The cryptic final lines rehearse the seven days of creation in Genesis: "Nor oyf eynemens ru veln zibn zayn vakh, / Un oyf zibn mol tog—zol nor eyn mol zayn nakht!" ("For every single rest, seven will keep watch / And for sevenfold day, let only one be night!").

Reading and translating these lines, I tried to imagine how Markish would have performed them. Esther Markish recalls Russian translators visiting their house to collaborate:

No sooner would a translator enter the room and I leave it than the air would be filled with shouts, in Russian and Yiddish, singing, stamping, and general clamor: Markish was working with the translator. . . . On one occasion, alarmed by a strange thud, I peered through the crack in the door. Markish was prone on the floor, arms wide, literally embracing it: the verses in question represented the author embracing the whole world, the entire universe.[46]

Though Esther Markish does not identify the poem he was translating in that anecdote, so many of Markish's lines yearn for this all-embracing kinship: "Es blit undzer erd mit shtol un mit roykh—/ A bruder di vayt un a bruder—di hoykh" ("Our earth buds with steel and smoke / The distance, a brother and a brother—the heights"). This is the very definition of pre-bordered space, as Nail writes: "A society without any kind of border, internal or external, is simply what we would call the earth or world: a pre-social, undivided surface. Accordingly, society is first and foremost a product of the borders that define it and the material conditions under which it is dividable. Only afterward are borders (re)produced by society. . . . The border has become the social condition necessary for the emergence of certain dominant social formations, not the other way around."[47] The sense of relentless traversal across great space forces the poema forward:

> On brokh un on broyz vert keyn zakh nit tseshtroyt,
> Nor der vos tsebrekht, der shtelt oyf un der boyt.
>
> . . . On a shturm hot di shif nokh dem yam nit farzukht,
> Nor di shif iz tsum geyn un der shturm—oyf adurkh!
>
> Nothing can spread without fracture and boil
> Only one who smashes can organize and build.
>
> Without storms, the ship can't taste the ocean
> The ship is made for movement, and the storm for piercing![48]

Markish's couplets often begin as near slogans and veer into abstraction, tempering bare utopianism with ambivalence or complex metaphor. Compare, for example, a verse from the anthem of the Jewish Labor Bund written by S. An-sky in 1902: "Tsuzamen, tsuzamen, di fon zi iz greyt / Zi flatert fun tsorn, fun blut iz zi reyt" ("Together, together, the banner is ready / It flaps with anger, it's red with blood"). The same tropes of readiness, bloody fervor, and flags reoccur in *The Man of Forty*, but Markish reorders them into anti-prescriptive lines.

These verses interweave the iconography of labor with the unboundedness of nature, creating a felt sense of being in the world beyond the romance of industrialization. Without borders, he aspires for comradeship with all life to become possible. Yet the passage in Esther Markish's memoir grows poignant when we consider the dissonance between her husband's gesture of embracing a borderless world and her own excluded position, eavesdropping through a crack in the door.

Markish's extended visual corpus of border-freedom served to praise Soviet leaders in later years. The 1938 collection *Foterlekhe erd* (Fatherly Earth) is emblazoned with a star and red flag on its title page and contains the poem *"Grenets-lid"* (Border-Poem), which reifies and nationalizes the enclosure of land. Its poetic speaker hails a horseback rider at the border, a gigantic protector figure: "No eagle can compete with them, / No lightning flash can pass where they are!"[49] As Thomas Nail notes, historically borders replaced the bodies of soldiers who had guarded a territory.[50] Here, the citizen-soldier is the physical embodiment of the border:

> Oyf di yamen—khvalyes zikh tsevign,
> In di heykhn—shotns fun farlend—
> S'iz der rand oyf festn shlos farziglt,
> S'zeynen shlisl—in getraye hent!
>
> S'vet keyn shand oyf undzer shverd nit faln
> Bay dem mindstn shpan fun undzer erd—
> S'hot undz ongezogt der khaver stalin,
> Er aleyn bagleyt hot undz aher!
>
> Upon the seas—waves fiercely rocked,
> In the heights—shadows of butchery
> The border is sealed and locked
> devoted hands hold its key!
>
> No shame will fall upon our sword
> at the merest span of our earth—
> Comrade Stalin has declared
> he alone accompanies us here!

The vaunted horseback rider is revealed to be "khaver stalin." *Khaver* is a markedly Jewish term for comrade, rather than the international *kamarad* or *genose*. It was a grim challenge to translate this inversion of Markish's familiar style and border-less ideal in service to his eventual executioner. Perhaps this translational

ache was shared by the Russian Jewish translator Aleksandr Golemba (pseudonym of Aleksandr Solomonovich Rapoport, 1922–1979), who worked on these
odes after Markish's execution and formal rehabilitation. Despite the critique of
backshadowing, translating Markish's paeans to Stalin remains stingingly painful, though it expresses his charge to survive by composing encomia. The space
between *"Grenets-lid"* and *Fertsikyeriker man* lies in the abyss between *grenets*
and *rand,* the border that circumscribes and the rim that pours over.

"THE CALENDAR OVERTURNED": *REVOLUTIONARY TEMPORALITY*

Breaching the borders of time heralds revolution in *The Man of Forty*. Nail
characterizes the timetable as "a border technology that both divides and prescribes the passage of social time and social space. . . . Thus the borders of the
timetable must be enforced just like any other border: curfews in the cities, prayer
and work in the monastery, and meals and visitation in the prison."[51] Timetables
and calendars are upended in *The Man of Forty* in the natural path of insurrec-
tion, as Walter Benjamin writes: "The consciousness of exploding the contin-
uum of history is peculiar to the revolutionary classes in the moment of their
action. The Great Revolution introduced a new calendar. The day on which the
calendar started functioned as a historical time-lapse camera. . . . During the evening of the first skirmishes, it turned out that the clock-towers were shot at independently and simultaneously in several places in Paris."[52] Between 1929 and
1940, Soviet temporality was transformed: the day of rest was desacralized and
changed from Sunday to one day within a five-day workweek. This new Communist temporality was imposed upon Jewish cyclical time as well, and Yiddish
newspapers printed daily timetables for studying Marxist texts based upon traditional devotional schedules.[53] Editors mapped state ideology upon internalized
schedules by refilling religious temporal structures with Communist content.

The poem's revolutionary temporality is not purely secular; it overturns
machine time on the path toward repairing Jewish cyclical and messianic time.
This fusion of Jewish-revolutionary time represents a Benjaminian modernist
move. The second book opens with a shuddering temporality:

> Es shit zikh der brokh un di horns gegurt
> Oyf shmelts un tsegli un oyf nayes geburt.
>
> Es brenen di oyvns getsundn fun frayheyt
> Un s'shtraln zikh oys—nit keyn teg, nor di tseyt!

Un mishmoyres zi shneydt, un mishmoyres zi bayt
In di roymen in dr'hoykh, in di shtrekes oyf vayt.

Durkh gezang fun bavegung, geverb un geboy,
In freyd fun vuks un farlust, durkh gebert un gebroykh.

Durkh dem mentshlekhn zayn, durkh dem mentshlekhn min,
In freyd fun der arbet, in freyd fun der mi!

Un zi geyt un zi shtaygt mit gezangikn takt:
—Rum tsu ot di velkhe hobn gevagt!

Rum tsu dem akhzer mit hamer in hant
Vos hot nit getsitert, vos hot nit gezamt,

Baym haldz funem gliver, baym haldz fun fargang
Un hot zikh farmostn aroyf—un derlangt!

Catastrophe cracks, forging
and pouring and smelting new horns.

Ovens burn, alight from freedom
radiating not days, but time!

Time oversees the reaping and replacing
in realms above, in stretches of distance.

Through song of movement, of verb and of form,
Through joy of growth and loss, through birth and through use.

Through human existence, through humankind,
In joy of labor, in joy of toil!

Move and rise with chanted cadence:
—Glory to those who were daring!

Glory to the cruel one, hammer in hand
who did not tremble, who did not tarry

At the throat of stasis, at the throat of the past
Who fixed aim—and strikes![54]

Mixed sheaves at harvest references biblical time and agricultural life ruled by
the seasons. Finkin discusses an image from an earlier Markish poem: a deserted
marketplace wall where "clocks hang, hairy like hacked-off heads of calves, / And

lick emptiness with the pendulum's back-and-forth."⁵⁵ As in that image, where clocks are suspended carcasses at the butcher's shop, the shattered machinery of time once had animal life. The confusion of secular or state time and biblical time is not merely a stylistic device but has political and psychological resonance. The calendar hangs wilting like a Dalí clock, but the speaker's consternation is real: "Es lign di teg in gevalger fun brokh— / Un vu iz do shabes, un vu iz do vokh?" ("Days wallow in brokenness— / Where is the sabbath, where is the week?") This is not an untroubled liberation from repressive hourly wage systems or absurd religious strictures; rather, the lines dramatize being cut adrift into desacralized time. The reference to a cruel figure, "Vos hot nit getsitert, vos hot nit gezamt" ("who did not tremble, who did not tarry"), inverts the messianic prayer of Habbakuk (2.3), "Though he tarry, he shall come." The final lines ascribe a loshn-koydesh word (*akhzer,* cruel one) to the figure who wields the hammer, that Communist icon: "Glory to the brute, hammer in hand / who did not tremble, who did not linger / At the throat of death, at the throat of the past / Who fixed aim—and strikes!" This ironic declamation indicts the brutality of those who would destroy the past or sever temporality from tradition. David Markish's Russian translation domesticates this satiric image into a folkloric one: the *akhzer* (cruel one) becomes a brave wanderer carrying only an empty sack (*pustaia kolomka*) and hammer, instead of a walking stick.⁵⁶ This poem contains a paradigmatic arc for Markish: he begins with lines worthy of the most emphatic futurist, but by its end he has judaized revolutionary time and troubled the premise of liberation by emphasizing the violence of its means.

"WHO BY HAMMER AND WHO BY SICKLE": DEBILITY AND EMBODIMENT

The Man of Forty captures bodies in extreme states and traumatized by war, in verbal counterpart to the graphically wounded figures of post–World War I expressionism. The stamina demanded to recite the poema might exceed the ill bodies it describes: How can a feverish throat recite epic poetry? This cleaves the debilitated bodies it represents from the kind of body required to perform it. The ephemeral and flamboyant masculine embodiment of *Shveln* is here revisualized through injury from war and pogroms. *The Man of Forty* was composed in a period when photographs of wounded bodies circulated among the Jewish public in newspapers and photo exhibitions. Elissa Bemporad notes that for one exhibition in 1923, "condemning the pogroms was in agreement with the Bolsheviks' official struggle against antisemitism. On the other hand, the same trend to overlook the Jewish identity of the victims and the antisemitic nature of the attacks . . . gradually infused and eventually came to dominate Soviet public discourse."[57] This exhibition was well-reviewed in *Pravda* and published in 1926 as an oversized photo album titled *Jewish Pogroms, 1918–1921*.[58] However, as Bemporad notes: "The book did not reproduce some of the most controversial photographs that could impinge on the politically sensitive issue of the identity of the victims, the perpetrators, and the profiteers," including wallets and boots cobbled from Torah scrolls and razed synagogues.[59] In the wider postwar context, artists appropriated technologies like newsreels to counter the glorification of war, from Picasso's headlines pasted into Cubist collage to the anarchist photographer Ernst Friedrich's *Krieg dem Kriege!* (*War Against War!*).[60] Friedrich's book—which Susan Sontag called "photography as shock therapy"—compiled two hundred photographs from German military and medical archives censored during wartime.[61] It closes with a sequence titled "The Face of War": twenty-four close-up photographs of soldiers with disfigured and maimed faces, each with an anti-militarist caption in German, French, English, and Dutch. *War Against War* subverts the grandiose visual style of military documentary, paralleling Markish's mock-epic couplets.

The Man of Forty disrupts iconographies of heroism with shocking images of soldiers' and civilians' debility. "Ven es rayst oyf a shlakht op a zelner di fis, / Iz khapt er zikh on mit di hent far der shpiz" ("When battle tears off a soldier's feet, / He hangs on to his bayonet with his hands"). Disability is not a mark of difference in this context, but the common and inevitable horizon of being. In Poem 40 of Part 1, the poetic speaker encounters the body of a soldier abandoned by the side of the road:

> Der tog zikh fartsit, zikh fartsit un fartsert,
> Un ver mit a hamer, un ver mit a serp.
>
> S'bafelt der hamoyn un mit zun er bashvert,
> Un ikh mit a zastup far keyversher erd.
>
> Iz farkhlyanet dos harts un mit fiber farzoymt.
> Vel ikh oyfgeyn tsu dir un dir zogn azoy:
>
> Itst mit dorshtike oygn di vaytn me mest
> Un tsu kvure vil keyner itst brengen keyn mes.
>
> Ligt der mes oyfn veg, s'iz vi shrift zayn gebeyn.
> S'zaynen foystn farshtart un tsum himl—di tseyn.

Nor di geyers farbaygeyn un tsrik kumen on,
Un dem mes unter pakhve farrukt m'hot a fon

Mit oyfshrift mit heln, mit oysyes royt:
—Der toyter in lebn zol lebn in toyt!

The day drags on, drags on and pines away
who by hammer and who by sickle.

Mobs command and swear on the sun
And I with a spade for burial earth.

The heart's flooded, stitched closed in fever.
I will rise up to you and tell you this:

Now with thirsty eyes measure the distance
No one wants to bear a corpse to burial.

The corpse lies on the path, bones like metal type
Fists frozen rigid, teeth toward heaven.

Only wanderers come and go
A flag shoved under the cadaver's armpit

Inscribed with gleaming red letters:
—May the one dead in life live long in death![62]

These verses undercut Jewish religious imagery with state idiom. The false sanctity of the fallen soldier is grotesquely shoved against the Hebraic *oysyes* (letters) of Jewish mysticism, colored red for blood and revolution. The corpses' bones resemble *shrift,* handwriting in a manuscript or the typographical letters placed on a printing press. The image echoes exhibition photographs of boots and wallets sewn from desecrated Torah scrolls. The refrain of the Yom Kippur prayer *Unetanneh tokef*—"who by water and who by fire, who by sword and who by beast"—is radically parodied with "Who by hammer, and who by sickle." Communist emblems become instruments of the death penalty for sins. The sole passersby are *geyers,* wandering messianic figures of Jewish lore; a devastated, apocalyptic landscape is populated only by corpses and these mythical wanderers. Markish satirizes the attempt to posthumously co-opt a soldier's body into an emblem: "A flag is shoved under the cadaver's armpit." The poetic speaker witnesses this attempt to give meaning and symbol to the immeasurability of death by the crude gesture of shoving a flag beneath the soldier's armpit—rather than burying the soldier's corpse under a flag. This image is as brutal as any in Friedrich's photo book.

David Markish's Russian translation shifts this poem from protest to elegy.[63] The Yiddish line "Lign der meys oyfn veg, s'iz vi shrift zayn gebeyn / S'zaynen foystn farshtart un tsum himl—di tseyn" becomes in Russian "Krichat' na doroge kostei pis'mena / I prosiatsia v zemliu zubov semena" ("the soldier's teeth do not face the sky but become seeds, begging to be returned to the earth as their corpse longs to be buried").[64] David Markish deletes the image of a national flag in the soldier-corpse's armpit, replacing it with the footsteps of indifferent people erasing the "cuneiform" of bones. The rhyme *royt/toyt* (red/dead) does not carry over to Russian, but the burning red letters here speak anew: "Let the *signs* of the departed live, speak!" The body becomes a semiotic system, its bones and teeth their own monuments of memory. The apparition of war-ravaged bodies rattles this highly expressionist passage in Part 2:

> Es shvartsn tsum himl zikh foystike festungs—
> Firshtokike kvorim far brider un shvester.
>
> Antkegn di fentserlekh—grinsn un nest,
> Un taykhn fun untn—di spre tsi der dniester.
>
> In shteynerne shtaygn fun khoyshekh farshtekt
> Hungern shvester tsu fertsiker teg.
>
> Tsu fertsiker teg un tsu fertsiker nekht
> Dos moyl nit ge'efnt un oyg—nit fartrert . . .
>
> Zey hungern herlekh un shtolts un getray
> Un khoven mit letstinke reges dem shtrayk.
>
> Mit letstinke reges fun lebn un layb,
> Nor dakh iz fun shteyn un der himl iz blay . . .
>
> In brust in farbrenter, in layb in fardarts,
> Shtelt op azoy shtil zikh un langzam dos harts.
>
> In dorshtikn fiber, in bren un in turem,
> Trikenen langzam di odern oys.
>
> N'bay nakht iber festung, bay nakht iber turem
> Onlaybike kumen zey libn dem shturem . . .

S'iz hel in arum, un s'iz likht umetum,
Un zey kern zikh mer in di shtaygn nit um.

Un nokh dem iz fintster fun droung di gas
Un s'shrayen di shteyner fun tsorn un has.

Un s'trogn zikh droendik gasn aleyn
Mit flamike fonen, mit flamen gebeyn.

Fortress-fists rise, blackening heaven
Four-storied graves for brothers and sisters.

Across small windows—foliage and nest,
Underneath, rivers: Spree stretching to Dniester.

In stony cages of forced darkness
Sisters hunger for forty days.

For forty days and forty nights
Mouth unopened and eye, untearful

They starve in splendor and pride and devotion
And rear the strike with their final moments.

With final moments of life and body
But the roof is stone and the sky is lead . . .

In burning breast, in withered body
Calm and slow, the heart stops.

In thirsty fever, in fire and ferment,
Veins slowly drain out.

At night over the fortress, at night over the spire
They come bodiless to sex the storm . . .

It's bright around them, it's bright everywhere
And they never return to their cages.

Later the street is dark with threat
Stones shriek with rage and hate.

Streets of menace carry along
Flaming flags, blazing skeletons.[65]

Famished inmates turn to hunger striking, and the temporal unit of "forty" transforms from a period of holy wandering into a prison sentence. David Markish's Russian translation heightens the anarchic image of the final couplet: "And the streets await, and the Law trembles / in the flame of bodies and the fire of banners" ("I ulitsy zhdut, i drozhit Zakon / v plamene tel i v pozhare znamion"). Marching skeletons and hungry rising spirits enter a cinematic sequence informed by the visual culture of anarchist agitation. Among those influences is likely the anti-militarist film *J'accuse* (1919) by Abel Gance, which was screened in the USSR.[66] Its final sequence lingers on the disfigured faces of uniformed soldiers, some chemically melted or with heads wrapped in white cotton. Skeletons appear among the crowd; the wounded masses are multiplied through a bug-eye lens. These men were a hidden population, nicknamed *les gueules cassess* (the broken mugs).[67] The mass dissemination of Gance's anarcho-expressionist film, Friedrich's *Krieg dem Kriege!*, and Tsernikover's pogrom photographs and testimonies documenting the pogroms inform the anti-militarist visual landscape of *The Man of Forty*. Markish's surging crowd of migrant laborers scenes appear as though filmed with Gance's fractal lens:

> Sun-browned and bronze-blinded,
> chestnut tree–bodied, bough-handed.
>
> Torn caps upon smokecurls of hair,
> wider than long is the twentieth year.
>
> Not by the sands and not by the border—
> in the middle of the day and at the road's center.
>
> Mountain-stretch boys, youth of the steppe—
> pathmakers straight from the cities they rep.
>
> They tear from the streets, like bootsoles their flesh.
> In one hand—a spade, in the other—bread.
>
> Storm-cloud kettles, smoke-filled kettles.
> Hands scatter paths through exalted pinnacles.
>
> For whom comes burden and for whom comes cheer,
> and asphalt flows in layer upon layer.
>
> It drowns in the deep, it drowns in the heights
> with pitch and with tar, with blood and with might.

My mouth's seamed in fever and hunger ache.
I rise to you and to you I will say:

> —We, path-drivers like brilliant horses,
> the span of the earth merely suffices for us.

> The distance the earth and the light of day—
> We joyfully await our revelers!

> A path in the future, a path falls unknown:
> —*Willkommen,* new generations, to visit our bones . . . ![68]

In the final couplet, Markish uses the German word *Willkommen* for ironic effect, a sardonic tendency which Pomerantz also noted.[69]

Amid the wounded masses and churning factories of these verses, erotic embodiment still courses through shattered bodies. Indeed, a primary aspect of the poema's resistant aesthetics is the search for pleasure and discovery of beauty in the world, amid its relentless brutality. *Hefker* again appears as erotic keyword: "Oyb broyt oyf der vog, oyb ru in der ray— / Zol meydl zayn hefker, zol libe zayn fray!" ("If bread's in the balance, if peace waits its turn— / Let a girl be wild [*hefker*], let love be free!")[70]

The second book of *The Man of Forty*—which Markish considered unfinished—grows denser and more obscure with political reference: bureaucratic agencies, diplomats, chancellors, Social Democrats, bishops, imperial eagles, and attachés appear in flashes, then dissolve into abstraction. Ownerless spaces and unbound horizons melt into bureaus and states. Here his vision of liberation hits the constraint of racial imagination: he gazes internationally, toward children laboring in the rice fields of China and India and, most graphically, the Black victims of lynching in the United States. These poems repeat racist caricatures and fetishized hero-figures of Soviet poster art, populated by giant striding Black men and rarely Black women. Part 2 names the brutality of U.S. lynchings and agricultural slave labor in India and China, portending apocalyptic global violence in a mystical-political sequence recalling late Blake. Poem 27 of Part 2 portrays the lynching of a Black man and racializes his suffering body horrifically, lingering on the image of tortured dark skin. Markish repeats the grotesque tropes found in Yiddish North American anti-lynching poetry; the description of this body lacks the densely metaphoric language with which *Di kupe* speaks of Jewish death.

The Man of Forty instrumentalizes the bodies of women as metaphors for earth, industry, and desire. Gender difference is not dissolved in the sweep of these verses, nor in Markish's other work. In Poem 13 of *To a Jewish Dancer* (1940), for example, a woman's hair is transformed into harp strings for the poetic narrator to strum, submitting her beauty to be used for male artistic virtuosity, as Yves Klein used his nude female models' hair as his brush. Markish celebrates industry through metaphors of sexual conquest:

> Yungfroyish rufn di trakhtn fun dr'erd:
> —Kumt tsu undz, kumt, un farlangt un bagert!

> It beckons like virgins, the earth's uterus:
> —With passion and lust, come, come to us![71]

From the innermost parts of the earth, wellsprings erupt; lust for production circulates from mine-shafts to mills, from Siberia to the Urals, and the throats of chimneys moan:

> Es fibern berg vi di hiftn fun dr'erd
> —Kumt tsu undz, kumt, un farlangt un bagert!

> Mountains grow feverish like the earth's hips:
> —Come to us, come, with desire and wish![72]

Does his ventriloquism of the land's lust for its own conquest ironize Soviet rhetoric? Markish's feminine metaphors for the earth's submission register uneasily: can his cry for universal brotherhood include other kinships? Or, in this vision, will sexist conventions persist after borders are abolished?

Following the suite of internationalist poems, *Fertsikyeriker*'s final pages return to the eroticism that gleams in the poema like shafts of light in gothic ruins:

> Un makhnes nokh makhnes in freyd kumen on.
> Me hert nit keyn fokh un keyn flater fun fon.

> S'iz ponimer hele, vi fonen kayor,
> Un ale iz farshtendlekh un zunik un klor.

> Un vint tsum badinen, un vint tsum bafel,
> Un keynem gemitn, un keynem gefelt!

> A tog vi a kavn tseshnitn oyf helft—
> Un s'shtromt fun im zaft, un s'shtromt fun im hel.

> Un zunenzaft gist zikh, zunenzaft kvelt,
> Un s'vilt oyf di hent itst zikh nemen di velt.

Pamelekh zi nemen, tsuzamen, in eynem.
—Ot dort iz a vund nokh, ot do tut nokh vey . . .

Ot do nit farheylt nokh, ot dort nokh a shram,
Un ergets nokh trifndik vundfleysh faran.

Az borves iz zi nokh, oyf gloz nokh ir trot,
Un s'shtekht zi der krants nokh fun dernerdik drot.

Un vu s'iz farvorlozt, un vu s'iz farbrent
Dokh vilt zi zikh nemen azoy oyf di hent.

Pamelekh zi nemen, pamelekh, in eynem—
Ot do iz a vund, ot do tut nokh vey . . .

Multitudes upon multitudes arrive with joy.
You hear no ripple of air, no flutter of flag

Faces bright as the flags of dawn
All is knowable here, sun-lit and clear.

And wind to serve, wind to command,
No one shunned, no one absent!

A day like a watermelon sliced open—
Juice streams out, bright streams out.

Sun-sap pours forth, sun-sap gushes,
You long to grab the whole world in your hands.

Slowly take her, together as one.
—Oh there's still a wound, here it still aches . . .

Here it's unhealed, ay, there's still a scar
somewhere a flesh wound's still oozing.

Barefoot still! Stepping on glass,
she's stung by a wreath of thorny wire.

There she's neglected, here she's singed
still you long to hold her in your arms.

Slowly take her, slowly as one—
Oh there's still a wound, here it still aches . . .[73]

Masses assemble, without ideology: "no flutter of flag / faces bright as the flags of dawn." In this moment of lucidity, banners and slogans are replaced by the irreducible human face, rebuking the earlier image of a flag shoved in the armpit of a corpse, reducing the sum of a life's sacrifice to a flag. The body of the earth remains libidinous, wounded, and barefoot. The image of stepping upon a "wreath of thorny wire" ("Az borves iz zi nokh, oyf gloz nokh ir trot, / Un s'shtekht zi der krants nokh fun dernerdik drot") evokes and disrupts the symbol of Jesus's crown of thorns: *drot* (wire) repeats Markish's electro-head, wires emerging from its neck, the fallen and unredeemed twentieth century. In David Markish's Russian translation, there is no trodden wreath of wire but "a crown of thorns stings his forehead," which foregrounds its messianic undertones.

The space between Peretz Markish's Yiddish and David Markish's Russian speaks of the dissonance between the text's internal poetics and the historical world it negotiates. In Poem 38, which closes *Fertsikyeriker man,* Peretz Markish uses no state vocabulary; nature and animals are replaced with industry and machines, but there is no nation-building, only unnamed *land* (land or territory). The ox is replaced by the tractor, and great mountains crack open like walnuts, making the land itself raw foodstuff. David Markish's Russian rendition appends national utopia, personified as a steel body:

> Day comes over the world like the tide.
> Its breath is the wind, and the wind is a call:
>
> "—The young country's slender body
> Needs legs forged of Bulat steel!"
>
> There, where the ox once pulled its plow,
> Let the tractor run, tall and thundering.
>
> And where it runs—for days on end,
> May its soot and fumes delight the peasant.[74]

The full stanza "The young country's slender [*stroinyi*] body / Needs legs forged of Bulat steel" has no equivalent in the Yiddish. In choosing to add the detail of Bulat steel to his Russian translation, David Markish trades on an alloy material with a long Russian lineage, used in medieval weaponry and perhaps adapted from Persian forging techniques. *Stroiyniy* connotes a muscular physique, sharing the root with "building construction," to echo the slogan *stroit' komunizm* (build communism). The image of a "young country" in need of legs makes the land in need of a man-made prosthetic: the nation is a bionic body forged from its territory. This relation between the land, the nation, and the body of the worker is elaborated in its final stanza:

> But the hands reach out like a pine forest—
> To raise the young country to the heavens.
>
> So year after year, let them compete:
> Kolkhoz against kolkhoz, factory against factory.[75]

Pine forests are replaced by factories, and the human body is likened to forests that once grew, each superseding the other. The Russian translation enlarges workshops to factories and farms. Peretz Markish's Yiddish word *tsekh* (guild or good company) is not carried into the Russian, whose word *tsekh* signifies the factory floor. Women and children disappear from the Russian translation, and disembodied "hands" are centered. The working body's need for material rapidly outstrips the land ("They're toiling efficiently, hand over hand . . . / There just isn't enough raw material yet").

Ending with the bionic nation, communist and anarchist elements coexist in complex tension. The Yiddish does not conclude with the reification of a named nation; its union of humanity and nature is no longer spiritual union, but supersession and replacement. Far from the ecotopian Caucasian mountains of *Yerushe*, *The Man of Forty* ends with industrial consummation. Read non-teleologically, the poema as a whole contains polyvalent politics, its anarchist aesthetics interpenetrating Soviet commitments. The Russian translation consistently foregrounds the hegemonic industrial voice of the poema. Peretz Markish's poetic structure often subverts the slogan of the first line through the irony of the second line; the Russian rendition extends the first line's vocal without the second line's following critique.

LEV SYRKIN'S ARTWORK IN THE MAN OF FORTY

Initially, I had assumed that Lev Syrkin's line drawing of a severed head embossed on the cover of *The Man of Forty* refers to the "electro-head" in Markish's *Khalyastre* manifesto. Broken wires protrude from its neck, with brow furrowed and chin stubbled; one of its amputated hands seems to grasp a clod of sprouting earth. I later learned from Syrkin's daughter Eva Belavsky that he had selected this image from an existing series titled *One Hundred Heads,* and it depicts the artist holding his own heart in his severed hand.[76] The two Russian Jewish men never met, and Syrkin selected drawings from his existing portfolio

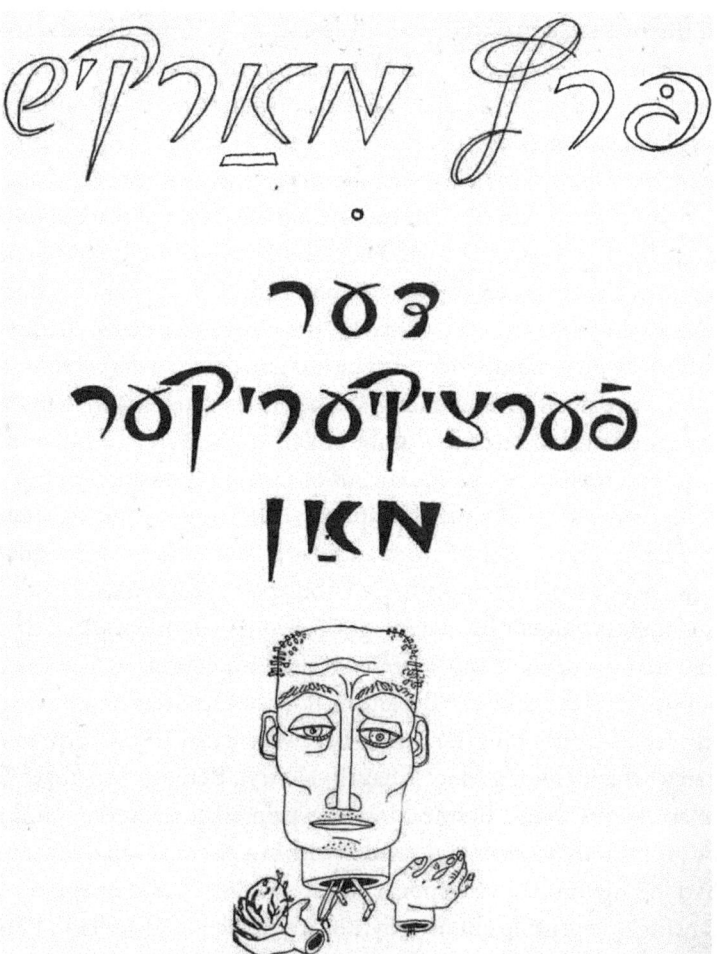

Lev Syrkin's image of an "electro-head" illustrates the cover of
The Man of Forty. (Courtesy of Lev Syrkin Estate)

for *The Man of Forty* after reading David Markish's Russian translation. As Gerald Nordland notes, these works "deal with the same themes of life experience—a parallel suite of drawings which show a startling common view, and they complement the poem with telling accuracy."[77] That the art precedes the poem—and the Russian translation precedes the Yiddish in print—reverses the expected chronology and hierarchy between art and letters, text and "illustration."

Syrkin's and Markish's visual imaginations resonate uncannily, representing perhaps representing as Syrkin's daughter remarked, a "mystical connection"

between the two unacquainted Russian Jewish men. From their densely metaphoric treatment of violence to visualizations of ritual time, Syrkin and Markish call and respond across media. Syrkin, though not religiously observant, in-
tegrates religious themes throughout. He gifted "Shabbat" (1978), another ink
drawing in *The Man of Forty,* to Menachem Mendel Schneerson, leader of the
Chabad-Lubavitch movement. The rabbi hung it in pride of place above his bed
throughout his life.[78] Facsimiles of Markish's handwriting beside Syrkin's ink
drawings show the two men's complete commitment to line: rarely does Markish cross out a single verse, and Syrkin does not correct the marks made with pen
and ink. Both of their handiwork must be imagined first in detail, fully committed to, and wrought in a single long stroke. Their symbolic systems visualize
Jewish temporality, bordered and unbounded landscapes of Zion and Russia,
and biblical intertextuality. To the corpus of Jewish idiom and symbology, Syrkin adds his own system of visual metaphors: a dancing, devouring alligator appears repeatedly, representing Soviet authoritarianism and the presence of the
devil, with a whole city in its mouth. Crumbling cities are crested by hourglasses,
suggesting their imminent fall; an image of a woman in orientalized dress dancing with a man in peasant cap represents the bifurcations of Russian society.
Their elongated faces evoke the Byzantine lines of Orthodox icons.

Syrkin (1929–2012) joins the cohort of Jewish artists who interpreted Markish's visual world, including Marc Chagall, Henryk Berlewi, and Yosef Chaikov.
The human figures found beside Markish's printed texts never stand straight
upon the ground; they hover and revolve within a circle or spiral, lifting off into
space. Syrkin's figures likewise appear to tilt within circular or spiral compositions, dancing or gesturing akimbo. Syrkin, a prolific muralist, had an epic sense
for scale and labor that suits Markish's utopian expanses. In the documentary
A Fool's Dream, directed by his son Daniel Syrkin, the artist appears delighted as
trucks rumble past his mosaic: "I like that. It belongs to every passerby. A worker
who works here for twenty years doesn't get tired of it. . . . I wanted to work
where Jews work, where Jewish workers work."[79] His sense of composition was
informed by Kazimir Malevich, Russian suprematism, and Goethe's theories of
color. Syrkin was nominated for the Lenin Prize, which Markish was awarded
and created the largest mural in Europe, two thousand square meters, as well
as the largest mural in Israel, on the wall of a factory near the Dead Sea. Syrkin's
microcosmic approach echoes Markish's abstracted imagery: examining a circle
that in fact depicts the eye of a huge fish in his factory mural, Syrkin explains,
"You can isolate any detail, and it becomes an abstract painting." His "practice
was based on Suprematist geometric forms and designs that oscillated between

Lev Syrkin, "Ivan and Maria," 1974, pen and ink on paper, 25 × 35 cm.
(Courtesy of Lev Syrkin Estate)

the macro and micro worlds. . . . Most of the compositions do not have clear
contours—they overflow the margins and endow the mosaic with dynamism
and vitality. The work's components are usually composed of a form within a
form, each of which constitutes a whole in itself."[80]

Syrkin's drawings are at once monumental and microcosmic. The compositions are often circular, curling at the edges into flags, ship sails, clouds, licking
flames. The space spans folkloric Russia and ancient Jerusalem, the domes of
Moscow appearing near the Mount of Olives. The first printed image in *The
Man of Forty* is filled with foreboding: a man with a Dostoevskian beard and a
woman with a villager's kerchief are framed within a yoke, its buckets broken
and tumbling, water spilling as a portent of catastrophe to come.[81] The motif
of the water-bearing yoke repeats in the final image selected to "illustrate" the
book, and it again unites a couple beneath a yoke—here, a reparative image of
a healed yoke. The female figure reclines, breasts exposed beneath a fantastical
collar. The couple's arms reach toward one another, around the yoke that rests
on their heads, resembling sabbath candlesticks. Her features are sparely drawn,
and he has a fleshy nose and lips, a Russian embroidered collar, and thick hand.
The rim of the image ripples and billows.

Lev Syrkin, "The Concertina," 1975, pen and ink on paper, 25 × 35 cm.
(Courtesy of Lev Syrkin Estate)

The juxtaposition of Syrkin's and Markish's lines generates cross-temporal exchanges. In one ink drawing, an androgynous, decadent poet with a fantastical hat holds an umbrella and lifts a tiny mouse in the other: "Famine."[82] In *Aesthetics of Struggle,* Markish also "ridicules the grotesque figure of the dandy that is dependent only on external forms of expression."[83] Another of Syrkin's striking compositions balances a man playing the concertina and a woman dancing with abandon. Its perspective hovers directly above the man, his face turned away; yet the woman who shares the page is seen frontally, as though we join her on the dance floor. Her garments are floridly Orientalized; he wears a peasant's cap. The concertina is the focal point, expanding beyond possibility, as though this modest instrument were granted infinite range. Perhaps this is a czarina dancing with the masses.[84] One of the most harrowing scenes evokes Guernica or, suggests Eva Belavsky, Max Beckmann's birth painting.[85] One female figure reclines, arms and legs spread, head thrown back; from her emerges a train.[86] The lines are interrupted, breaking the usual long gestural figure of Syrkin's women. And in the final image of *The Man of Forty,* despite its utopian structure, a bar-

Lev Syrkin, "The Agony," 1975, pen and ink on paper, 25 × 35 cm.
(Courtesy of Lev Syrkin Estate)

rier remains between the two lovers, and ambivalent faces appear as hidden details. This rhymes with the ending of Markish's work, an intensely erotic vision
within which pain persists in the form of glass beneath bare feet, like a groom
crushing a glass during the wedding.

The metaphoric flights of violence in Markish's verse sear Syrkin's line drawings, particularly in the giant figure of Mother Russia. With kerchief on her
head and sickle on her back, a patched coat revealing her undergarments, she
leaps in midair, the flag held aloft in her hand summoning a highway of souls
from the village. At her side, an Orthodox church tilts like the Tower of Pisa,
and women draw water from a village well. Balancing the composition, on the
left is a cluster of houses and a bottle of vodka with a flag at the top, like a Mo-
lotov cocktail.

During our conversation, Eva Belavsky pulled down the copy of *Fertsik-*
yeriker man that her father had annotated and read part of his inscriptions, written on June 12, 1984, while they traveled in Europe:

> This trip would have never happened, had your parents not broken free
> from the grim country that had destroyed Yiddish culture. . . .

Peretz Markish was thinking about Russian affairs in the Jewish language. And in my drawings, I was thinking in Russian about our Jewish
fate. . . .

My drawings for this book are not illustrations but my own poem
about the past; I want to believe that you, our children, will never have
to live through it.[87]

Belavsky emphasized the significance of Syrkin's inscribing *The Man of Forty* in
Basel, site of the First Zionist Congress in 1897. Tracing Markish's visions of
liberation across the linked realms of temporality, territory, and embodiment
remains a partial reading of this enigmatic, exhilarating text, which speaks in the
highest language of Communist ideals to David Markish, Zionist aims for Lev
Syrkin, and anarchist limitlessness to this translator.

Written by a deportee behind Earth's longest border, the poema prefigures a
restless space with "no flutter of flag," where the earth exceeds and overthrows
its borders. As the anarchist reviewer Ahrne Goldberg wrote in 1923, Markish
"storms the Yiddish Bastille" and "sings with wind and hurricanes, with the creative unrest of a furious world . . . carrying within himself the strengths of Pro-

Lev Syrkin, "The Village," pen and ink on paper, 17.5 × 25 cm.
(Courtesy of Lev Syrkin Estate)

metheus to hasten and scorch worlds and build other, more beautiful worlds in their place."[88] Goldberg's reading of Markish shows that "for anarchists, the act of interpretation is also a creative act."[89] Markish's reclamation of religious genealogy and luminous inhabitation of *atsind* (nowness) remain both explosively modernist and profoundly Jewish. In spite of—or perhaps to spite—Soviet state ownership of time, of his time, Markish's writing prefigures another temporality, neither an untroubled utopia deferred after the revolution nor a co-opted past, but a present containing all possibility within itself, despite it all: "A day like a watermelon sliced open—Juice streams out, bright streams out."

PART FOUR

Language Politics

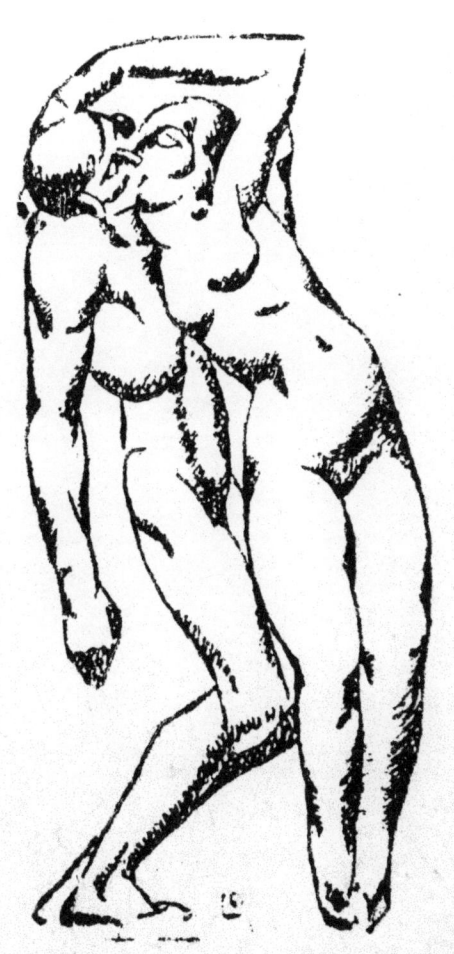

CHAPTER VII

"*Language Is Migrant*"

TRANSLATION AND DEPORTATION

MULTILINGUALISM AND FREE SPEECH LAW: ABRAMS V. UNITED STATES

Mollie Steimer gazed out from the high window. Below lay East Broadway, perhaps glowing with night cafeterias, Seward Park shadowed by treetops, workers arriving by the hundreds, voices rising. Steimer held sheafs of broadsides of *Frayheyt* (Freedom) in her hands. Its motto was an anarchist reworking of a maxim used by Henry David Thoreau: "Yene regirung iz di beste, velkhe regirt in gantsn nit" (That government is best which governs not at all). Perhaps she sorted the pamphlets—clutching the Yiddish ones in one hand, English in the other—and released them, like the sails of white ships down East Broadway. The *Frayheyt* group was so prodigious at rooftop distribution that a rumor arose: the Yiddish anarchists of Manhattan had their own aircraft![1]

The *Frayheyt* pamphlets called for a general strike against production of ammunitions that would be used against Russian revolutionaries in a military intervention by President Woodrow Wilson. Factory workers picked up the scattered broadsides and called the police; one of the editors, Hyman Rosansky, was beaten into a confession about his comrades' whereabouts.[2] By afternoon, headlines blared: "Seditious Circulars Scattered in Streets"; "Wilson Attacked in Circulars from Roofs of East Side." Law enforcement had pursued the *Frayheyt* editors for months, but the group remained elusive. After the Espionage Act passed in 1917 and printers refused to publish their circulars, they began using a small hand-press in their shared flat in Harlem and hand-delivered copies to city mailboxes under cover of night.[3] Police arrested the editors and severely beat Jacob Schwartz, author of the Yiddish pamphlet. The arresting officers were unable to read Yiddish themselves.[4]

Yiddish anarchist language politics were less a matter of habitus or multiculturalism than a tactic of negotiating state censorship. The Frayheyt editors' propagandistic strategy reflected their language politics, which questioned: How can a monolingual court assure free speech when dissidence is expressed in a minor language? The first major prosecution of writers under the Sedition Act was *Abrams v. United States,* 250 U.S. 616, which charged Steimer and her Russian comrades in a trial fraught with erroneous translations. With a majority of 7–2, the court upheld the decision that the Espionage Act does not violate the First Amendment.[5] Steimer was sentenced to fifteen years in prison and a $500 fine and ultimately deported in 1921 in a prisoner exchange, whose details were never disclosed to her.[6] David Rabban argues that "the *Abrams* dissent marked the transformation of [Oliver Wendell] Holmes and [Louis D.] Brandeis into defenders of free speech."[7] Crucially, this crackdown on the radical press unfolded in an age of mass multilingual printing. In Manhattan in 1913, there were more than 280 book binderies; by 1917, these employed about 4,000 men and 5,000 women, who produced all manner of pamphlets, books, calendars, and other printed matter through arduous work.[8]

Upon immigrating to New York City from Dunaivtsi, Ukraine, Steimer quickly became radicalized by working in a factory and reading Kropotkin, Bakunin, and Goldman. She joined a group of about twenty anarchists who printed *Frayheyt,* including the Russian-born Jacob Abrams (1886–1953), who had married a survivor of the Triangle Shirtwaist fire. At the center of the case was *Frayheyt*'s manifesto, printed in two editions of five thousand copies in both English and Yiddish. The Yiddish pamphlet was only translated after the anarchists were arrested, and the courtroom translation had a number of errors.[9] The English text was written by Sam Lipman, who, like all the *Frayheyt* writers, was not a native speaker of English. When taking him into custody, Yiddish-illiterate police officers asked whether the two pamphlet versions said the same thing. The editor, Hyman Lachowsky, replied, "There are some words a little different, but they are the same." However, the Yiddish version by Jacob Schwartz was more strident, demanding a general strike in support of the Russian revolutionaries: "Let the government not frighten you with its wild penalties of imprisonment, hanging and shooting.... Three hundred years the Romanovs have taught us how to fight. Let all rulers remember this, from the smallest to the biggest despot, that the hand of the revolutionary will not tremble in the fight. Woe to those who stand in the way of progress! Solidarity lives. [Signed,] REBELS." It confronts its readers in the second person, demanding a new international kinship of the working class: "Workers in the ammunition factories, you are producing bullets, bayonets, cannon, to murder not only the Germans, but also your dearest, best, who are in Russia and are fighting for freedom." The English version demanded: "Will you allow the Russian Revolution to be crushed? YOU; yes, we mean YOU, the people of America! . . . The Russian Revolution cries: 'WORKERS OF THE WORLD! AWAKE! RISE! PUT DOWN YOUR ENEMY AND MINE!' Yes, friends, there is only one enemy of the workers of the world and that is CAPITALISM."[10]

Frayheyt's English-language text recorded its editors' speech patterns. Lines such as "Three hundred years had the Romanoff dynasty taught us how to fight" use Yiddish syntax, with the verb in the second position of the sentence. The English manifesto also includes Yiddish colloquialisms such as "God forbid" and emphatic repetitive syntax ("The destruction of the Russian Revolution, that is the politics of the march to Russia"). Its metaphors are mixed and highly emotive ("Will you be calm spectators to the fleecing blood from the hearts of the best sons of Russia?"). The English pamphlet expresses the language of an Ashkenazi immigrant to readers attuned to accent.

Federal judge Henry DeLamar Clayton, Jr., aligned with President Wilson on most issues, save two: women's suffrage and literacy tests for immigrants, both of which figured in Steimer's case.[11] Clayton maintained that literacy tests would reduce American workers' competition from the "cheap pauper labor of Europe."[12] Richard Polenberg notes, "In 1916, as he empaneled a grand jury in New York City, Clayton declared that even naturalized citizens who 'unfairly' criticized the government 'should get off the face of the earth, or at least go back to the country they left. . . . I have no sympathy with any naturalized citizen who is given to carping criticism of this Government or who cannot say that he loves America first, last, and forever.'"[13] Not only the "foreignness" of Yiddish but the "foreignness" of their accented English was implicated.

Steimer and Abrams were represented by Harry Weinberger, who also defended Goldman, the Mexican revolutionary Ricardo Flores Magón, and the writers Djuna Barnes and Eugene O'Neill.[14] In "A Rebel's Interrupted Autobiography" (1942), Weinberger introduces himself with a patriotic flourish: "I was born of Jewish parents in New York City in 1886, the same year the people of the United States erected the Statue of Liberty in New York Harbor."[15] Weinberger was a charismatic fighter for the First Amendment in cultural and legal spheres.[16] He produced Sholem Asch's lesbian sex-worker romance *God of Vengeance* (*Got fun nekome*) on Broadway in 1923. When an English translation of Asch's play faced fines and charges of obscenity, Weinberger defended it in court with little support from the American Civil Liberties Union, ultimately winning an appeal in the New York State Court of Appeals.[17]

Schwartz died the night before the trial in the hospital ward of Bellevue prison, where the influenza pandemic ran rampant. Official records attribute his death to influenza; his comrades asserted that he was "brutally murdered" by the police.[18] In a letter written from his cell following his torture and interrogation, Schwartz nonetheless wrote defiantly: "What are the red spots of blood on our clothings in comparison with the greatness of our Ideal! Our Ideal is the future. They are the Past."[19] In addition to this English letter, Schwartz left in his Tombs cell a Yiddish note: "Farewell, comrades. When you appear before the court I will be with you no longer. Struggle without fear, fight bravely. I am sorry I have to leave you. But this is life itself."[20] Steimer recalled watching detectives leave Schwartz's cell after torturing him and the sight of a bloody handkerchief across his mouth.[21] Memorial rallies and a Russian funeral march were held for Schwartz on the anniversary of his death; John Reed recited poetry and mourners sang revolutionary songs as they streamed into the streets.[22]

Abrams and Steimer used the courtroom as a platform for propaganda, in the tradition of Haymarket. Steimer defined anarchism plainspokenly:

> By anarchism I understand a new social order, where no group of people shall be in power, no group of people shall be governed by another group of people. Individual freedom shall prevail in the full sense of the word. Private ownership shall be abolished. Every person shall have an equal opportunity to develop himself well, both mentally and physically. We shall not have to struggle for our daily existence as we do now. No one shall live on the product of others. Every person shall produce as much as he can, and enjoy as much as he needs—receive according to his need. Instead of striving to get money, we shall strive towards education, towards knowledge. While at present the people of the world are divided into various groups, calling themselves nations, while one nation defies another—in most cases considers the others as competitive—we, the workers of the world, shall stretch out our hands towards each other with brotherly love. To the fulfillment of this idea I shall devote all my energy, and, if necessary, render my life for it.[23]

Steimer explains anarchism to the court as the process of freedom-seeking and social flourishing. She views "brotherly love" not as a distant philosophical ideal but a goal achievable through mutual aid; universal kinship rather than citizenship can transform social relations. Her defense does not oppose law as an institution, as had occurred in earlier trials of anarchists. Many deportees had fervently hoped that, unlike the Russian Empire, the United States would guarantee their freedom of speech in order to organize for working-class liberation. Their court testimonies hailed free speech as an American ideal—albeit one not yet realized.[24] Abrams referred to "our forefathers of the American Revolution," for example, to which Judge Clayton responded, "Do you mean to refer to the fathers of this nation as your forefathers? Well, I guess we can leave that out, too, for Washington and the others are not on trial here." Abrams elaborated: "I have respect for them. We are a big human family, and I say 'our forefathers.' Those that stand for the people, I call them fathers."[25] Like Parsons at the Haymarket trial, the defendants appealed to the First Amendment, which converged with anarchist ideals. This phenomenon was particular to the United States, unlike tactics advanced by Errico Malatesta and others in response to European anti-semitism and fascism.[26]

Ultimately the *Frayheyt* editors Mollie Steimer, Jacob Abrams, Hyman Lachowsky, and Samuel Lipman were charged with sedition in the 1918 Supreme Court case *Abrams v. United States* 250 U.S. 616, which ruled 7–2 that the Espionage Act does not violate the First Amendment. Other members of *Frayheyt* and their comrades organized a group that succeeded in freeing the four from prison, at the cost of their deportation to Russia. Steimer herself objected to the petition for amnesty, writing to Weinberger: "I do not want any pardon. The word 'pardon' drills my ears and affects my sense of right, which is bad already." She objected to deportation on the basis of her belief that "each person shall live where he or she chooses": "No individual has the right to send me out of this, or of any country!"[27] It took a few attempts to move Steimer to Ellis Island: first she refused to be moved until all political prisoners were free.[28] Then she refused to be transported during a railroad strike, declaring "I'm not going to go on a train that's led by scabs."[29] Wardens were forced to wait ten days longer for the strike to end. She was deported on the *S.S. Estonia* on November 24, 1921, with Samuel Lipman, Hyman Lachowsky, and Jack Abrams, accompanied by his wife, Mary. When they arrived, Bolsheviks had already repressed the Kronstadt rebellion, and Emma Goldman and Alexander Berkman had already departed, disillusioned.[30]

Steimer, Abrams, Berkman, and other deportees faced a tragic trajectory, their attempts at anti-military speech instigating a series of deportations from multiple nations. Anarchist free speech must then be understood as a trans-national struggle, with First Amendment law representing only one link. Avrich notes that the Union of Russian Workers and other groups' main organizers were "only to be imprisoned or shot in the cellars of the Bolshevik secret police. Victims of the Red Scare in America, they ended as victims of the Red Terror in Russia."[31] In November 1922, Steimer was arrested in the Soviet Union for "participating in an underground organization which is rendering aid to the imprisoned Anarchists and of having connections with Europe and America."[32] Abrams and Steimer, deported from the United States for criticizing capitalism and militarism, were then expelled from the Soviet Union in 1923 for criticizing Bolshevism.

During exile in Berlin, Steimer wrote that her second expulsion was far more painful than her deportation from the United States. She criticized the Bolshevik regime: "Espionage overshadows all thought, all creative effort and action.... Thousands of workers, students, men and women of high intellectual attainments, as well as undeveloped but intelligent peasants, are languishing today in Soviet prisons. The world is told they are counter-revolutionists and bandits. Though they are the most idealistic and revolutionary flower of Russia, they are charged with all sorts of false charges before the world."[33] Her anarchist critique of speech repression extended from the rooftops of Manhattan through France, Germany, and Soviet Russia, where she was continually deported for anti-militarism and anti-authoritarianism.

After two decades in Paris and Berlin, Steimer traveled to Mexico in 1942 with a Nansen passport, the document issued by the League of Nations to stateless subjects of the former Russian Empire.[34] There, Abrams became indispensable to Jewish community culture and opened a successful printing shop. Friends hailed his contributions in the material labor of printing, rather than through writing or composition: "If he himself didn't write stylish Yiddish, it didn't matter—his colleagues stylized his passionate writing for him."[35] Both Steimer and Abrams—and their fights—were remembered reverently. The Mexican Yiddish poet Isaac Berliner, who had befriended Abrams and cared for him during his illness, wrote in his memorial book: "I don't now want to seek the synthesis of Abrams, the human being and the Jew. Abrams was very far from Jewish tradition and national Jewishness. His motto—an equal world for everyone—did not allow him to single himself out from the ordinary world. Therefore, the Jewishness inside him didn't smolder separately; rather, it became an integral part of the human race."[36] Steimer's memorial book, *Toda Una Vida de Lucha: La Rebellion de Una Anarquista Condenada Por Ambos Imperios* (A Lifetime of

Struggle: The Rebellion of an Anarchist Condemned by Both Empires), includes Juan Goytisolo, the Spanish poet. More than fifty years later, Hilda Kovner, a member of *Frayheyt,* reminisced, "That was holy work, you know, to distribute our literature, to spread the word."[37]

GENDERING SEDITION: EMMA GOLDMAN
AND LANGUAGE POLITICS

Since the rise of anti-statist movements and the mass exile of French Communards to the South Pacific, deportation has disciplined anarchists and controlled the press.[38] Among the U.S. deportees of 1919 were Alexander Berkman and Emma Goldman, the editors of the English-language anarchist journal *Mother Earth,* for agitating against conscription. Two years earlier, Goldman had been charged under the Comstock Laws for lecturing in Yiddish on birth control. The Sedition Act extended the Espionage Act of 1917, which criminalized "willfully" obstructing military recruitment, "insubordination, disloyalty, mutiny, or refusal of duty."

Charges of sedition and obscenity hinged not only on *what* was said but also on the linguistic and gendered expression of these Jewish anarchists' speech— particularly of the women. Only two cases of federal censorship of Yiddish material are documented: *Abrams v. United States* and a sexual health pamphlet. The cases involving Abrams, Steimer, Berkman, and Goldman established legal precedent against multilingual anti-war sentiment, which linked "obscenity" and "sedition" as forms of unprotected speech: by advocating against militarism and compulsory reproductive labor, Steimer and comrades threatened the production and enlistment of new soldiers. These trials are linked to anarchist uses of language not primarily as expressions of ethnic identity but as strategies to elude state censorship and surveillance. The anarchists demanded full autonomy of the body: freedom of movement, speech, and reproduction, and refusal of conscription. The court decisions in Yiddish free speech cases disciplined the transgression of a *discursive* border by deportation across geographic borders.

Anarchist ephemera implicated in free speech trials—courtroom testimony, prison newspapers, orations, and pamphlets—countered hostile media representations of radical immigrants. Despite the crackdown on anti-militarist writers, the multilingual radical press persisted in spaces of incarceration, as deportees in Ellis Island's detention center produced handwritten newspapers. While many studies focus on racialization and antisemitism in these prosecutions, centering multilingualism highlights the relation between linguistic and political hegemony and court monolingualism. These cases reveal the complexity of immigrant language usage: dissidents' multilingualism offered the possibility of evading censorship, though they still faced preemptive arrests of people in diglossic communities by monolingual police. In the courtroom, Yiddish encountered English-language hegemony, in which judges' literacy tests and anxiety about "foreignness" informed court rulings.

The Steimer-Abrams case linked obscenity and sedition as forms of unprotected speech: by advocating against munitions factories, enlistment, and coercive reproduction, Steimer and her comrades threatened militarism and the generation of new soldiers. Though they held opposing views on universal suffrage, Emma Goldman was, like Steimer, keenly supportive of women's reproductive rights. Her sentences for supporting abortion healthcare and opposing militarism followed in quick succession. Goldman was arrested in 1916 for speaking on birth control in Yiddish, for which she served about three weeks.[39] She then served two years for protesting conscription; after her release she was immediately re-arrested by order of J. Edgar Hoover, then director of intelligence for the U.S. Department of Justice. Hoover persuaded the court to deny Goldman's claims to citizenship, and she was deported under the 1918 Alien Act.

During their trials, the court and sensational press fixated upon Goldman's and Steimer's identities as Jewish women. Judge Clayton questioned Steimer and her fellow defendants about "free-love" activity, seeking to humiliate them.[40] One newspaper described Steimer's appearance "as plump as an anarchist bomb," at once hypersexualizing and militarizing her body.[41] Goldman was subjected to the same treatment, as Clare Hemmings notes: "Newspaper reporting portrayed Goldman in ways that secured the representational links between foreignness and political violence, but also simultaneously reduced that threat through a focus on her femininity."[42] Steimer occupies a complex position in a consideration of the paradox of female citizenship: she was at once prosecuted for her anarchism, which opposes enfranchisement as the primary guarantor of human rights, even as she faced other anarchists' censure for her affirmative position on women's suffrage. Like the work of Yevzerov Merison, Goldman's reproductive labor praxis encompassed propagandizing in multiple languages, nursing, and midwifery, even arranging an abortion for her comrade Hilda Adel. Her partner Ben Reitman was a gynecologist serving sex workers in Chicago, and Chaim Weinberg points to the presence of Jewish sex workers at anarchist meetings in Pittsburgh.

Although Jewish culture was historically permissive of free speech, religious taboos against slanderous speech (*loshn-hore*) are crucial cultural practices.[43] Little attention has been given to Goldman's language politics and strategic use of multilingualism. Clare Hemmings offers a closely observed analysis of Goldman's racialization but simplifies her linguistic strategy.[44] In a fictional sequence of letters composed as creative responses to the historical letters Goldman received from her romantic friend Almeda Sperry, Hemmings imagines Goldman writing in 1912: "I have never understood comrades' resistance to spreading the word in whatever tongues we can, as though Yiddish or Russian were somehow purer—such absurd nostalgia for countries that never did them any favors!"[45] Hemmings's imagination of Goldman's language politics nods to Goldman's strategic approach to propagandizing, while it flattens the affective and literary aspects of her actual language use. Hemmings's "vocalization" of Goldman displaces Yiddish and Russian into the nostalgic past, whereas Goldman deployed her multilingualism in complex ways to elude the Comstock Laws, and her non–English-native linguistic identity informed her racialization and sexualization.

Beginning at least in 1908, Emma Goldman lectured in Yiddish on reproductive health topics.[46] These speeches were delivered in Toronto, New York, Los Angeles, and elsewhere, with titles such as "Marriage and the Lot of Children Among the Poor" and "Sex Sterilization of Criminals." For the series where she spoke in both English and Yiddish, the difference is pronounced: in July 1913, for example, her Yiddish lectures included the title "Should the Poor Have Many Children," with no equivalent subject in English.[47] In one letter, she praises Jewish audiences as more sexually enlightened: "I had a very good Jewish meeting Friday night where I spoke on the subject of sex. The audience was unusually earnest. It is always very difficult and embarrassing to talk on things that seem so simple and natural before indiscriminate crowds. They usually come to get some erotic sensation. But I must say that the audience on Friday night put me at ease at once. The discussion too was interesting. If only the English lectures are anything like the Jewish the struggle would not be so hard."[48]

Despite her strategic usage, Goldman's relationship to Yiddish was ambivalent. She reportedly spoke it less confidently than Russian, English, and French, but more so than Spanish.[49] Newsreel footage of Goldman reveals a sharp mid-Atlantic cadence without either Yiddish or Russian accent.[50] Goldman was likely dyslexic and hired typists whenever possible.[51] Although Goldman praised the efforts of the non-Jewish editor Rudolf Rocker in learning Yiddish, she did not conceptualize it as a "workers' language" nor use the rhetoric of Yiddish cultural movements. Observers reported that she preferred to speak in a "plain German," which may mean that she predominantly used the "international" linguistic components of Yiddish, rather than loshn-koydesh. Others recall her speaking pas-

sionately in Yiddish to crowds of eight hundred people, in commemoration of
the Haymarket Affair.[52]

Goldman's letters are filled with Yiddishisms, which may reflect the texture
of her everyday speech. In a note to Mark Mratchnyi in London on January 5,
1937, she writes: "Here is a long megille for the Freie Arb. Shtimme and the
Spanish Revolution." A *megile* is a Purim scroll and, colloquially, signifies a long
story. In another letter to Mratchnyi, written February 4, 1938, on CNT-FAI
letterhead, she jokes about his assimilation using Yiddish phrases: "How is Johanna quite Americanized isn't she? And you, ein ganzer Yankee, was?" (And
you, a real Yankee, eh?) Goldman's letters reveal a native Yiddish speaker translating her thoughts into English, through her usage of punctuation ("they watch
closely, everything, that I do") and dropping prepositions ("in playing dominos," "I sold 800 $ literature"). Her letter to Van Valkenburgh on March 19, 1927
reveals Yiddish syntax: "But who is Liber that one should care?"

In *Living My Life* (1931), Goldman describes her return to lecturing about
literature in Yiddish at smaller events, probably in 1928: "[These friends were]
enthusiastic Judaists, who gathered the Yiddish intelligentsia to attend my lecture on Walt Whitman at their home. They were proud that I was one of their
race, they reiterated. It was worth coming back to Montreal to reach their Yiddish hearts by the grace of the *goi* Walt Whitman."[53] Goldman does not say
whether *she* was "proud that I was one of their race," and she plays on the ambiguity of *yidish,* which could be either "Jewish" or "Yiddish." She dubbed Whitman "the Liberator of Sex" and praised his representations of "the beauty and
wholesomeness of sex . . . freed from the rags and tatters of hypocrisy."[54] No letters in Yiddish from Goldman to her lover Leon Malmed have been located;
her correspondence with him included mainly telegrams. Leon Malmed and his
wife, however, corresponded entirely in Yiddish.[55]

Goldman used Yiddish as a primary language for discussions of sexuality
and circulation of banned material, which led to her sentence for delivering
birth control lectures—in part because it was *not* in English. Yet Goldman vacillated between lecturing in Yiddish to mass assemblies and denying all knowledge of "zhargon."[56] Her literary aesthetic was often interpreted by English-
language critics as a backward-looking Romanticism that compared unfavorably
to the avant-garde. Despite Goldman's often negative views of Yiddish, her
English-language lectures and editorials on art were strongly informed by the
Sweatshop poets. In her 1915 lecture "The Modern Drama as a Mirror of Individual, Class and Social Rebellion Against the Tyranny of the Past," delivered in
English in the resplendent Fine Arts Building in Chicago, Goldman discussed

the Yiddish playwrights Jacob Gordin, Sholem Asch, David Pinski, and Max Nordau.[57]

Whereas Yiddish and German were often found spoken in the same radical spaces, Yiddish and English tended to be proximate as *literary* languages. While Johann Most successfully communicated with Yiddish-speaking audiences through his fiery German, Goldman's attempts to reciprocate were received with incomprehension, according to observers from the Immigration and Naturalization Service:

> The Hall was crowded to the doors by Yiddish speaking people, but owing to the fact that the lecture was given in German, instead of Yiddish, as it was announced, there was a spirit of discontent, and I heard rumors of regret by many people here, saying that they could not follow her. At the end of the lecture Miss Goldman invited the audience to ask her questions and that she would endeavor to answer them. But save for a few very silly questions asked by a couple of young men, who it could be easily perceived could not follow the trend of her lecture, none cared to ask any questions. She scored the women present for the lack of interest displayed by them, by not coming forward and debate with her upon questions paramount to their own welfare, but after waiting a considerable length of time, for answers which failed to come forth, the meeting was closed.[58]

Why would Goldman prefer lecturing in less-intelligible German than in fluent Yiddish? In a letter written in 1916 to a friend who helped arrange her lectures, Goldman even denied knowing Yiddish:

> Of course, I should prefer English meetings. I do not care for Jewish ones, especially since I do not speak Jargon and they will understand English, about as well, as German and also because I want to interest the people all over the Country in our Mag. M. E. [*Mother Earth*] and therefore want to appeal to an English-speaking public. However, I have no objections to one Jewish meeting. You could therefore, have two English and one Jewish gathering.[59]

In another letter, Goldman verges on antisemitic caricatures of mercenary Jews:

> Fr A S always opposed going into the unions, has opposed every strike, every public event. Has acted cowardly, when courage was needed. . . . True there are not many American Comrades, but the few, know at least,

what Anarchism means. They do not sell their Anarchism in real estate, or in playing dominos in restaurants. They live Anarchism and thereby they are having a moral influence, of greater more lasting value, than 10 publications of F Ar S. Did you ever hear the American press or police make a fuss over that paper, or the Jewish propaganda, or Mr Yanovsky? Certainly not. Why do they watch closely, everything, I do? Because I carry our ideas among the Americans, before thousands of people. The fact, that I sold 800 $ literature on my last tour, particularly in cities where there are but few foreigners, shows that there are American interested in Anarchism people who read and that is more, than can be said of the F Arb St gang.[60]

Goldman disparages the *Fraye arbeter shtime* "gang" as beneath surveillance. Despite her aversion to its "provincialism," Yiddish offered some benefits for propagandists. Goldman used Yiddish strategically for discussions of sexuality, in a period when sending information regarding birth control through the mail was highly prosecutable. Margaret Sanger also wrote for Goldman's paper *Mother Earth* and used the anarchist slogan "No Gods! No Masters!" on the masthead of her publication *The Woman Rebel.* Both Goldman and Sanger were arrested for protesting the Comstock Laws, which banned the distribution of information on contraceptives. They framed birth control as an issue of labor, not morality: during the period of Sanger's and Goldman's writing, there were more than 2,000 brothels in the area between Murray Hill and Gramercy Park in New York City. Sex workers there earned $50 per week, in comparison to female garment workers' wages of $6–12 per week.[61]

Goldman's second incarceration in New York City resulted from her speeches on birth control, delivered both in English and Yiddish. After her trial on April 20, 1916, the anarchist Leonard D. Abbott wrote, "This time her offense was that she exposed the evils of indiscriminate and incessant breeding and that she told the poor, in language they could understand, how they might limit their families."[62] In his description of the trial, Abbott notes the discrepancies between how her language use was understood:

> The lecture for which Emma Goldman had been arrested had been delivered at the New Star Casino in New York on February 8th. She had given the same lecture in English and in Jewish half a hundred times in cities throughout the country. Two detectives were put on the stand to testify as to what they had heard. They were so ignorant that they had not known how to spell correctly the words of the indictment they

had framed in connection with Emma Goldman's arrest, and their testimony was inaccurate. They declared that Emma Goldman had spoken at the New Star Casino in German, whereas she had actually spoken in Yiddish. She could have made more than she did of this error, but she refused to take advantage of technicalities and preferred to keep to the main issue.[63]

Abbott's reportage of the trial emphasizes the illiteracy of the detectives, in contrast to Goldman's expertise in multiple languages. It seems that she chose not to shame the prosecutors, a decision consistent with the anti-classism of her original speech and her class analysis of health education access throughout the trial—or perhaps she wished to minimize her public association with Yiddish. Following her sentence of fifteen days in the workhouse of Queen's County Jail, the district attorney's office told the press: "This office has no fault to find with the expression of any honest opinion given in a decent manner. The gravamen of the charge is not the discussion of birth control, but the indecency of the manner in which the subject was presented to a promiscuous audience, in which children of tender years were permitted to be present."[64] In this formulation, Goldman's "manner" and Jewish audience—not her material—are racialized as excessive and rendered indecently mixed. Goldman delivered a class analysis of the situation: "I have simply given to the poorer women in my audiences information that any wealthy woman can obtain secretly from her physician, who does not fear prosecution." The court maintained that the prosecution did not censor sex information but disciplined its transmission: the offense was located in an immigrant woman speaking "Jewish" to an audience figured as excessive in their ethnicity, age distribution, and sexuality. In this trial, the *language itself* of "free speech" was at issue. Though we have no recordings of these speeches, anarchist papers advertised the titles, dates, and locations of these lectures. Accounts of lecture attendees paint a fuller picture of anarchist sociality. While the papers were material artifacts of labor, speeches were a key component of agitation and social life. Their prosecution entailed free speech struggle, and their language politics follow the pattern of printed bilingual matter.

Goldman disdained those who used Yiddish as a buffer between radical subcultures and the vulnerability of mainstream visibility. In a letter from 1906 cosigned with Alexander Berkman, she casts *Frayer arbeter shtime* editor Yanovsky's views as shamefully cautious. The letter concerns Leon Czolgosz, the Polish-American who assassinated President McKinley in 1901. Although Czolgosz never organized with the anarchist movement, Goldman defended his "propaganda of the deed" in *Fraye gezelshaft* (Goldman's article was in fact published in Chicago's English-language anarchist paper *Free Society,* 1901) as the inevitable product of his society; the publication led to her arrest.[65] Goldman and Berkman write, "I think Yanovsky & the Fr. A. Stimme are becoming entirely too 'respectable,' too anxious about 'good public opinion.' It is this fear of adverse public sentiment that created the principle 'Religion is a private affair.' "[66] Although Czolgosz was not Jewish, Goldman and Berkman's letter demonstrates other Jews' anxiety about his reflecting poorly on them. Their anxiety may have resulted from Russian pogroms following the assassination of Tsar Alexander II. This letter also reveals that Goldman and Berkman closely read *Fraye arbeter shtime* and Yiddish media, even if they did not contribute to it beyond Goldman's Yiddish lectures sponsored by that newspaper. Berkman and Goldman understated the risks faced by Yiddish-writing anarchists; despite their "cautiousness," *Fraye arbeter shtime*'s writers were attacked by a mob after the McKinley assassination.[67]

In later years, Goldman refused to speak Yiddish in public whatsoever; she claimed that she wanted the detectives tailing her to know exactly what she was saying.[68] Perhaps she also sought to eliminate linguistic difference as a step toward eliminating social inequality. Despite her objections to its perceived provincialism, Yiddish benefited Goldman as propagandist. Of the surviving transcribed Yiddish lectures by Goldman, half concern sexuality, including *Gebirts-kontrol fun sotsialn shtandpunkt* (Birth Control from a Social Perspective) and *Heyrat un fraye libe* (Marriage and Free Love).[69] Isidore Wisotzky details the dangerous logistics of circulating birth control information at that time:

[I] was given my first difficult assignment: to publish a Yiddish pamphlet (it was also printed in English) on *Birth Control.* This was against the law. Bill Sanger, the husband of Margaret Sanger, was sentenced to jail for passing out this type of literature. Emma Goldman and Dr. Reitman also went to jail for the same crime. Anthony Comstock, the keeper of American morals at that time, saw to it.[70] One of our friends, a doctor, made a good, simplified translation in Yiddish. All I needed now was a printer to do the job. Finally I found one. However, there were two conditions: one, he had to have cash before he started the job and two, I had to be in the printing shop while the pamphlet was being set up and printed. The minute it got off the press, I was to take it out. The deal made, I ordered ten thousand pamphlets. We agreed on the price and time. . . . As soon as the job was done, we packed it up and took the load to his room where we made bundles of 500 each. We then notified our comrades, each at a different time, to come and pick up his bundle for distribution. Every baby carriage on the East Side, Harlem, Bronx, Brownsville, Williamsburg, got a birth control pamphlet. . . . It was a successful job. No arrests. The pamphlets were well distributed. But how beautiful it would be to live to see the day when the U.S. government is interested in birth control aid.[71]

Wisotzky's direct-to-carriage strategy for disseminating the pamphlets recalls the logistics of the *Frayheyt* case in strategizing bilingualism and translation.

Ultimately it was not the charge of obscenity but anti-militarism that decided Goldman's and Berkman's expulsion. The office of their journal *Mother Earth* was among the first to be ransacked in 1917, and Hoover confiscated Goldman's library to study the contours of the Left before destroying it.[72] Berkman recounts that "raids of public gatherings, of offices, and private dwelling places, accomplished with utmost brutality and uncalled for violence, are of daily occurrence throughout the United States. . . . FREE press has been abolished, and every radical paper that dares speak out, is summarily suppressed. . . . Books and whole libraries of 'radical centers' are confiscated, even text books of arithmetic or geography torn to shreds, furniture destroyed, pianos and victrolas smashed to kindling wood."[73] On December 21, 1920, 246 men and three women were deported on the *USAT Buford*, dubbed the "Red Ark."[74] At least 184 of the *Buford*'s passengers were members of the Union of Russian Workers, an anarchist organization formed in New York City by refugees from the 1905 Russian Revolution.[75] The entire editorial board of their Russian-language paper *Khleb i Volia* (Bread and Freedom) was deported on the *Buford* as well.[76] *Khleb i Volia*, whose name honored Kropotkin, had criticized the U.S. government for oppressing African Americans and the labor movement.[77] Adolf Schnabel, the Russian anarchist and editor of *Nabat* (Alarm Bell, 1918), was also deported on the *Buford*. Goldman's early excoriation of "the principle of government by deportation" proved prescient.[78] The acting secretary of the Department of Labor, Louis F. Post, approved Berkman's deportation[79] but refused to sign the warrants for nearly three thousand other alleged immigrant radicals arrested in Palmer raids, halting their deportations.[80] Yiddish papers dedicated front-page coverage to the unfolding Palmer raids.[81] Like Steimer's expulsion, Goldman's deportation was one chapter in a continuing transnational campaign for autonomous speech, negotiating language and the limits of citizenship.

On the threshold of his deportation, Berkman composed "with pencil and scraps of paper concealed behind the persons of friends who had come to say good-bye at the Ellis Island Deportation Station" an essay titled "DEPORTATION—Its Meaning and Menace."[82] This text reasons similarly to the courtroom testimony of Parsons and Goldman, arguing that even canonical authors such as Lincoln, Thoreau, and Jefferson would now transgress the Criminal Anarchy Law and Espionage Law; they appealed to American exceptionalism by defamiliarizing the national canon. Berkman concludes his farewell manifesto rousingly: "Seekers of the slaveless world, speak from your heart.[83] . . . The only true mastery is in you, the working class, in your power to feed and clothe the world and make it joyous. . . . Allow no suppression of the freedom of thought and speech."[84]

THE ELLIS ISLAND SOVIET: MULTILINGUAL PRISON NEWSPAPERS AND MIGRATORY AESTHETICS

Amid the anti-immigrant panic and mass deportations of the early twentieth century, the Lublin-born sweatshop worker Jacob Glatshteyn wrote a poem in Yiddish titled "1919":

> Lately, there's no trace left
> Of Yankl, son of Yitskhok,
> But for a tiny round dot
> That rolls crazily through the streets
> With hooked-on, clumsy limbs.
> The lord-above surrounded
> The whole world with heaven-blue
> And there is no escape.
> Everywhere "Extras!" fall from above
> And squash my watery head.
> And someone's long tongue
> Has stained my glasses for good with a smear of red,
> And red, red, red.
> You see:
> One of these days something will explode in my head,
> Ignite there with a dull crash
> And leave behind a heap of dirty ashes.
> And I, the tiny dot,
> Will spin in ether for eternities,
> Wrapped in red veils.[85]

Glatshteyn imprints the year with calamity. The poem opens with a traditional genealogical formula of identity: "Yankl, son of Yitskhok" is the familiar form of "Jacob, son of Isaac," biblical figures and the real names of Glatshteyn and his father. From this formulaic opening, the poem disintegrates into images of modern alienation, migration, and bodily diffusion, until all that remains is an essential, stubborn "tiny dot" (*kaylekhdike pintele*) of self, unrooted and "spinning in ether." Glatshteyn sardonically describes the political claustrophobia of daily life: "Everywhere 'Extras!' fall from above / And squash my watery head." The poetic speaker feels besieged by the calls of newspaper vendors, bellowed out as though prophecy. Gazing through sullied (*baflekt*) eyeglasses, the world appears awash in "red, / And red, red, red"—the color of revolution, blood, and the Red Scare.[86]

Glatshteyn's "1919" dramatizes the political consciousness shaping Ashkenazi migrant readers' daily lives during the Palmer raids. By 1920, Ellis Island was packed with hundreds of radicals awaiting deportation from detention centers across the United States. According to the Hebrew Immigrant Aid Society (HIAS), 1 percent of 119,036 Jewish immigrants were deported between July 1, 1920, and June 30, 1921.[87] One of the most remarkable documents produced at Ellis Island was *Gazeta* or the *Island of Tears Gazette,* a multilingual anarchist tribune written by hand by people awaiting deportation. German, Russian, Lithuanian, Yiddish, English, and other languages coexist on the page. Each issue's masthead is calligraphically emblazoned with gothic lettering or formed from sketches of tree branches, as though detention papers were illuminated manuscripts. Four issues from January 1920 are extant. The inmate-editors declared that here, finally, behind bars, they were free of censorship and could at last practice "real freedom of speech."[88] The paper records the procedures and decisions of tribunal meetings, and Kenyon Zimmer notes that "detainees instituted 'full Communism' among themselves, with the self-proclaimed 'Ellis Island Soviet' collecting voluntary weekly contributions" to purchase food from the canteen and distribute to those in need. One *Gazeta* article describes the detention center as the Commune, invoking the Paris Commune, a fortress of resistance within the city: 'the spirit of Communism is daily unfolding itself here on Ellis Island.' "[89]

Each surviving issue of *Gazeta* begins with Russian, adding Lithuanian, English, Yiddish, Ukrainian, and other languages written by different hands. The first page records a resolution "Passed at the General Meetings Which Took Place on the 5th and 6th of January 1920 on the *Island of Tears* in rooms 204 and 206." It implores "Comrade Workers!": "We are sure that the time is close when

the American proletariat will extend its hand to the proletariats of all countries
in the fight for the liberation of the workers from the capitalist system—a system of oppression, violence and slavery. Long live Soviet Russia! Long live the
Socialist Revolution!"[90] Like *Frayheyt, Gazeta* is largely composed in the second
person: "Because the ruling classes are also trying to dissolve the classes loyally
connected to the proletariat, through a man's unworthy politics, at this hour
I am calling the workers of the world to unity. Workers! Different beliefs and
nations forge the bond that holds the earth together." With the same urgent
temporality, editors implore readers to "Read the ISLAND OF TEARS every
day." News and reports are dispatched, including communications with "the
Bolshevik movement of Great Britain" and this portentous note: "There are stubborn rumors on the island that a ship will depart on Saturday evening, loaded
with comrades from the island, to Soviet Russia."[91]

The majority of *Gazeta* is written in Russian, with Lithuanian, Yiddish, and
English "pages" or features. One banner announces the "English Page," followed
by the block hand-lettered title "Six Days that Shook Ellis Island," vividly nar-
rating daily detention center life:

> Between bad stomachs and the U.S. Dept of Justice it is difficult to say
> which is causing more trouble to the officials at Ellis Island. A week ago
> they did not figure on having so many "Reds," here. Now that they stay a
> while and go away muttering, "Damn these Bolsheviks, we can't under-
> stand them.["] Of course they can't understand us, not even if they live a
> thousand years. . . .
>
> It must be admitted that the U.S. Dept. of Justice is working very
> hard to destroy Communist ideas. Instead of destroying Communist
> principles and ideas they are rather helping to build them up. Our orga-
> nization here is a miniature of a Commune. The basis of existence is the
> predominance of the Collective spirit as opposed to the spirit of individ-
> ualism. So far has this principle developed that it is becoming difficult to
> tell the characteristics of one comrade from that of another.
>
> Touching and interesting scenes are witnessed every minute of the
> day. When we first arrived here a shave was a great luxury. A comrade
> receives a razor from home, without any invitations a line is formed
> [and] every comrade is shaved. Another luxury is that of rye bread, a
> comrade receives some of this bread from home and distributes it to the
> other comrades. Another comrade receives cigarettes half he keeps, half
> goes to the Commune. We receive word that the lady comrades are in

need of money, before one can count three $61 is raised and sent to our lady comrades. These instances can be multiplied at infinitum.

The writer emphasizes mutual aid among prisoners and attends to the mechanics of detainees' language diversity:

> There are those nations who express their instinct for music through the individual, such as France and Italy. There are those nations who express their instinct for music through the people as a whole. The beauty of Russian music lies in the folk and revolutionary songs. The most wonderful spectacle is that of the Russian comrades singing their songs. They constantly interrupt and tell us that we make too much noise. Well, we can account for this, "He who has no soul for music is either a scoundrel or a fool." And so the spirit of Communism is daily unfolding itself here on Ellis Island with the officials gaping and mumbling to themselves. "Damn those Bolsheviks, we can't understand them."[92]

This striking passage juxtaposes uncomprehending guards and officials with the revolutionary spirit of multilingual communists. A jab at France and Italy for their "individualist" musical sensibilities is followed by a rousing image of Russian captives singing folk songs together. Despite the language barrier, it is implied, the other radicals can enjoy the music, which registers only as noise to the monolingual guards. The Russian-language edition records the music-making of a certain renowned cell: "Very interesting concerts take place in room 204 after dinner. The best talents of the local colony take part." These accounts of deportees' singing recall Steimer's loud performance of revolutionary songs during her incarceration—a common tactic to rouse spirits and antagonize wardens.[93]

Gazeta records the minutiae of life, centering cooperative sociality. The German section contains editorials, minutes from a meeting, outreach to German prisoners, the proceedings of a "court" and its attendant debate, election, and committee formation. Editors eagerly reached out to German readers for contributions. Another "Note" is signed by one "Brother Spartacus": "Editorials, poems, experiences, and funny comedies are requested to be sent to the headquarters of this publication for publication under the 'German Page.'"[94] As was common in anarchist papers, the genres of the anecdote, joke, and vignette were emphasized, despite (or to spite) their carceral context. The Russian section solicits submissions for a humor department, and its tone remains gallows-humorous even in reporting mundane events, under the title "Humor and Satire." After radicals were quarantined on Ellis Island, the Romanian Jewish anarchist Shmuel Marcus (later known as Marcus Graham) organized another newspaper, titled *Ellis Island Anarchist Weekly*. This one was also handwritten in pencil, but only in English. His was an outward-facing project: its editor "hoped the paper would circulate amongst the nonpolitical immigrants detained on the island, and that they would write questions and continue their dialogues with the anarchists about the views espoused therein."[95]

In print, as in speech, multiple languages coexisted in radical spaces of forced convergence. *Gazeta* records the multilingual space of the detention center and also reflects spaces formed by the anarchist movement in the world outside. As with *Frayheyt*, multilingualism is both utilitarian and literary, a strategy and an artistic effect, seeking to maximize outreach but also reflecting the particularity of each ethnic experience—not a translation, but a series of originals. The emerging category of "migratory aesthetics" offers a framework for considering the archival writing of deportees. Catherine M. Lord and Sam Durrant describe migratory aesthetics as representations of liminality and movement, "drawing attention to those who are caught, even frozen, in transition, between lives and countries, unable to lay claim to citizenship; not so much subjects-in-process as subjects-on-hold, subjects-in-stasis whose freedom to move is violently circumscribed."[96] This addresses the experience not only of deportation but its prelude of detention. "Perhaps the greatest contribution of migratory aesthetics," argues Miguel Á. Hernández Navarro, "is the importance given to traces in their material, sensitive, perceptible, aesthetic sense."[97] These materials draw attention to the temporality of deportation: the period of incarceration beforehand, the duration of a court trial, the sea passage, and the returns often attempted.

A capacious reading of "migrant aesthetics" would include oratory, humor, pamphlets, and multilingual broadsides in all stages of translation, admitting not only high modernism such as Glatshteyn's poetry but also ephemera into the canon of migration literature. To read Glatshteyn's "1919" together with the prison papers of Ellis Island reveals surprising evidence of the primacy of print in Yiddish immigrant life. Seeking to escape the overdetermined ideology of newspapers, Glatshteyn's poetic speaker abstracts imagery—turning the modernist kaleidoscope to a fine blur—to represent the habitus of migration and the perception of one's essence (*pintele*) as unceded. Though Glatshteyn himself was not identified with anarchist movements, reading his work with a diasporic anarchist lens refocuses his investment in a new migratory aesthetics that seeks to unbind any fixed or imposed ideology. It is difficult to imagine a more evocative image of history's bombardment of the self than Glatshteyn's line: "Every-where 'Extras!' fall from above / And squash my watery head."

The humor of migratory aesthetics scorns maudlin images of the deportee. Upon learning that the tycoon Henry Frick (whom he had attempted to assassinate in revenge for unleashing Pinkertons upon striking miners) had died before Berkman's impending deportation, he remarked to a friend, "I'm glad he left the country before me."[98] *Gazeta* called for readers to perform a similarly defiant affect, declaring: "On *The Island of Tears* not a single one of us has shed a single tear. And this is in the normal order of things: Communist revolutionaries do not cry. . . . They also lead the fight, they fight with their prison-keepers. And even if this seems like a petty fight at first glance—the fight for a piece of soap, for a towel, for better treatment—but it speaks to their strength [and] it speaks to their rebellious spirit that strikes at the bars of the iron grate."[99] *Gazeta*'s editors remarked on the irony of practicing uncensored speech from within a detention center on the threshold of deportation. Indeed, during the nearly month-long voyage, the *Buford*'s self-organized militants enthralled and even converted a few of their guards to take up anarchist ideals by the time they landed.[100] In spaces of constraint—in detention centers and deportation ships themselves—anarchist speech persisted and, ironically, encountered less regulation than it had in surveilled common spaces of the metropolis.

VISUALIZING THE DISSIDENT JEWISH DEPORTEE

One of the most powerful languages at play in the multilingual press was the visual language of cartoons. Cartoons visualized and disseminated specters of "Judeo-Bolshevism," the essentialized association between Jewish individuals and Communism.[101] Following the Russian Revolution of 1905, a cartoon series called "Fizzboomski" appeared, starring a hapless would-be Slavic assassin with cap and beard[102]—a visual riff on the antisemitic caricature.[103] Another cartoon illustrated the *Buford* departing as Uncle Sam waves from a pier, coattails flapping as he declares sarcastically, "It is more blessed to give than receive"; on board the ship, the cartoonist has drawn a scuffle of legs and arms, as though the deportees immediately began a melee on deck.

Deportation tableaux were imagined, illustrated, and staged across media. In 1978, a newsreel was unearthed from the Yukon tundra. Protected from combustion by burial in permafrost, the nitrate film reel includes a clip titled "America Bids Farewell to 'Red' Agitators."[104] Its title card announces, "More than 300 undesirables from all parts of the country start for Ellis Island there to board the 'Soviet Ark' for deportation to Europe." The decayed film's images crackle at the edge, as though surrounded by flames. We see a throng of men walk along a pier in Jersey City, carrying small suitcases, packages, and in one man's hands, a guitar. Intertitles describe them as "undesirables from all parts of the country." One man stands out from the rest, visually striking with his moustache, round spectacles, and high-buttoned shirt, clutching a leather bag. In both this footage and still photographs of the embarkment, he directly returns the camera's gaze. As he stands poised to step off the pier onto a waiting barge, intertitles interrupt: "'Good-bye and (CENSORED)!'—the cops heave a sigh of relief." Six men in police uniform or civilian suits wave contemptuously toward the water, laughing. The clip then cuts to a rickety, unseaworthy-looking ferry, its tugboat blowing steam as it pulls out of the harbor. The decks are empty; neither sailor nor deportee looks back.[105]

The newsreel delivers a conventionally cinematic scene, from the officers' jollity to the stricken faces of the deportees. Since their inception, newsreels were constructed pastiches, often packaged to falsely represent historical events. An early reel, for example, passed off a random gray-haired man to viewers as Alfred Dreyfus.[106] A closer look at this newsreel reveals the handiwork of its editors. First, the number of deportees was inflated by the intertitles: 249 Russian citizens, not 300, boarded the *Buford*. The sixty-two military staff onboard are not shown. Though the "America Bids Farewell" clip carried the image of deportees further than the reach of their own radical press' circulation, the newsreel's staging invites viewers to identify with the officers who remain on the pier; the camera does not follow the deportees onto the ship to reveal its constrained spaces or the sociality or conversation amongst these men. While the extent to which this scene may have been directed by cameramen is difficult to confirm, even through its framing, viewers are nonetheless confronted by the faces and penetrating gazes of the deportees. In "The Russian Tragedy," Berkman emphasized the severity of their treatment as prisoners aboard the "leaky old tub" of the Buford throughout their month-long journey, revealing the spaces and experiences unseen in news footage.

Compare the spectacle of the officers triumphantly waving farewell to "Reds" departing Jersey City for Ellis Island with Goldman's account of the scene at 4 a.m., as the deportees were marched onto the ship: "Deep snow lay on the ground; the air was cut by a biting wind. A row of armed civilians and soldiers stood along the road. . . . One by one the deportees marched, flanked on each side by the uniformed men, curses and threats accompanying the thud of their feet on the frozen ground."[107] The *Buford*'s mission was so significant that a delegation including J. Edgar Hoover and several members of Congress traveled to New York to accompany the ferry, including Representative Albert Johnson of Washington State, chair of the House Committee on Immigration and Naturalization, known as "an outspoken anti-Semite, a Ku Klux Klan favorite, and an ardent opponent of immigration."[108] While the actual congressional architects of deportation remained invisible observers, the newsreel's actor-police provided a proxy of power that audience members were invited to identify with. In an ironic twist, the *Buford* ended its career as a Hollywood prop, serving as the set for Buster Keaton's film *The Navigator* (1924).

Despite the image of the Jew as eternally racialized foreigner, Steimer, Berkman, and Goldman refrain from accusing the court of antisemitism, instead appealing to American ideals of free speech and liberty. Through allusion and metaphor, however, they identify refugeehood itself as a Jewish condition, placing their experience of expulsion within a historical genealogy of Jewish diaspora. In "A Woman Without a Country," Goldman casts refugees of all religions as "veritable Wandering Jews" who are "adrift in this Christian world of ours." Jewish identity here is an embodiment of stateless modernity, even as the conclusion of that essay reaches toward an unrealized vision of American liberty.

Rather than explicitly naming antisemitism as a factor in their deportations, defendants spoke in code. At a federal hearing on deportation, Goldman compared the proceedings' "very spirit" to "a revival of the ancient days of the Spanish Inquisition or the more recently defunct Third Degree system of Czarist Russia."[109] Goldman likens her antagonists to "drastic Prussian methods" and "American Cossacks,[110] known as the State Constabulary."[111] Goldman remarks that, since America "has begun to acquire colonial possessions, in contradiction of the principles she stood for over a century, it will not be difficult to find an American Siberia once the precedent of banishment is established"; this statement references federal aspirations to send U.S. citizens to Guam.[112] This critique via analogy also appears in a letter from *Frayheyt*'s editor Jacob Schwartz written on September 5, 1918, to his comrades, composed in the New York prison known as the Tombs: "Our arrest could be compared with the Spanish Inquisition and the blackest pages of man's brutality to man. . . . For our declaration that we are Anarchists and one of us a Socialist, we had to endure the most horrible tortures which the Twentieth Century will not be able to erase."[113] Steimer, Goldman, Schwartz, and others inscribe their experience of ethnic persecution within historical memory of anti-Jewish campaigns, even as their ideals reach toward universal liberation. Rather than making discrimination legible to the external world, they proceed through metaphor, allusion, and "accent," expressing another form of cultural diglossia: the observance of taboos on what may be uttered aloud, and to whom.

The study of language politics illuminates how linguistic difference informed First Amendment trials: at stake was not only what was said, but what language it was spoken in. From Judge Clayton's literacy tests and anti-suffragism to the New York City police's targeting of the underground Yiddish press, anti-militarist and reproductive speech were both charged in gendered and racialized campaigns. The twinning of sedition and obscenity charges confirmed anarchists' critique of both discursive and geographic borders. By attending to historical questions of language politics, migratory aesthetics, and translation, we may better hear their contemporary echoes. The racialized politics of language difference applied to Yiddish and Russian speakers persists today, through the targeting of speakers of Spanish, Arabic, and Indigenous South American languages.[114] Thomas Nail argues, "We should think about borders not just as dividing lines between countries but as cultural and aesthetic structures that also have effects on legal policy, law enforcement, electoral politics, and thus the lives and deaths of migrants. This is why we need to actively refuse the cultural and aesthetic criminalization of migrants and develop a new political aesthetics of the migrant image."[115] Nail notes that "so much of migration and criminalization politics happens before the confrontation at the border and transversally across borders. Thus, the circulation of media images has its own kind of migration and its own kind of borders that are not necessarily spatially or temporally congruent with the migrant bodies at the border or in detention. There is simply no way to fully understand migration politics and criminalization without understanding migrant images as part of the process—confronting their own barriers and waging their confrontations."[116] Strategically using courtroom statements, orations, and handwritten newspapers, the Russian anarchists "waged their confrontations" against deportation and contributed to a genealogy of borderless, anti-deportation critique. Their histories demonstrate that struggles for free speech were—and remain—inseparable from multilingualism.

CHAPTER VIII

"Multitongued Languaging"
ANARCHIST LINGUISTICS

Were Yiddish anarchists concerned with the question of a Jewish national language? Did they participate in language reform movements? How did the immigrant labor movement's multilingualism function in organizing spaces and print? Was *anarchist* multilingualism distinct among Jewish multilingualism or diglossia? Intrigued by these questions, I arranged an interview with Audrey Goodfriend (1920–2013). Known in the San Francisco Bay Area for founding the Walden School along the principles of Ferrer's Modern School, Goodfriend was a lifelong anarchist and a friend of Kenneth Rexroth and Emma Goldman. Goodfriend's parents raised her speaking Yiddish in the Sholem Aleichem Houses and were part of *Fraye arbeter shtime*'s circle; she identified as a "red-and-black diaper baby." Informed that Goodfriend was fond of ending meetings by singing the Internationale, I memorized all the verses in English and two different versions of the Yiddish anthem from flashcards, loathe to bungle the moment. When I asked whether she thought that a sense of "Yiddish nationalism" or affective attachment to their native language prevailed among the editors of *Fraye arbeter shtime*, Goodfriend snapped in response: "We published in Yiddish simply because that was the language we spoke best. What are you, an academic?"[1]

Goodfriend's reply demonstrates her linguistic pragmatism. She echoes the *Fraye arbeter shtime* editor Joseph Cohen's "Anarchist view" of language, which he elaborates in a memoir about trying to build an anarchist farming colony in Michigan: "I maintained that all languages, like all people, are equal, and that each individual has the right to live and speak in the way he wishes. At the same time, I pointed out that language has no particular sanctity which justifies making it a fetish or a cause of dispute. Indeed, in my opinion the only criterion was convenience."[2] Goodfriend's pointed remark echoed the literary ideology of the *In-zikhistn* (Introspectivist) manifesto of 1919: "Mir shraybn yidish vayl mir zaynen yidish!" ("We write Yiddish as long are we are Yiddish/Jewish.")[3]

Anita Norich describes Yiddish language politics as "the very definition of current discussions of multiculturalism and transnationalism."[4] The anarchists, however, approached language not (only) as cultural expression or habitus but as a tool for remaking the world. This chapter examines how Yiddish anarchists approached language ideology, utopianism, multilingual praxis, philology, and immigrant socialization. The heterogeneity of anarchist language politics aligns with larger patterns of anarchists' resistance to articulating and enforcing a single ideology. Overall, they avoided ascribing a single ideology to Yiddish, while they used language choice strategically to evade surveillance. Their wariness toward linguistic singularity reflected a multilingual movement and allowed greater attachment toward Hebrew, where other Jewish leftists drew a line before religiosity.

THE AGE OF UTOPIAN LINGUISTICS

Jewish political movements of the nineteenth and twentieth centuries were linguistic movements as well. Zionists advocated for the "revival" of Hebrew, inspired by the Litvak lexicographer Eliezer Ben-Yehuda and organized by formal language councils.[5] Der Algemeyner Yidisher Arbeter Bund (the General Jewish Workers' Union, or the Bund) claimed Yiddish as the workers' international language, organizing in that language across Russia, Lithuania, and Poland.[6] Chaim Zhitlovsky and like-minded Socialist representatives to the 1908 Czernovitz conference debated whether Yiddish ought to be designated "*a* language of the Jewish nation" or "*the* language of the Jewish nation."[7] The Bund "vigorously ward[ed] off attempts to cultivate Hebrew culture in Poland at the expense of the original Yiddish culture."[8] As Amelia Glaser notes, "The fragile 'diaspora nationalism' championed by the Bund relied not on the idea of a state but on the uniting powers of a textual tradition, including folklore, literature, and language."[9] The most stringent bid for Yiddish exclusivity was proposed by the Bundist leader Esther Frumkina, who became a high-ranking member of the Soviet intelligentsia.[10] In his 1897 essay *"Farvos davke yidish?"* ("Why Only Yiddish?"), Chaim Zhitlovsky calls for "Jewish intellectuals to end their estrangement from the Jewish 'folk,' to build Yiddish culture, and to build socialism in Yiddish."[11] Madeleine Cohen notes that the Bund's path toward a single-language ideology evolved over several years, as the "founding generation of Bundists were largely not native Yiddish speakers, but rather Russian speakers. These were organizers whose first agitational projects included teaching Jewish factory workers Russian, so that they could become part of the revolutionary movement."[12] Bundist single-language ideology, then, was a move against the multilingualism of its context. Soviet Yiddishists altered orthography to diminish its loshn-koydesh component and cut ties to German, then associated with fascism.[13] Jewish language choice remains ideologically charged into the twenty-first century: the Satmar sect of Hasidim, for example, speaks Yiddish as a language of separation within Israel as they eschew voting for the Knesset.[14]

Jewish linguistic politicization unfolded within imperial and expansionist language movements of the era. Soviet language reformers, avowedly motivated by a desire for pedagogical simplicity, changed Arabic, Latin, Georgian, and other alphabets to Cyrillic.[15] During the same period, Turkish reformers abandoned the Arabic alphabet and purged the language of words derived from Persian and Arabic.[16] Ataturk's new state demanded that Turkish be spoken, pressuring Ladino-speaking families to assimilate and identify as "Turks of Jewish faith," rather than Jews.[17] One anarchist response to these language reform movements was a turn toward language utopianism, particularly in Russia. Ruth Kinna writes: "For anarchists, utopias are about action. . . . Utopianism is not treated as an abstract concept or method, nor as a literary genre or place—because that is not how anarchists have understood the idea. Utopia, [Uri] Gordon notes, 'has always meant something more than a hypothetical exercise in designing a perfect society.' As a revolutionary idea, utopia is instead linked to the principle of prefiguration."[18] Language utopianism proposed inventing new languages to prefigure how they aspired to be and speak, rather than reforming orthography or altering an existing corpus of vocabulary. The anarchist linguists wagered that if language can be repaired, perhaps society could be as well.

In Russia, Volf Lvovich Gordin (or Ze'ev Volf) pioneered a brand of linguistic theory at once fantastical and mathematical. V. L. Gordin (brother of the Yiddish writer and editor Abba Gordin) invented the language AO, for which he provided "sophisticated" grammar books and extensive bilingual dictionaries. The first page of its grammar book declared: "There is no god, no nature. Talk like humans, use 'AO.'" His pen name Beobi (meaning "Human," written $1 + o_1\sqrt{}$) was coined from AO's literal terms for "Society-Me." Gordin's invention "eventually became the world's first language for interplanetary travel among Mos-

cow's anarcho-cosmists of the later 1920s. . . . AO offered a compact circle of
logical meanings that its adepts believed would make perfect sense in outer
space."[19] Michael G. Smith notes, "True to the anarchist ethic, V. L.'s new language altogether dispensed with gender (signifying male oppression), as well as
possessive cases and possessive pronouns and the genitive case (signifying property relations)."[20] Gordin's linguistic search "echoed the poetic experiments" of
Zaum, the experiments in sound symbolism and language creation carried out
by Russian futurist poets.[21] The conceptual artist Yevgeniy Fiks's installation
"Yiddish Cosmos" (2018) presents Gordin as a "Cosmopolitan in Space," the-
matizing the links between Jewish diasporic language and Moscow's First International exhibition of AO in 1927.[22]

More famous than Gordin's utopian language is Esperanto, created by
Białystok-born Ludovik Lazarus Zamenhof (1859–1917), who termed his project *Hilelismo* and envisioned it uniting humankind by offering two-way trans-
latability to all languages.[23] Before inventing Esperanto, Zamenhof first attempted to "modernize" Yiddish with Latin characters to develop a "new Jewish
language"—predating by decades Soviet orthography and standardization by
the YIVO Institute for Jewish Research.[24] Brigid O'Keeffe has argued that
Zamenhof launched Esperanto as "a means of solving the Jewish Question" and
"offered Esperanto as a program for uniting all the world's peoples into a moral
community of global citizens bound together by a shared international auxiliary
language and universalist ethics."[25]

The USSR invested in the Soviet Esperanto Union, which "promoted Russian proletarian internationalism by way of labor unions and pen pals." In France,
a faction of the Anarcho-Esperantists called the Non-Nationalist Association
(*Sennacieco Asocio Tutmondo*) dedicated themselves to a borderless world. Another French anarcho-syndicalist, Victor Coissac, proposed "an interplanetary
language of mathematics and geometry for future space travel," and organized a
commune that endured from 1911 to 1935. Cuba held an Esperanto conference
in 1990 to great celebration, and Fidel Castro briefly addressed the crowd in
Esperanto. (In 2018, traveling in Havana, I happened to place a book on Esperanto on a bar, which sparked the interest of several others keen to learn, and
I relinquished the book.) The earlier support for Esperanto waned, and widespread repression of the language across Western Europe began in 1922, when
France banned its being taught in schools; in 1936, Germany and Portugal
banned Esperanto itself. The rise of Stalinism led to the arrests and executions
of many Esperantists in 1937, and it was forbidden as the "product of bourgeois
internationalism and cosmopolitanism."[26]

Jewish anarchists responded ambivalently to the Esperantist movement. The German anarchist Gustav Landauer fiercely opposed Esperanto on the grounds that this "artificial product" would homogenize the human variety of world literatures. In a pamphlet titled "Do Not Learn Esperanto!" he diagnoses Zamenhof's strategy of unifying language as a misrecognition of the root of inequity:

> Anarchists need to understand that the basis of both individual life and human coexistence is something that cannot be invented. It is something that has to grow. Society as a voluntary union of humanity, for example, has grown. Nowadays, this union has been *over*grown by a dreadful artificial product, the state. The people's languages and dialects have also grown. It is sad that different languages are often cited as excuses for hostilities between nation states. It would be even sadder, however, if humans really believed that the diversity of languages was the reason for disunity. Ineradicable, real difference does not only exist between peoples, it exists between all human beings. . . . Total equality is not only impossible; it would also be dreadful.[27]

Landauer's emphasis on the vital importance of *difference* marks a vision of utopia built on heterogeneity. Like Kropotkin's affirmation of "the little nations," Landauer rejects the idea of universal language: "The diversity of languages is nothing to be lamented. Even less so it is something we can abolish. What we need to abolish are the conditions that keep humans from learning foreign languages. Are anarchists not always opposed to palliatives and gradual improvements within the state and capitalist society? Esperanto is nothing but that—and it is a particularly ugly, useless, and dangerous palliative."[28]

In her report from the International Anarchist Congress in Amsterdam in 1907, Goldman weighs in on the Esperanto question in the context of a multilingual organizing space: "No doubt, much could have been gained at the Congress had all the delegates known Esperanto, as the interpretations from the French, Dutch and German consumed a tremendous amount of time. But to believe that an arbitrary, mechanical language can ever replace anything that has grown out of the soil, the life and the customs of a people, is to be sectarian indeed."[29]

The French Communard Louise Michel also fiercely criticized Esperanto, on the grounds of its "artificiality" and obstruction of learning others' languages, particularly Indigenous languages.[30] Michel was one of few convict Communards exiled to New Caledonia who learned the Kanak language and fought against

France in the 1878 uprising. She identified their anti-colonialism with the aims of the Paris Commune and, through studying their language and music, attempted to become a collaborator in both artistic and political senses. Carolyn J. Eichner writes, "[Michel] has also garnered notable respect for her translation and transcription of Kanak tales, for the way she preserved the sound and rhythm of the stories and recognized them as an oral literature. . . . The Kanak valorization of Michel reflects a transtemporal understanding of political solidarity and allegiance. Rising above her vocabulary linking them to the stone age and Medieval Europe (historically specific language undoubtedly denigrating and offensive), contemporary Kanak have demonstrated a willingness to view Michel—a historical figure—historically. Just as she analogized Kanak life to past eras, seeking to better present the New Caledonians to the European world, many 21st-century Kanak have recognized the historical specificity of Michel's language, reading through it to find its radical and liberatory intent."[31] This decolonial approach to anarchist language politics represents an alternative to Esperanto's utopian universalism, echoing Landauer's declaration: "What we need to abolish are the conditions that keep humans from learning foreign languages."

Did the Yiddish language *itself* inspire or inform anarchist language politics? As a diasporic language, its formal characteristics lend themselves to poetic innovation. The poet and literary historian Benjamin Harshav (Hrushovski) writes, "Yiddish always was an *open language,* moving in and out of its component languages and absorbing more or less of their vocabularies, depending on the group of speakers, genre of discourse, and circumstances."[32] Harshav refers to the linguist Max Weinreich's term *komponentn-visikayt,* or "component-consciousness," the awareness among Yiddish speakers and writers of the linguistic origins of the words they choose.[33] A poet can play off readers' *komponentn-visikayt* by juxtaposing words of different etymologies, producing great nuance and texture. As Harshav writes, "Yiddish literature developed a profound grasp of this interaction and play of components and used it as a major source of semantic and stylistic variation and impact."[34]

Weinreich emphasizes the impact of Yiddish on co-territorial languages, attending to words adopted into non-Jewish languages and surviving post-expulsions.[35] What Yankev Glatshteyn termed *altsetsungte shprakheray,* the "multitongued languaging" of Yiddish, inspired a diasporic *poetics* drawn from its linguistic components and internal heterogeneity.[36] This "openness"—inherent or potential, projected or constructed—affected how Yiddish anarchists conceptualized their language politics. In counterpart to this linguistic openness is *lehavdl-loshn,* "language of separation."[37] Max Weinreich writes, "There are words applied to Jews (or even neutrally, when no differentiation is intended), and these have parallel series that has to begin with a derogatory connotation or one of disgust."[38] *Lehavdl* is also used as an exclamation, a verbal barrier between subjects that should not be spoken of in the same breath. This separatist component of the language agitated some speakers' universalism. A Soviet publisher of Mani Leyb's poetry, for example, replaced terms from *lehavdl-loshn* such as *goyim* with *nit-yidn* (non-Jews).[39] When Soviet publishers removed any traces of a derogatory shadow-meaning, they sought to resolve the tension between their internationalism and *lehavdl-loshn.* Within several years, however, the Communist regime sought to "resolve" that tension not by internal erasure of the language of difference, but by banning Yiddish and Hebrew, as it did during World War I.[40]

How anarchists interpreted the "openness" and "separateness" of Yiddish defined their language politics in relation to acculturation and assimilation. Alexander Harkavy centered the "openness" of Yiddish and balanced it against American acculturation. Rabbi Yankev Meyer Zalkind, on the other hand, centered the closedness of Yiddish as a ward against English assimilation. The case studies of these two anarchist linguists reframe the "Jewish language debate" beyond nationalism and instead around axes of assimilation, acculturation, and strategy.

"FOR THIS LANGUAGE I LIVE": ALEXANDER HARKAVY

Alexander Harkavy was foundational in establishing modern Yiddish philology, but his contributions to the anarchist movement as editor, essayist, and translator have largely gone unstudied. Harkavy (1863–1939) was born in Navaredok in the Russian Empire, now Belarus, to an intellectual family connected to the influential Romm printing press in Vilna.[41] His Hebrew memoirs of 1935 recall that, as a very young boy, he "felt a powerful love for the language of our people."[42] Family lore claims that their name is derived from the word *kartavyi,* a speech impediment affecting pronunciation of the guttural *r*—a striking patronymic for a linguist.[43] Harkavy's early research concerned documentary evidence of early Jewish presence in Poland: hundreds of coins inscribed in Hebrew and Slavic, completely in Hebrew characters, found near Gniezno in the twelfth or thirteenth century, and medieval Hebrew manuscripts with Slavic glosses. Harkavy tended to ascribe even recognizably Czech glosses to Russian, "cementing the ancient association of Jews with early Slavic, or Russian, language and culture."[44] Around 1882, Harkavy met the poet Dovid Edelshtat in Liverpool, England, en route to the United States. Harkavy studied languages in Minsk before immigrating to New York City in 1882 with the Am Olam movement, which advocated for spiritual and cultural Jewish nationalism.

Harkavy's project of acculturation extended to writing histories of the United States. Among these is *Kolumbus, oder, di entdekung fun amerike* (Columbus, or the Discovery of America), an undated 34-page booklet published in New York City. Harkavy recounts Columbus's sea journeys in a dramatic register, perhaps to prepare immigrants for literacy or citizenship tests. His mention of Taino and Arawak people is minimal; he only states that Columbus dubbed "the wild original inhabitants of America" (*di vilde urshpringlikhe aynvoyner fun amerike*) Indians because he thought he was in India. Harkavy does name the cacique Guanacanagari, but short shrift is given to non-European perspectives of encounter in this pedagogical material.[45]

Harkavy wrote best-selling works addressing immigrant populations, such as his trilingual Yiddish-Hebrew-English dictionaries and *brivnshteler* (book of letter-writing templates). Anarchist thought informed his expansive linguistic approach, which, as Dovid Katz contends, "defies labels."[46] Katz locates Harkavy as a central architect of the field of modern Yiddish linguistics: "To understand the full impact of Harkavy as a founder of Yiddishism, it is important to bear in mind that his 1886 Yiddishist pamphlet appeared at a time (preceding Y. L. Peretz's literary debut) and in a place (America) where a pamphlet on behalf of the Yiddish language was both intellectually revolutionary and journalistically sensational."[47] Framing Harkavy as an anarchist makes him an outlier in the field of Yiddish philology. Barry Trachtenberg's *Revolutionary Roots of Modern Yiddish, 1903–1917* (2008) places Shmuel Charney, Nokhem Shtif, and the Marxist Zionist leader Ber Borochov at the center of the development of a "Yiddish science" in Russia, bound up in the discourse of national languages: "The first practitioners of *Yidishe visnshaft* . . . hoped to refashion Russian Jewry as a modern nation with a mature language and culture that deserved the same collective rights and autonomy demanded by other nations in the empire."[48] Although Harkavy was born in the Russian Empire and studied linguistics there, he did not participate in this discourse of national minority language politics. These stakes shifted rapidly after his immigration to New York, as David Shneer notes: "In Eastern Europe, the language wars were put on hold during World War I, when Hebrew and Yiddish language was banned by the Russian Empire, and communication across large distances became much more difficult. But the tensions between [Hebraists and Yiddishists] and the modern and nationalist pressures toward a single Jewish language exploded once tsarist power imploded."[49]

In North America, Harkavy avoided the existential risks confronting European Yiddishists. There, Harkavy contributed to the anarchist newspapers *Fraye arbeter shtime, Fraye gezelshaft*, and others, and translated European anarchist philosophers such as Élisée Reclus for *Fraye gezelshaft*. Harkavy also founded his own nonpartisan radical newspaper, *Der nayer gayst* (The New Spirit), which he edited until 1898, when the editorship was transferred to B. Gorin (Yitskhok Goyde). *Der nayer gayst* featured articles by a variety of leftists.[50] In a *daytshmerish*-laden editorial published in October 1897, Harkavy announces his vision: "Our ideal was a free newspaper—free of party structures . . . it can only educate and uplift the spirit."[51] Harkavy does not indict the political party system but proposes an alternative to "progressive party organs" as he politely "recognize[s] their great worth." His journal will combine "belletristic literature," "avant-garde ideas," "various scholarly articles," "polemics on major questions"— all, he emphasizes, in Yiddish. Harkavy's tone is diplomatic, except for his references to spirituality as an "amusement." The expansive ideal of a single newspaper as microcosm of the Left, open to submissions from all, contrasts with the "one-sidedness" of single-party newspapers. This heterogeneity and lack of concern for ideological purity marked the anarchist press in different regions and periods, from the first joint Socialist-Anarchist effort in 1890 to the Russian avant-garde *Anarkhiia*. Harkavy also worked in Montreal as a Hebrew teacher and published Canada's first Yiddish newspaper, *Di tsayt* (Time), practicing linguistic ecumenicalism in a period of national contention.[52]

Harkavy's linguistic articles in *Der nayer gayst* concerned the relationships between words of varying base components and etymologies.[53] Using now-common pedagogical techniques, he relates clusters of concepts across Yiddish, German, and Hebrew loanwords. From the word *bavegenen* (to move) he teaches *vandern* (Yiddish for "to wander, migrate"). He places these words alongside נוד (*nod*, Hebrew for "nomadic"), which he claims derives from יד (Jew). In this schema, where identity is determined by etymology, the Jew is essentially nomadic or diasporic! Harkavy also relates the connection between *vayb* (wife) and *veber* (weaver) and *vebl* (linen). He notes that German housewives tended to spin wool and relates this to the English term "spinster." Russian women were also associated with harvesting corn, from which they earned their own term: Russian women walk in the fields, unlike the domestic spinning of the English and German. This article on loanwords has a remarkable denouement. In tracing the vocabulary of possession across Ladino, Italian, French, German, biblical Hebrew, and Yiddish, Harkavy flourishes a multilingual pun:

> Another example. We would like to know something about the history of property. Let us contemplate the designation of this concept in languages. In the Romance dialect of Ladino, property is called "rauba."[54] This word comes from the stem "raub." (The Medieval Romance languages were mixed with German root-words.) Its significance is therefore *royb* (robbery)! In Italian, an item of property is *roba* (also from the same root); in French, the word *robe* (garment or dress) derives from the same root [*shoyresh*].[55] (Clothing was considered a main article of property.) And from that word, we have another French term *derober* (rob, plunder). The German word *Vermögen*[56] stems from *megn, makht* (power). That also stinks a bit of robbery; the Hebrew word [*hon*] (*fermegn,* fortune) descends without doubt from [*hunot*] (*beroybn,* to deceive, cheat), from the language [le'honutam me'akhurzetam] (defraud the estate/inheritance), Ezekiel 46:18. Not in vain did Proudhon say: *La propriété, c'est le vol* (*Eygntum iz royb*)—property is theft.[57]

Harkavy expresses his linguistic view of loanwords using the vocabulary of anarchist thought. This differs from neutral characterizations of diasporic multilingualism and internal *komponentn-visikayt,* such as that of Benjamin Harshav, who argues that while not every Yiddish writer was a "multilingual walking library, Yiddish poetry as a whole stood at an unusual intersection, attuning its antenna to 'Culture' and open to winds from all sides."[58] Contrast Harshav's description of the "openness" of Yiddish with Harkavy's pointed passage. Kenyon Zimmer interprets this article as "playfully combin[ing] his linguistic research with his political sympathies by invoking the French anarchist Pierre-Joseph Proudhon":

> In other words, no language is the exclusive property of a particular people, an argument that echoes Proudhon's view that only the product of one's labor constitutes legitimate private property, while everything else is a collective resource. In an era when language was often the basis for defining "national" groups, this was a nod to a cosmopolitan conception of identity.[59] . . .
>
> . . . In his view, Yiddish and Yiddish culture formed the basis of Jews' identity as a people. This was a thoroughly anti-essentialist definition of Jewishness; as Harkavy's article on word borrowing attests, languages and

cultures are not isolated, impermeable, or unchanging, and his emphasis on bilingualism highlights the possibility of multiple and elective attachments.[60]

Harkavy's cheeky genealogy of "property" was Jewishly *multilingual,* including Ladino and Yiddish and flaunting his Torah learning—in the same edition of a newspaper where he refers to religion as "an amusement"! This Jewish multilingualism is evident from his early involvement in Am Olam's Hebraic back-to-the-land philosophy to his inclusion of Hebrew in his trilingual dictionary. Harkavy's multilingual punning not only reflects his cosmopolitan identity but *performs* his multivalent language politics for the reader. As Hélène Cixous said:

> We are cultivated beings: our language is an inheritance; on the one hand, to the extent that it's the result of a history that we study in philology, it is itself made up of sediments of a great many languages. . . . We go on unwittingly using a language that speaks much more richly than we ever consciously realize, such that even when we are very primitive in our expression, a well-trained ear can hear in an apparently simple statement layers and layers of resonances, whether or not you can hear the hum of etymology behind it. . . . An author is all the better for the fact that she has been cultivated like a piece of land, for the fact that her language has been elaborated by a number of other languages since the dawn of time.[61]

By mapping loanwords, Harkavy helps his readers listen more deeply for the "hum of etymology." For a diasporic language without an attendant piece of land, Cixous's metaphor describes the cultivation of a "portable homeland."

Harkavy's popular dictionaries went through about thirty editions. First to appear was his *Folshtendiges English-Yiddish Verterbukh* (Complete English-Yiddish Dictionary, with an added title "English-Jewish Dictionary"), published in New York in 1891. Another, *English-yidish verterbukh* (English-Yiddish Dictionary), was published in 1898, followed in 1925 by the trilingual *Yiddish-English-Hebrew Dictionary.* These dictionaries generated much discussion in Russian and Hebrew periodicals.[62] He also began a Yiddish-Yiddish dictionary titled *Yidish folks-verterbukh* (Jewish People's Dictionary), which remained unfinished and unpublished, apart from an excerpt that appeared in *YIVO-Bleter* in Vilna in 1931.[63] As with any reference work, the author's social location is revealed through choices of what to include. Harkavy included Americanisms, such as the expression "A. K." (slang for *alter kaker,* which he euphemistically defines as an "unfit person").[64] In the original dictionary (1891), Harkavy notes that he "introduces some of the technical and scientific terms now common to all Indo-European languages." In a study of scientific Yiddish dictionaries, Stephen M. Cohen writes, "An examination of the English wordlist shows a rich concentration of mathematical, physical, astronomical, and biological terms, but a relative paucity in the chemical area."[65] Still, in the scientific realm, Harkavy's work presaged later specialist Yiddish dictionaries. These works helped shape the development of Yiddish as a spoken language, and the dictionary assumed a significant role in readers' lives. Harkavy's work is saluted in "Gedalye's Dictionary," a poem by Leah Zazulyer about her uncle's language struggles:

> . . . In his old Harkavy dictionary
> that I inherited, every other page
> was illuminated in a fine monk's script—his new language,
> his old language,
> his inner language.[66]

He also published a series of "Americana," likely informed by his work as a social worker with the Hebrew Immigrant Aid Society.[67]

Harkavy's success continued with his best-selling *Harkavy's amerikanisher brivnshteler* (1902), its title attesting to his name recognition. The Yiddish genre of *brivnshteler* (letter-writing manuals) dates to the European Renaissance, and Hebrew-language collections date to the sixteenth century.[68] Harkavy's *brivnshteler* fit with other Yiddish instructional material for new immigrants while following a traditional Jewish genre. Harkavy's introduction expresses his hope to satisfy immigrants' social needs, addressing topics of concern for businessmen, family members, and lovers. He was uniquely positioned to speak to new immigrants, as he had also worked from 1904 to 1909 for the Hebrew Immigrant Aid Society on Ellis Island, teaching American history and the Constitution in Yiddish.[69] The letter templates include suggestions for such scenarios as "From a lady to a gentleman, complaining of faithlessness" and "From a gentleman to a lady offering to release her from an engagement, on account of heavy business loans." He offers various possibilities for each response: "a kind reply," "a stern reply," and so forth.[70] In the first case, the lady's jealousy was proven baseless; in the second, she assures the letter-writer that she does not love him for his fortune, and so its loss does not sway her affection. This suggests that the right answer to the situation is not to marry for money, subtly instilling comradely behaviors among his readers. Harkavy's letter-templates were embedded in the genre of Yiddish cultural pedagogy for new immigrants, which also included such domestic genres as cookbooks and sexual education pamphlets.[71] Yiddish

radio shows on the New York station WEVD (named for Eugene V. Debs) offered advice to callers, and the *Forverts* newspaper offered an advice column,
often taking up writers' questions related to communication. Such media codify
intimate and sincere expression not as "natural" or original but as social reitera-
tions of a nearly fixed form that can be modified for the sake of cultivating new
forms of sociality. This format is akin to the *tkhines-bikhe:* constructed as wom-
en's spontaneous outpourings of prayer, they were in fact printed books, complete with "stage directions" instructing worshippers on the correct moment to
cry. The letters-to-the-editor pages of anarchist newspapers also served as a kind
of *brivnshteler,* demonstrating proper modes of public comradeship and discourse. Goldman's memoir likewise offered a grand template of liberation, and
many anarchists cited her life as the inspiration for their own paths. From memoirs to radio shows counseling the lovelorn, the genre of Yiddish advice was ripe
for reinvention as a tool of socialist acculturation.

Elisheva Carlebach, a historian of Yiddish correspondence, writes: "Letters
are the precursors to the world's newspapers, and they carried vital information
about communal and personal events, maintaining the bonds of familiarity over
great distance."[72] Carlebach emphasizes the constructedness of the letter form
and refutes the idea that these documents are "the closest thing we have to
speech, from which it seems to flow."[73] Yet in a surveillance culture where police
regularly transcribed anarchist lectures, speech *became* writing. Emma Goldman's letters were sometimes written in code, especially in the late 1920s, "to
escape the gaze of prison and post office censors."[74] Charles von Onselen details
police forces' usage of Yiddish-speaking officers as infiltrators among Jewish
radicals, sometimes framing or otherwise falsely implicating them.[75] The mass
popularity of Harkavy's letter-writing guides reveals the potential for radical
acculturation within this form, seeing the moment of immigration as an opportunity for new, more comradely socialization. Across his trilingual dictionary,
bilingual *brivnshteler,* and scholarship on loanwords, Harkavy's practice of
language politics was both ideological and aimed to support practical survival.
Harkavy supported the multilingual program of co-territorial languages, without diminishing his commitment to Yiddish, of which he wrote: "For this language I live."[76]

ANARCHIST PHILOLOGY: RABBI Y. M. ZALKIND

Shvartsbard's mentor Rabbi Dr. Yankev Meyer Zalkind (Jacob Meir Salkind)
encompassed the breadth of possible identities for a Yiddishist in the early twen-

tieth century: he was at once an Orthodox rabbi and fierce anarchist, a classical philologist and rabble-rouser, an anti-militarist and settler, a conscientious objector and an assassin's mentor. Zalkind developed a political philosophy of anarchism from his study of Talmudic ethics, retaining the particularity of Jewish identity and cultural autonomy within a vision of life liberated from capitalism, militarism, statism, and institutional oppression. Zalkind's expansive politics confounds the binary of religious conservatism versus leftist atheism, anticipating the rise of the "spiritual Left" and critiques of political secularism. His contemporaries remarked that his political imagination "breached every boundary":

> [While many individuals hold many radical divergent views,] in all such examples, we are able to locate the central point of that person's thought in which its roots burrow and from which its fundamental stem grows. . . . Jacob Meir Salkind's thought . . . had no such point. Rather, it had many centers at once. . . . He was a man of contradictions who breached every boundary . . . or so it appeared to us; he himself saw no contradiction at all. For him, everything grew from a single stalk. . . . He did not pass from camp to camp, from Zionism to Socialism and Anarchism, from Hebraism to Yiddishism, from faith to heresy, from piety to libertinism. . . . Rather, he inhabited all these camps at once, he thought every thought at once, entertained every belief at once, inhaled every atmosphere in a single breath and perceived no inconsistency in it.[77]

Even within scholarship on London's radical Yiddish milieu, Zalkind's contributions remain largely unstudied.[78] Recognized early as a *"flam-fayerdik ile"* (intense child prodigy), Zalkind is said to have mastered between twenty-one and thirty ancient and five modern languages.[79] He was dubbed *der go'en anarkhist* (the anarchist sage). His philological studies include prayer books with grammatical annotations, a linguistic analysis of the Song of Songs, and a translation of a Hebrew-Yiddish dictionary; his secular translations include the works of Molière and the French anarchist Sébastien Faure. He left a number of large projects unfinished or unpublished, including a history of the Jewish press and *Di filosofye fun anarkhizm* (The Philosophy of Anarchism). Zalkind's grandest undertaking was rendering the Talmud into Yiddish, which consumed more than twenty years of his life. Zalkind was said to have published more than one thousand newspaper articles and editorials in Russian, Ladino, Hebrew, and other languages, and he continued to lecture at salons for the religious anarchist community until his later years.[80] Like Harkavy, he articulated an anarchist linguistics that venerated Jewish languages; unlike his North American comrade, he rejected the project of acculturation and assimilation.

Rather than retrofitting secular radicalism or "judaizing" anarchism, Zalkind articulated his anti-statism through its convergences with Jewish scripture while fiercely opposing contemporaneous anarchist strains of atheism, universalism, and antisemitism. Uniting his pedagogical aims and rabbinic training, Zalkind devoted himself to translating and disseminating religious and philological texts in Yiddish and Hebrew. Zalkind, with Arn-Leyb Bisko, edited one of the few Yiddish-Hebrew dictionaries published in the early twentieth century, *Milon male veshalem zhargoni-ivri* (1913). The dictionary was later retitled to replace "zhargoni-ivri" with "Yehudi-Ivri," re-translating the term for "Yiddish" from the more informal, loaded *zhargon* (jargon) to the higher-register *yehudi*.[81]

Zalkind wrote his dissertation at the University of Bern in 1905, titled *Die Peschitta Zu Schir-Haschirim: Textkritisch in irhem Verhältnisse zu Mt. Und LXX Untersucht* (The Peschita [Syriac translation] of the Song of Songs: Examined Through Textual Criticism and in Its Relation to Mt. [Matthew] and LXX [the Septuagint]). Zalkind wrote in German on Peschitta, which he considered "sisters" to the Septuagint and Vulgate "and even the Targum." The dissertation's dedication page uses a combination of German, Yiddish and Hebraic conventions and Jewish calendar dates, signifying and establishing a Jewish genealogy: "Dem ewigen andenken meines lieben unvergesslichen Vaters, M. J. L. Salkind n'e gest. am 17 Ellul 5658, in kindlicher Liebe un Dankbarkeit, Gewidmet vom Verfasser": "In eternal memory of my beloved unforgettable father M. J. L. Salkind, may his soul rest in paradise, passed away on September 8, 1898, dedicated by the author with childlike love and gratitude." This dedication is a site of Jewish multilingualism, calling to multiple audiences: his professors at the University of Bern, his readers in the Jewish world, and his family. With this philological background, Zalkind turned to his most ambitious project: translating the Talmud into Yiddish. His choice to translate into Yiddish rather than Hebrew caused the poet Bialik—once his study partner at Volozhin Yeshiva—to implore, "Please, with your abundant mercy, uproot your dwelling from the Yiddish to the Hebrew!"[82]

The first volume of Zalkind's Yiddish Talmud appeared in London in 1922. The literary critic Shmuel Charney hailed Zalkind's translation as written "in a mekhayedik-yidisher shprakh" (in a delightful Yiddish rendition), which in later volumes became even more "pure and refined."[83] In the introduction to *Berakhot,* the first volume of his *Talmud bavli—gemore in yidish,* Zalkind names himself as the "translator and clarifier" (*iberzetser un derklerer*), a responsibility that he does not take lightly. Zalkind claims that his translation is "strongly literal, even when the style suffers for it," yet he has "taken pains to create a piece of work that would be accessible for all, useful for the beginner as well as for scholars." Pirush is "the main point, grounded in the explanations of Rashi, Tosefot, Maharsha, Rabeinu Yonah, and the armor-bearers (*noyse-keylim*) of Talmud."[84] In the introduction to Pe'ah, Zalkind explains, "We always aimed through our work not to make a '*visnshaftlekhe*' publication for specialists resounding with textual criticism, but to give ordinary Jews who want to 'learn' the possibility of clear understanding. Too many details would only distract, instead of helping them to learn the Mishnah." Zalkind employed a "scientific, Western" methodology to appeal to the post-yeshiva London and Tel Aviv generation of the 1920s, while excoriating the Jewish community for drifting from tradition. Zalkind positions himself as enlightening the reader with scientific clarity, noting that the *pirush* "is built, in the main, on the explanations of Rashi, Tosafot, Maharsha, Rabenu Yona, and other 'commentaries on the Talmud,'" but in certain places "we found it appropriate to offer our own opinion as well."[85]

Between 1922 and 1932, Zalkind published Yiddish translations of *Berakhot* (Blessings) from the Babylonian Talmud, and *Pe'ah* (Corner [of a Field]), *Demai* (Doubtfully Tithed Crops), and *Kil'ayim* (Hybrid) from the Jerusalem Talmud. *Pe'ah* discusses ethics in agriculture, including hospitality toward travelers, redistribution of crops to the poor, and the commandment not to reap the corners of one's fields. The desire to make *halakhah* more accessible drove many popular Yiddish publications of texts from the previous centuries, including *tkhines* (prayers) and the *Tsenerene* (a literary retelling of the Hebrew Bible) intended primarily for women. For Zalkind, concern about access to scripture is related to class, rather than gender, and he aimed to make labor law accessible to laborers themselves. *Pe'ah* has to do with the immediate redistribution of wealth, while *hefker*, surplus or abandoned property that may be gathered up by the poor, figures as a goal—the prospect of an abandoned field open for all to harvest.

The last tractate Zalkind published was *Kil'ayim* (Mixtures, 1932), which concerns the laws of agriculture, the mixing of species, and borders between property—subjects of particular interest to an anarchist questioning borders and property. Of the tractate *Kil'ayim*, Jacob Neusner notes: "In choosing to consider as orderly that which appears to be in order, Mishnah effectively makes the point that the boundaries of order are established by human beings. The standards of ordinary perception, and not the way things 'actually are,' decide the final status of objects."[86] Having earned a degree in agronomy in Glasgow with the aim of working the land in Palestine, Zalkind would have taken particular interest in this tractate. Indeed, the edition includes a large fold-out map of the land of Israel, designating the sites of settlements in Yiddish. Zalkind's *Kil'ayim* lists its subscribers by name and region, which reveals that his work circulated in London, Glasgow, Manchester, Grand Rapids, Detroit, Milwaukee, Jersey City, New York, Cleveland, Switzerland, and France. Nearly 760 subscribers are named, most with the honorific "Dr.," "Prof.," or "Herr" (Sir). Synagogues and groups such as the Kobrin Aid Union are included as supporters, pointing to Zalkind's reach beyond radical circles.

Shvartsbard paints an abject portrait of Zalkind laboring over translations in seclusion for two decades:

> A few years ago, when Dr. Zalkind published his first *Gemore Berakhot* in Yiddish, I earnestly asked him a question: "How much time did it take you, my dear Zalkind, to translate Berakhot with Perush?"—"Two and a half years." His wife was sitting there and called out, "You must count the nights that you were awake—you forgot to count those." Thus, if you encounter the usually ebullient Zalkind sitting and dozing in the afternoon, it's no wonder. . . .
>
> —Twenty years of difficult work! No sleep, no life, isolated from everyone, estranged and ignored by others—as long as he accomplished his life's dream and created a work that will exist in the future, what counted was his monumental work.[87]

This portrait of a man consumed by the act of translation is corroborated by Zalkind's own fiery introduction. He describes the sacrifices he made for scholarship (leaving out being oblivious to his wife). The introduction lambasts Jewish communities for slackening their devotion to Talmud and falling for modern luxuries:

> It took an entire two and a half years until, thank God, I finished a new volume of my Talmud in Yiddish and could release the fourth volume, tractate *Kil'ayim*. I feel that I owe an explanation to my good friends, who recognized the value of my work and waited with impatience for the publication of this volume. I want them to know that the delay is— God forbid!—not the result of indolence or negligence on my part. The delay resulted from my becoming in debt up to my neck to the printer, after the translation was ready—and by necessity, I must transform from

an author into a book peddler, scrambling up a thousand steps and rap-
ping at a hundred doors to inquire whether there are still Jews here interested in the article that one calls Talmud. For that reason, thanks to the
subversive tendencies and ignorance of Jewish knowledge [*ameratses*]
which intruded upon our lives and demolished the patriarchal Jewish
lifestyle with its holy solemnity, in the modern Jewish house there is a
place for pianos, gramophones, radios, and whatnot, but not for the se-
forim cupboard once the pride of the old Jewish home.[88]

Zalkind laments that "even if there still remain survivors [*sheyres-hapleytes*] who
respect Jewish books," this community is "split between two hostile groups engaged in a bitter struggle": one side are "so-called radicals, who tremble at the
thought that, God forbid, they might be suspected of clericalism"; the other
side are those "who believe that, based on the merits of the little reading they
consumed in their childhood, they became distinguished scholars for their whole
lives, and that in general, while engrossed in the gates of impurity of all kinds of
parties and politics, we have no more time for the study of Torah." Zalkind recounts his "months of hard work and sleepless nights until the new volume was
prepared"; although his "glass is filled with bitterness and humiliation," he gives
thanks for the "spiritual, edenic bliss that I enjoyed while writing this volume
for the public! Is that not enough pure compensation for all that I have endured?
Should that also in the future be a source of consolation in hours of despair and
disappointment for the apathy of 'the People of the Book' to their books and
scribes? . . . I do not have enough words to thank the God of Israel, that he found
me worthy to entrust me with a such holy (though difficult) mission—the mission to distribute his holy word amongst a wide strata of his people, unblocking
for them the life-source which sustained a hundred generations of Jews [with
the] strength of giants." Zalkind concludes:

> I heard his voice in the desert of our modern Jewish life and I felt upon
> my lips the ardor of his holy fire. . . . I know that I am too small to have
> earned such favor and joy; therefore, so long as it remains his will to
> protect the soul he breathed into me, I will not cease to write and pub-
> lish one tractate after the other, not even when I become tired. He, the
> Knower of All Thoughts, understands what a difficult sacrifice it is for
> people with a little self-dignity and pride in their lineage [*yikhes-shtolts*]
> to keep climbing up a thousand stairways and rapping on a hundred
> doors, searching for Jews who comprehend that the Talmud is and was
> and always will be the sine-qua-non condition of our national survival,

and that his teaching must therefore be granted the same position of honor in our time as in the lives of our parents.[89]

Zalkind associates "politics and parties" with the "gates of impurity" (*sha'arey tum'ah* in Hebrew), raising Talmud transcendently above the modern state and the indignities of contemporary Jewish life. In Shvartsbard's account of their conversations, Zalkind was driven by Jewish pride, ardent defiance against European Christian scholars, and hope that less-learned Jews might be enlightened:

> We must not wait until the non-Jews grow to fear us. We must learn further with our children the Talmud, the Yiddish scholarship and morals, the Talmud must become popular and accessible to every Jew, not only for the select [*yekhidey-sgule*]. . . .
>
> It must become clear to each why the Jesuits so greatly persecuted the Talmud in the Middle Ages, exterminated it, and burned it together with its readers. . . .
>
> And strikingly: when Dr. Zalkind came to Berlin to the great German scholars of the last age of his Gemore in Yiddish, the non-Jewish scholar did not know to heap praise on the work and amused himself for a few hours by speaking about the theme of the Talmud. At the end, the scholar asked him a question: "Are you a Jew or a Christian?" Zalkind wondered at the question. "I ask this to you," the German expert confessed, "because many Christians come to me, who now study Talmud in the original."[90]

When Zalkind reveals that the roots of the ethical texts they had studied were in fact found in the Pirke Avot, the antisemitic Swiss scholars and students are "taught a hard lesson." Shvartsbard declares with pride that Zalkind proves Jews are not *pkhodim* (cowards) and impresses the non-Jewish colleagues with his "multifaceted, polylinguistic" knowledge. While secular universalist anarchists of his time envisioned the liberation of land through its unbordering, Zalkind devoted himself to the study and translation of *Kil'ayim*. This rabbinic tractate on agriculture codifies relations to the earth through specific practices and prohibitions against altering plants (such as grafting, interbreeding, or weaving different fibers together). Zalkind's religious politics stand against the universalist dissolution of difference, then, instead derived from a "fervent love for God, his people, his Torah, his land." Proudhon wrote that "property is theft," referring to the theft of profit from workers' labor; Zalkind's rendering of property law appeals to a religious understanding of land as temporarily loaned by God. Just as one may only disrupt the roots of another's plants to the depth of three hand-widths, without controlling the land's depths, so too would Zalkind's readers come to understand property as contingent, worthy of respect but not worship.

Jewish language politics expresses an ideology of time, and Zalkind's politics of language aimed to de-corrupt modernity. Zalkind's comrade Rudolf Rocker wrote, "I am an anarchist not because I believe anarchism is the final goal, but because there is no such thing as a final goal. Freedom will lead us to continually wider and expanding understanding and to new social forms of life. To think that we have reached the end of our progress is to enchain ourselves in dogmas, and that always leads to tyrannies."[91] Rocker critiques deferral and messianism, distinguishing anarchist time from communist revolutionary horizons. Like Rocker, Zalkind rejected the idea of absolute revolution, writing in 1921:

> Even the society of the new dawn will have its anarchists, for even in the morning people will not be free. Even in the morning, the struggle toward what is new and different will express itself in a new struggle and new forms of suffering. Anarchism is a perpetual struggle that does not end with any one victory. The anarchist is an eternal wanderer into infinity.[92]

Zalkind refuses the totality of both religious messianism and communist revolution, transforming the trope of the Jewish "eternal wanderer" into an anarchist figure.

Zalkind claimed Jewish textual tradition as fuel for struggle against assimilation, nationalism, militarism, capitalism, and antisemitism. Jewish anarchist aesthetics continually adapted forms and structures of traditional life, reifying them even in anti-religious practices (such as Yom Kippur Balls, seder parodies, and satirical prayer books learned even in their heresy). In contrast to speculative tendencies, Zalkind labored throughout his life at philology and translation, the literary practice of touching past time. Zalkind's radical temporality rejects secularism as the determining mark of modernity. In an *Arbeter fraynd* essay from 1920, Zalkind writes: "The past is a cemetery for dead dreams. The future is a nursery where fresh dreams grow. The present is like a volcano; it is covered with extinguished dreams, beneath which rumbles fresh, hot, boiling lava that searches for an opening."[93] In describing life as an eternally turbulent state of hope, Zalkind channels the Yiddish modernist poetics of his era, shattering linear time into new forms capable of transmitting revolutionary euphoria. Claiming a Talmudic genealogy for anarchism was an anti-assimilationist strategy, reaching from a radical present moment into Jewish deep time to displace secular, capitalist, and Christian temporalities. Zalkind's language politics casts translation as the labor of religious devotion.

NON-JEWISH YIDDISH ANARCHISM:
ROCKER AND DE CLEYRE

In the United States and England, non-Jews were at times compelled to learn Yiddish as part of their leadership within Jewish anarchist communities. Most renowned of these were Rudolf Rocker (1873–1958) in London and Voltairine de Cleyre (1866–1912) in Philadelphia. Rocker, dubbed the "anarchist rabbi," learned Yiddish to edit *Arbeter fraynd* and published translations, essays, and memoirs in Yiddish. Rocker's accomplishments included establishing the Jewish Bakers Union, organizing protests of 25,000 people, and leading the successful general strike of 3,000 Jewish tailors in 1912.[94] De Cleyre, a prodigious poet and orator educated in a Catholic convent, learned Yiddish to participate more fully in radical circles.

Coalitions between immigrants necessitated multiple languages within organizing spaces. Johann Most addressed Yiddish-speaking audiences in German, as historian Paul Avrich describes: "He could enthrall with his revolutionary passion even those Jews—the vast majority—with only a shaky grasp of the German in which he spoke. His sharp phrases, noted Israel Kopeloff, a member of the Pioneers of Liberty in New York, had 'the impact of the bombs and dynamite' of which he so often spoke; and he had only to give the word, so it seemed, and 'the audience would rush to build barricades and begin the revolution.' "[95] The linguistic intimacy between German and Yiddish permitted their coexistence within organizing spaces. Consider as well the disparate *Yiddishes* determined by dialect, linguistic component, and register. Leon Kobrin, writing for the New York *Morgn frayheyt* in 1942, describes a debate between an unnamed social democrat and Chaim Weinberg, the confidant of Voltairine de Cleyre:

> The social democrat attempted to show what a good and fine speaker he was, so he spoke a Germanized Yiddish and used the words *niemals* and *sondern* and *abwahl* and *tat,* and other such words that our Yiddish long ago sent back to the Germans. Thereby he got very impassioned and excited, and he shouted until he became so hoarse that no one could hear his closing words. And Weinberg answered him so calmly and with such a clear, wonderful Yiddish for those days, compared with the Germanized language of the other fellow![96]

While Most's oratory transcended linguistic barriers for Yiddish speakers, Yiddish-speaking lecturers using heavy *daytshmerish* fared worse. Kobrin's quip about "such words that our Yiddish long ago sent back to the Germans," though not especially accurate historically, echoes James Joyce's remark, "I'll give [the English] back their language. They really needn't worry and scold so much. . . . I'm not destroying it for good!"[97] Weinberg rejects *daytshmerish* in favor of simple oratory as an aesthetic choice toward anti-classism: if *daytshmerish* was the dialect of social democrats, then Weinberg intentionally chose *poshete verter* (plain words) in a bid for accessibility.

The linguistic texture of Yiddish anarchist newspapers was varied and internally heterogeneous, presaging the move of modern linguists away from prescriptive norms, toward descriptive theory. Moshe Goncharok notes, "Until *Fraye arbeter shtime* turned 50, it had a great readership—the greatest part coming from Russia. One could find Russian folk sayings and idioms in the texts and articles, as well as in letters from readers."[98] *Fraye arbeter shtime* also favored a *daytshmerish* style, considered elegant or "international" at the time. This was common among the Sweatshop poets who, as Benjamin Harshav notes, "used an array of lofty German words to poeticize the language of their verse and to lift the spirits of the sweatshop APREYters ('operators,' from American): the poetic MOND ('moon,' from German), substituted for the everyday Yiddish LEVONE; MEER ("sea," from German) for YAM; ZEL ('soul,' from the German SEELE), for the Yiddish NESHOME; and its unconventional counterpart, VEL (from WELLE, "welle") rather than KHVALYE."[99] One example of anarchist preference for Germanic vocabulary is *Fraye arbeter shtime*'s use of *genose*, spelled with an extra *samekh* for the S, rather than the Hebraic *khaver*, for "comrade." Tony Michels explains that this new vocabulary of revolution often confused "the uninitiated, who mistook the abbreviated word for comrade, *gen.* (*genose*), to mean a military general. Many immigrants were surprised: 'Who knew there were so many Jewish war heroes in the United States?' "[100] In both print and speech, then, *daytshmerish* posed challenges for those wanting to telegraph both sophistication and anti-classism. In other circles, *daytshmerish* created the opposite effect, feigning bourgeois affiliation. Isidore Wisotzky recalls the process of acculturation into Yiddish radicalism and the new vocabulary it demanded "to become conversant":

> I stepped into a new world of thoughts and ideas and a lingo that I frankly did not understand clearly. Strange to me were the conversations, debates, discussion and words like "sabotage," "the social revolution," "Socialism," "Anarchism," "Syndicalism," "Marx," "Engles," "Prudon," "Commonwealth," "Bakunin," "Kropotkin," "Direct Action," "Political Action," "Beaurocracy" [*sic*], "Capitalism," etc.[101]

The Yiddish spoken by radicals was internally heterogeneous in orthography and dialect, as well as the ethnicity of its leaders.

Another prominent non-Jew who learned Yiddish was Voltairine de Cleyre, the poet, polemicist, former Catholic convent student, and teacher whom Emma Goldman called "the most gifted and brilliant anarchist woman America ever produced."[102] De Cleyre (1866–1912) learned Yiddish primarily to teach English. She writes in a letter of 1911 to *Fraye arbeter shtime* editor S. Yanovsky, whom she addresses as "brother": "Enclosed, please find report for *F. A. S.* as to the [Mexican Liberal Defense Committee]. . . . I have an article in this month's *Mother Earth,* on the Mex. Revolt. Maybe you will want to translate it. I am too lazy to write two!"[103] De Cleyre idealized Jewish anarchists affectionately, describing them as "the most liberal minded and active comrades in the movement as well as the most transcendental dreamers."[104] Despite (or because of) this tendency toward idealization, she fretted about understanding her Jewish comrades. Another letter to an unnamed confidant (likely Joseph Cohen) expresses her alienation:[105]

> Midnight, Friday.
> Dear Comrade:—
>   All evening I have been thinking about your words: "You will never understand them, and they will never understand you." Why is it? I have known those people for eighteen years, and I have not understood them!! Why did I not? Is it because I am so different that I have no key at all to understand them? Why, why are we so different?—What makes them see honor in one direction, and I in another? I cannot understand. I think and think, and I cannot get any further. To me certain things are very simple and very plain; there can be no question at all. And to them these things do not appear. Why? Why? Are we really of such different instincts altogether? . . . Is it because they [Jews], with a thousand years of Talmudic sophistry behind them, while I am a "*goye* [written in Hebrew letters] with the blood of Puritans and fanatics in me"; because you also are a Jew, and you do understand me, I think. Then where is it, where is it? Why do we think so differently? . . . The State and all that it can do, I do not mind; it does not bewilder me; but to find my own people strangers has made things slip around me. And I always come back to the same question: why are we so different? Have I all my life gone on with a fool's dream, and never knowing what people meant when they talked. V. de Cleyre.[106]

De Cleyre suffered from depression, and this letter suggests exacerbated social anxiety about her standing with Jewish anarchists. Her use of "sophistry" to describe Talmudic reasoning is not positive; nor is it clear whom she is quoting when she refers to herself as a "*goye* [non-Jewish woman] with the blood of Puritans and fanatics in me." De Cleyre finds herself dismayed that social reality diverges from her ideal of unity across ethnic difference: "to find my own people strangers has made things slip around me. And I always come back to the same question: why are we so different?"

In contrast to De Cleyre's anxiety about personal comradeship with Jews, Rudolf Rocker—a German-born former Catholic partnered with a Jewish woman—did not romanticize or essentialize Jews as a people: "When the Nazi movement in Germany raised the Jewish question I felt that I must oppose my knowledge and experience of the Jews against that terrible barbarity.... I never held that Jews are the salt of the earth. But certainly they are none of the terrible things of which the Nazis, in their search for a scapegoat, accused them. Antisemitism has always been a weapon of the reactionary forces."[107] Rudolf Rocker raised his son, the visual artist Fermin Rocker, in a multilingual milieu and spoke German at their London home. He was named in honor of the Spanish anarchist and mayor of Cádiz, Fermín Salvochea y Álvarez (1842–1907)—a further gesture of the family's multilingualism. Fermin Rocker described his father as least comfortable addressing a crowd in English due to his strong German accent, and he would do so only after a few years in the United States in the mid-1930s. Fermin Rocker recalls that he communicated in German with some Yiddish elements with the parents of his Jewish mother, Milly Witcop. Fermin Rocker's own speech in his oral history is dotted with Yiddish, such as when he refers to himself and his cousin as "the *mamzerim*" (illegitimate children), as his parents opposed marriage. In *The London Years* (1956), a memoir written in plainspoken Yiddish, Rudolf Rocker describes working with a Yiddish anarchist group formed by Russian-Jewish students in Paris. In its first years, they spoke Russian at meetings; as the group attracted more Jewish workers, they switched to Yiddish, which initially posed difficulties for older members. In an oral history, Fermin Rocker reflected on the linguistic diversity of his father's circle:

> From reading *The London Years,* one gets the somewhat erroneous impression that it was almost exclusively a Jewish milieu, which it wasn't—because up in that flat, which was 32 Dunston Houses, you heard all kinds of languages: French, Italian, Spanish.... Any time there was any kind of injustice, which God knows there were plenty of, Spaniards would come. My father had a working knowledge of Spanish, his French was quite

acceptable, and you see there too, he was one of the few in the East End who could converse with these people in their father tongue, so you see he was at least as interested in those people and their goings-on as in the Whitechapel events.[108]

Fermin Rocker emphasized that "to think of him as a spokesperson for the East End Jews is really a bit erroneous," although he "moved away from his own [German] compatriots, a breed with whom he never really got along very well. . . . [He] found a much more congenial atmosphere among the Jews of the East End." As with Spivak and Michel's anti-colonial framework of language acquisition, both Jews and non-Jews learned Yiddish as practical solidarity and affirmation of the "little nations" of the anarchist movement.

Yiddish anarchist language politics spanned the utopianism of Esperanto and AO, Harkavy's secularism and Zalkind's piety, and the practical strategies of Steimer, Goldman, De Cleyre, and Rocker. Few Jewish anarchists rejected English, as European movements turned away from Russian or Hebrew. Harkavy's best-selling *brivnshteler* did not advocate English as replacement for Yiddish; his letters placed the two languages beside each other, as Dovid Katz underscored when he pointed to Harkavy's "unique ability to balance the need for Americanization with Yiddishist loyalty."[109] The waves of Jewish anarchist language politics varied by geographic location, shaped by co-territorial languages and state linguistic hegemony. The United States had no anti-Yiddish government policy analogous to the attempted eradication of its Indigenous languages, nor was Yiddish publication banned as in the Soviet Union or regulated as in Israel. Further research is needed on anarchist language politics in Russia, Poland, South America, and elsewhere.

A further intriguing transmission point of anarchist linguistics is represented by Noam Chomsky. As a young person, he lived in Philadelphia and at age twelve traveled to New York City to engage with Yiddish anarchist spaces.[110] In later years, he befriended the Yiddishists Alex Erlich and Shoska Erlich, whom he called "the last living Bundists who stayed true to the founding ideas." Considering this genealogy of anarchist linguists—from Gordin to Harkavy, Zalkind to Chomsky, son of the first American Zionist Hebraist and someone who spent time as a child listening to the Yiddish-speaking editors in the *Fraye arbeter shtime* offices—suggests that metalinguistics are prototypically anarchist.[111]

These accounts demonstrate the heterogeneity of Jewish anarchist language politics: having divested from the idea of a state and, therefore, from any monolingual hegemony, their theorizations ranged from Zalkind's Talmud translation to Harkavy's triglossic acculturation projects to De Cleyre's and Rocker's non-ethnic pragmatism. By proliferating attachments to the "minor," these anarchist linguists, editors, and organizers practiced the cultural defiance of "little nations" that Kropotkin had hailed in his Yiddish introduction to *Mutual Aid*: "All that I have learned in my life . . . convinced me that the most certain path to bring about harmony from the striving of various nations, is—for each part of humanity to develop and enrich the language spoken by the masses of that part of humanity. . . . [Multilingualism] is the surest way to enrich our general heritage [*yerushe*] from all nationalities and tribes, which have special value for philosophy, theory, poetry and art." Rather than embracing the universal language "solutions" of Esperanto, Bundism, Zionism, Soviet orthography projects, or other single-language ideologies, the Yiddish anarchists elaborated a politics resonant with contemporary decolonial approaches to language.

Singing Antifascism with Jewlia Eisenberg

The fervor for justice can be like a religious
calling, if your religion is freedom.

—Jewlia Eisenberg

Standing behind a harmonium in a red dress and tall bouffant, flanked by the members of her band Charming Hostess, Jewlia Eisenberg presented her work-in-progress *The Ginzburg Geography* to an audience at the University of California, Los Angeles, in 2013.[1] This project represented a "radical cartography" of the lives, writing, and cities of Leone and Natalia Ginzburg, "famous for their intellectual brilliance and resistance to Mussolini's fascist state." Clad in the red and black of anarcho-syndicalist flags, Charming Hostess opened the set with a hand-clapping workers' song in northern Italian dialect that "comes so much out of the agricultural rhythms of the land, maps these things in place." Eisenberg then introduced the song "Revolution in Borgo San Costanzo," drawn from Natalia Ginzburg's *All Our Yesterdays* (1952):

> This is the book that she wrote under a pseudonym while she was in exile in Abruzzo. It's about a small town called Borgo San Constanzo, but that's not a real town. It's really about her life in Pizzoli in Abruzzo. She talks about, "What does it mean? What does revolution mean, actually— and is it gonna be fun? What will happen?" In the book, it seems like for some of us, revolution is about figuring out just very basic questions around land ownership from the marchese—boring, really—but to some people, that's interesting! That's how we know that revolution means different things to different people.[2]

Eisenberg extracts lyrics from Ginzburg's dense passage about the relationship in "a fairly wretched village" between a doctor who "took no interest in illness and the schoolmistress [who] took no interest in teaching," as they face their political-temperamental differences:

> Anna, at the mention of revolution, woke up and asked if he would allow her to take part in the revolution with him. But to Cenzo Rena, starting a revolution meant going to the municipal office and pulling out all the old deeds crumbling in the drawers, and making the Marchesa disgorge money for improving the drainage and setting up a dispensary, with an active doctor who would not let himself crumble away. All these were things that at present seemed like a dream, because fascism was in power and fascism wanted people to let themselves crumble away. This kind of revolution did not please Anna.[3]

From Ginzburg's portrait of mundane life and desire collide with revolution, Eisenberg sings the heart of the matter:

> Revolution, revolution
> After the war, a revolution
> Can I be in the revolution with you?

Her voice growls the first syllable of "revolution," then trills flirtatiously, and finally ascends to cantorial heights as she implores, "Can I be in the revolution with you?" The next verse pivots on the surreal lustiness of Ginzburg's text:

> Your revolution seems kind of dull
> I want fighting, escapes from rooftops
> Perhaps I'm an insect and you are a leaf
> But how can we not be outside good and evil?

Like Markish's technique of epic subversion, Eisenberg's narrative voice resists a single prescriptive command just before the threshold when poetic language would harden into slogan. The declarative line "After the war, a revolution" ends with a statement of desire that tumbles into a startling metaphor. The eroticism of revolution is Eisenberg's great topic; permitting desire to enter spaces of resistance inoculates language from becoming doctrinaire or coercive. She sings of revolutionaries unremoved from daily life, even as they long to make the horizons blossom and the borders vanish.

Eisenberg lived and sang anthemically. Born in 1970, she grew up in the Starrett City housing development in East New York, raised by a militant Marxist cadre of the United Community Center. Her best friend introduced her to anarcho-syndicalism in high school. In 1988, she enrolled at the University of California, Berkeley, to study music and history; there, she lived in the radical Barrington co-op and moved toward anarchist politics, organizing an anarchist film series with the bassist Devin Hoff. Like many twentieth-century Jewish anarchists, Eisenberg's politics arced from hardline communist origins toward heterogeneously anarchist modes of thought, art, spirituality, and action. Taking pleasure in melting ideological contradictions, her music drew from religious liturgy, queer poetry, and radical history, with such diverse inspirations as Asja Lācis, Babylonian domestic amulets, the Song of Songs, and Sephardic cooking songs. Across these projects, she listened keenly to the lived histories of Jewish women and perceived the electric pulses of anarchist movement that signaled across time and territory. Her collaborations included Charming Hostess with cellist Marika Hughes and Book of J with the blues and cantorial scholar Jeremiah Lockwood.[4] A performer dripping femme swagger in red Fluevog boots and feather eyelashes, Eisenberg's voice could be heard for a half-mile, projecting revolutionary queer femininity.

The four elements of Jewish anarchist diasporism charted in this book—
elegy, genealogy, modernism, and language politics—orbit through Eisenberg's
borderfree musical cosmos. When speaking of political organizing, she often
insisted: "Diversity of tactics!" Her musical methodologies embodied tactical
diversity as well, delving into leftist ballads and piyyutim (Hebrew liturgical
poems) equally. Her archival research practiced genealogical recovery, and her
lay leadership innovated "noncoercive ritual" pedagogies. Eisenberg expressed
her polyglot hunger through a dizzying number of languages: Aramaic, Ladino, Yiddish, Hebrew, Italian, Bulgarian, Romanian, Turkish, English, Latin,
and more.

One of her early anarchist interventions into the Jewish musical canon is
"Klezsex," on Charming Hostess's first album, *Eat* (1999), which reinterprets
the popular song *"Di grine kuzine"* (My Greenhorn Cousin). Written in 1921 by
A. Schwartz and Hyman Prizant, the seven stanzas of *"Di grine kuzine"* tell the
story of an immigrant woman's ruin from her youthful arrival in the United
States to her physical decline as she labors for long years in a millinery shop. Its
lyrics are macaronic, laced with linguistically unfused Americanisms: *zhob,
peyde, nekst-dorke* (job, payday, next-door neighbor). It puns on "greenhorn":
"Di bekelekh, di royte pomerantsn, / Hobn zikh shoyn oysgegrint in gantsn"
(Her cheeks, red oranges / became completely green), as "becoming green" represented American assimilation. In the final verse, the greenhorn cousin curses
"Columbus' land." *"Di grine kuzine"* was a hit, performed both cynically in full
and patriotically with its final stanzas excised.

Charming Hostess's "Klezsex" opens with an anxious clarinet line, followed
by dense, trilling vocals spat quicker than speech. Eisenberg uses the original
melody but sings only the final stanza of *"Di grine kuzine"*:

> Haynt, az ikh bagegn mayn kuzine
> Un ikh freg zi: Vos zhe makhstu, grine?
> Entfert zi mir mit a krumer mine:
> Az brenen zol kolombuses medine!

> Today, when I meet my cousin
> and ask her: What's up, greenhorn?
> She answers with a grimace:
> Columbus' land can burn!

Haynt, haynt, haynt. Today, today, today. There is no moment of "before," no
narrative fall. The greenhorn's expression is idiomatically "crooked," without poi-

Jewlia Eisenberg holds a red and black sign (the colors of
anarcho-syndicalist flags) with the Yiddish phrase "*Mir veln
zey iberlebn*" and the caption "We will outlive them with
intersectional anti-fascism." (Courtesy of AnMarie Rodgers)

gnant intimations of former beauty, as male writers have often described women's
aging faces. What served as a furious climax in the version written one hundred
years ago becomes not a punchline of despair but a story of the unchanging structure of labor extraction. Yiddish song often repeats the final two lines of a stanza,
a structure heightened by Eisenberg's repetition of the final stanza alone. The
music is iterative, static as funk. A stanza sung four times without variation becomes an insistent protest. Without internal translation or any English-language
hint of its social critique, the YouTube video evokes comments from viewers who
praise its "great dance energy!"—and they are not wrong.

This genre of ironic immigrant lament undergirds Stephen Sondheim's lyrics to "I Like to Live in America." *West Side Story* was originally based on the play *Abie's Irish Rose* and titled "East Side Story." Its composers made non-Jewish characters ventriloquize the historically specific tone of *"Di grine kuzine,"* and Sondheim admitted: "I've never even known a Puerto Rican."[5] The long echo chamber of Yiddish theater was displaced into Nuyorican stereotypes invented by its gay Jewish songwriters. Unlike Sondheim's transference, however, Eisenberg's setting of *"Di grine kuzine"* upends the teleology of liberal immigration narrative. There is no longer an arc toward redemption or disillusionment, only the singers' presence and their trilling indictment of "Columbus' land."

Among Eisenberg's performances of radical Yiddish music is Dovid Edelshtat's "Mayn Tsavoe" (My Oath), recorded around 2016 with David Shneer, her close friend and collaborator in multiple antifascist song projects.[6] They sing beside Edelshtat's gravestone in Colorado, which is engraved with that Yiddish poem.[7] "Mayn Tsavoe" was one of three songs Edelshtat composed in 1899; it was used by revolutionary organizations in Russia as popular propaganda. The tsarist government arrested any workers they could find with copies of Edelshtat's songs.[8] The poet H. Leivick recalled hearing a fellow prisoner in Siberia singing "Mayn Tsavoe" to protest a hanging.[9] The anarchist editor S. Yanovsky recalled how a "stoic" worker in New York once gained strength from reciting this poem and brought a workers' gathering to tears.[10] The communal reading of Edelshtat's poetry functioned as protest and public.

As Shneer sings in Yiddish, Eisenberg plays a small Casio keyboard and harmonizes wordlessly. They sing all four stanzas as Edelshtat published them, repeating the last two lines of each. Edelshtat's poetic speaker begins by addressing comrades who will outlive him, in Aaron Kramer's translation:

> O gute fraynd ven ikh vel shtarbn
> Trogt tsu mayn keyver undzer fon
> Di fraye fon mit royte farbn
> Bashpritst mit blut fun arbetsman

> Oh comrades mine, when I am dead
> carry our banner to my grave:
> the freedom-banner—flaming red
> with all the blood that workers gave.[11]

Only the last line of the final stanza is sung in English by Shneer:

> Un ven ikh her di shverdn klingen
> In letstn kamf fun blut un shmarts

Tsum folk vel ikh fun keyver zingen
Un vel bagaystern zayn harts

I will sing to the people
from the grave inspire their hearts.

Aaron Kramer's translation of the final stanza emphasizes the liminality of the revolutionary poet-prophet, who somehow hears and sings from beyond the door of death:

And when I hear a cannon sound
the final siege of want and pain,
my song shall trumpet from the ground
and set the people's heart aflame!

As Edelshtat elegized Parsons and the Haymarket martyrs, "Mayn Tsavoe" links the poet with those who sing his words beyond death. The anarchist elegy becomes a call to action, placing the performer and poet into the kinship of mourners. By visiting Edelshtat's grave and singing there, Shneer and Eisenberg enact this ritual remembrance.

In May 2022, fourteen months after Eisenberg passed from a rare GATA-2 genetic mutation, Charming Hostess released *The Ginzburg Geography* on John Zorn's Tsadik label. Eisenberg had begun developing the project in 2012 and delayed her bone marrow transplant to record as much of it as physically possible. Produced by Marika Hughes and Max Baloian, her bandmates completed the album using her research notes and vocals from performances over several years. The sound of Eisenberg's voice in different songs reflects her changing health. Eisenberg's liner notes declare: "Because of the Ginzburgs' connection to the culture and values of people who work the land, I wanted part of the music to echo the work chants and lifecycle songs from Abruzzo and Piemonte. I wanted to honor Justice and Liberty by being in conversation with anti-fascist music. . . . I wanted to touch on how the fervor for justice can be like a religious calling, if your religion is freedom, and also acknowledge their Jewish heritage, using threads of Jewish and Catholic devotional music." Through juxtapositions of traditional song and modernist text, the album illuminates how questions of justice, liberty, and place might be answered. *The Ginzburg Geography* segues from rice workers' labor songs to Woody Guthrie's "All You Fascists Bound to Lose" to records of historical shock. The song "La Situazione" sets a text written by Leone Ginzburg on the day Nazi tanks rolled into Rome: "The duty of every Italian is just this one: hunt down the Germans, sabotage their methods of communication, do not believe alarmist news. Do not be discouraged, ever. The duty of Italians is to not be discouraged ever."

In the 2013 performance at UCLA, Eisenberg explained the research behind "Marciar, Marciar," seeking out women's voices and acknowledging the absences even within radical archives:

> I did a taxonomy of partisan songs as part of preparation for this project. . . . I listened to hundreds of Italian partisan songs. And one of the interesting things is that they are about the military experiences of partisans, or they are about fighting. . . . This next song we are about to sing is about *girls who like partisans*. There are no songs about people who are killed for editing the anti-fascist newspaper. So think of this project as that.[12]

In an interview with the podcast radio613 in 2014, Eisenberg noted that the only Italian antifascist song she had previously known was "Bella Ciao."[13] She was delighted to discover how alive communal song traditions remained: "One of the things that's special about Italy is that when they honor World War II veterans, . . . people keep up the tradition of singing anti-fascist songs. . . . We don't come together and sing folk songs in America; it's not practiced. But in Italy, young people still know them, so it wasn't hard to learn."

Eisenberg describes the lyrics of "Marciar, Marciar" as representing an erotic, nonhierarchical feminism within the everyday world:

> One [song] we do, I really love. It's called "Marciar Marciar," March March. And it's from the point of view of a girl who is watching a partisan walk away to go to the front. Part of why I like it is that it captures the unusual situation of a woman objectifying a man as he walks. She likes the way he walks, how he walks with such a strength. . . . Then the point of view shifts to the workday: "We don't have lieutenants, we don't have captains, we have no chain of command. This is the ideal army." Then the last line: "I want to marry a partisan!" So this kind of flows back and forth, between a nonhierarchical revolutionary structure and—"That's sexy, I want to marry that!"

As in "Klezsex," Eisenberg's setting excavates the anarchist current within a song. Her "Marciar, Marciar" inverts the order of the stanzas, beginning with its ending call: "There is no lieutenant or captain / Neither colonel nor general / . . . I want to marry a partisan." The martial ballad denies hierarchy and asserts desire, accompanied by raucous horns.

Introducing their rendition "La Lega" (The Union), Eisenberg explains its origins and translates the Italian lyrics for the audience:

It's actually a song of the Mondina, of the rice workers of the north. Once again tuning into the folk culture, into the songs of the workers to get a sense of place of these different areas. I love the words for this 'cause there's some communist women that I really love. These are songs of some great, great working women. Their words are: "Just 'cause we're women, we're not afraid. For the love of our children, we're going to build this union, and then, *La La, the union will rise.*" Socialists want freedom.

(Which—some do, some don't. I do, but I'm an anarchist! Faked you out there!)

The next verse is: "If freedom doesn't come, it's because there's not enough unity. The scabs and the bosses, they're kind of tight, so we should kill them all." Then the final verse is: "Just because women were not afraid. We've got big mouths that's gonna defend us. . . . "

Even the *la la la* part, it's very obvious. So please sing along. When people say "sing along," probably most [of] the time they don't mean it. But we actually mean it. So please, go ahead and dance and sing along. If you can't get those words, just go *la la la*. It's really from your mouth to God's ear.

With that line of stage patter, Eisenberg references the Hasidic tale of the naïve boy who tosses the outpourings of his heart into the air as prayer. Markish analogized the pure Hasidic boy to Mayakovsky's futurist outpourings; Eisenberg transposes the tale to singing along with an Italian women's militant union song. Although the 2013 performance follows the traditional lyrics, Eisenberg's album recording adapts the repeated phrase "E noialtri socialisti" (And we socialists) to include *socialisti, anarchici, comunisti, femministe,* expanding the varieties of antifascist identities who fought with the Ginzburgs.

Eisenberg's music maps a diasporic anarchism capacious enough to invite in Jewish and non-Jewish mysticism, steadfast feminism, queer love, and revolutionary militancy. The introduction of this book, written before we lost her, proposed regarding archival ephemera as an anarchist form that reflects the precarity of working life and documents everyday practices of comradeship through their fleeting forms. Please admit to this archive alongside close readings of Jewlia's songs these unphotographed images as well: a circle of faces lit by strings of light under a sukkah in Oakland, singing labor ballads to honor her father,

Martin, a Brooklyn labor organizer, on his yortsayt. An explosive moment in the darkened Brooklyn club Barbès when, after performing a union anthem, she followed it with "The Loco-Motion." Floating in a lake in summer by the Latvian border, my eyesight blurry without glasses, her bouffant piled high like an impressionist muse, her voice carrying over bright water. Lying on Riis Beach in the Rockaways in spangled swimsuits, reading Saidiya Hartman and Frank Bidart aloud, sand blowing into the pages as she made me repeat lines, finding different beats in them each time. During the months of her hospitalization, we read Anne Boyer's poetry by Zoom, as I smoked eggplants over the stovetop and longed to share them with her. In any text she listened until she found its music. And throughout the first year of her memorialization, she taught through the pedagogies of grief and elegy. Eisenberg lived and sang a diasporic anarchism which opens.

Notes

ACKNOWLEDGMENTS

1. Jacques Rancière, "Aesthetic Separation, Aesthetic Community: Scenes from the Aesthetic Regime of Art." Lecture at the University of Amsterdam, June 2006.

INTRODUCTION

1. Reuben Brainin (1862–1939) wrote in Hebrew and Yiddish. In addition to this profile of Goldman, he published interviews with S. Abramovitsh, Y. L. Perets, Max Nordau, Albert Einstein, and other notable Jewish public figures. See *Tsum Hundertstn Geborntog fun Reuben Brainin: Zamlbukh* (New York: Ikuf, 1962), 125–126.
2. Author's translation of Reuben Brainin, "*Fun shabes biz shabes,*" 1935. Full publication information is missing from the newspaper clipping. Courtesy of the Emma Goldman Papers Project, Berkeley, California. Unless otherwise noted, all translations are by the author.
3. Brainin recognizes her "Jewish eyes" and *khutspe* (swagger or insolence); other journalists racialized her "face of a Slav" or "mouth of a worker and the eyes of an enthusiast." His description mixes admiration and denigration ("Now for the first time I glimpsed the face of the lady, who was not young and was not graceful. Her round face still had hidden in it the traces of past beauty"), typical of journalists who interpreted Goldman's body as if it were a manifesto. On the press's racialization and sexualization of Goldman, see Clare Hemmings, *Considering Emma Goldman: Feminist Political Ambivalence and the Imaginative Archive* (Durham: Duke University Press, 2016), 110–114.
4. See also Mina Grauer, "Anarcho-Nationalism: Anarchist Attitudes Towards Jewish Nationalism and Zionism," *Modern Judaism* 14, no. 1 (February 1994): 1–19.

5. Emma Goldman, *Emma Goldman: A Documentary History of the American Years,* vol. 2, ed. Candace Falk and Barry Pateman (Champaign: University of Illinois Press, 2012), 42 n158.

6. Ruth Kinna, *The Government of No One: The Theory and Practice of Anarchism* (New York: Penguin, 2019), 83. Giorgio Agamben, "We Refugees," *Symposium* 49, no. 2 (Summer 1995): 114–119.

7. Jean Varlet, "The Explosion," in *Anarchism: A Documentary History of Libertarian Ideas,* ed. Robert Graham (Montreal: Black Rose Books, 2005), 22.

8. Quoted in Robert Graham, *We Do Not Fear Anarchy, We Invoke It!: The First International and the Origins of the Anarchist Movement* (Stirling, U.K.: AK Press, 2015), 241.

9. Quoted in Ruth Kinna, *Kropotkin: Reviewing the Classical Anarchist Tradition* (Edinburgh: Edinburgh University Press, 2016), 157.

10. Allison Schachter, *Diasporic Modernisms: Hebrew and Yiddish Literature in the Twentieth Century* (New York: Oxford University Press, 2011), 33.

11. H. Burgin, "*Vos iz anarkhizm? A kurtser leson in sotsyalizm*" (What Is Anarchism? A Short Lesson in Socialism), *Forverts,* New York, Sunday, March 23, 1919, 2.

12. Jesse Cohn, "'Don't Trust Anybody, Not Even Us': Kafka's Realism as Anarchist Modernism," *Studies in 20th & 21st Century Literature* 35, no. 2 (2011). Ginsberg links his participation in the Industrial Workers of the World with nostalgia for previous generations of Jewish anarchists when he confesses: "America I feel sentimental about the Wobblies" ("America," in *Collected Poems, 1947–1980* [New York: HarperCollins, 2001]). Ginsberg praises nonviolent Czech anarchists and family activism: "The YIPPIES were a paraphrase of the YIPSELS [Young People's Socialist League, founded in 1907], a socialist organization of the 1920s that my mother belonged to. . . . Our purpose was to project some kind of rock n' roll enthusiasm, Dada anarchism, humor and festival of life." In "Anarchism and Revolution in Amerikkka, an interview with Allen Ginsberg," *Drunken Boat,* no. 1, ed. Max Blechman (1994), collected in *Revolutionary Romanticism: A Drunken Boat Anthology,* ed. Max Blechman (San Francisco: City Lights, 2001).

13. Decision on the John Turner case, *Turner v. Williams,* 194 U.S. 279.

14. Kenyon Zimmer, *Immigrants Against the State: Yiddish and Italian Anarchism in America* (Champaign: University of Illinois Press, 2015), 1.

15. Emma Goldman, *Living My Life,* vol. 1 ([1931] New York: Dover Publications, 2013), 165.

16. Rocker, *The London Years* ([1956] Nottingham: Five Leaves Publications, 2005), 66.

17. I. S. Grossman-Roshchin, *Biloye,* no. 27/28 (1924), 172–182.

18. Paul Avrich, *The Haymarket Tragedy* (Princeton: Princeton University Press, 1984). Kenyon Zimmer, "Haymarket and the Rise of Syndicalism," in *The Palgrave Handbook of Anarchism,* ed. Matthew Adams and Carl Levy (London: Palgrave Macmillan, 2018), 353–364.

19. Ori Kritz, *The Poetics of Anarchy: David Edelshtat's Revolutionary Poetry* (Berlin: Peter Lang GmbH, Internationaler Verlag der Wissenschaften, 1997), 101.

20. Correspondence with Edelshtat's descendant Bob Telson, 2021.

21. *Sing, Stranger: A Century of American Yiddish Poetry—A Historical Anthology,* ed. Benjamin Harshav, trans. Barbara Harshav and Benjamin Harshav (Stanford: Stanford University Press, 2006), 13.

22. See Binyamin Hunyadi, "The Meshuggener Philosopher and the Crippled Shlimazl: Satire in the Anarchist Yiddish Press," lecture at YIVO Institute for Jewish Research, November 18, 2019.

23. Moshe Goncharok, *On the History of the Yiddish Anarchist Press* (Jerusalem: Farlag "Problemen," 1997).

24. Paul Avrich, *Anarchist Portraits* (Princeton: Princeton University Press, 1990), 179.

25. Avrich, *Anarchist Portraits,* 183.

26. Avrich, *Anarchist Portraits,* 183.

27. Avrich, *Anarchist Portraits,* 183.

28. See Introduction to Anna Elena Torres and Kenyon Zimmer, eds., *With Freedom in Our Ears: Histories of Jewish Anarchism* (Chicago: University of Illinois Press, 2023).

29. Introduction to Torres and Zimmer, *With Freedom in Our Ears.*

30. The largest and oldest English-language publishing house is Freedom Press in London's East End, founded in 1886, which also ran a paper titled *Freedom.*

31. See Yael Chaver, *What Must Be Forgotten: The Survival of Yiddish in Zionist Palestine* (Syracuse: Syracuse University Press, 2004).

32. For further circulation data see Kenyon Zimmer, "American Anarchist Periodical Circulation Data, 1880–1940" (2014). https://www.academia.edu/7715169/American_Anarchist_Periodical_Circulation_Data_1880_1940.

33. Interview with Friedrich's grandson Tommy Spree in Wedding, Berlin, Summer 2018.

34. Avrich, *The Anarchists in the Russian Revolution* (Ithaca: Cornell University Press, 1973), 49–52.

35. The last editor of *Problemen* was Yosef Luden, whose brother Itzhak Luden edited the Yiddish Bundist paper *Lebens-Fragen* for forty-three years, until it folded in 2014.

36. Kathy Ferguson, "Anarchist Printers and Presses: Material Circuits of Politics," *Political Theory* 42, no. 4 (August 2014): 392.

37. Ferguson, "Anarchist Printers and Presses," 407.

38. Wisotzky, "Such a Life" (typewritten manuscript), Box 1, Folder 5, Joseph A. Labadie Collection, Special Collections Research Center, University of Michigan Library, Ann Arbor, 15–16.

39. See Avrich, *Anarchist Portraits;* Goncharok, *On the History of the Yiddish Anarchist Press.*

40. "The Little Review," Modernist Journals Project, https://modjourn.org/journal/little-review/.

41. Margaret Anderson, *My Thirty Years' War* (New York: Covici Friede, 1930), 54.

42. Cited in *Félix Fénéon: The Anarchist and the Avant-garde,* ed. Starr Figura, Isabelle Cahn, and Philippe Peltier (New York: Museum of Modern Art, 2020), 22–23.

43. Patricia Leighten, "Fénéon's Anarchist Avant-Gardism," in Figura, Cahn, and Peltier, *Félix Fénéon: The Anarchist and the Avant-garde,* 95.

44. André Breton, "La Claire Tour" in *La Clé des champs* (Paris, January 11, 1952), and Jean-Jacques Pauvert (1967), 42. See also A. T. Kingsmith, Julian von Bargen, Karen Bridget Murray, and Robert Latham, *The Radical Left and Social Transformation: Strategies of Augmentation and Reorganization* (London: Taylor and Francis, 2020).

45. Robert A. Varisco, "Anarchy and Resistance in Tristan Tzara's 'The Gas Heart,' " *Modern Drama* 40, no. 1 (1997).

46. Tom Sandqvist, *Dada East: The Romanians of Cabaret Voltaire* (Cambridge: MIT Press, 2006). Alfred Bodenheimer, "Dada Judaism: The Avant-Garde in First World War Zurich," in *Jewish Aspects in Avant-Garde: Between Rebellion and Revelation,* ed. Mark Helber and Sami Sjöberg (Berlin: De Gruyter, 2017). Varisco notes that "Tzara" could also be understood as a reversal of "eretz" or "aretz," the Hebrew word for "land," thus reversing the Romanian term "tara" (land). "Dada Judaism," 27.

47. Dovid Katz, Introduction to *Menke: The Complete Yiddish Poems,* trans. Benjamin Harshav and Barbara Harshav (New York: The Smith, 2005), xxxvii.

48. "*Notitsn vegn naye bikher,*" *Frayhayt* (April 25, 1932), 5. Cited by Dovid Katz, Introduction to *Menke,* xxxvii.

49. Chaim Krul, "*Minyaturn.* Menke Katz" [Miniatures. Menke Katz] in *Fraye arbeter shtime,* September 4, 1936. Cited by Dovid Katz, Introduction to *Menke,* xliv.

50. See Nina Gurianova, *The Aesthetics of Anarchy: Art and Ideology in the Early Russian Avant-Garde* (Berkeley: University of California Press, 2012).

51. On anarcho-Zionism and anarcho-Judaism, see Hayyim Rothman, *No masters but God: Portraits of Anarcho-Judaism* (Manchester: Manchester University Press, 2021).

52. P. Nyers, "Abject Cosmopolitanism: The Politics of Protection in the Anti-deportation Movement," *Third World Quarterly* 24, no. 6 (2003): 1069–1093.

53. Harsha Walia, *Border and Rule: Global Migration, Capitalism, and the Rise of Racist Nationalism* (Chicago: Haymarket Books, 2021), 5.

54. See Mark Rifkin, *Beyond Settler Time: Temporal Sovereignty and Indigenous Self-Determination* (Durham: Duke University Press, 2017).

55. See "*Antisemit, das geht nicht unter Menschen,*" in *Anarchistische Positionen zu Antisemitismus, Zionismus und Israel,* Band 1–2, ed. Jürgen Mümken and Siegbert Wolf (Lich/Hessen: Edition AV, 2014); Frédéric Krier, *Sozialismus für Kleinbürger: Pierre-Joseph Proudhon—Wegbereiter des Dritten Reiches* (Köln: Böhlau, 2009).

56. Dominique F. Miething, "Antisemitism in the Anarchist Tradition," *Anarchist Studies* 26, no. 1 (2017): 106.

57. P. J. Proudhon, *Carnets de P. J. Proudhon,* ed. Pierre Hauptmann and Mitchell Abidor, trans. Mitchell Abidor (Paris: M. Rivière, 1960).

58. *God and the State* (1871) was translated into French by Carlo Cafiero and Élisée Reclus in 1882. A corrected English translation was issued in 1910. Yanovsky translated from the earlier version.

59. Eliyahu Stern, *Jewish Materialism: The Intellectual Revolution of the 1870s* (New Haven: Yale University Press, 2018), 140.

60. Mikhail Bakunin, *God and the State,* in *The Selected Works of Mikhail Aleksandrovich Bakunin* (N.p.: Library of Alexandria, undated), 74.

61. Bakunin, *Got un der shtat,* trans. Saul Yanovsky (Lidz: Lidzer anarkhiṣṭishe grupe, 1901), 89.

62. Daniel Blatman, "Bund," in *The YIVO Encyclopedia of Jews in Eastern Europe* (New York: YIVO Institute for Jewish Research, 2010).

63. Sarah Abrevaya Stein, *Extraterritorial Dreams: European Citizenship, Sephardi Jews, and the Ottoman Twentieth Century* (Chicago: University of Chicago Press, 2016), 5.

64. Abrevaya Stein, *Extraterritorial Dreams,* 11.

65. A nurse named Lini/Lena Moerkirk de Vries (Fuhr) of Sephardi Dutch background wrote the memoir *Up from the Cellar* (1979).

66. "1399 Max Nash aka Nunez/Nashitz—Sephardi from 13 Clarence Gdns, Clarence Rd, Hackney, London—KIA Ebro/Gandesa July/Aug 1st 1938 by a sniper." https://www.marxists.org/subject/jewish/spanjews.pdf.

67. Jeff Lesser, *Rethinking Jewish-Latin Americans* (Albuquerque: University of New Mexico Press, 2008).

68. Christine Temin, "Pissarro: Lifelong Anarchist," *Art New England* 32, no. 5 (2011).

69. Kathleen Adler, *Camille Pissarro: A Biography* (New York: St. Martin's Press, 1977), 124–125.

70. On the socialist Ladino press, see Devin Naar's forthcoming work.

71. Kinna, *The Government of No One,* 38.

72. Hemmings, *Considering Emma Goldman,* 110–114.

73. Reed Ingalls, "No Self, No Masters: An Interview with Author of *The Nation on No Map: Black Anarchism and Abolition* and Activist William C. Anderson." March 14, 2022. https://noselvesnomasters.com/2022/03/14/zen-and-the-anarchism-of-blackness/.

74. Ruth Wilson Gilmore, interview with Chenjerai Kumanyika, Intercepted, June 10, 2020. https://theintercept.com/2020/06/10/ruth-wilson-gilmore-makes-the-case-for-abolition/.

75. Reed W. Ingalls, "Zen and the Anarchism of Blackness: An Interview with Author & Activist William C. Anderson." March 14, 2022. https://noselvesnomasters.com/2022/03/14/zen-and-the-anarchism-of-blackness/.

76. Walter Benjamin, "Ministry of the Interior," in *One-Way Street* (Cambridge, Mass.: Harvard University Press, 2016), 31–32.

77. Ruth Kinna, "Utopianism and Prefiguration," in *Political Uses of Utopia: New Marxist, Anarchist, and Radical Democratic Perspectives,* ed. S. Chrostowska and J. Ingram (New York: Columbia University Press, 2016), 198–218, 200.

78. Cindy Barukh Milstein, *Anarchism and Its Aspirations* (Edinburgh and Oakland: AK Press/IAS, 2010), 68.

79. Uri Gordon, "Prefigurative Politics Between Ethical Practice and Absent Promise," *Political Studies* 66, no. 2 (2018): 521–537.

80. Jayna Brown, *Black Utopias: Speculative Life and the Music of Other Worlds* (Durham: Duke University Press, 2021), 158.

81. Amelia Glaser, *Songs in Dark Times: Yiddish Poetry of Struggle from Scottsboro to Palestine* (Cambridge: Harvard University Press, 2020), ix.

82. Theresa Warburton, *Other Worlds Here: Honoring Native Women's Writing in Contemporary Anarchist Movements* (Evanston: Northwestern University Press, 2021), 25.

83. Brandon Benallie, "Life, Freedom, and Ethics: Kropotkin Now!—Saturday Session 2B" lecture, February 11, 2021. https://www.youtube.com/watch?v=aURs174ZMIU.

84. On Marx's impact on anarchist thought, see Graham, *We Do Not Fear Anarchy, We Invoke It!* and Y. A. Maryson [Merison], *Principles of Anarchism* (New York: Jewish Anarchist Federation of America, 1935).

85. Bellini, *St. Francis in the Desert,* c. 1480.

86. Graeber's final essay was his introduction to Kropotkin, *Mutual Aid: An Illuminated Factor of Evolution* (Oakland: AK Press, 2021), 24.

87. *Encyclopaedia Britannica* (1905), s.v. "Anarchism."

88. Jacob Isaac Segal, *Kropotkin-zamlbukh: gevidmeṭ dem finf un tsvantsiḳṭn yortsayṭ zinṭ dem ṭoyṭ fun P. A. Kropoṭkin* (Buenos Aires: Grupe Dovid Edelshtat, 1947).

89. Paul Avrich, "Kropotkin in America," *International Review of Social History* 25, no. 1 (1980): 13.

90. Dr. A. Mukdoyni, "Sholem Shvartsbard," *Lodzher Morgnblat,* June 30, 1926, 47. Shvartsbard, *In'm loyf fun yorn* (In the Tide of Time, Sholem Shvartsbard Komitet, Chicago: 1934), trans. Kelly Johnson, 291.

91. Avrich, "Kropotkin in America," 14.

92. Reprinted in *Centennial Expressions on Peter Kropotkin 1842–1942 By Pertinent Thinkers* ([1942] Los Angeles: Rocker Publications, 1962), 13.

93. Y. A. Merison, *Gegenzaytige hilf: bay khayes un menshen, als a faktor fun entviklung* (New York: Kropotkin Literature Society, 1913), vii.

94. As the articles that constitute *Mutual Aid* were originally composed in English, presumably Kropotkin's seven-page introduction to the 1913 Yiddish edition was translated into Yiddish by Merison.

95. The insight on "little nationalities" was offered by Raya Shapiro in conversation, March 2022.

96. Kropotkin, Introduction to Merison, *Gegenzaytige hilf,* 2–3.

97. Gustav Landauer, *Revolution and Other Writings: A Political Reader* (Oakland: PM Press, 2010), epigram. Landauer was significant for Herman Frank, an editor of *Fraye arbeter shtime,* who translated his work.

98. Landauer, *Revolution and Other Writings,* 25.

99. Butler, "The Anarchist Turn," conference, New School, New York, May 5, 2011. http://www.newschoolphilosophy.com/arendtschurmann-symposium/anarchist-.

100. Rebecca Solnit, *A Paradise Built in Hell: The Extraordinary Communities That Arise in Disaster* (New York: Penguin, 2010), 10.

101. Saidiya Hartman, *Wayward Lives, Beautiful Experiments: Intimate Histories of Riotous Black Girls, Troublesome Women, and Queer Radicals* (New York: W. W. Norton, 2019). Gómez-Barris, *The Extractive Zone* (Durham: Duke University Press: 2017).

102. Saidiya Hartman, "The Anarchy of Colored Girls Assembled in a Riotous Manner," *South Atlantic Quarterly* 117, no. 3 (July 2018): 471.

103. Conferences (such as "Kropotkin Now!" in February 2021) grappled with Kropotkin's legacy as an anthropologist. Hartman characterizes Black mutual aid as invisible to anarchist scholarship ("The Anarchy of Colored Girls Assembled in a Riotous Manner," 2).

104. Dean Spade, *Mutual Aid: Building Solidarity During This Crisis (And the Next!)* (London: Verso, 2020). See also Big Door Brigade's Mutual Aid Toolbox, https://bigdoorbrigade.com/mutual-aid-toolbox/.

105. Léopold Lambert, "Interview: Making Abolition Geography in California's Central Valley with Ruth Wilson Gilmore," *Funambulist* 21 (January–February 2019).

106. Colin Ward, *Anarchy in Action* (Crows Nest, Australia: George Allen and Unwin, 1973), 15.

107. Landauer's daughter Brigitte Hausberger quoted by Paul Avrich in *Anarchist Voices: An Oral History of Anarchism in America* (Princeton: Princeton University Press, 1995), 33.

108. See Julian Levinson, "Walt Whitman Among the Yiddish Poets," *Tikkun* 18, no. 5, and Leonard Prager, "Walt Whitman in Yiddish," *Walt Whitman Quarterly Review* 1, no. 3 (December 1983).

109. Quoted in Terrence Kissack, *Free Comrades* (Chico, Calif.: AK Press, 2008), 69.

110. Kissack, *Free Comrades,* 70.

111. Kissack, *Free Comrades,* 72.

112. Prager, "Walt Whitman in Yiddish," 22–35.

113. Whitman's first German translator was Ferdinand Freiligrath, a friend of Marx and Engels.

114. See also Fahri Öz, "Drum-Taps: Whitman's Problematic Legacy as a War Poet," *IAFOR Journal of Literature and Librarianship* 5, no. 1 (Autumn 2016).

115. Goldman, "Walt Whitman" (incomplete manuscript). Emma Goldman Papers Project: Microfilm Edition, reel 54. Subsequent quotations from Goldman's unpublished essay are taken from this source.

116. Whitman, "For You O Democracy," *Leaves of Grass: A Textual Variorum of the Printed Poems, 1855–1856* (New York: NYU Press, 2008), 375.

117. See Theresa Warburton, *Other Worlds Here: Honoring Native Women's Writing in Contemporary Anarchist Movements.*

118. Gustav Landauer, "Anarchism in Germany," in *Anarchism in Germany and Other Essays,* trans. and ed. Stephen Bender and Gabriel Kuhn (San Francisco: Barbary Coast Publishing Collective, 2005).

119. Landauer, "Schwache Stattsmänner, Schwächeres Volk!" *Der Sozialist,* June 1910.

120. Mark Doty, "The Question of Homoeroticism in Whitman's Poetry: Mark Doty on Sexuality and 'Unspeakability' in *Leaves of Grass*," *Lit Hub,* April 14, 2020.

121. Mark Doty, *What Is the Grass: Walt Whitman in My Life* (New York: W. W. Norton, 2020).

122. Michael Robertson, *The Last Utopians: Four Late Nineteenth-Century Visionaries and Their Legacy* (Princeton: Princeton University Press, 2018), 159.

123. "Mariame Kaba: Everything Worthwhile Is Done with Other People," interview with Eve L. Ewing, *Adi* (Fall 2019). Taylor Mac, "Whitman in the Woods," AllArts/PBS 2021. https://www.pbs.org/show/taylor-mac-whitman-woods/.

124. Goldman, *Living My Life,* vol. 1, 168.

125. Charles J. Stivale, "Louise Michel's Poetry of Existence and Revolt," *Tulsa Studies in Women's Literature* 5, no. 1 (Spring 1986), 41–61. Carolyn Eichner, "Language of Imperialism, Language of Liberation: Louise Michel and the Kanak-French Colonial Encounter," *Feminist Studies* 45 (2019).

126. Bullitt Lowry and Elizabeth Ellington Gunter, "Translator's Introduction," in *Red Virgin: Memoirs of Louise Michel* (Tuscaloosa: University Alabama Press, 2003), xi.

127. Margaret Anderson, "Emma Goldman in Chicago," *Mother Earth* 9 (1914): 320.

128. Kritz, *The Poetics of Anarchy: David Edelshtat's Revolutionary Poetry,* 44.

129. Isaac Bashevis Singer, "Father Becomes an Anarchist," in *More Stories from My Father's Court,* trans. Curt Leviant (New York: Farrar, Straus and Giroux, 2000), 193–200. Isaac Singer, "Job," *New Yorker,* August 13, 2012, https://www.newyorker.com/books/page-turner/job.

130. Miriam Karpilove, *Diary of a Lonely Girl, or The Battle Against Free Love,* trans. Jessica Kirzane (New York: Syracuse University Press, 2020), 151.

131. Jeffrey Veidlinger, *In the Midst of Civilized Europe: The Pogroms of 1918–1921 and the Onset of the Holocaust* (New York: Metropolitan, 2021). On pogroms and "neglect" as a category of violence, see also Harriet Murav, "Archive of Violence: Neighbors, Strangers, and Creatures in Itsik Kipnis' *Months and Days," Quest: Issues in Contemporary Jewish History,* no. 15 (August 2019).

132. Michael Nevins, "Henry Torrès, 'Defender of Jewish Assassins,'" *Felshtin Society,* November 16, 2013. http://felshtin.org/henry-torres-defender-of-jewish-assassins/.

133. Kelly Johnson, "Sholem Schwarzbard: Biography of a Jewish Assassin" (PhD diss., Harvard University, 2012), 263.

134. Dovid Bergelson, *Geklibene verk,* 8 vols. (Vilne: B. Kletskin, 1928–1930), vol. 5; *Shturemteg, Dertseylung* (1930); vol. 6, 177. Translation by Joachim Neugroschel, in *Shadows of Berlin: The Berlin Stories of Dovid Bergelson* (San Francisco: City Lights, 2005), 21–44.

135. Harriet Murav, *David Bergelson's Strange New World: Untimeliness and Futurity* (Bloomington: Indiana University Press: 2019), 158.

136. Zimmer, *Immigrants Against the State,* 34.

137. Carolin Kosuch, "We Are Too Far Ahead to Be Understood," in *Anarchism and the Avant-Garde: Radical Arts and Politics in Perspective,* ed. Carolin Kosuch (Leiden: Brill Publishers, 2019), 167.

138. Flores Magón, "Carta del 30 de noviembre de 1920." Antorcha Biblioteca Virtual. http://www.antorcha.net/biblioteca_virtual/politica/epis/carta_elena_30_noviembre_1920 .html. Also cited by Jesse Cohn in "What Is Anarchist Literary Theory?" 4.

139. Translation by Aaron Kramer, performing for WBAI, 15:41. https://media.sas.upenn .edu/pennsound/authors/Kramer-A/Kramer-Aaron_Complete-Recording_Poets -Of-The-Sweatshop-I-Winchevsky-Edelshtat_WBAI_11–18–61.mp3.

140. Kramer papers, Joseph A. Labadie Collection, Special Collections Research Center, University of Michigan Library, Ann Arbor. See also Aaron Kramer, *A Century of Yiddish Poetry* (New York: Cornwall Books, 1989), 60.

141. Gurianova, *Aesthetics of Anarchy,* 2.

142. I follow Chana Kronfeld's characterization of modernist trend affiliations in *On the Margins of Modernism: Decentering Literary Dynamics* (Berkeley: University of California Press, 1996), 12.

143. Robert Darnton, *The Forbidden Best-sellers of Pre-revolutionary France* (New York: W. W. Norton & Co., 1996), 300.

144. Robertson, *The Last Utopians,* 117.

145. Adrienne Maree Brown and Walidah Imarisha, eds., *Octavia's Brood: Science Fiction Stories from Social Justice Movements* (Chico, Calif.: AK Press, 2015), 3.

146. Margaret Killjoy, "The Anarchist Utopian Imagination," *Fifth Estate,* no. 389 (Summer 2013).

147. Sidra DeKoven Ezrahi, *Booking Passage: Exile and Homecoming in the Modern Jewish Imagination* (Berkeley: University of California Press, 2000), 270.

148. Jayna Brown, *Black Utopias: Speculative Life and the Music of Other Worlds* (Durham: Duke University Press, 2021), 113.

149. Brown, *Black Utopias,* 178.

150. P. Kropotkin, "Anarchist Morality," Part VI, 1897. Reprinted in Kropotkin, *Fugitive Writings* (Montreal: Black Rose Books, 2021), 142.

151. Alexandra Schwartz, "Believe You Me," *New Yorker*, May 8, 2017, 93.

152. Humphrey Carpenter, *W. H. Auden: A Biography* (London: Farber and Farber, 2011), 41.

153. Grace Paley, *Just As I Thought* (Farrar, Straus and Giroux, 2014), 194.

154. Kropotkin, *Ethics: Origin and Development* (Montreal: Black Rose Books, 1992), 6.

155. Grace Paley, "Therefore," Begin Again: Collected Poems (New York: Farrar Straus Giroux, 2000), 174.

156. Paley, "Feelings in the Presence of the Sight and Sound of the Bread and Puppet Theater," in *A Grace Paley Reader: Stories, Essays, and Poetry by Grace Paley, ed. Kevin Bowen and Nora Paley* (New York: Farrar, Straus and Giroux, 2017), 303.

157. Grace Paley, "A Poem About Storytelling," in Bowen and Paley, *A Grace Paley Reader,* 326–327.

158. Paley, "Responsibility," in Bowen and Paley, *A Grace Paley Reader,* 345. Reprinted with permission of Macmillan and Union Literary.

159. "Grace Paley: An Interview by Joann Gardner," *American Poetry Review* (March 1994): 19–24.

160. Merle Bachman, *Recovering "Yiddishland": Threshold Moments in American Literature* (New York: Syracuse University Press: 2008), 180.

161. Kenneth Rexroth, "Again at Waldheim," *Retort* 1, no. 1 (Winter 1942): 27–32. Reprinted in *The Complete Poems of Kenneth Rexroth* (Port Townsend, Wash.: Copper Canyon Press, 2003), 221.

162. Grace Paley, "Faith in a Tree," in Bowen and Paley, *A Grace Paley Reader,* 92.

163. Cohn, "'Don't Trust Anybody, Not Even Us': Kafka's Realism as Anarchist Modernism," 119.

164. Dadoun is quoted in Jesse Cohn, "What Is Anarchist Literary Theory?" *Anarchist Studies* 15, no. 2 (Autumn/Winter 2007), 115 (Cohn's translation).

165. Berl Kagan, "Borekh Rivkin," in *Leksikon Fun Yidish-shraybers: Mit Hesofes Un Tikunim Tsum Leksikon Fun Der Nayer Yidisher Literatur, Un 5,800 Psevdonimen* (Amherst: National Yiddish Book Center, 2001). Translated by Joshua Fogel, *Yiddish Leksikon.* http://yleksikon.blogspot.com/2019/06/borekh-rivkin.html.

166. B. Rivkin, *A gloybn far umgloybike* (A Belief for Unbelievers) (New York, 1947). See also Eliui Damm, "On Rivkin's Ideas," in Torres and Zimmer, *With Freedom in Our Ears.*

167. Kagan, "Rivkin."

168. Kagan, "Rivkin."

169. B. Rivkin, *Grunt-tendentsn fund der yidisher literatur in amerike* (New York: Ikuf Farlag, 1948), 148–151.

170. Translation by Eliui Damm and author.

171. A. Litvak, *"Di rol fun der revolutsyoner lid in der arbeter bavegung,"* in *Yidishe literatur,* ed. N. Oyslander et al. (Kiev, 1928), 324.

CHAPTER 1. "SUBTERRANEAN FIRE"

1. Zimmer, *Immigrants Against the State,* 3.
2. A Yiddish version of Haymarket speeches introduced by Alexander Berkman appeared on November 11, 1933, coinciding with the anniversary of the executions: *Barimte redes fun di shikago'er martirer* (*Famous Speeches by the Chicago Martyrs*), trans. A. Frumkin (New York: Amshol-Kropotkin Group, 1933).
3. Paul Avrich and Karen Avrich, *Sasha and Emma: The Anarchist Odyssey of Alexander Berkman and Emma Goldman* (Cambridge: Belknap Press of Harvard University Press, 2012), 22.
4. Kalman Marmor, *Dovid Edelshtat* [Yiddish] (New York: YKUF Farlag, 1950), 41.
5. John Samuel Lorber, "*Tsum Folk Vel Ikh Fun Keyver Zingen:* I Will Sing to the People from the Grave; The Emotions of Protest in the Songs of Dovid Edelshtat" (master's thesis, Vanderbilt University, 2015), 27. N. Goldberg, *"Pionere der frayheyt," Geshikhte fun der yidisher arbeter bavegung in di fareynike shtatn,* ed. Tcherikower, 305, quoted in Ori Kritz, *The Poetics of Anarchy: David Edelshtat's Revolutionary Poetry* (Berlin: Peter Lang, 1997), 23–25, 31–37.
6. Karen Rosenberg, "The Cult of Self-Sacrifice in Yiddish Anarchism and Saul Yanovsky's *The First Years of Jewish Libertarian Socialism,*" in *Yiddish and the Left: Papers of the Third Mendel Friedman International Conference on Yiddish,* ed. Gennady Estraikh and Mikhail Krutikov (London: Routledge, 2017), 185.
7. Blaine McKinley, "'A Religion of the New Time': Anarchist Memorials to the Haymarket Martyrs, 1888–1917," *Labor History* 28, no. 3 (1987): 390.
8. Kritz, *The Poetics of Anarchy,* 388.
9. Goldman, "The Crime of the 11th of November," *Mother Earth,* November 1911, 265.
10. Shelley Streeby, *Radical Sensations: World Movements, Violence, and Visual Culture* (Durham: Duke University Press, 2013).
11. Nelson Algren, *Chicago: City on the Make* (New York: Doubleday, 1951), 75.
12. Streeby, *Radical Sensations,* 85–86.
13. James Green, *Death in the Haymarket: A Story of Chicago, the First Labor Movement, and the Bombing That Divided Gilded Age America* (New York: Anchor Books, 2006), 310–311.
14. Kathryn J. Oberdeck, "A Response to Shelley Streeby," *American Literary History* 19, no. 2 (Summer 2007), 434–437.
15. Avrich, *Haymarket Tragedy,* 10.
16. David R. Roediger and Franklin Rosemont, *Haymarket Scrapbook* (Chicago: C. H. Kerr, 1986), 112.
17. *Haymarket Scrapbook,* 163.
18. Zimmer, "Anarchist Newspapers and Periodicals 1872–1940," Mapping American Social Movements Through the 20th Century, University of Washington. https://depts.washington.edu/moves/anarchist_map-newspapers.shtml
19. Caleb Crain, "The Terror Last Time: What Happened at Haymarket," *New Yorker,* March 5, 2006.
20. Crain, "The Terror Last Time."

21. Albert Parsons, "Autobiography of Albert R. Parsons," in *Autobiographies of the Haymarket Martyrs,* ed. Philip S. Foner (New York: Pathfinder Press, 1969), 65.

22. Avrich, *Haymarket Tragedy,* 192.

23. Kritz, *The Poetics of Anarchy,* 101.

24. Kritz, *The Poetics of Anarchy,* 131–132.

25. McKinley, "'A Religion of the New Time,'" 386–400.

26. Kristin Boudreau, "Elegies for the Haymarket Anarchists," *American Literature* 77, no. 2 (2005): 319–347, 338.

27. Re'ee Hagay, "'Mourners Are the Soundtrack of Life': Mourning, Time, and Aesthetic Geographies of the South in a Mizrahi Singer's Antibiography," *Comparative Studies of South Asia, Africa, and the Middle East,* forthcoming.

28. Esther Schor, *Bearing the Dead: The British Culture of Mourning from the Enlightenment to Victoria* (Princeton: Princeton University Press, 1994), 97.

29. Jahan Ramazani, *Poetry of Mourning: The Modern Elegy from Hardy to Heaney* (Chicago: University of Chicago Press, 1994), xi.

30. Claudia Rankine, "The Condition of Black Life Is One of Mourning," *New York Times,* June 22, 2015.

31. Shulchan Aruch, Yoreh Deah 444:1.

32. Moshe Halbertal, "Eikhah and the Stance of Lamentation," in *Lament in Jewish Thought,* ed. Illit Ferber and Paula Schwebel (Berlin: De Gruyter, 2014), 6.

33. A. Frumkin, trans., *Barimte redes fun di shikago'er martirer* (New York: Amshol-Kropotkin Grupe, 1933).

34. Avrich, *Haymarket Tragedy,* 1.

35. Crain, "The Terror Last Time."

36. Avrich, *Haymarket Tragedy,* 256.

37. Avrich, *Haymarket Tragedy,* 256.

38. Avrich, *Haymarket Tragedy,* 292.

39. Blaine McKinley, "Anarchist Jeremiads: American Anarchists and American History," *Journal of American Culture* 6, no. 2 (June 1983): 3.

40. Lucy Parsons's speech appeared in the *Kansas City Journal,* December 21, 1886.

41. Edelshtat, "Albert Parsons," first published in *Fraye arbeter shtime,* November 7, 1890.

42. Translations from Edelshtat's Haymarket poem cycle are by the author.

43. Edelshtat, "Louis Lingg," *Fraye arbeter shtime,* October 24, 1890, 1.

44. Voltairine De Cleyre and Paul Avrich, *The First Mayday: The Haymarket Speeches, 1895–1910* (New York: Cienfuegos Press, Libertarian Book Club, 1980), 2–5, 36.

45. H. Lippold, "Louis Lingg," in *Der Anarchist,* St. Louis (November 11 1889). I thank Tom Goyens for sharing this poem and Nick Wilkins for translating it (June 2020).

46. Kritz, *The Poetics of Anarchy,* 113.

47. Edelshtat, *Shriften* (New York: Arbeyter fraynd, *Fraye arbeyter shtime,* 1925), 7.

48. *Daily Alta California,* November 11, 1887, vol. 42, no. 13951, California Digital Newspaper Collection, University of California, Riverside.

49. Albert R. Parsons, *Anarchism: Its Philosophy and Scientific Basis* (Chicago: Lucy Parsons, 1887), 56.

50. Edelshtat, "August Spies," lines 25–32; lines 13–16.

51. Edelshtat, "11th of November," line 20.
52. Saul Yanovsky, *Ershte yorn fun yidishn frayhaytlekhn sotsializm, oytobiografishe zikhroynes fun a pioner un boyer fun der yidisher anarkhistisher bavegung in england un amerike* (Fraye arbeter shtime, New York: 1948), 195. Translation by John Samuel Lorber, in *"Tsum Folk Vel Ikh Fun Keyver Zingen,"* 44.
53. Goldman, *Living My Life,* vol. 1, 50–62.
54. Basil Dahl [Yosef Bovshover], *To the Toilers and Other Verses,* trans. Rose Freeman-Ishill (Berkeley Heights, N.J.: Oriole Press, 1928), 38–43. Basil Dahl, *"Tsum ondenkung fun dovid edelshtat,"* in *Gezamlte shriften: poezye un proza,* ed. Joseph Bovshover (New York: Fraye arbeter shtime, 1911), 52–56.
55. Aaron Kramer, "Complete Recording of the Poets of the Sweatshop." Third broadcast in series, WBAI, New York, N.Y., February 25, 1962. Penn Sound Archive. https://media .sas.upenn.edu/pennsound/authors/Kramer-A/Kramer-Aaron_Complete-Recording _Poets-Of-The-Sweatshop-III-Joseph-Bovshover_WBAI_2–25–62.mp3.
56. Sadie Edelstadt, the daughter of Annie and Abe Edelstadt, helped organize Goldman's lectures in Butte, Montana (*Mother Earth,* July 1912).
57. Luden, *Flamen: Meditatsyes in ferzn* (Flames: Meditations in Verse) (Tel Aviv: Problemen, 1983), 77.
58. Luden, *Flamen,* 11.
59. Kathryn Hellerstein, "Malka Heifetz Tussman," Jewish Women's Archive, https://jwa .org/encyclopedia/article/tussman-malka-heifetz.
60. Hellerstein, "Malka Heifetz Tussman."
61. Heifetz Tussman, *Am I Also You?* (Berkeley: Tree Books, 1977), 9.
62. Hellerstein, "Heifetz Tussman."
63. I am grateful to Shawn Wilbur for sharing a scan of *The Alarm* and to Kathryn Hellerstein for her insight on Heifetz Tussman.
64. Nina van Zandt Spies, Preface to *August Spies' Autobiography* (Chicago, 1887).
65. *Haymarket Scrapbook,* 181.
66. Cited in Kristin Boudreau, *The Spectacle of Death: Populist Literary Responses to American Capital Cases* (Buffalo, N.Y.: Prometheus Books, 2006), 93–94.
67. Rosenberg, "The Cult of Self-Sacrifice," 190.
68. Records of the Joint Legislative Committee to Investigate Seditious Activities, *Margaret Sanger Microfilm,* C16:1035, New York State Archives.
69. Rachel Hui-Chi Hsu, *Emma Goldman, "Mother Earth," and the Anarchist Awakening* (Notre Dame, Ind.: University of Notre Dame Press, 2021).
70. V. Dolen and Lucy Parsons, "The Martyrs of 1886," *Alarm,* November 1915.
71. Heifetz Tussman, "A Young Mother's Reflections," *Alarm* 1, no. 1, November 1915, 4.
72. Silvia Federici, *Caliban and the Witch: Women, the Body, and Primitive Accumulation* (New York: Autonomedia, 2004), 97.
73. *The Alarm* 1, no. 2, November 1915. The same issue also contained this passage from Kropotkin's "Why We Are Anarchists": "We do not advocate Communism and Anarchy because we imagine men to be better than they really are; if we had angels among us we might be tempted to entrust to them the task of organising us, though doubtless even *they* would show the clovenhoof very soon. But it is just because we take men as they are

that we say: 'Do not entrust them with the governing of you. This or that despicable minister might have been an excellent man if power had not been given to him. The only way of arriving at harmony of interests is by a society without exploiters and without rulers.' It is precisely because men are not angels that we say, 'Let us arrange matters so that each man may see his interests bound up with the interests of others, then you will no longer have to fear his evil passions.' "

74. Margaret C. Anderson, "The Challenge of Emma Goldman," *Little Review* 3 (Chicago, May 1914): 5–9.

75. Emma Goldman Papers Project chronology of lectures for 1914 and 1915, 28–36. https://www.lib.berkeley.edu/goldman/pdfs/EG-AGuideToHerLife_Chronology1901–1919.pdf.

76. Heifetz Tussman, "My Shop Mate," *Alarm* 1, no. 3, December 1915, 4.

77. Helft undz trogn dem baner dem roytn / Forverts, durkh shturem, durkh finstere nekht! / Helft undz vorhayt un likht tsu farshpreytn / Tsvishn umvisende, elente knekht!

78. Quoted in Harshav and Harshav, *Sing, Stranger*, 21.

79. Poem by Chaim Plotkin, translated by Aaron Kramer. Kramer's papers, Joseph A. Labadie Collection, Special Collections Research Center, University of Michigan Library, Ann Arbor.

80. Elizabeth Freeman, *Beside You in Time: Sense Methods and Queer Sociabilities in the American Nineteenth Century* (Durham: Duke University Press, 2019), 3.

81. Elaine Scarry, *The Body in Pain: The Making and Unmaking of the World* (New York: Oxford University Press, 1987), 4.

82. Harshav and Harshav, *Sing, Stranger*, 21.

83. Teko Sāso, *November 11*, Sound Cloud Audio, November 11, 2015. https://tekosaso.bandcamp.com/album/november-eleven. Louis Lingg and the Bombs, "Louis Lingg, Anarchist," *Live at L'AJB*, recorded November 25, 2017.

84. Devin Ray Hoff, *Solo Bass*, 2008.

85. George Woodcock, "Elegy for an Anarchist," *London Review of Books* 6, no. 1 (January 19, 1984), 20–22.

86. Rexroth, "Again at Waldheim," 27–32.

87. Jesse Cohn, *Underground Passages: Anarchist Resistance Culture, 1848–2011* (Stirling, U.K.: AK Press, 2015).

88. Kritz, *The Poetics of Anarchy*, 124.

CHAPTER 2. "A GREAT CLEAVER CUT THROUGH AMERICA"

1. Bruce Watson, *Sacco and Vanzetti: The Men, the Murders, and the Judgment of Mankind* (New York: Penguin, 2007), 347.

2. Mark Mratchnyi Papers, Box 1, Folder 26, Joseph A. Labadie Collection, University of Michigan Library, Ann Arbor.

3. Jordan Finkin, "Sacco-Vanzetti Poems and Yiddish American Identity," in *Choosing Yiddish: New Frontiers of Language and Culture*, ed. Lara Rabinovitch, Shiri Goren, and Hannah Pressman (Detroit: Wayne State University Press, 2012), 47.

4. Allen Ginsberg, "America," in *Howl and Other Poems* (San Francisco: City Lights, 1956), unnumbered.

5. John Dos Passos, *The Big Money* (New York: Harcourt, Brace, 1936), 451.

6. Woodcock, "Elegy for an Anarchist," 20–22.

7. Yiddish poems responding to the case appeared in the communist *Proletpen* and the *In-zikh* journal by N. B. Minkov, Aaron Glantz-Leyeles, Moyshe-Leyb Halpern, Yankev Glatshteyn, and others. Upton Sinclair's *Boston: A Documentary Novel* was translated as *Boston: di tragedye fun Sacco un Vanzetti* (1930) in Warsaw, and Howard Fast's *The Passion of Sacco and Vanzetti: A New England Legend* was translated into Hebrew in 1921. In Buenos Aires, Nechemias Zucker published *In nomen fun gerekhtikayt: tragedye in dray aktn (En Nombre de la Justicia,* 1935) and Melekh Epshtayn's *Sacco-Vanzetti: di geshikhte fun zeyer martirertum* (1927). Nathan Asch, son of the Yiddish writer Sholem Asch, wrote *Pay Day* (1930), a compact, plotless novel set on the night of Sacco and Vanzetti's execution. See also Walter Kalaidjian, *The Cambridge Companion to American Modernism* (Cambridge: Cambridge University Press, 2006), 43.

8. I follow Chana Kronfeld's metaphor for the transmission of Jewish literary history as a rope with multiple overlapping threads (*On the Margins of Modernism,* 63).

9. Goldman to Van Valkenburgh, April 27, 1927, Box 1, Emma Goldman Papers, Joseph A. Labadie Collection, Special Collections Research Center, University of Michigan Library, Ann Arbor.

10. Yosef (Joseph) Cohen, *Di yidish-anarkhistishe bavegung in amerike: historisher iberblik un perzenlekhe iberlebungen* (The Jewish Anarchist Movement in America: A Historical Review and Personal Reminiscences) (Philadelphia: Workmen's Circle, 1945), 533.

11. Melekh Epstein, *Sako-Vanzeti di geshikhte fun zeyer martirertum* (New York: Yidisher sektsye vorkers partey, 1927), 27.

12. Ramazani, *Poetry of Mourning,* 361.

13. On Sacco and Vanzetti's allegiance to the militant Galleani, see Avrich, *Sacco and Vanzetti: The Anarchist Background* (Princeton: Princeton University Press, 1991).

14. Yankev Glatshteyn, *Kredos* (New York: Yidish lebn, 1929).

15. Yankev Glatshteyn, "Sacco and Vanzetti's Monday," trans. Lawrence Rosenwald, *In geveb: A Journal of Yiddish Studies* (May 2016). https://ingeveb.org/texts-and-translations /sacco-and-vanzettis-monday.

16. Bartolomeo Vanzetti, *Story of a Proletarian Life,* trans. Eugene Lyons (Boston: Sacco-Vanzetti Defense Committee, 1923).

17. In Bovshover's "A Song to the People," factory walls' border suffuses the world, producing no difference between inside and outside: "Lift up your eyes and see the factory walls that grow, / Where workers saw and plane and weave and knit and sew, / And forge and file and carve and chisel and sand and brace, / And create wares and create riches for the human race." In Harshav and Harshav, *Sing, Stranger,* 72.

18. Lawrence Rosenwald, "On Jacob Glatstein's Sacco and Vanzetti Poem," *Studies in American Jewish Literature (1981–)* 34, no. 1 (2015): 27.

19. Finkin, "Sacco-Vanzetti Poems," 56.

20. Yankev Glatshteyn, "Sacco and Vanzetti's Monday," trans. Lawrence Rosenwald, *In geveb: A Journal of Yiddish Studies* (May 2016). https://ingeveb.org/texts-and-translations /sacco-and-vanzettis-monday. All subsequent quotations from this work are taken from Rosenwald's translation.

21. Van Valkenburgh to Emma Goldman, "NEW MOVE IN S V CASE," n.d., c. 1927, Box 2,

Folder 7, Joseph A. Labadie Collection, Special Collections Research Center, University of Michigan Library, Ann Arbor.

22. Yosl Grinshpan, "Vanzetti's Ghost," in *Proletpen: America's Rebel Yiddish Poets*, ed. Amelia Glaser and David Weintraub (Madison: University of Wisconsin Press,; Coral Gables, Fla.: Dora Teitelboim Center for Yiddish Culture, 2005), 77–79.

23. John Dos Passos, "'They Are Dead Now': Eulogy for Sacco and Vanzetti," *New Masses*, October 1927.

24. Arturo Giovannitti, "The Walker," in *Others for 1919: An Anthology of the New Verse*, ed. Alfred Kreymborg (New York: Nicholas L. Brown, 1920), 44–51.

25. Elias Canetti, *Crowds and Power*, trans. Carol Stewart (London: Victor Gollancz Ltd, 1962), 298.

26. Quoted in Louis Joughin and Edmund M. Morgan, *The Legacy of Sacco and Vanzetti* (Princeton: Princeton University Press, 2015).

27. Glatshteyn's needle imagery recurs in "The Baron Tells of His Last Experience," recasting acts of labor as magic. See Harshav and Harshav, *Sing, Stranger*, 438–439.

28. Harshav and Harshav, *Sing, Stranger*, 27.

29. Ruth Rubin performs the song *"Mit a nodl, on a nodl"* for Smithsonian Folkways: http://www.folkways.si.edu/ruth-rubin/mit-a-nodl-oh-a-nodl-with-a-needle-without-a-needle/judaica/music/track/smithsonian.

30. Morris Rosenfeld, "Two Songs from the Ghetto," trans. Florence Kiper, in *Mother Earth* 8, no. 3 (May 1913), 67. On Rosenfeld see also Harshav and Harshav, *Sing, Stranger*, 20.

31. See also Morris Rosenfeld, "The Millionaire of Tears," trans. Harshav and Harshav, in *Sing, Stranger*, 7.

32. Gurianova, *Aesthetics of Anarchy*, 62.

33. "Houdini: Art and Magic," Contemporary Jewish Museum of San Francisco, 2012.

34. Kronfeld, *On the Margins of Modernism*, 165.

35. Benjamin Harshav, *The Meaning of Yiddish* (Berkeley: University of California Press, 1990), 107.

36. Halpern, *Moyshe-Leyb Halpern* (New York: Aroysgegebn fun Moyshe Leyb Halpern Komitet, 1934), 57–58.

37. Author's translation. For other translations, see Benjamin Harshav and Barbara Harshav, *American Yiddish Poetry: A Bilingual Anthology* (Berkeley: University of California Press, 1986), 437–439, and John Hollander in *Penguin Book of Yiddish Verse*, ed. Irving Howe, Ruth Wisse, and Chone Shmeruk (New York: Viking, 1987), 212.

38. "Sacco-Vanzetti" was collected posthumously (1934).

39. Mel Chen, *Animacies: Biopolitics, Racial Mattering, and Queer Affect* (Durham: Duke University Press, 2012), 42.

40. Author's translation of Halpern, *"Der gasnpoyker"* (The Street-Drummer). For a full translation of the poem, see John Hollander in Howe et al., *Penguin Book of Yiddish Verse*, 168.

41. Finkin, "Sacco-Vanzetti Poems," 58.

42. Howe et al., *Penguin Book of Yiddish Verse*, 212.

43. Lawrence Rosenwald, "Politics, Religion, and Some Poems About Sacco and Vanzetti," in *The Turn Around Religion in America: Literature, Culture, and the Work of Sacvan Bercovitch*, ed. Michael Kramer and Nan Goodman (Farnham, U.K.: Ashgate Publishing, 2011), 274.

44. Finkin, "Sacco-Vanzetti Poems," 52.

45. Amelia Glaser, *Songs in Dark Times*, 4.

46. Glaser, *Songs in Dark Times*, 18–19.

47. Glaser, *Songs in Dark Times*, 251–252.

48. Elaine Leeder, oral historian of Pesotta. Conversation, June 10, 2021.

49. Footage, "Funeral Procession of Sacco and Vanzetti: August 28, 1927; Narration: Robert D'Atilio." https://www.youtube.com/watch?v=J3YHuBeMc9M.

50. "Funeral Procession of Sacco and Vanzetti."

51. Michael A. Cohen Papers, YIVO Institute for Jewish Research, New York City, RG 313.

52. Goldman to Van Valkenburgh, April 27, 1927, Box 1, Emma Goldman Papers, Joseph A. Labadie Collection, Special Collections Research Center, University of Michigan Library, Ann Arbor.

53. Goldman to Van Valkenburgh, June 30, 1927.

54. Van Valkenburgh to Goldman, July 11, 1927.

55. Marc Miller, *Representing the Immigrant Experience: Morris Rosenfeld and the Emergence of Yiddish Literature in America* (New York: Syracuse University Press, 2007), 40–41.

56. Halpern founded *Di vokh* with comrades who broke from the Communist paper *Frayheyt* in 1929 over the Communist Party's response to the Hebron Massacre. See Harshav and Harshav, *American Yiddish Poetry: A Bilingual Anthology*, 391.

57. Levinson, "Modernism from Below: Moyshe-Leyb Halpern and the Situation of Yiddish Poetry," *Jewish Social Studies* 10, no. 3 (Spring/Summer 2004), 143–160, 153.

58. Author's translation of Halpern, "Salute," which was first published in Di *Vokh* (New York City), January 24, 1930.

59. Countee Cullen, "The Black Christ," *The Black Christ and Other Poems* (New York: Harper, 1929).

60. Trans. Harshav and Harshav, *American Yiddish Poetry: A Bilingual Anthology*, 431.

61. Levinson, "Modernism from Below: Moyshe-Leyb Halpern and the Situation of Yiddish Poetry," 143–160.

62. Wisse, "A Yiddish Poet in America," *Commentary* (July 1980), 39.

63. Parker Bright, demonstration at the Whitney Museum of American Art, 2017.

64. *The Letters of Sacco and Vanzetti*, ed. Marion Denman Frankfurter (New York: Penguin, 2007), 285.

65. Countee Cullen, *On These I Stand: An Anthology of the Best Poems of Countee Cullen Selected by Himself and Including Six New Poems Never Before Published* (New York: Harper, 1947), 160.

66. Moyshe-Leyb Halpern (1919), "A Nakht," in *A Little Love in Big Manhattan*, ed. Ruth Wisse (Cambridge: Harvard University Press, 1988), 96.

67. Trans. Aaron Kramer, Joseph A. Labadie Collection, Special Collections Research Center, University of Michigan Library, Ann Arbor. See also Kramer, *A Century of Yiddish Poetry*, 132–133.

68. Michael Topp, *Sacco and Vanzetti Case* (Boston: Bedford/St. Martin's, 2005), 46.

69. Nicola Sacco and Bartolomeo Vanzetti, *The Letters of Sacco and Vanzetti* (New York: Viking, 1928), 207–208.

70. See Sacco and Vanzetti, *Letters*, 51–54. Sacco's letter to his son (1927) was set to music by Pete Seeger in 1951, commissioned by Moses Asch.

71. Sacco and Vanzetti, *Letters,* 52.

72. Sacco and Vanzetti, *Letters,* 53.

73. Guthrie quoted in Seeger, *Where Have All the Flowers Gone: A Singer's Stories, Songs, Seeds, Robberies* (Bethlehem, Pa.: Sing Out, 1993), 92.

74. Sacco and Vanzetti, *Letters,* 53.

75. Vanzetti, *Story of a Proletarian Life,* 9.

76. Glaser, *Songs in Dark Times,* 251.

77. Harshav and Harshav, *Sing, Stranger,* 21.

78. Graeber, *Anarchy—In a Manner of Speaking* (Zurich: Diaphanes Anarchies, 2021), 92.

79. In "The Cult of Self-Sacrifice in Yiddish Anarchism and Saul Yanovsky's *The First Years of Jewish Libertarian Socialism,*" Karen Rosenberg characterizes the popularity of elegies as evidence of a pervasive rhetoric of martyrdom.

80. Martín Espada, "I Now Pronounce You Dead," *Massachusetts Review* 58, no. 4 (Winter 2017): 667. I thank Martín Espada for permission to reprint the poem.

81. Emily Wojcik, interview with Martín Espada, *Massachusetts Review* blog, January 18, 2018, https://www.massreview.org/node/6383.

82. Avrich, *The Haymarket Tragedy,* 393.

CHAPTER 3. "ANARCHISM BY OUR GRANDMOTHERS"

1. Asya Ferdâ, "Anarchism in the Work of Aurora Levins Morales," in *Writing Off the Hyphen: New Critical Perspectives on the Literature of the Puerto Rican Diaspora* (Seattle: University of Washington Press, May 2008), 107–124.

2. Aurora Levins Morales, "The Historian as Curandera," in *Medicine Stories: Essays for Radicals* (Durham: Duke University Press, 2019), 24.

3. See Wendy Brown on Foucault, *Politics Out of History* (Princeton: Princeton University Press, 2001).

4. ChaeRan Freeze, "*Yikhes,*" in *YIVO Encyclopedia of Jews in Eastern Europe,* ed. Gershon David Hundert (New Haven: Yale University Press, 2010).

5. Joseph (Yosef) Cohen, *Di yidish anarkhistishe-bavegung in amerike* (The Jewish Anarchist Movement in America, 1945); Saul Yanovsky, *Ershte yorn fun yidishn frayhaytlekhn sotsializm: oytobiografishe zikhroynes fun a pyoner un boyer fun der yidisher anarkhistisher bavegung in England un Amerike* (The Early Years of Jewish Liberationist Socialism: Autobiographical Memoirs by a Pioneer and Builder of the Jewish Anarchist Movement in England and America, 1948); and Yosef Luden, *Kurtse geshikhte fun anarkhistishe gedank* (A Short History of Anarchist Thought, Tel Aviv, 1984).

6. See George Ciccariello-Maher, "An Anarchism That Is Not Anarchism: Notes Toward a Critique of Anarchist Imperialism," in *How Not to Be Governed: Readings and Interpretations from a Critical Anarchist Left* (Lanham, Md.: Lexington Books, 2011), chapter 3.

7. See Mark Rifkin, *Beyond Settler Time: Temporal Sovereignty and Indigenous Self-Determination* (Durham: Duke University Press, 2017).

8. See also Theresa Warburton, "Coming to Terms: Rethinking Popular Approaches to Anarchism and Feminism," *Perspectives on Anarchist Theory,* no. 29 (January 2017).

9. Sally Roesch Wagner, *The Women's Suffrage Movement* (New York: Penguin Classics,

2019) and *Sisters in Spirit: Haudenosaunee (Iroquois) Influence on Early American Feminists* (Summertown, Tenn.: Native Voices Books, 2001).

10. Her name would be transliterated from the Yiddish as "Katherine" and appears in other English-language works as Katarina.

11. On racism in gynecology during Yevzerov Merison's era see C. Riley Snorton, *Black on Both Sides: A Racial History of Trans Identity* (Minneapolis: University of Minnesota Press, 2017). Yevzerov was likely rejected from Dr. Marion Sims's program for being a woman.

12. Berl Kagan, "Katerina Merison-Yevzerov," in *Yiddish Leksikon.*

13. Tony Michels, *A Fire in Their Hearts: Yiddish Socialists in New York* (Cambridge: Harvard University Press, 2005), 152.

14. Kagan, "Katerina Merison-Yevzerov." See translation by Khayim Leyb Fuks at http://yleksikon.blogspot.com/2017/11/katerina-merison-yevzerov.html.

15. Moshe Goncharok, *Tsu der geshikte fun der anarkhistisher prese oyf yidish* (On the History of the Yiddish Anarchist Press) (Jerusalem: Problemen, 1997).

16. Yevzerov, "*Di sotsyale lane fun di froyen,*" *Fraye gezelshaft* (Free Society), no. 4 (February 1900).

17. I thank Ayelet Brinn for sharing this article.

18. "Suffrage's High Cost, Effect on Elections Nil," *New York Times,* November 4, 1917, cited in Steven Cassedy, ed. *Building the Future: Jewish Immigrant Intellectuals and the Making of Tsukunft* (New York: Holmes and Meier, 1999), 177.

19. Katarina Yevzerov, "The American Women's Movement and the Victory for Women in the Last Elections," cited and translated in Cassedy, *Building the Future,* 197. Yevzerov refers to the streets where the German Reichstag and British Westminster Hall are located.

20. Cassedy, *Building the Future,* 200.

21. R. Edelsohn, "Hunger Striking in America," *Mother Earth* 9, no. 7 (September 1914).

22. Cassedy, *Building the Future,* 198.

23. Goldman, *Anarchism and Other Essays,* 3rd ed. (New York: Mother Earth Publishing, 1917), 106.

24. Letter to Joseph Cohen, February 27, 1911. De Cleyre files, YIVO Institute for Jewish Research, New York City.

25. Zimmer, *Immigrants Against the State,* 35.

26. Cassedy, *Building the Future,* 177.

27. Yevzerov, *Di froy in der gezelshaft* (Women in Society) (New York: Fraye gezelshaft, 1900), 8.

28. Zimmer, *Immigrants Against the State,* 44.

29. Cassedy, *Building the Future,* 194.

30. Warburton, *Other Worlds Here,* 117.

31. See J. Kēhaulani Kauanui, "The Politics of Indigeneity, Anarchist Praxis, and Decolonization," *Anarchist Developments in Cultural Studies,* no. 1 (2021).

32. Yevzerov, *Di froy,* 28.

33. *Badekn* is a dramatic moment of the Jewish marriage ceremony when the groom veils the bride.

34. Yevzerov, *Di froy,* 28.

35. Yosef (Joseph) Cohen, *Di yidish-anarkhistishe bavegung in Amerike: Historisher iberblik un perzenlakhe iberlebungen* (The Jewish Anarchist Movement in America: A Historical Overview and Personal Reminiscences) (Philadelphia: Workmen's Circle, 1945).

36. See also Samuel J. Spinner, *Jewish Primitivism* (Stanford: Stanford University Press, 2021).

37. See Sally Roesch Wagner, *Sisters in Spirit*.

38. Judith K. Brown, "Economic Organization and the Position of Women Among the Iroquois," *Ethnohistory* 17, no. 3/4 (Summer/Autumn 1970), 151–167.

39. Brandon Benallie (Dinétah), "Mutual Aid Is Reality," lecture at the conference "Life, Freedom, and Ethics—Kropotkin Now!" February 5, 2021.

40. Warburton, "Coming to Terms: Rethinking Popular Approaches to Anarchism and Feminism." https://anarchiststudies.org/coming-to-terms/.

41. Warburton, *Other Worlds Here,* 122.

42. Yevzerov, *Di froy,* 10.

43. Yevzerov refers to *hetaerae* (freeborn courtesans), who worked in brothels often run by women.

44. Yevzerov, *Di froy,* 10.

45. Yevzerov, *Di froy,* 00. See also Zimmer, *Immigrants Against the State,* 44.

46. Yevzerov, *Di froy,* 45.

47. Others cite Greek thinkers as prototypical anarchists: Lazar Lipotkin claims Zeno and the Stoics in *The Russian Anarchist Movement in North America,* trans. and ed. Malcolm Archibald (Edmonton: Black Cat Press, 2019), 5.

48. Yevzerov, *Di froy,* 78.

49. See also the biography by the poet M. A. Suhl, *Ernestine L. Rose: Women's Rights Pioneer* (New York: Biblio Press, 1990).

50. Yevzerov, *Di froy,* 74.

51. Carol A. Kolmerten. *The American Life of Ernestine L. Rose* (Syracuse: Syracuse University Press, 1999), 179.

52. *American Feminism: Key Source Documents, 1848–1920,* ed. Janet Beer, Katherine Joslin, and Anne Trudgill (London: Routledge, 2002), 244.

53. Yevzerov, *Di froy,* 82. Yevzerov uses the *daytshmerish* term *unabhängig* (independently).

54. On Lebensboym's pseudonyms, see Abraham [Avrom] Novershtern, "'Who Would Have Believed That a Bronze Statue Can Weep': The Poetry of Anna Margolin," *Prooftexts* 10, no. 3 (September 1990): 435.

55. Ayelet Brinn, "Beyond the Women's Section: Rosa Lebensboym, Female Journalists, and the American Yiddish Press," *American Jewish History* 104, no. 2/3 (April/July 2020): 348.

56. Brinn, "Beyond the Women's Section," 351–354.

57. Reuben Iceland, *Fun unzer friling: literarische zikhroynes un portretn* (New York: Aroysgegebn fun R. Azland Yoyvl Komitet, Miami Bitsh, Farlag Inzl, 1954), 152.

58. Iceland, *Fun unzer friling,* 143.

59. Brinn, "Beyond the Women's Section," 350.

60. Norma Fain Pratt, "Anna Margolin's *Lider:* A Study in Women's History, Autobiography, and Poetry," *Studies in American Jewish Literature,* no. 3 (1983): 11–25.

61. Rosa Lebensboym, *"Di froyen un der krieg,"* *Der tog,* June 25, 1915. Trans. Ayelet Brinn in "Beyond the Women's Section," 360.

62. Anna Margolin, *Literarishe bleter,* January 31, 1930, 19. See also Brinn, "Beyond the Women's Section," 361.

63. Anna Margolin, *Literarishe bleter,* June 11, 1915.

64. Accounts differ; this visit may have occurred as early as 1908. Leonard Prager, *Yiddish Culture in Britain: A Guide* (Berlin: Verlag Peter Lang, 1990), 437.

65. Faith Jones, "Anna Margolin (21 January 1887–29 June 1952)," in *Writers in Yiddish,* ed. Joseph Sherman, *Dictionary of Literary Biography,* vol. 333 (Farmington Hills, Mich.: Gale, 2007), 163–173.

66. Iceland, *Fun undzer friling,* 153.

67. Reuben Iceland, *From Our Springtime: Literary Memoirs and Portraits of Yiddish New York,* trans. Gerald Marcus (Syracuse: Syracuse University Press, 2013), 143–144.

68. Iceland, *From Our Springtime,* 144.

69. Novershtern, "Who Would Have Believed," 437.

70. Abraham Novershtern, *"Anna Margolin—materialn tsu ir poetisher geshtalt,"* *YIVO Bleter* New Series Band I (1991): 145.

71. Margolin, *Drunk from the Bitter Truth: The Poems of Anna Margolin,* ed. and trans. Shirley Kumove (New York: State University of New York Press, 2017), 109. Reprinted with permission of the translator and SUNY Press.

72. Trans. Kumove, *Drunk from the Bitter Truth,* 11.

73. Trans. Kumove, *Drunk from the Bitter Truth,* 173.

74. Author's translation from the version printed in Margolin, *Lider* (New York: Orion Press, 1929), 111. For another interpretation and version of this poem, see Robert Wolf's translation in Novershtern, "Who Would Have Believed," 438–439.

75. Wolf, in Novershtern, "Who Would Have Believed," 439.

76. See also Kathryn Hellerstein's critique, "Translating as a Feminist: Reconceiving Anna Margolin," *Prooftexts* 20, no. 1–2 (Winter/Spring 2000): 191–208. Melissa Weininger, "A Poetic Paradox: Gender and Self in Anna Margolin's Mary Cycle," *In geveb: A Journal of Yiddish Studies* (May 2017).

77. Translated by Kathryn Hellerstein, in *Jewish American Literature: A Norton Anthology,* ed. Jules Chametzky (New York: Norton, 2001), 265. Reprinted with permission of the translator.

78. Weiman Kelman, *Queer Expectations: A Genealogy of Jewish Women's Poetry* (Albany: State University of New York Press, 2018), 35.

79. David L. Eng, with Judith Halberstam and José Esteban Muñoz, "What's Queer About Queer Studies Now?" Introduction in *Social Text* 84–85 (Fall–Winter 2005): 4.

80. Weiman Kelman, *Queer Expectations,* 35.

81. Carolyn Dinshaw, Lee Edelman, Roderick A. Ferguson, et al., "Theorizing Queer Temporalities: A Roundtable Discussion," *GLQ: A Journal of Lesbian and Gay Studies* 13, no. 2–3 (2007): 177–195. See also Dinshaw, *Getting Medieval Sexualities and Communities, Pre-and Postmodern,* Series Q (Durham: Duke University Press, 1999).

82. Dinshaw, Edelman, Ferguson, et al., "Theorizing Queer Temporalities," 2.

83. Jafari Allen, "Black/Queer/Diaspora at the Current Conjuncture," *GLQ: A Journal of Lesbian and Gay Studies* 18, no. 2–3: 215.

84. Jafari Allen, "Black/Queer/Diaspora," 237.

85. Margolin, *Lider,* 6.

86. Kramer papers, Labadie Collection. See also Kramer, *A Century of Yiddish Poetry,* 135–136.

87. Joseph Leftwich, ed. and trans., *The Golden Peacock: A Worldwide Treasury of Yiddish Poetry* (New York: T. Yoseloff, 1961), 6.

88. Iceland, *From Our Springtime,* 152.

89. Pratt, "Anna Margolin's *Lider,*" 15.

90. Kramer, a lifelong leftist, is the rare critic to cite Margolin's close connection with Kropotkin. Kramer's anthology eschews the usual periodization of Sweatshop, *Di Yunge,* and *In-zikh* schools in favor of a "First Golden Age," "Second Golden Age," etc.

91. Trans. Kumove, *Drunk from the Bitter Truth,* 165.

92. Trans. Kumove, *Drunk from the Bitter Truth,* 165.

93. Gertrude Stein, *Three Lives* (New York: Simon and Schuster, 2002), 70. The phrase "negro sunshine" is repeated several times in *Three Lives.*

94. Cited by Faith Jones, in Sherman, *Writers in Yiddish,* 167.

95. Trans. Kumove, *Drunk from the Bitter Truth,* 269.

96. Margolin, *Lider,* 104; author's translation.

97. Trans. Kumove, *Drunk from the Bitter Truth,* 13.

98. Novershtern, "Who Would Have Believed," 455.

99. Trans. Kumove, *Drunk from the Bitter Truth,* 15.

100. Barbara Mann, "Picturing the Poetry of Anna Margolin," *Modern Language Quarterly* 63, no. 4 (2002): 501-536.

101. *Antologye Mityest-Mayriv,* 1932–1933, ed. Mattes Deitch, B. Ben Shalom, Shloime Schwartz, Tordros Geller, and M. Ziporin (Chicago: M. Ceshinsky, 1933).

102. Heifetz Tussman, *Am I Also You?,* trans. Marcia Falk (Berkeley: Tree West Coast Print Center, 1977), 6.

103. Heifetz Tussman, *Bleter Faln Not (Leaves Do Not Fall)* (Tel Aviv: Yisroel bukh, 1972), cited and translated in Benjamin Harshav and Barbara Harshav, *American Yiddish Poetry: A Bilingual Anthology,* (Berkeley: University of California Press, 1986), 599–603.

104. Heifetz Tussman, "Like the Root." Translated by Marcia Falk in *With Teeth in the Earth: Selected Poems of Malka Heifetz Tussman* (Detroit: Wayne State University, 1992), 120. Reprinted with permission of the translator.

105. Heifetz Tussman, *Lider* (Los Angeles: Malkah Ḥofets-Ṭuzman bukh ḳomiṭeṭ, 1949), 106.

106. "I Am Woman" by Heifetz Tussman, translated by Marcia Falk, in *With Teeth in the Earth,* 50–51. Another version of this translation was published in *Lilith* magazine on September 19, 1987. The text is identical, but the line breaks are shorter, following the briefer Yiddish lines.

107. Tal Ilan, "Rachel, Wife of Rabbi Akiva," in *Jewish Women: A Comprehensive Historical Encyclopedia* (Brookline: Jewish Women's Archive, 2009).

108. Nikki Giovanni, "Ego Tripping (there may be a reason why)," in *Ego Tripping and Other Poems for Young Readers* (Cambridge, U.K.: ProQuest Information and Learning, 2004).

109. Molly Fraser, "The Endless Road of 'The Self': Malka Heifetz Tussman," December 10, 2019, citing *Lilith* 17 (Fall 1987): 21.

110. Mujeres Creando, "An Interview with Mujeres Creando," in *Quiet Rumours: An Anarcha-Feminist Reader,* 3rd edition, Dark Star Collective (Oakland: AK Press, 2012), 126. (Confederación Nacional del Trabajo is the confederation of anarcho-syndicalist unions founded in Barcelona in 1910.)

CHAPTER 4. "THE PROPHETS WERE SOCIALISTS"

1. David Wengrow and David Graeber, *The Dawn of Everything* (New York: Farrar, Straus and Giroux, 2021), 10.

2. Carolyn Nakamura, "Untenable History." *Offshoot,* March 13, 2022.

3. Esther Dolgoff, the wife of Sam Dolgoff, prepared a handwritten 808-page translation manuscript, now held in the Kate Sharpley Library.

4. Saul Yanovsky, *Ershte yorn fun yidishn frayheytlekhn sotsializm: oytobiografishe zikhroynes fun a pyoner un boyer fun der yidisher anarkhistisher bavegung in England un Amerike* (New York City, 1948).

5. Yosef Luden, *Kurtse geshikhte fun anarkhistishe gedank* (Tel Aviv: Problemen, 1984).

6. Herman Frank, *Anarkho-sotsyalistishe ideyen un bavegungen bay yidn, historishe un teoretishe aynfirung* (Anarcho-socialist ideas and movements among Jews: historical and theoretical introduction) (Paris: Fraye Tribune, 1951).

7. Yosef (Joseph) Cohen, *Di yidish-anarkhistishe bavegung in Amerike: historisher iberblik un perzenlekhe iberlebungen* (Philadelphia: Workmen's Circle, 1945).

8. Esther Dolgoff's handwritten translation, 13.

9. Esther Dolgoff's handwritten translation, 14.

10. Cohen appeals to readers to donate historical materials or oral histories to the librarian Agnes Inglis of the Labadie Collection, founded by the anarchist Joseph Labadie (1850–1933).

11. Mikhail Aleksandrovich Bakunin, *God and the State* (1883), in *Selected Writings [of] Michael Bakunin* (London: Cape, 1973), 112.

12. Kropotkin writes, "The mutual-aid tendency in man has so remote an origin, and is so deeply interwoven with all the past evolution of the human race, that it has been maintained by mankind up to the present time, notwithstanding all vicissitudes of history." *Mutual Aid* ([1902] Boston: Extending Horizons Books, 2005), 180.

13. Esther Dolgoff's handwritten translation, 30.

14. Biographical note, Central Archives for the History of the Jewish People, http://cahjp .nli.org.il/webfm_send/995.

15. Before it closed, *Problemen* appeared in Tel Aviv bimonthly and had a circulation of 300 to subscribers in Canada, Argentina, Paris, Israel, Denmark, and Sweden.

16. Yosef Luden, *Kurtse geshikhte fun anarkhistishe gedank* (Brief History of Anarchist Thought) (Tel-Aviv: Problemen, 1984), 5. All translations of *Kurtse geshikhte* are the author's.

17. On Taoism and anarchism, see Peter Marshall, *Demanding the Impossible: A History of Anarchism* (Oakland: PM Press, 2012).

18. Luden, *Kurtse geshikhte*, 11. The person whom Luden refers to as "Alexander David" was actually the French-Belgian anarchist Alexandra David Néel, who published *The Theory of the Individual in Chinese Philosophy: Yang-Chou* after traveling to Lhasa in 1924. She was the first European woman to visit Tibet's capital. In 1899, her anarchist treatise was prefaced by Elisée Reclus.

19. Judges 8:23.

20. Micah 4:4.

21. Hosea 10:13, "Ye have plowed wickedness, ye have reaped iniquity; ye have eaten the fruit of lies" (King James Bible).

22. Luden references Zechariah 4:6, using two of the loshn-koydesh words from the Hebrew verse. Luden makes the passive Hebrew verse active: "This is the word of the Lord unto Zerubbabel, saying: Not by might, nor by power, but by My spirit, said the Lord of hosts."

23. Luden's nostalgia for a time when *ba'al* meant "man" without connotations of dominance or possession is shared by Abraham Joshua Heschel, who recalls (or constructs) a period when the Hebrew word *davar* meant "word," without meaning a material thing. Susan A. Handelman, *The Slayer of Moses: The Emergence of Rabbinic Interpretation in Modern Literary Theory* (Albany: State University of New York Press), 3–5.

24. Luden, *Kurtse geshikhte*, 12–13.

25. Luden, *Kurtse geshikhte*, 14.

26. Luden writes: "The characteristics of the development of the communes by the Dead Sea were the negation of an earthly king and the hope of a heavenly king. To the Essenes, domination was a sin. According to the first Christians, in the Book of Corinthians (Book of the Apostles) chapter one, line 24 says: 'He (the messiah) will negate the government, each domination of might. He (the messiah) will alone be king.' The new social order of the first Jewish-Christians was a collective. In the history of the apostles, it says: 'All believers lived in a Hebrew society and distributed their property between all, others sold their possessions and distributed gold, each according only to his necessity.'" Luden refers to Apostles 2:45–46 (*Kurtse geshikhte*, 16.)

27. Daniel Boyarin and Jonathan Boyarin, "Diaspora: Generation and the Ground of Jewish Identity," *Critical Inquiry* 19, no. 4 (Summer 1993): 718. Luden's anarchist reading of the Prophets is akin to the Boyarins' claim that "the dialectical struggle between anti-royalism and royalism persists throughout the course and formative career of the Old Testament as its structuring force" (717).

28. Boyarin and Boyarin, "Diaspora," 715.

29. Luden, *Kurtse geshikhte*, 13.

30. Luden, *Flamen* (Tel-Aviv: Farlag *Problemen*, 1983), 6.

31. Luden, *"Mayn shtot,"* in *Gezamlte lider*, vol. 2 (Tel Aviv: Farlag *Problemen*, 1990), 253; author's translation.

32. Roger Berkowitz, "'The Angry Jew Has Gotten His Revenge': Hannah Arendt on Revenge and Reconciliation," *Philosophical Topics* 39, no. 2 (2011): 1–20.

33. Shvartsbard, *In'm loyf fun yorn* (1933), 30. Translated in Kelly Johnson, "Sholem Schwarzbard: Biography of a Jewish Assassin," 36–37.

34. Schwarzbard [Shvartsbard], "Shtil iz di nakht . . . " (Quiet Is the Night), in *Troymen un virklekhkeyt* (Dreams and Reality, Paris, 1920), 65–66. Trans. Johnson, "Sholem Schwarzbard," 80.

35. Elias Tchernikower Collection, Polonnoye (Polonne) (Folder 629A) Mizrakh Yidisher Historisher Arkhiv, RG 80, Center for Jewish History, YIVO Archive, New York City.

36. See A. E. Torres, "The Anarchist Sage/*Der Go'en Anarkhist:* Rabbi Yankev-Meir Zalkind and Religious Genealogies of Anarchism," *In geveb: A Journal of Yiddish Studies* (February 2019).

37. Shvartsbard, *"Farn yungn dor,"* translated by the author.

38. Saul S. Friedman, *Pogromchik: The Assassination of Simon Petlura* (New York: Hart, 1976), 86.

39. On the aftereffects of the "Age of Attentats," see Richard Bach Jensen, "The Decline of Anarchist Terrorism, 1900–1930s," in *The Battle Against Anarchist Terrorism: An International History, 1878–1934* (Cambridge: Cambridge University Press, 2014), 349.

40. *Der shos oyf Petluran—Shvartsbard's protses* (The Shot at Petliura—Shvartsbard's Trial) features portraits of Petliura, Shvartsbard, and Torrès and includes dramatic quotations: "Petliura is a murderer and I was his judge!" ("Groshen-Bibliotek," Warsaw). Amsterdam: International Institute of Social History, 43.

41. I thank David Mazower for locating this image.

42. Johnson, "Sholem Schwarzbard," 58. Johnson (730) quotes Shmuel Charney's review of Shvartsbard's poetry in *Dreams and Reality: At War with Myself* and *In the Tide of Times* (*Tsukunft*, August 1934).

43. Anna Shvartsbard, *"Di neyterin"* (The Seamstress). *Fraye arbeter shtime* (October 15, 1948), 10. See YIVO folder of handwritten poems by Anna Shvartsbard (undated; 1939, 1943–1945, 1948), RG 85 Shalom Schwartzbard Papers (Tcherikower Archive), Folder 905.

44. Yosef Hayim Yerushalmi, *Zakhor: Jewish History and Jewish Memory* (Seattle: University of Washington Press, 1982), 96.

45. Yerushalmi, *Zakhor,* 96.

46. Sholem Shvartsbard, *"Di rede vos ikh hob nit gehaltn"* (The Speech I Never Gave), in Shvartsbard, *In'm loyf fun yorn,* trans. Kelly Johnson, "Sholem Schwarzbard," 308–315.

47. In a letter from the front, Shvartsbard tells his father of a conversion experience to a Jewish God that he associates with the warriors of Ephraim, Aaron and Gideon, "the brave women Judith and Delilah," and Jonathan: "Go to the gates of Jerusalem and gather together the brave, old heroes, those who defended the gates of the city . . . " *In krig mit zikh aleyn* (Chicago: Sholem Shvartsbard komitet, 1933), 133. Translated in Johnson, "Sholem Schwarzbard," 81. Shvartsbard's memoir also cites Bar Kochba as an inspiration.

48. Johnson, "Sholem Schwarzbard," 44.

49. Emma Goldman, *Living My Life,* vol. 1, 370.

50. Prison letter, Sholem Shvartsbard Collection, Folder 883, YIVO Archives.

51. Shvartsbard, *In'm loyf fun yorn,* 291.

52. Jonathan Kirsch, *The Short, Strange Life of Herschel Grynszpan: A Boy Avenger, a Nazi Diplomat, and a Murder in Paris* (New York: Liveright, 2014), 11.

53. In a 1921 editorial in *Arbeter fraynd,* Zalkind lambasted the Zionist Revisionist leader Jabotinsky for his agreement with Petliura. This passage expresses Zalkind's concern about possible alliances between nationalists such as Jabotinsky and Petliura. Although he does not advocate retaliation against Petliura explicitly and condemns "revenge upon the innocent" (Jews under Bolshevism), Zalkind does rule out nationalist responses to pogroms (*"Briv un barikhten: entfer fun di redaktor," Arbeter fraynd,* December 31, 1921, 7).

54. Sholem Shvartsbard, *"Dr. Yankev Meyer Zalkind un zayn gemore oyf yidish,"* in *Moment* (Warsaw: January 20, 1929), 5. (No such monument seems locatable in Père Lachaise.)

55. Shvartsbard, *"Dr. Yankev Meyer Zalkind un zayn gemore oyf yidish,"* 5.

56. *"On refuse à Schwartzbard l'entré en Syrie et en Palestine,"* in *Israël* (April 3, 1928), cited in Johnson, "Sholem Schwarzbard," 234.

57. Isidore Wisotzky, "Such a Life" (typewritten manuscript), 270, Box 1, Folder 5, Joseph A. Labadie Collection, Special Collections Research Center, University of Michigan Library, Ann Arbor.

CHAPTER 5. "MY HEART HAS NO ROOF"

1. Peretz Markish, *"Tsu keynem nit,"* in *Shpigl oyf a shteyn,* ed. Chone Shmeruk (Jersualem: Universitah ha-Ivrit, 1987), 443. I am grateful to Markish's descendants for permission to translate and reprint his writings. Unless otherwise noted, all translations of his work and of other sources are by the author.

2. Sergei Narovchatov, *Stikhotvoreniia i poemy* (Leningrad: Sovetskii pisatel' [Soviet writer], 1969), 6.

3. Markish, *"Milkhome,"* in Narovchatov, *Stikhotvoreniia i poemy,* 12.

4. Elie Wiesel, "Some Words About Peretz Markish," *Jewish Frontier* (August–September, 1981), translated from French by Mitchell Cohen.

5. Astrid Deuber-Mankowsky, "Peretz Markish (1895–1952): Modern Marxist and Yiddishist," in *Makers of Jewish Modernity: Thinkers, Leaders, and the World They Made,* ed. Jacques Picard, Jacques Revel, Michael Steinberg, and Idith Zertal (Princeton: Princeton University Press, 2016), 329.

6. "Pogroms perpetrated by Nestor Makhno forces" (Folder 29), Mizrakh Yidisher Historisher Arkhiv, RG 80.pdf, Center for Jewish History, YIVO Archives.

7. Ida Mett, "Memories of Makhno," 1948; reprinted in *Oppositions: Some Anarchist Writing of Ida Mett* (Steimer Press, 2021). https://steimerpress.noblogs.org/.

8. Max Nomad, *Apostles of Revolution* (Boston: Little Brown, 1939).

9. Joseph Nedava, "Abba Gordin: A Portrait of a Jewish Anarchist," *Soviet Jewish Affairs* 4, no. 2 (1974): 73–79.

10. Avrich notes that in Guliai-Pole, Makhno's Military-Revolutionary Council set up communes of up to 300 members each, who "operated the communes on the basis of full equality and accepted the Kropotkinian principle of mutual aid as their fundamental tenet" (Paul Avrich, *The Russian Anarchists* [Oakland: AK Press, 2005], 214). Similar communes sprang up in Guliai-Pole in 1905 and 1917, forming a rare continuity between Russian anarchist generations. Alexandre Skirda, *Nestor Makhno: Anarchy's Cossack* (Oakland: AK Press, 2004), 339.

11. Esther Markish, *The Long Return,* trans. D. I. Goldstein (New York: Ballantine, 1978), 12.

12. Shimon Markish and Maria Rubins, "David Markish (24 September 1938–)," in *Dictionary of Literary Biography*, vol. 317 (Farmington Hills, Mich.: Gale, 2005), 212.

13. For bibliographies of Markish's work, see *Captive of the Dawn: The Life and Work of Peretz Markish*, ed. Joseph Sherman, Gennady Estraikh, Jordan Finkin, and David Shneer (Oxford: Legenda, 2011) and David Shneer, "Peretz Markish (7 December 1895–12 August 1952). Joseph Sherman, "Writers in Yiddish," *Dictionary of Literary Biography*, vol. 333, 174–179.

14. Sutzkever was also offered a Stalin Prize but "felt that a net was being cast around [him]" and feared that he would be prevented from leaving the country. Joshua Rubenstein and Vladimir Pavlovich Naumov, *Stalin's Secret Pogrom: The Postwar Inquisition of the Jewish Anti-Fascist Committee* (New Haven: Yale University Press, 2005), 64.

15. See Kronfeld, "Murdered Modernisms: Peretz Markish and the Legacy of Soviet Yiddish Poetry," in Sherman et al., *Captive of the Dawn*.

16. Anna Akhmatova translated his ode to Dovid Bergelson into Russian, included in a 1957 anthology. http://www.languages-study.com/yiddish/markishlider.html.

17. Esther Markish, *The Long Return*, 246.

18. Ahrne Goldberg, *Vegn perets markish's lektsye* (Regarding Peretz Markish's Lecture), *Arbeter fraynd* (January 1923), 5.

19. David Frishman (1859–1922) was a literary critic, translator, and poet. As editor of Hebrew literary journals in Warsaw, he championed Bialik, Y. L. Peretz, and others.

20. Goldberg, *Vegn perets markish's lektsye*, 5.

21. Alexander Pomerantz, *Inzshenern fun neshomes: di shrayber un bikher fun der Idisher Sovetisher literatur* (Engineers of Souls) (New York: o. fg., 1943), 5.

22. Pomerantz, *Inzshenern fun neshomes*, 6–7.

23. Pomerantz, *Inzshenern fun neshomes*, 7.

24. Pomerantz, *Inzshenern fun neshomes*, 9.

25. Pomerantz, *Inzshenern fun neshomes*, 16.

26. Pomerantz, *Inzshenern fun neshomes*, 17.

27. Alexander Pomerantz, *Di sovetishe haruge malkhes, tsu zeyer 10tn yortsayt, vegn dem tragishn goyrl fun di yidishe shraybers un der yidisher literatur in sovetnland* (Buenos Aires: YIVO, 1962), 162–171.

28. Elazar Elhanan, "'Rear the Head Like a Middle Finger . . . And Pierce the Heavens': The Long Poem as a Site of Blasphemy, Obscenity, and Friendship in the Works of Peretz Markish and Uri Tsevi Greenberg," *Dibur Literary Journal* 4 (Spring 2017): 55.

29. Seth Wolitz, "Markish's Radyo (1922): Yiddish Modernism as Agitprop," in Sherman et al., *Captive of the Dawn*, 104.

30. Translated in Laëtitia Tordjman, "Challenging the Literary Community: The Warsaw Yiddish Avant-Garde and Khalyastre," in *Jewish Aspects in Avant-Garde: Between Rebellion and Revelation*, ed. Mark Gelber and Sami Sjöberg (Berlin: De Gruyter, 2017), 88.

31. Cited and translated in Elhanan, "Rear the Head," 55–56.

32. Judith Butler, "Queer Anarchism and Anarchists Against the Wall" (paper presented at "The Anarchist Turn" conference, New School, Manhattan, May 5, 2011).

33. Frida Zak, "When Peretz Markish Came to Polonne," oral history gathered by *AHEYM*:

Archives of Historical and Ethnographical Yiddish Memories, Bloomington, Indiana. https://www.youtube.com/watch?v=XiPJPmm2xxk.

34. Peretz Markish, *Farbaygeyendik: eseyen* (Vilna: Bikherlager bay der tsentraler yidisher shul-organizatsye, 1921).

35. Amelia Glaser, *Jews and Ukrainians in Russia's Literary Borderlands: From the Shtetl Fair to the Petersburg Bookshop* (Evanston: Northwestern University Press, 2012), 145–146.

36. Markish, *Farbaygeyendik,* 15–19.

37. Mikhail Bakunin, "Die Reaktion in Deutschland. Ein Fragment von einem Franzosen," in *Deutsche Jahrbücher fur Wissenschaft and Kunst,* ed. Arnold Ruge (Leipzig: October 17th–21st, 1842), 247–251.

38. Group of Anarcho-Futurists, "*Shturmovoi, opustoshaiushchii manifest anarkho-futuristov,*" *K Svetu* (Kharkov), March 14, 1919, 1, trans. Paul Avrich, *The Anarchists in the Russian Revolution* (Ithaca: Cornell University Press, 1973), 54.

39. Markish, *Shveln* (Thresholds), (Kiev: Yidisher folks farlag, 1919), 9.

40. Markish, *Shveln,* 11.

41. Markish, *Shveln,* 15.

42. Markish, *Shveln,* 16.

43. See Kronfeld's translation, "Murdered Modernisms," 197–198.

44. See Madeleine Cohen, "Here and Now: The Modernist Poetics of Do'ikayt" (PhD diss., University of California, Berkeley, 2016).

45. See Vladimir Markov, *Russian Futurism: A History* (Berkeley: University of California Press, 1968).

46. Bengt Jangfeldt, *Mayakovsky: A Biography* (Chicago: University of Chicago Press, 2014), 104–105; Gurianova, *Aesthetics of Anarchy,* 8, 91–92, 216.

47. Avrich, "Russian Anarchists and the Civil War," *Russian Review* 27, no. 3 (July 1968): 296–306.

48. Esther Markish, *The Long Return,* 83.

49. Roy Greenwald, "Pogrom and Avant-Garde: Peretz Markish's *Di kupe*" *Jewish Social Studies* 16, no. 3 (2010): 67.

50. V. V. Mayakovsky, "Commentaries to A Cloud in Tousers," in *The Complete V. V. Mayakovsky in 13 Volumes,* vol.1 (Moscow: Khudozhestvennaya Literatura, 1957).

51. Glaser, *Jews and Ukrainians,* 111–112.

52. Glaser, *Jews and Ukrainians,* 147.

53. Ilya Ehrenbourg, *Les Gens, les années, la vie* (Lyon: Parangon/Vs, 2008), 494–498.

54. Connor Doak, "One Man's Meat is Another Man's Poetry: Masculinity and Metaphor in the Work of Vladimir Maiakovskii," *Modernism/modernity* 20, no. 2 (2013): 239–264. See also Doak, "The Poetics of Masculinity: Rereading Vladimir Mayakovsky" (lecture at the University of British Columbia, Vancouver, 19 Dec. 2019).

55. Doak, "One Man's Meat Is Another Man's Poetry," 239–264.

56. Translation of this stanza by Yael Chaver, "Jewish Radicalism: Hebrew in Peretz Markish's Early Poetry," in Sherman et al., *Captive of the Dawn,* 18–19. I thank Chaver for permission to cite it.

57. Chaver, "Jewish Radicalism," 19.

58. Markish (1926) in *Shpigl oyf a shteyn,* 462.

59. Walt Whitman, "Song of Myself," in *Walt Whitman's Song of Myself: A Sourcebook and Critical Edition* (London: Taylor and Francis, 2013), 164.

60. Seth Wolitz, "'Di Khalyastre,' the Yiddish Modernist Movement in Poland: An Overview," *Yiddish* 4, no. 3 (1981): 5–20, 11.

61. Jordan Finkin, "The Lighter Side of Babel: Peretz Markish's Urban Poetics," in Sherman et al., *Captive of the Dawn,* 38.

62. Naomi Brenner, *Lingering Bilingualism: Modern Hebrew and Yiddish Literatures in Contact* (Syracuse: Syracuse University Press, 2015), 64–71. See also Gerald J. Blidstein, *Notes on Hefker Bet-Din Hefker in Talmudic and Medieval Law* (Philadelphia: Temple University Press, 1973).

63. Kronfeld, "Murdered Modernisms," 198–199.

64. Markish, "Maestoso Patetico" (1922), in *Shpigl oyf a shteyn,* 429.

65. Karolina Szymaniak, "Language of Dispersion and Confusion: Peretz Markish's Manifestos from the Khalyastre Period," in Sherman et al., *Captive of the Dawn,* 79.

66. Szymaniak, "Language of Dispersion and Confusion," 79.

67. Oral history, *AHEYM: Archives of Historical and Ethnographical Yiddish Memories,* Bloomington, Indiana. http://www.indiana.edu/~aheym/archives.php?filter=person& f2=occupation&f3=social%20worker.

68. "The Earth Is Trembling": Édouard Glissant in conversation with Hans Ulrich Obrist. December 20, 2021. In *Archipelago* (Isolarii, 2021). Trans. Emma Ramadan.

69. Alla Rosenfeld, "Nationhood, Internationalism, and Transnationality: Henryk Berlewi Within the Network of the European Avant-garde" (Merrill C. Berman Collection, 2019), 14.

70. Greenwald, "Pogrom and Avant-Garde," 81.

71. Greenwald, "Pogrom and Avant-Garde," 79.

72. Nokhem Oyslender, "*A kapitel zikhroynes vegn Peretz Markishen,*" *Di yidishe gas* 2 (1993), 49–75. Cited by Greenwald, "Pogrom and Avant-Garde," 82.

73. Markish, *Di kupe* (*The Heap*), trans. Barnett Zumoff (Sovietskaya, Russia: Orenburg, 2015), 11.

74. Jeffrey Veidlinger, conversation on *In the Midst of Civilized Europe: The Pogroms of 1918–1921 and the Onset of the Holocaust* (New York: Metropolitan, 2021).

75. Elye Tsherikover Collection, Horodich (Folder 639D) Mizrakh Yidisher Historisher Arkhiv, RG 80, YIVO Archives.

76. Tsherikover, *Antisemitizm un pogromen in Ukraine in di yorn 1917–1918* (Antisemitism and Pogroms in the Ukraine in the years 1917–1918) (Berlin: Yidisher literarisher farlag, 1923) and *Di Ukrainer pogromen in yor 1919* (The Ukrainian Pogroms in 1919) (New York: YIVO Institute for Jewish Research, 1965).

77. Elhanan, "Rear the Head,"; Glaser, *Jews and Ukrainians;* Greenwald, "Pogrom and Avant-Garde," 66; David G. Roskies, "The Pogrom Poem and the Literature of Destruction," *Notre Dame English Journal* 11, no. 2 (1979): 89–113; Seth L. Wolitz, "A Yiddish Modernist Dirge: *Di kupe* of Peretz Markish," in Sherman et al., *Captive of the Dawn,* 229–241.

78. Glaser, *Jews and Ukrainians,* xvii.

79. Greenwald, "Pogrom and Avant-Garde," 74.

80. Elhanan, "Rear the Head," 54.

81. Elhanan, "Rear the Head," 63–64.

82. Elhanan, "Rear the Head," 63–64.

83. Jay Geller, *Bestiarium Judaicum: Unnatural Histories of the Jews* (New York: Fordham University Press, 2017).

84. Jack Halberstam, *Wild Things: The Disorder of Desire* (Durham: Duke University Press, 2020), 77–78.

85. Halberstam, *Wild Things,* 77–78.

86. Zumoff translation, *The Heap,* 38.

87. Zumoff translation, *The Heap,* 30.

88. Markish, *Di kupe* (Kiev, 1922), 23 (Hebrew pagination).

89. Zumoff translation, *The Heap,* 43.

90. Zumoff translation, *The Heap,* 20.

91. Greenwald, "Pogrom and Avant-Garde," 73.

92. Seth Wolitz, " 'Di Khalyastre,' the Yiddish Modernist Movement in Poland," 11.

93. Markish, "*In droysn*" in *Shpigl oyf a shteyn,* 387.

94. See David Shneer and Robert Adler Peckerar, "Peretz Markish (1895–1952)," in *Makers of Jewish Modernity: Thinkers, Artist, Leaders, and the World They Made,* ed. Jacques Picard, Jacques Revel, Michael P. Steinberg, and Idith Zertal (Princeton: Princeton University Press: 2016), 332.

95. Peretz Markish, "*Ovnt-shpatsir,*" in *Yerushe* (Inheritance), trans. Mary Schulman 140. Reprinted with permission of Mawenzi House (formerly TSAR Publications).

96. Markish, *Yerushe,* 148–149, trans. Mary Schulman.

97. Markish, "Figaro," *Yerushe,* 150–151.

98. Markish, "The Bat," *Yerushe,* 154–155.

CHAPTER 6. "THE BORDER, A WOUND"

1. Esther Markish, *The Long Return,* 154. See also Elias Schulman, "Peretz Markish's 'Secret Poem,' " *Jewish Quarterly* 29, no. 1 (1981): 23–24. I thank David Markish and his son Peretz Markish for permitting me to cite and translate these poems. I am especially grateful to Chana Kronfeld for her thoughtful comments on the translation and to Harriet Murav and Amelia Glaser for their readings. Raya Shapiro provided key assistance with Russian translation.

2. David Markish, *Sorokaletnii* (Man of Forty) *СТИХОТВОРЕНИЯ и поэмы* (Stikhotvoreniia i poemy) (Leningrad, 1968). https://lechaim.ru/events/sorokaletnij-na-vse-vremena/.

3. Peretz Markish, *Der fertsikyeriker man* (Tel Aviv: Farlag Y. L. Perets, 1978). David Markish published a Russian translation in *Stikhotvoreniia i poemy* (Leningrad: Poet's Library, 1969).

4. Markish family, Afterword to *Fertsikyeriker,* 128.

5. Markish family, Afterword to *Fertsikyeriker,* 131.

6. Chana Kronfeld, "Murdered Modernisms: Peretz Markish and the Legacy of Soviet Yiddish Poetry," in Sherman et al., *Captive of the Dawn,* 204.

7. The word for happiness used here is *schast'e. Evreiskoe schast'e* (Jewish Happiness), also translated as "Jewish luck," is the title of a 1925 Soviet film starring Markish's comrade Solomon Mikhoels. *Evreiskoe schast'e,* then, is an ironic set phrase denoting bad luck.

8. Narovchatov, *Stikhotvoreniia i poemy* (Leningrad: *Sovetskii pisatel'* [Soviet writer], 1969), 24–25. Translation by Raya Shapiro.

9. Avraham Novershtern, "Markish, Perets," trans. Rebecca Margolis, *YIVO Encyclopedia of Jews in Eastern Europe,* 2010, https://yivoencyclopedia.org/article.aspx/Markish _Perets.

10. Markish, *Fertsikyeriker,* 71.

11. All translations from *Der fertsikyeriker man* are the author's own.

12. Harriet Murav, "Jewish Responses to Violence: Necropolitics, *Hefker,* and Yiddish Literature of the 1920s" (forthcoming). Accessed via correspondence with the author.

13. Giorgio Agamben, "We Refugees," *Symposium* 49, no. 2 (Summer 1995): 114–119.

14. *Umru* was also a key term for Soviet Yiddish writer Izi Kharik. See Madeleine Cohen, "Here and Now: The Modernist Poetics of Do'ikayt," 50.

15. Karolina Szymaniak, "The Language of Dispersion and Confusion," in Sherman et al., *Captive of the Dawn,* 66–87.

16. On the successive waves of Soviet Yiddish language reform, see Gennady Estraikh, *Soviet Yiddish: Language Planning and Linguistic Development* (Oxford: Oxford University Press, 1999).

17. "In the verses of Markish, 'The Caucasus,' the joyful radiance of Caucasian nature is contrasted with the bitter experiences of the author: 'At the foot of a mountain, in stony torpidness, I, brought here by my grief, had to sit in mourning for that which had been destroyed, obliterated in the suffering of millennia.'" *Revelations from the Russian Archives: Documents in English Translation,* ed. Diane P. Koenker and Ronald D. Bachman (Washington, D.C.: Library of Congress, 1997), 222.

18. Esther Markish notes, "The censor, moreover, threw several poems out of the collection: 'Jerusalem,' 'Galilee,' a few chapters of 'The War'—all of which were seen as infused with Jewish nationalism—and, it goes without saying, 'To Mikhoels—Eternal Light.'" Markish, *The Long Return,* 250. The poem "To Mikhoels—Eternal Light" saluted his friend Shlomo Mikhoels, the Yiddish actor and antifascist organizer. This poem, saturated with traditional Jewish imagery, named Mikhoels's death as murder at Stalin's command.

19. Max Weinreich, *History of the Yiddish Language,* vol. 1 (Chicago: University of Chicago Press, 1980), A228.

20. David Shneer, *Yiddish and the Creation of Soviet Jewish Culture: 1918–1930* (Cambridge: Cambridge University Press, 2004), 39.

21. Photograph, Item 24545, Blavatnik Archive, New York, https://www.blavatnikarchive .org/item/24545.

22. Esther Markish, *The Long Return,* 250.

23. These lines echo part of the verse published in *Shveln:* "Un yung iz nokh der tog, / un bloy iz nokh di hoykh, / un frish iz nokh der vint, / un ikh bin nokh a kind!" (10).

24. Narovchatov, *Stikhotvoreniia i poemy,* 9.

25. Shimon Markish and Maria Rubins, "David Markish (24 September 1938–)," 209.

26. I thank Raya Shapiro for their insights on David Markish's Russian translation in this section. Correspondence, May 2021.

27. Translation to English from David Markish's Russian, adapted from Raya Shapiro.

28. David Markish, "*Forty Years—For All Time,*" *Lechaim* (in Russian), January 2, 2021, https://lechaim.ru/events/sorokaletnij-na-vse-vremena/.

29. Shapiro, conversation and collaborative draft, summer 2021.

30. Alan Dowty, *Closed Borders: The Contemporary Assault on Freedom of Movement* (New Haven: Yale University Press, 1987), 66.

31. Gennady Estraikh, *In Harness: Yiddish Writers' Romance with Communism* (Syracuse: Syracuse University Press, 2005), 150.

32. Markish, Poem 6, Part 2, *Fertsikyeriker,* 76.

33. Markish, Poem 9, Part 2, *Fertsikyeriker,* 81.

34. Markish, Poem 10, Part 2, *Fertsikyeriker,* 82.

35. Zumoff translation, *The Heap,* 43.

36. Zumoff translation, *The Heap,* 36.

37. Markish, Poem 14, Part 2, *Fertsikyeriker,* 88.

38. Thomas Nail, *Theory of the Border* (Oxford: Oxford University Press, 2016), 7.

39. Markish, Poem 33, Part 1, *Fertsikyeriker,* 55.

40. I thank Raya Shapiro for sharing this insight.

41. Markish, Poem 3, Part 1, *Fertsikyeriker,* 73.

42. See also Harriet Murav, *Music from a Speeding Train: Jewish Literature in Post-Revolution Russia* (Stanford: Stanford University Press, 2011).

43. Markish, Poem 6, Part 2, *Fertsikyeriker,* 76.

44. Markish, Poem 30, Part 2, *Fertsikyeriker,* 00.

45. Jordan Finkin, "Constellating Hebrew and Yiddish Modernism: The Example of Markish and Shlonsky," *Journal of Modern Jewish Studies* 8, no. 1 (March 2009): 7.

46. Esther Markish, *The Long Return,* 57.

47. Nail, *Theory of the Border,* 4.

48. Markish, Poem 18, Part 1, *Fertsikyeriker,* 32.

49. Markish, "*Grenets-lid,*" *Foterlekhe erd* (Kiev: Melukhe-Farlag, 1938), 171.

50. Nail, *Theory of the Border,* 69–71.

51. Nail, *Theory of the Border,* 104–105.

52. Walter Benjamin, "On the Concept of History," trans. Harry Zohn, in *Selected Writings of Walter Benjamin,* vol. 4, 1938–1940, ed. Howard Eiland and Michael W. Jennings (Cambridge: Belknap Press of Harvard University, 2003), 397.

53. Anna Shternshis, *Soviet and Kosher: Jewish Popular Culture in the Soviet Union, 1923–1939* (Bloomington: Indiana University Press, 2006).

54. Markish, Poem 1, Part 2, *Fertsikyeriker,* 71.

55. Translated in Jordan Finkin, *An Inch or Two of Time: Time and Space in Jewish Modernism* (University Park: Pennsylvania State University Press, 2015).

56. David Markish translates this line: "Derznuvshemu slava! On shel nalegke—/ Pustaya kotomka da molot v ruke."

57. Elissa Bemporad, *Legacy of Blood: Jews, Pogroms, and Ritual Murder in the Lands of the Soviets* (New York: Oxford University Press, 2019), 69.

58. Z. S. Ostrovsky, *Jewish Pogroms* [Evreiskie pogromy] *1918–1921* (Moscow: School and Book, 1927).

59. Bemporad, *Legacy of Blood*, 71.

60. Friedrich likely refers to the pacifist ideology of William James's "The Moral Equivalent of War" (1906). Leftist intellectuals predicted it would sway public opinion against war; veterans sued public galleries displaying the photographs and police raided bookstores. By 1930, the book had ten German editions and was translated into several languages, defining the iconography of anti-militarism.

61. Susan Sontag, "Looking at War: Photography's View of Devastation and Death," *New Yorker*, December 9, 2002.

62. Markish, Poem 40, Part 2, *Fertsikyeriker*, 64.

63. See the bibliography in Shimon Markish and Maria Rubins, "David Markish (24 September 1938–)" in "Twentieth-Century Russian Emigre Writers," *Dictionary of Literary Biography*, vol. 317, 206–214.

64. The last two lines are translated: "No krasnye bukvy zovut [call out] i goryat / 'Pust' znaki ushedshykh zhivut, govoryat [speak]!"

65. Markish, Poem 18, Part 2, *Fertsikyeriker*, 92.

66. The film was distributed in Russia by Nordisk and became highly influential for filmmakers in Moscow. Abel Gance stated that its purpose was "to show the horror of war and consecrate to the execration of the ages those who are responsible." Gance, *Prisme* (Paris: Librairie Gallimard, 1930), 164. Gance's politics vacillated between pacifism and militancy, and he joined the Comite International de defense de l'Union Sovietique; Steven Philip Kramer, Review of Norman King's *Abel Gance: Politics of Spectacle*, *Literature/Film Quarterly* 13, no. 4 (1985): 275–276.

67. The actors were two thousand soldiers on eight-day leave from the front in Verdun; 80 percent of them were killed upon returning. Gance again explored the figure of the anti-miltarist poet in *La Fin du Monde* (1930), set after an international anarchist revolution. Gance played the hero, who reads passages from Kropotkin aloud.

68. Markish, Poem 7, Part 2, *Fertsikyeriker man*, 79.

69. Pomerantz, *Di sovetishe haruge malkhes, tsu zeyer 10tn yortsayt, vegn dem tragishn goyrl fun di yidishe shraybers un der yidisher literatur in sovetnland* (Buenos Aires: YIVO, 1962), 5. The sarcastic "Willkomen" appears again: "Welcome, brothers, from across borders!" (9).

70. Markish, Poem 21, Part 2, *Fertsikyeriker*, 38.

71. Markish, Poem 34, Part 2, *Fertsikyeriker*, 116.

72. Markish, Poem 34, Part 2, *Fertsikyeriker*, 116.

73. Markish, Poem 36, Part 2, *Fertsikyeriker*, 120.

74. David Markish, "*Sorokaletnii*," in *Stikhotvoreniia i poemy*, 576. Bulat steel is an alloy of steel and carbon (also called red steel) forged with a technique from Iran, thus representing "east-west synthesis."

75. Translation by Raya Shapiro, June 2021.

76. This section draws from my correspondence with Syrkin's children, Daniel Syrkin and Eva Belavsky, in particular an extended conversation on March 9, 2021. I am grateful for their generosity. The image that I initially read as an "electro-head" is titled "Ideology,"

c. 1960s, felt-tip pen, ink on paper, 80 x 60 cm. See Gerald Nordland, *Lev Syrkin* (Jerusalem: Prisma Press, 1998), 15, 99.

77. Nordland, *Lev Syrkin,* 15.

78. Eva Belavsky interview, March 2021.

79. Daniel Syrkin and Ido Syrkin, *A Fool's Dream* (documentary, Israel, 2007).

80. "Lev Syrkin: I Have Set My Rainbow" (exhibition catalogue 2012), 17. Curated by Dina Grossman, Ben-Gurion University of the Negev, Trumpeldor Gallery.

81. The drawing is Syrkin's "Ivan and Maria" (1974). Pen and ink on paper, 25 cm x 35 cm. See Nordland, *Lev Syrkin,* 139.

82. Syrkin, illustration, *Fertsikyeriker,* 24.

83. Szymaniak, "Language of Dispersion and Confusion," in Sherman et al., *Captive of the Dawn,* 82.

84. Syrkin, "The Concertina," 1975. Pen and ink on paper, 25 x 35 cm. See Nordland, *Lev Syrkin,* 145.

85. Reproduced in Markish, *Fertsikyeriker,* 109.

86. Syrkin, "The Agony," 1975. Pen and ink on paper, 25 x 35 cm. See Nordland, *Lev Syrkin,* 149.

87. Eva Belavsky translated her father's Russian inscription. Correspondence, August 2021.

88. Ahrne Goldberg, "*Vegn Perets Markish's Lektsye,*" 5.

89. Jesse Cohn, "What Is Anarchist Literary Theory?" *Anarchist Studies* 15, no. 2 (2007): 127.

CHAPTER 7. "LANGUAGE IS MIGRANT"

1. Joseph Spivak, "The Life's Journey of Jacob Abrams," in *The J. Abrams Book,* trans. Ruth Murphy (Mexico City: La Voz Israelita de México, 1956; reprint, Rebecca Nestle, 2016), 8.

2. "A Memoir About Jack Abrams by Mollie Steimer" (1930), translated from the Yiddish by Esther Dolgoff, in *Fighters for Anarchism: Mollie Steimer and Senya Fleshin,* ed. Abe Bluestein (St. Louis: Left Bank Books, 1983), 82.

3. Mollie Steimer, "To Twenty Years in Prison," in *J. Abrams Book,* 36.

4. Zosa Szajkowski, "Double Jeopardy: The Abrams Case of 1919," *American Jewish Archives* 23 (April 1971).

5. For the Holmes dissent, which Brandeis joined, see *Abrams v. United States,* 250 U.S. 616 (1919).

6. Steimer, "A Memoir About Jack Abrams," in Bluestein, *Fighters for Anarchism,* 84.

7. David Rabban, *Free Speech in Its Forgotten Years* (Cambridge: Cambridge University Press, 1997), 343.

8. Richard Polenberg, *Fighting Faiths: The Abrams Case, the Supreme Court, and Free Speech* (Ithaca: Cornell University Press, 1987), 11.

9. Translation of *Frayheyt*'s Yiddish pamphlet by Chana Kronfeld in Polenberg, *Fighting Faiths.*

10. English text: http://www.rightsmatter.org/teachers/Abrams.pdf.

11. Richard Polenberg, "Progressivism and Anarchism: Judge Henry D. Clayton and the Abrams Trial," *Law and History Review* 3, no. 2 (Autumn 1985): 397–408.

12. *Congressional Record,* 62nd Congress, 3rd Session (February 19, 1913), 3418, cited in Polenberg, "Progressivism," 402.

13. Polenberg, "Progressivism," 402.

14. Joshua Lambert, "Unclean Lips" (PhD diss., New York University, 2009), 20.

15. Harry Weinberger, "A Rebel's Interrupted Autobiography: A Personal Document on the Impact of War on One Who Has Made a Lifelong Fight Against It," *American Journal of Economics and Sociology* 2, no. 1 (October 1942).

16. Weinberger's *Liberty of the Press* (Berkeley Heights: Oriole Press, 1934) argued through comparison to John Peter Zenger's 1735 libel case that twentieth-century Americans had abandoned their commitment to free speech. Edward J. O'Toole, "The Liberty of the Press (Book Review)," *St. John's Law Review* 9, no. 2 (May 1935).

17. Mike Cummings, "Defending an 'Indecent' Play: 'The God of Vengeance' in the Yale University Library archives," *Yale News,* October 15, 2015.

18. Steimer, in Bluestein, *Fighters for Anarchism,* 7.

19. Cited in Polenberg, *Fighting Faiths,* 89.

20. Cited in Polenberg, *Fighting Faiths,* 89.

21. Steimer, "A Memoir About Jack Abrams," in Bluestein, *Fighters for Anarchism,* 82.

22. Polenberg, *Fighting Faiths,* 94

23. Avrich, *Anarchist Portraits,* 218.

24. Goldman, "Woman Without a Country," *Mother Earth* 4, no. 3 (May 1909).

25. Steimer and Fleshil, in Bluestein, *Fighters for Anarchism,* 8.

26. Errico Malatesta, "The Two Freedoms," trans. Andrew Hoyt, *La Questione Sociale* (November 1899).

27. Eric L. Goldstein, "Mollie Steimer," *Jewish Women: A Comprehensive Historical Encyclopedia* (Brookline: Jewish Women's Archive, 2009).

28. *Defiance: Anarchist Statements Before Judge and Jury* (Olympia, Wash.: Detritus Books, 2019), 129.

29. "Statement by Mollie Steimer in the Film *Anarchism in America* (1980)," in Bluestein, *Fighters for Anarchism,* 28.

30. Avrich, "Anarchist Lives: Mollie Steimer (1897–1980) and Simon (Senya) Fleshil (1894–1981)," in Bluestein, *Fighters for Anarchism,* 13.

31. Avrich, *Anarchist Voices,* 174.

32. Steimer, Affidavit, in Bluestein, *Fighters for Anarchism,* 29.

33. Mollie Steimer, "On Leaving Russia," *Freedom* (January 1924; reprint, Cienfuegos Press Anarchist Review, no. 4, 1978).

34. Steve J. Shore, "Forever an Anarchist: Mollie Steimer," *Women of Liberty* 135 (September 2019), 279.

35. M. Rubinstein, "J. Abrams and His Role in Jewish Mexico," *The J. Abrams Book,* 15.

36. I. Berliner, "Over a Quarter Century of Community Work in Mexico," in *The J. Abrams Book,* 50.

37. Polenberg, *Fighting Faiths,* 22.

38. In 1871, after the Paris Commune was crushed and twenty thousand people were killed, France deported about 4,500 communard survivors to New Caledonia, a Melanesian

colony one thousand miles from Australia. See John Merriman, *Massacre: The Life and Death of the Paris Commune* (New York: Basic Books, 2014).

39. "Emma Goldman Extended Timeline," Emma Goldman Papers Project at Berkeley University. https://libcom.org/history/emma-goldman-extended-timeline.

40. Avrich, "Anarchist Lives," in Bluestein, *Fighters for Anarchism*, 7.

41. "Mollie Steimer Gets Six Months in Workhouse," *Evening World* (1919), 18.

42. Hemmings, *Considering Emma Goldman*, 109.

43. Moshe Carmilly-Weinberger, *Censorship and Freedom of Expression in Jewish History* (New York: Sepher-Hermon Press and Yeshiva University Press, 1977).

44. Hemmings, *Considering Emma Goldman*, 87.

45. Hemmings, *Considering Emma Goldman*, 188.

46. "Emma Goldman Extended Timeline," Emma Goldman Papers Project.

47. See J. Richards, *The Fury Archives: Female Citizenship, Human Rights, and the International Avant-Gardes* (New York: Columbia University Press, 2020).

48. Goldman letter, February 3, 1935. Labadie Collection, University of Michigan, Ann Arbor.

49. Kathy Ferguson, *Emma Goldman: Political Thinking in the Streets* (Lanham, Md.: Rowman and Littlefield, 2011), 105.

50. Steven Fischler and Joel Sucher, *Anarchism in America* (Brooklyn: Pacific Street Films, 1983).

51. Goldman, *Living My Life*, vol. 1, 688. See also Ferguson, *Emma Goldman: Political Thinking in the Streets*, 124 n123.

52. Goldman, *Emma Goldman: A Documentary History of the American Years*, vol. 2, *Making Speech Free, 1902–1909*, ed. Candace Falk et al. (Champaign: University of Illinois Press, 2008), 269.

53. Goldman, *Living My Life*, vol. 1, chapter 56. Goldman lectured in Yiddish on Whitman in a private home in Montreal in February 1928.

54. Goldman (1916), 2. Unfinished manuscript titled "Walt Whitman," in *The Emma Goldman Papers: A Microfilm Edition*, ed. Candace Falk with Ronald J. Zboray et al., reel 54.

55. Courtesy of Debbie Rose, Toronto.

56. *Zhargon* (jargon) is a derogatory term for Yiddish in some contexts.

57. Emma Goldman Papers Project, "A Guide to Her Life: Chronology," 32.

58. Report for the Immigration and Naturalization Service by interpreter Louis P. Domas, cited in Goldman, *Documentary History*, vol. 2, 272.

59. Goldman to Nunia Berman Seldes, *Documentary History*, vol. 2, 193.

60. Goldman, *Documentary History*, vol. 2, 358.

61. Jean H. Baker, *Margaret Sanger: A Life of Passion* (New York: Hill and Wang, 2011), 58.

62. Leonard D. Abbott, "Reflections on Emma Goldman's Trial," *Mother Earth* 11 (May 1916), 504.

63. Abbott, "Reflections on Emma Goldman's Trial," 504.

64. Abbott, "Reflections on Emma Goldman's Trial," 504.

65. Emma Goldman, "The Tragedy at Buffalo," *Free Society*, October 6, 1901.

66. Goldman, *Documentary History*, vol. 2, 200.

67. Ferguson, *Emma Goldman: Political Thinking*, 62.

68. Conversation with Barry Pateman, 2007.

69. Reizbaum, "Yiddish Modernisms: Red Emma Goldman," *Modern Fiction Studies* 51, no. 2 (Summer 2005): 456–481, 477.

70. Anarchists such as Ezra Heywood—publisher of the pamphlet *Cupid's Yokes* and founder of the stunningly idealistic New England Anti-Death League—were arrested under the Comstock laws in 1878 for circulating birth control information.

71. Wisotzky, "Such a Life," 270, Box 1, Folder 5, Joseph A. Labadie Collection, Special Collections Research Center, University of Michigan Library, Ann Arbor.

72. United States National Archives, Record Group 60, via the Emma Goldman Papers.

73. Alexander Berkman and Emma Goldman, *Deportation, Its Meaning and Menace: Last Message to the People of America* (Ellis Island, N.Y.: ME Fitzgerald, 1919).

74. The women were Emma Goldman, Dora Lipkin, and eighteen-year-old Ethel Bernstein.

75. Grueter, "Red Scare Scholarship, Class Conflict, and the Case of the Anarchist Union of Russian Workers, 1919," *Journal for the Study of Radicalism* 11, no. 1 (Spring 2017): 53–82.

76. This included editor Peter Bianki, Nikifor (Hyman) Perkus of Cleveland, two Shatz brothers, and Arthur Katz. Avrich, *Anarchist Voices*, 199.

77. Grueter, "Red Scare Scholarship," 56.

78. Emma Goldman, *The Social Significance of Modern Drama* (Boston: Gorham Press, 1914).

79. See Louis F. Post, *The Deportations Delirium of Nineteen-Twenty: A Personal Narrative of an Historic Official Experience* (New York: Charles H. Kerr, 1923).

80. Matthew Guariglia, "Wrench in the Deportation Machine: Louis F. Post's Objection to Mechanized Red Scare Bureaucracy, *Journal of American Ethnic History* 38, no. 1 (Fall 2018): 62–77. Adam Hochschild, "When America Tried to Deport Its Radicals," *New Yorker*, November 4, 2019. https://www.newyorker.com/magazine/2019/11/11/when-america-tried-to-deport-its-radicals.

81. "Radical Non-Citizens Will Be Deported. Attorney General Palmer demonstrates that the 7,000 members of the Union of Russian Workers in America plan an armed revolt in every major city—detectives reveal false production materials for dynamite bombs. 585 'Reds' arrested in 15 cities." *Morgn zhurnal*, November 9, 1919.

82. Robert Minor, introduction to Berkman and Goldman, *Deportation, Its Meaning and Menace*.

83. On Goldman's use of the term "slave," see the chapter "Race and Internationalism" in Hemmings, *Considering Emma Goldman*.

84. Berkman and Goldman, *Deportation, Its Meaning and Menace*.

85. Glatshteyn, "1919." Translated by Kathryn Hellerstein and Benjamin Harshav, in *Jewish American Literature: A Norton Anthology*, ed. Jules Chametzky (New York: Norton, 2001), 371. Quoted with permission of the translator.

86. On Kabbalistic colors, see Gershom Scholem, "Colours and Their Symbolism in Jewish Tradition and Mysticism," trans. Johanna Pick Marguilies, *Diogenes* 109 (1980): 64–76.

87. Zosa Szajkowski, *The Impact of the 1919–20 Red Scare on American Jews* (Brooklyn: Ktav Publishing, 1974), 13.

88. Kenyon Zimmer, "The Voyage of the *Buford:* Political Deportations and the Making and Unmaking of America's First Red Scare," in *Deportation in the Americas: Histories of Exclusion and Resistance* (Arlington: Texas A&M University Press, 2018), 147.

89. *Gazeta,* multilingual handwritten newspaper, four issues, January 2–8, 1920. Courtesy of the New York Public Library.

90. *"Island of Tears Gazette,* Edited by the Commune, A daily tribune. Wednesday, Jan. 7 1920," 11–12. Translation from the Russian and Ukrainian by Zackary King, commissioned by Kenyon Zimmer for his forthcoming book on the *Buford* deportation. I thank them for sharing this research.

91. *Gazeta,* January 1920.

92. *Gazeta,* January 1920.

93. Avrich, *Anarchist Portraits,* 219–220.

94. *Gazeta,* January 1920, translation from German by Nick Wilkins, spring 2020.

95. Andrew Cornell, *Unruly Equality: U.S. Anarchism in the Twentieth Century* (Oakland: University of California Press, 2016), 130.

96. Catherine M. Lord and Sam Durrant, eds., *Essays in Migratory Aesthetics: Cultural Practices Between Migration and Art-making* (Leiden, Amsterdam: Brill | Rodopi, 2007), 11–12.

97. Miguel Á. Hernández Navarro, "Migratory Aesthetics," in *Encyclopedia of Aesthetics* (2nd ed.), ed. Michael Kelly (Oxford: Oxford University Press, 2014).

98. Gabriel Javsicas in Avrich, *Anarchist Portraits,* 47.

99. *Gazeta,* January 2–8, 1920.

100. Zimmer, "Voyage of the *Buford,*" 150–151.

101. See Paul Hanebrink, *A Specter Haunting Europe: The Myth of Judeo-Bolshevism* (Cambridge: Belknap Press of Harvard University, 2018).

102. Reynolds Hahamovitch, "Towards the Jewish Revolution: Yiddish Anarchists in New York City, 1901–1906" (master's thesis, Central European University, 2018), 114–115.

103. John J. Appel, "Jews in American Caricature: 1820–1914," *American Jewish History* 71, no. 1 (1981): 103–133.

104. 22320 Library and Archives Canada, "International News Vol 1, Issue 52: [excerpt] (1919)," 11:11, April 13, 2015. https://www.youtube.com/watch?v=tBStypKmqto&ab _channel=LibraryandArchivesCanada.

105. This newsreel appears in Bill Morrison's extraordinary film *Dawson City: Frozen Time* (New York: Picture Palace Pictures, 2017), which documents the story of a Canadian Gold Rush city just south of the arctic circle. In the 1900s, Dawson City received hundreds of nitrate film prints to entertain a population of 100,000 prospectors. Those films and newsreels were preserved in permafrost and uncovered by accident in 1978, revealing a cache of 533 nitrate films. I thank Morrison for sharing this footage, in which he identified Berkman.

106. Raymond Fielding, *The American Newsreel: A Complete History, 1911–1967,* 2nd ed. (Jefferson, N.C.: McFarland and Company, 2011), 8.

107. Hochschild, "When America Tried to Deport Its Radicals."

108. Hochschild, "When America Tried to Deport Its Radicals."

109. Goldman, "Statement by Emma Goldman at the Federal Hearing In Re Deportation.

New York, October 27, 1919." Bruce Broderius literature collection, SC006. University of Northern Colorado.

110. See David Fishman, "The Politics of Yiddish in Tsarist Russia," in *From Ancient Israel to Modern Judaism: Intellect in Quest of Understanding. Essays in Honor of Marvin Fox,* ed. Ernest S. Frerichs, Jacob Neusner, and Nahum M. Sarna (Providence: Brown University Press, 1989). On Soviet censorship see David Shneer, *Yiddish and the Creation of Soviet Jewish Culture, 1918–1930* (Cambridge: Cambridge University Press, 2004).

111. Goldman, "Statement at the Federal Hearing re Deportation," New York, October 27, 1919.

112. Hochschild, "When America Tried to Deport Its Radicals."

113. Szajkowski, *The Impact of the 1919–20 Red Scare on American Jews,* 5.

114. On errors in court translation of Arabic, see Susan M. Akram and Kevin R. Johnson, "Race, Civil Rights, and Immigration Law After September 11, 2001: The Targeting of Arabs and Muslims." http://www.law.nyu.edu/sites/default/files/ecm_pro_065053 .pdf. On detention of Spanish-speakers, see Amy Beth Hanson, "2 detained for speaking Spanish settle border patrol lawsuit," *AP News,* November 24, 2020. On translators of Indigenous South American languages, see Ashley Cleek, "The government says Border Patrol Agents in the Southwest speak Spanish—but many migrants speak Indigenous languages," *The World,* July 3, 2018.

115. Thomas Nail, "Guilty Before Trial: The Image of the Criminal Migrant," University of Oxford Faculty of Law, April 9, 2019. https://blogs.law.ox.ac.uk/research-subject -groups/centre-criminology/centreborder-criminologies/blog/2019/04/guilty-trial.

116. Nail, "Guilty Before Trial."

CHAPTER 8. "MULTITONGUED LANGUAGING"

1. Interview with Audrey Goodfriend in summer 2007, Oakland, California, while apprenticing with the Emma Goldman Papers Project.

2. See Joseph (Yosef) Cohen, *In Quest of Heaven: The Story of the Sunrise Co-Operative Farm Community* ([1957] reprint, Calif.: Factory School, 2007).

3. Harshav and Harshav, *American Yiddish Poetry: A Bilingual Anthology,* 774–784.

4. Anita Norich, "Writing on the Edge," in *Choosing Yiddish: New Frontiers of Language and Culture,* ed. Lara Rabinovitch, Shiri Goren, and Hannah S. Pressman (Detroit: Wayne State University Press, 2012), 11.

5. See Scott B. Saulson, *Institutionalized Language Planning: Documents and Analysis of Revival of Hebrew* (Berlin: Walter de Gruyter, 1979).

6. Ron Kuzar, *Hebrew and Zionism: A Discourse Analytic Cultural Study* (Berlin: Walter de Gruyter, 2001).

7. *Czernovitz at 100: The First Yiddish Language Conference in Historical Perspective,* ed. Joshua A. Fogel and Keith Weiser (Lanham, Md.: Lexington Books, 2010).

8. Daniel Blatman, "Bund," *YIVO Encyclopedia of Jews in Eastern Europe.* http://www .yivoencyclopedia.org/article.aspx/Bund.

9. Glaser, *Songs in Dark Times,* 23.

10. Glaser, *Songs in Dark Times,* 23.

11. Chaim Zhitlowsky, " 'A Jew to Jews' and 'Why Only Yiddish?' " in *Jews and Diaspora*

Nationalism: Writings on Jewish Peoplehood in Europe and the United States, ed. Simon Rabinovitch (Waltham, Mass.: Brandeis University Press, 2012), 82.

12. Madeleine Cohen, "Here and Now: The Modernist Poetics of Do'ikayt," 15.

13. See Gennady Estraikh, *Soviet Yiddish: Language Planning and Linguistic Development.*

14. See R' Zalman Leib Teitelbaum exhorting a mass gathering not to vote. Mea She'arim, January 2013, https://www.youtube.com/watch?v=Nkb8_E8aVLA.

15. Ivan G. Iliev, "Short History of the Cyrillic Alphabet," *International Journal of Russian Studies,* no. 2 (2013/14).

16. See Geoffrey Lewis, *The Turkish Language Reform: A Catastrophic Success* (Oxford: Oxford University Press, 2002).

17. Nesi Altaras, "Sephardic Jews in Turkey Were Told to Assimilate. Today's Generation Is Reclaiming Its Identity Through the Ladino Language," Stroum Center for Jewish Studies, July 21, 2020.

18. Ruth Kinna, "Utopianism and Prefiguration" (Loughborough: Loughborough University, 2016), 1. https://hdl.handle.net/2134/19278.

19. Michael G. Smith, *Rockets and Revolution: A Cultural History of Early Spaceflight,* (Lincoln: University of Nebraska Press, 2014), 131.

20. Smith, *Rockets and Revolution,* 131.

21. Sarah Marks and Mat Savelli, eds., *Psychiatry in Communist Europe* (London: Palgrave Macmillan, 2015), n48.

22. Yevgeniy Fiks, https://blokmagazine.com/yiddish-cosmos-by-yevgeniy-fiks-at-stanton -street-shul/

23. Esther Schor, "Esperanto—A Jewish Story," *Pakn-treger* (Winter 2009).

24. Schor, "Esperanto—A Jewish Story."

25. Brigid O'Keeffe, "An International Language for an Empire of Humanity: L. L. Zamenhof and the Imperial Russian Origins of Esperanto," *East European Jewish Affairs* 49, no. 1 (2019): 1.

26. Will Firth, "Esperanto and Anarchism," *Lexikon der Anarchie* (Verlag Schwarzer Nachtschatten, 1998). Translated and expanded for the Anarchist Library, https://theanarchist library.org/library/will-firth-esperanto-and-anarchism.

27. Gustav Landauer, "Do Not Learn Esperanto!" in *Revolution and Other Writings,* 277.

28. Landauer, "Do Not Learn Esperanto!"

29. Emma Goldman, *Mother Earth* (October 1907), 308.

30. Carolyn J. Eichner, "Civilization vs Solidarity: Louise Michel and the Kanaks," *Salvage,* 22 May 2017. Carolyn J. Eichner, "Language of Imperialism, Language of Liberation: Louise Michel and the Kanak-French Colonial Encounter," *Feminist Studies* 45, no. 2 (2019).

31. Eichner, "Civilization vs Solidarity: Louise Michel and the Kanaks." https://salvage .zone/in-print/civilization-vs-solidarity-louise-michel-and-the-kanaks/.

32. Benjamin Harshav, *The Meaning of Yiddish,* 28.

33. Max Weinreich, *Geshikhte fun der yidisher shprakh* (New York: Workmens Circle, 1973), 2, 318. Weinreich, *History of the Yiddish Language,* trans. Shlomo Noble (Chicago: University of Chicago Press, 1980), 656.

34. Harshav, *Meaning of Yiddish,* 40.

35. Weinreich, *History of the Yiddish Language*, A-660.

36. Yankev Glatshteyn, "Zing Ladino," *Yidishtaytshn* (Warsaw: Farlag Brzoza, 1937), 291.

37. Harshav identifies another aspect, *fusion*, as counterpart to *linguistic openness*.

38. Weinreich, *History of the Yiddish Language*, 185.

39. Weinreich, *History of the Yiddish Language*, A228.

40. David Shneer, *Yiddish and the Creation of Soviet Jewish Culture*, 39.

41. The Romm press was established in 1799 and published continuously in Vilna until World War II, supporting the development of modern Yiddish literature.

42. Dovid Katz, "Alexander Harkavy and His Trilingual Dictionary," in *Yiddish-English-Hebrew Dictionary*, ed. Alexander Harkavy (New York: YIVO Institute for Jewish Research and Schocken Books, 1988), ix.

43. Katz, "Alexander Harkavy and His Trilingual Dictionary," vii.

44. Lily Kahn and Aaron D. Rubin, *Handbook of Jewish Languages* (Leiden: Brill, 2015), 600.

45. Alexander Harkavy, *Kolumbus, oder, di entdekung fun amerike* (Columbus, or the Discovery of America) (New York: Hebrew Publishing, 19-?), 15.

46. Katz, "Alexander Harkavy," xv.

47. Katz, "Alexander Harkavy,," ix.

48. Barry Trachtenberg, *Revolutionary Roots of Modern Yiddish, 1903–1917* (Syracuse: Syracuse University Press, 2008), 5.

49. Shneer, *Yiddish and the Creation of Soviet Jewish Culture*, 39.

50. Zimmer, *Immigrants Against the State*, 27.

51. Harkavy, *"Erklerung fun der redaktsyon"* (Statement from the Editor), *Der nayer gayst* (October 1897), 1.

52. Katz, "Alexander Harkavy," x.

53. Harkavy, *Der nayer gayst*, 20.

54. The *Concise Ladino-English/English-Ladino* dictionary gives "rovar" (similar to Spanish "robar") as "to steal."

55. Harkavy alternates between loshn-koydesh grammatical terms.

56. Also Yiddish for "riches, fortune." *Farmegn* is estate or property.

57. Quotation marks, italics, or parentheses preserve the languages cited by Harkavy.

58. Harshav, *Meaning of Yiddish*, 165.

59. Zimmer, *Immigrants Against the State*, 27.

60. Zimmer, *Immigrants Against the State*, 42.

61. Hélène Cixous, *White Ink: Interviews on Sex, Text, and Politics* (New York: Columbia University Press, 2008), 12.

62. Rubin and Kahn, *Handbook of Jewish Languages*, 600.

63. Borekh Tshubinski, "Alexander Harkavy," *Yiddish Leksikon*, February 29, 2016.

64. Julius G. Rothenberg, "Some Idioms from the Yiddish," *American Speech* 18, no. 1 (February 1943): 45.

65. Stephen M. Cohen, "Chemical Literature in Yiddish: A Bridge Between the Shtetl and the Secular World," *Aleph*, no. 7 (2007): 225.

66. Rita Falbel (interviewer) and Leah Zazulyer, "The Uses of Language," *Bridges* 16, no. 1 (Spring 2011): 133–142. Quoted with permission of her son Ian Watson.

67. The "Americana" series included *Kolumbus, di antdekung fun amerike* (Columbus, the discovery of America) (1892); *Vashington, der ershter prezident fun di fareyntigte shtatn* (Washington, the first president of the United States) (1892); *Konstitutsyon fun di fareynigte shtatn* (Constitution of the United States), English text and Yiddish translation (1897); *Der sitzen* (The citizen), laws on naturalization in the States (1899; revised edition, 1922); Tshubinksi, "Alexander Harkavy."

68. Alice Nakhimovsky and Roberta Newman, "Brivnshtelers," *YIVO Encyclopedia for Jews in Eastern Europe,* http://www.yivoencyclopedia.org/article.aspx/Brivnshtelers.

69. Katz, "Alexander Harkavy," x.

70. Alexander Harkavy, *Harkavy's amerikanisher brivnshteler* (New York, 1902), 161–162.

71. Eli Lederhendler, "Guides for the Perplexed: Sex, Manners, and Mores for the Yiddish Reader in America," *Modern Judaism* 11, no. 3 (October 1991): 321–341.

72. Elisheva Carlebach, *Palaces of Time: Jewish Calendar and Culture in Early Modern Europe* (Cambridge: Harvard University Press, 2011), 116.

73. Carlebach, *Palaces of Time,* 114.

74. Goldman, *Emma Goldman: A Documentary History of the American Years,* vol. 2, ed. Candace Falk et al. (Urbana: University of Illinois Press, 2008), 6.

75. Charles von Onselen, "Jewish Police Informers in the Atlantic World, 1880–1914." *Historical Journal* 50, no. 1 (2007): 119–44.

76. Katz, "Alexander Harkavy," vi.

77. M. Kleinman, "Concerning Jacob Meir Salkind, a Week After His Passing" (Ya'kov Meir Zalkind: Le-Yom Ha-Shevi'I Le-Moto), Davar (March 1, 1938), 9. Translated by Hayyim Rothman, in *No masters but God,* 36.

78. Shvartsbard, "*Dr. Yankev Meyer Zalkind un zayn gemore af yidish,*" *Der moment,* January 20, 1929, 5. David Biale, "Gershom Scholem on nihilism and anarchism," *Rethinking History* 19, no. 1 (2015): 61–71. Sam Brody, *Martin Buber's Theopolitics* (Bloomington: Indiana University Press, 2018); and Paul Mendes-Flohr, Anya Mali, and Hanna Delf von Wolzogen, eds., *Gustav Landauer: Anarchist and Jew* (Berlin: De Gruyter, 2014). Neither Rocker's memoir *The London Years* (London: Robert Anscombe, 1956) nor W. J. Fishman's *East End Jewish Radicals, 1875–1914* (London: Duckworth, 1975) mentions Zalkind.

79. Itskhok Kharlash, "Yankev Meyer Zalkind," in *Der Leksikon fun der nayer yidisher literatur,* vol. 3, ed. Shmuel (Niger) Charney and Jacob Shatsky (New York: Marsten Press, 1960), 535.

80. Moshe Goncharok, "The Fate of Jewish Anarchists" (Sud'by evreiskikh anarkhistov; Судьбы еврейских анархистов), http://www.jewniverse.ru/biher/goncharok/anarchie /8.html.

81. Arn-Leyb Bisko and Zalkind, eds., *Milon male veshalem zhargoni-ivri* (London: Narodski, 1913). See also Shimeon Brisman, *A History and Guide to Judaic Dictionaries and Concordances* (Hoboken, N.J.: Ktav, 2000), 140.

82. Chaim Nachman Bialik, letter to Zalkind, January 19, 1931, in *Igrot H. N. Bialik* (Tel Aviv: Dvir, 1939), 5:134–135.

83. Shmuel Charney, *Bleter geshikhte fun der yidisher literatur* (New York: Alveltlekhn yidishn kultur-kongres, 1959), 203–207.

84. Yankev Meyer Zalkind, *Talmud Bavli (Gemore in Idish): Iberzetst un erklehrt fun Ya'akov Me'ir Zalkind* (London: B. Veinberg, 1928).

85. Zalkind, *Talmud Bavli,* 11.

86. Jacob Neusner, ed., *The Talmud of the Land of Israel,* vol. 4, *Ki'layim* (Chicago: University of Chicago Press, 1990), 3.

87. Shvartsbard, "*Dr. Yankev Meyer Zalkind un zayn gemore oyf yidish,*" 20.

88. Yankev Meyer Zalkind, foreword to *Ki'layim* in *Talmud Bavli: Gemore in Idish,* vol. 4 (London: Vainberg, 1932). Translation by the author.

89. Zalkind, foreword to *Ki'layim.*

90. Shvartsbard, "*Dr. Yankev Meyer Zalkind un zayn gemore oyf yidish,*" 5.

91. Rocker, *The London Years,* 111.

92. Zalkind, "*Anarkhism un shmerts,*" *Arbeter fraynd,* March 26, 1921, 4–5. Translated in Rothman, "The Case of Jacob Meir Salkind," 20.

93. Zalkind, "*Anarkhism un shmerts,*" 20.

94. William J. Fishman, *Jewish Radicals: From Czarist Shtetl to London Ghetto* (New York: Pantheon Books, 1974), 295–299.

95. Avrich, *Anarchist Voices,* 4.

96. Quoted in Chaim Leib Weinberg, *Forty Years in the Struggle: The Memoirs of a Jewish Anarchist,* trans. Naomi Cohen (Duluth, Minn.: Litwin Books, 2008), 155.

97. Robert Deming, ed., *James Joyce,* vol. 2, *1928–1941* (London: Routledge, 1997), 418.

98. Moshe Goncharok, *Tsu der geshikte fun der anarkhistisher prese oyf yidish* (Jerusalem: Problemen, 1997). Translation by the author.

99. Harshav, *Meaning of Yiddish,* 62.

100. Tony Michels, *A Fire in Their Hearts: Yiddish Socialists in New York* (Cambridge: Harvard University Press, 2009), 112–113.

101. Wisotzky, "Such a Life," 58.

102. Goldman, reflecting on the day they met in Philadelphia in 1893. Emma Goldman, "Voltairine de Cleyre" (Berkeley Heights, N.J.: Oriole Press, 1932).

103. De Cleyre letter, August 5, 1911, Yanovsky papers, International Institute of Social History Archive, Amsterdam. She was treasurer of the Mexican Liberal Defense Conference, Chicago.

104. A. J. Brigati, ed., *The Voltairine de Cleyre Reader* (Oakland: AK Press, 2004), ii.

105. Letters in her archive address Joseph Cohen primarily and periodically S. Yanovsky. This one was likely written to Cohen, which Robert Helms confirms. (Email correspondence with Helms, June 2016.)

106. Voltairine de Cleyre files, YIVO Archives, Folder 7, YIVO Institute for Jewish Research, New York.

107. Rocker, *The London Years,* 64.

108. Fermin Rocker interviewed by Andrew Whitehead, *Andrew Whitehead Oral History Interviews with Political Radicals,* 1985.09.27, audio recording accessed at the British Library.

109. Katz, "Alexander Harkavy," xvii.

110. Chomsky recalls: "Though the native language of my parents was Yiddish, I almost never heard a word. In the Kulturkampf of the day in the Jewish community, they were

deeply immersed in the Hebrew side. . . . At the same time, independently, I developed a strong interest in anarchism. As a child, was visiting the office of Freie Arbeiter Stimme at Union Square in New York, read Rocker early on, but somehow never connected it properly. The Hebrew background was I guess too strong. . . . I spent much of the time on 4th Avenue from Union Square down poking around second-hand bookstores—it was a very different city then. Some were run by anarchist refugees from Spain. Spent time there talking to—meaning listening to—the owners and picking up materials, which I later used in writing about Spanish anarchism, most [of] them unavailable until recently. Also spent time at the [*Fraye arbeter shtime*] office in Union Square. Same experience. But the cultural and age gap was huge, despite my quite passionate interest in the topic, not shared by anyone I knew so I never could talk about it." Chomsky, personal correspondence, September 14, 2019.

111. Chomsky, Preface to Rudolf Rocker, *Anarcho-Syndicalism* (Oakland: AK Press, 2004).

CODA

1. The Charming Hostess musicians at this performance were Jewlia Eisenberg, Jason Ditzian, Cynthia Taylor, and Laura Inserra. I am grateful to AnMarie Rodgers and John Zorn for permission to quote Jewlia Eisenberg's words.

2. Https://www.youtube.com/watch?v=ZEpZZ1uYowE&t=9s.

3. Natalia Ginzburg, *All Our Yesterdays,* trans. Angus Davidson ([1952] New York: Simon and Schuster, 2016), 153.

4. Jason Ditzian, "mapping the journey." https://www.charminghostess.com/jewlia-bio. See also "The Dig," a visual timeline of Eisenberg's life and work. https://www.charming hostess.com/timeline.

5. Jordyn Haime, "Jews were behind the original 'West Side Story' and today's remake. Should they be?" *Times of Israel,* December 12, 2021. https://www.timesofisrael.com /jews-were-behind-the-original-west-side-story-and-todays-remake-should-they-be/.

6. Shneer was a professor of Jewish studies at the University of Colorado, Boulder. His death from brain cancer preceded Eisenberg's death by four months. See also Erin Faigin, "Anti-fascist Yiddish Song: Shneer and Eisenberg on Lin Jaldati." *In geveb: A Journal of Yiddish Studies* (February 2016). https://ingeveb.org/blog/anti-fascist-yiddish -song.

7. "Mayn Tsavoe sung by David Shneer z"l & Jewlia Eisenberg z"l at David Edelstadt grave in Denver." https://www.youtube.com/watch?v=pwV2ePo1Z90.

8. Marmor, *Dovid Edelshtat,* 50. Cited by Lorber, "*Tsum Folk Vel Ikh Fun Keyver Zingen,*" 43.

9. YIVO Institute for Jewish Research. *In Love and in Struggle: The Musical Legacy of the Jewish Labor Bund* (New York: YIVO, 1999), liner notes 6. Cited by Lorber, "*Tsum Folk Vel Ikh Fun Keyver Zingen,*" 57.

10. Yanovsky, *Ershte yorn fun yidishn frayhaytlekhn sotsializm, oytobiografishe zikhroynes fun a pioner un boyer fun der yidisher anarkhistisher bavegung in england un amerike,* 195. Translation by Lorber, "*Tsum Folk Vel Ikh Fun Keyver Zingen,*" 44.

11. Kramer papers, Labadie Collection. See also Kramer, *A Century of Yiddish Poetry,* 60.

12. Charming Hostess performs *The Ginzburg Geography* at UCLA. Musicians: Jewlia

Eisenberg, Jason Ditzian, Cynthia Taylor, and Laura Inserra. https://www.youtube.com
/watch?v=ZEpZZ1uYowE&t=9s.

13. "Ginzburg Geographies w/ Jewlia Eisenberg of Charming Hostess," radio613 podcast.
https://open.spotify.com/episode/56NecPjhdG9zRkgQiwTaFf?si=2AeQruDxQwiKx
EeXn4FPtg&nd=1.

Index